THE DIVINE PLAYER

Jacket

Kṛṣṇa defeating Kāliya

THE DIVINE PLAYER

(A Study of Kṛṣṇa Līlā)

DAVID R. KINSLEY

MOTILAL BANARSIDASS
Delhi :: Varanasi :: Patna

Indological Publishers and Booksellers
Head Office: BUNGALOW ROAD, JAWAHAR NAGAR, DELHI-7
Branches : 1. CHOWK, VARANASI-1 (U.P.)
2. ASHOK RAJPATH, PATNA-4 (BIHAR)

ISBN 0 89684 019 0

First Edition : *Delhi*, 1979

Price : Rs. 65

Printed in India

BY SHANTILAL JAIN, AT SHRI JAINENDRA PRESS, A-45, PHASE-I, INDUSTRIAL AREA, NARAINA, NEW DELHI-28 AND PUBLISHED BY NARENDRA PRAKASH JAIN, FOR MOTILAL BANARSIDASS, BUNGALOW ROAD, JAWAHAR NAGAR, DELHI-7

ACKNOWLEDGEMENTS

It is now my pleasant task to thank those who have helped and encouraged me in this study. Although I have thanked several of these people personally, I should like to acknowledge their help publicly and formally.

I owe a debt of gratitude, first of all, to my professors at the University of Chicago, who unstintingly gave of their time and effort on my behalf. To Professors Mircea Eliade, Edward C. Dimock, and Charles Long I am most grateful. I am particularly grateful to Professor Joseph Kitagawa, who, although he was not an official member of my Ph.D. committee, took the time to read my dissertation and provide me with helpful criticisms and encouragement.

While writing my dissertation in Calcutta and doing further research on the cultic aspects of Vaiṣṇavism, it was my good fortune to meet several people who subsequently helped me to become familiar with the more inaccessible aspects of the faith as lived. To the *brahmacārīs* of the Caitanya Research Institute, and to the head of that institute, Tridaṇḍi Swāmī Bhakti Vilās Tīrtha Mahārāj, I am grateful for accepting me both as an interested scholar and as a friend and for permitting me free access to their library and devotional services. I am also grateful to Bhakti Probaji, a lay devotee of Kṛṣṇa, who invited my wife and me to regularly attend his informal, weekly *kirtan* meetings in his small, crowded, but nevertheless always friendly home worship room. There we were not treated as aloof observers but as fellow playmates of Kṛṣṇa and were always invited to sing, dance, and play instruments in praise of the Blue Lord.

Among others who were particularly helpful during my stay in Calcutta I should like to mention Tarun Mitra of the American Institute of Indian Studies, Professor Naresh Guha, and Dr. and Mrs. Rabin Sinha. In many ways these people in particular made our adjustment to a strange country and a bewildering city pleasant and exciting.

Shortly after my arrival in Calcutta it was my great good fortune to meet Tridib Ghosh. For the remainder of my stay in

India hewas my indispensible guide and research assistant. He located and translated with me several important Bengali sources on various aspects of the Kṛṣṇa cult in Bengal, acted as my guide and translator on many occasions, and introduced me to people both within and outside the Kṛṣṇa cult. Without his help it would have been extremely difficult, if not impossible, to have gained access to the life of the cult as quickly and thoroughly as I did.

I owe a note of thanks to the Office of Education of the U.S. Department of Health, Education, and Welfare for awarding me a Fulbright-Hays Graduate Fellowship for study in India. Without the first-hand knowledge of the Kṛṣṇa cult that was gained during my stay in India, this study would not have been possible.

Finally, I should like to acknowledge the help and encouragement I have received from my wife, Carolyn. She took upon herself the tedious responsibility of copyediting and typing the entire dissertation, thus freeing me from the more thankless and wearying aspects of scholarship. It was my wife, too, who during those bleak periods of my research, when my work sometimes seemed futile and dreary, reminded me in one way or another that, after all, man's end is not, perhaps, to work but to play; who many times enabled me to return to the task at hand with an outlook that made the whole business fun again. I dedicate this study to her, my helpmate and playmate.

CONTENTS

INTRODUCTION

For the smile of the gods gave to the things of the cosmos their being and their power to continue.
—Proclus in his commentary on the *Timaeus*

This dissertation is directed at understanding a problem that has interested me for some time: the relationship between play and religion. While this study does not pretend to be a definitive work on the subject, the problem is treated consistently throughout in the context of Indian religion.

It is my feeling that in previous studies the question of the relationship of play to religion has been posed in such a way as to neglect the central issue: the apparent significance of play itself as a positive religious symbol and activity. Religion, for example, has been compared to play in that both involve make-believe, or pretending. The conclusion drawn from such a comparison is often a negative one: that religion represents a childish stage in man's upward evolution to adulthood as a species. I think the comparison between the make-believe world of play and the "other" world of religion is valid, but I think that the real significance of the similarity lies in the fact that in both play and religion man exercises and is captured by his world-creating, imaginative faculty. And I am indeed reluctant to call this faculty a vestigial aspect of man's racial childhood.

The relationship between play and religion has also been studied from a developmental point of view. A rather vigorous debate, for example, has centered on the question of which phenomenon, play or religion, precedes or develops into the other. While it is clear that games play a part in certain rituals, and that certain games have become ritualized, and while it is certainly interesting, not to say enlightening, to know the history of how this comes about in particular situations, to pose the question in such developmental terms does little to inform us about what makes play an appropriate religious expression in and of itself.

The important fact to keep in mind, I think, is that in many traditions play *is* an appropriate religious expression. As a symbol of divine activity and as cultic activity, play clearly bears a positive relationship to religion generally. This is obviously clearer in some religions than in others, but its relative disperse-ment does not justify treating the problem in evolutionary or developmental terms. Play does not, for example, dominate so-called primitive religions, nor is it an uncommon feature of divine or cultic activity in the so-called high religions. The key to the relationship between the two phenomena, I think, is best understood by the fact that play participates in and expresses otherness. There is in or about play something that suggests the vital essence of religion itself.

There is in religion, or in the religions, an irreducible element. There is what might be called a vertical referent that is characteristic of religion generally. In the history of the history of religions this has been given various names in an attempt to define it more exactly. Otto called it the Holy; Van der Leeuw, Power; and Eliade, the Sacred, or the distinction between the sacred and the profane. Whatever we may call it, it is generally apprehended and expressed as something other. Indeed, "otherness" is perhaps the best term to describe this feature of religion.

An almost universal characteristic of otherness is its transcendence and unconditioned nature. The gods, for example, are *super*natural. They are not limited by human frailty or hindrances. They express the unconditioned or transcendent nature of otherness in terms of knowledge (omniscience), spacelessness (the ability to change form at will, to be in more than one place at one time, or to be omnipresent), timelessness (the gods are frequently in the prime of youth, very old, or eternal), deathlessness (immortality), creativity, and power (omnipotence).[1]

These characteristics are what might be called classic features of the divine. In almost every religious tradition the gods are gods because they are characterized by these features. In Hinduism the gods clearly possess all these classic features of divinity,

[1]The prefix "omni" of course must be understood as relative given the multiplicity of cultures and religions in the history of religions. Vis-à-vis different cultures and religions, for example, a particular god may seem at once both very powerful and very weak and lowly.

yet it is also apparent that the Hindu gods are further characterized by their playful nature.

While play is perhaps not a classic feature of the divine in all religions, in Hinduism it is typical of the gods and represents, I think, an appropriate expression of the unconditioned and transcendent nature of the divine in India.

While the great variety of activities and phenomena that are called play makes it difficult to supply a simple, all-encompassing definition of the word, there are obvious characteristics of play that make it especially suitable to the divine sphere. Play, just as much as power, knowledge, and eternity, expresses the truth that the gods are not limited. For play expresses freedom; it is carefree and relatively unmotivated. Play is done for the fun of it, for no ulterior reason. As opposed to most other types of activity, it is intrinsically satisfying rather than instrumental. It is an end in itself. The gods act, but their acts cannot be understood simply within the structures of theological or ethical systems. In their complete otherness, their actions can only be called *līlā*, which may be translated as "sport," "play," or "dalliance." To say that the gods act to satisfy any desire, to save man from injustice, even to free man from bondage, is to pretend to comprehend something that simply cannot be understood by man. The gods are entirely complete. They need and desire nothing. Their activity, therefore, is appropriately called *līlā*. And *līlā* is different from, or "other" than, the world of here and now that is dominated by cause and effect, where man is forced to act out of necessity.

In the Hindu religious tradition the importance of play as divine activity indicates that play is a positive activity, an activity that partakes of the other realm of the gods. In the human sphere, therefore, it is not surprising that play is also understood as a peculiarly religious activity in man's religious quest. Play itself, and many activities that share important characteristics with play, are central to Hindu cult, and particularly to the *bhakti* cults of North India. Play and playful activities such as dancing, singing, emotional frenzy, and madness signify that man has exploded the confines of his pragmatic, utilitarian nature and entered an "other" realm of freedom. They signify that he has transcended the ordinary and participates in the extraordinary.

In Hindu cult, particularly the *bhakti* cults, the mark of a great devotee is often the "uselessness" of his life. This is especially clear in the lives of the saints, who frequently behave like children, madmen, or drunkards and who are often depicted as being incapable of looking after themselves in the pragmatic world. As members of their society, they are quite unproductive. Their lives are mere ornaments. They are often incapable of sustained work or of acting in an orderly manner at all. They do not act according to the laws of cause and effect, so their actions appear motiveless and aimless. Indeed, they are in many ways like the gods because they do not work but play.

This study will proceed, then, by first discussing the play of the gods. By illustrating its importance to and variety in the divine sphere it will be shown that play is considered a special activity in the Hindu tradition, an activity that is peculiarly appropriate to divinity. In this discussion I shall treat the god Kṛṣṇa at length, as he is both one of the most popular Hindu gods and the most playful. I shall then proceed to discuss the place of play in Hindu cult in order to show the positive role of play, and activities that share important characteristics with play, in man's religious quest. I shall treat separately the lives of various Hindu saints, as they are both paradigmatic for man's devotional life and illustrative of the freed man. The saints have transcended the human condition and have entered the divine sphere, and an important indication of this fact is the spontaneous and superfluous nature of their lives. Finally, I shall discuss a few examples of play in non-Hindu religious traditions to show that play is also considered appropriate to the divine and cultic spheres outside India.

CHAPTER I

PLAY AS DIVINE ACTIVITY IN HINDUISM

A. *The Play of Creation and the World Dance*

In the *Bhagavadgītā* Kṛṣṇa addresses Arjuna and suggests a perspective from which the activity of Indian gods can be understood as play.

> For Me, son of Pṛthā, there is nothing to be done
> In the three worlds whatsoever,
> Nothing unattained to be attained;
> And yet I still continue in action.[1]

Viṣṇu, as Kṛṣṇa, is entirely complete.[2] He desires nothing and needs nothing. Yet he continues to act. Because this is so his actions are not to be understood as instrumental; they are not the result of cause and effect. There is nothing desired nor anything to be achieved. Divine actions as such proceed from a fullness, an overflowing abundance. And so they are properly called play.

Play as divine activity in India is commonly seen in creation. In the *Brahma-sūtra* of Bādarāyaṇa we read: "(Creation is) not (possible for Brahman) on account of having a motive. But, as in ordinary life, creation is mere sport (to Brahman)."[3]

---

[1] 3.22; *The Bhagavad Gītā*, trans. Franklin Edgerton (New York: Harper & Row, 1964), p. 20.

[2] It might seem, given this view of God, that he would remain motionless, content to enjoy his fulness in stillness. And of course the divine or the Absolute in India is pictured in just this way frequently. The serenity of the Buddha, the calm of the *yogin* and his paradigm the meditating Śiva, and the ineffable totality of the attributeless Brahman of the *advaita* school are typical of the Indian vision of the divine.

[3] II.1.32-33; Bādarāyaṇa, *The Brahma Sūtra: The Philosophy of Spiritual Life*, trans. and ed. S. Radhakrishnan (London: George Allen & Unwin, 1960), pp. 361-62. Another famous passage that speaks of Brahman creating the world in sport is found in *Manu-smṛti* 1.80: "The Manvantaras, the creations and destructions (of the world, are) numberless; sporting, as it were, Brahman repeats this again and again." *The Laws of Manu*, trans. G. Bühler (Delhi: Motilal Banarsidass, 1967), p. 22.

In his commentary on this verse Radhakrishnan says that "God cannot have a motive or a need for creating the universe for he is all-sufficient." Brahman is like "men in high position, who have no unfulfilled desires, [and thus] indulge in sport."[1] Śaṅkara, in his commentary on this verse, compares Brahman's creative activity to breathing, which "goes on without reference to any extraneous purpose, merely following the law of its own nature. So also creation proceeds from the nature of the Supreme without reference to any purpose."[2] In a similar vein, Baladeva, also commenting on this verse, says that Brahman's *līlā* "is the overflow of the joy within. As in ordinary life, a man full of cheerfulness on awakening from sound sleep dances about without any motive or need but simply from the fullness of spirit, so is the case with the creation of the world by God."[3]

This view of creation as the play of God is beautifully portrayed in the Vaiṣṇava version of the creation of the world. Viṣṇu creates the world while lying asleep on the cosmic serpent Ananta (or Śeṣa) in the middle of the primordial ocean. During his sleep a lotus grows from his navel and the demiurge Brahmā is created, who in turn creates the world. Creation here is seen as a pointless, effortless reflex of God. He creates the entire universe while asleep; he dreams the universe into existence, as it were.[4]

In the logic of the Sāṁkhya system Viṣṇu's creativity is also spoken of as his play with Prakṛti. "The Lord is of transcendent glory and is fully merged in the enjoyment of Himself. Only at times in revelling vein He doth join with Prakriti, wherefrom issues forth the flow of creation."[5]

---

[1]*Brahma-sūtra*, commentary on II. 1. 32-33 (Bādarāyaṇa, p. 362).

[2]*Ibid.*, commentary on II. 1. 33.

[3]*Ibid.*

[4]See the *Matsya-purāṇa* 167. 1-25; *Matsya Purāṇam*, trans. A Taluqdar of Oudh (Allahabad: Sudhindra Nath Vasu, 1916), Part II, pp. 130-31. *Harivaṁśa* 50.11; *Harivamsha*, trans. Manmatha Nath Dutt (Calcutta: Elysium Press, 1897), p.217. *Bhāgavata-purāṇa* I.3.1-5; *The Srimad-Bhāgavatam of Krishna-Dwaipayana Vyasa*, trans. J. M. Sanyal (5 vols.; 2d. ed., Vols. I, IV, V; 3d. ed., Vols. II, III; Calcutta: Oriental Publishing Co., 2d ed., n.d.; 3d. ed., 1965), I, 8.

[5]*Bhāgavata-purāṇa* I.9.32 (I, 39). See also III.26.3-4 (I, 119).

The ancient sage Mārkaṇḍeya was once permitted to see the great Viṣṇu before the creation of the world. In this remarkable vision the sage is inhaled by the sleeping Viṣṇu and upon entering the god's body sees all the universes.[1] Upon being exhaled Mārkaṇḍeya has another extraordinary sight of Viṣṇu. He sees the creator in the form of a small boy on a branch of a banyan tree. "He was seen playing all by himself without any anxiety in the universe bereft of creation."[2] Then he begins to create the universe. "In that great ocean, the great place of pilgrimage, the infallible Hari, the creator of all the worlds, plays for some time and brings forth out of his navel a wonderful lotus of a thousand petals shining like the sun."[3]

The *Harivaṁśa* also refers to this image of Viṣṇu playing in the primordial waters. "Thereupon, for the purpose of creating creatures the Eternal Hari lay in the great ocean, and sporting in diverse ways, attained to great delight."[4] And the *Viṣṇu-purāṇa* also pictures Viṣṇu as a sporting boy. "Vishṇu being thus discrete and indiscrete substance, spirit, and time, sports like a playful boy, as you shall learn by listening to his frolics."[5]

Both the image of the sleeping Viṣṇu spinning the world into being from his dreams and the image of the solitary boy creating the world amid his play suggest a spontaneous, unpremeditated creation. The world does not appear to be purposely fashioned but is brought into being as a result of reflex or overabundance.[6]

---

[1]The goddess Mahāmāyā is also said to hold the universe within her belly. *Mahānirvāṇa-tantra* XIII. 242; *The Great Liberation* (*Mahānirvāṇa Tantra*), trans. Arthur Avalon (John Woodroffe) (4th ed.; Madras: Ganesh & Co., 1963), p. 410.

[2]*Matsya-purāṇa* 167.31 (Part II, p.131).

[3]*Ibid.* 168.14-15 (Part II, p.133).

[4]*Harivaṁśa*, Bhaviṣya Parva 11.15 (p.847).

[5]I.2.18; *The Vishṇu Purāṇa*, trans. H. H. Wilson (3d ed.; Calcutta: Punthi Pustak, 1961), p. 9.

[6]Cf. Alan Watts, *Beyond Theology*: *The Art of Godmanship* (New York: Pantheon Books, 1964), p. 25: "The Hindu God is shown, not as a technician, but as a being with many arms and many faces, a cosmic centipede of fantastic dexterity moving innumerable limbs without, however, having to *think* about it, to know how it is done. In just the same way, we move

In Vaiṣṇava tradition the *avatāras* of Viṣṇu are central. From time to time Viṣṇu incarnates himself, or a part of himself, to maintain the balance of good and evil in the world, to uphold the *dharma* of the age. In his various *avatāras* Viṣṇu may be said to act as a savior in the Hindu tradition. While this may sound like a very serious business, especially to a student of the Christian tradition, it is often stated in Hindu scriptures that Viṣṇu's *avatāras* are simply his way of amusing himself. In the *Bhāgavata-purāṇa*, for example, we read: "Whenever there is waning of Dharma and waxing of sin, the Supreme Lord Sri Hari incarnates himself. There is no reason for the birth and act of the Lord of the Universe, except for enjoying his own illusive powers."[1]

When the world was forcibly taken beneath the primordial waters by a demon, Viṣṇu became a boar ostensibly to rescue the earth. The *Matsya-purāṇa*, however, says Viṣṇu became a boar simply to amuse himself. "Then the Lord manifested Himself as a boar that He might enjoy the playing in waters."[2] Again, in the *Bhāgavata-purāṇa*, Kṛṣṇa's parents address him at his birth: "O Lord, verily we cannot conceive any other cause of thy birth, except in thy sportive humour; for thou art not attached to this Earth."[3] The same scripture says: "He, in his kindness and playful revels, manifested Himself as *Brahma*, . . . *Rudra*," etc.[4] And finally, "Like an actor acting on the stage, He assumed and renounced His different forms such as a Fish and others."[5]

It is certainly clear in the Vaiṣṇava scriptures that Viṣṇu's *avatāras* serve to relieve the world of its burden, to restore the balance of *dharma* and *adharma*. But these passages make it clear that Viṣṇu does not act from necessity or from any clear motive. One does not get the idea of a just god acting out of moral outrage, or a compassionate god bestowing

our own arms and legs, beat our hearts, shape our bones, constellate our nervous systems, and grow our hair with astounding efficiency and yet without needing to explain it. Indeed, thinking about these processes often interferes with them, just as the actor or dancer falters when he is too conscious of himself."

[1]*Bhāgavata-purāṇa* IX. 24. 56 (III, 262).

[2]*Matsya-purāṇa* 248. 64 (Part II, p. 282).

[3]*Bhāgavata-purāṇa* X.2.39 (IV, 12).

[4]*Ibid.* I. 1. 17 (I, 4).

[5]*Ibid.* I. 15. 35 (I, 66).

mercy, although these elements are not entirely lacking. Restoration of the moral order often seems a mere by-product of Viṣṇu's play. In the following passage from the *Viṣṇu-purāṇa* Viṣṇu's incarnations are seen as rhythmical and natural: "The multifarious forms of that manifold being encounter and succeed one another, night and day, like waves of the sea."[1] The play of waves on the ocean surface is a fitting description of Viṣṇu's *avatāras*.[2] His incarnations never act once and for all but follow upon one another, flirting with and flitting about the world as much in response to some inherent, playful urge for aimless display as for the good of the world.

The creation of the world in the Śaivite tradition is similarly spontaneous and playful. Śiva, the king of dancers, brings about the creation of the world by means of dancing.[3] In the *Mahābhārata* he is addressed as follows: "Thou art

---

[1]*Viṣṇu-purāṇa* V. 1. 20 (p. 396).

[2]This imagery is nicely expressed in a song recited by Narendra (Vivekānanda), one of Rāmakṛṣṇa's disciples: "Upon the Sea of Blissful Awareness waves of ecstatic love arise: / Rapture divine ! Play of God's bliss ! / Oh, how enthralling ! / Wondrous waves of the sweetness of God, ever new and ever enchanting, / Rise on the surface, ever assuming / forms ever fresh. / Then once more in the Great Communion all are merged, as the barrier walls / Of time and space dissolve and vanish: / Dance then, O Mind ! / Dance in delight with hands upraised, chanting Lord Hari's holy name." M. [Mahendranath Gupta], *The Gospel of Sri Ramakrishna*, trans. Swami Nikhilananda (New York: Ramakrishna-Vivekananda Center, 1942), p. 705. The theme of rhythmic motion underlying the creation and destruction of the universe is also clear in vss. 6-7 from the *Kāma-kalā-vilāsa* describing the interaction between Śiva and Śakti, who "in their secret mutual enjoyment, are now expanding and now contracting. They are the Cause of the creation of the Word (*Vāk*) and Meaning (*Artha*), now entering and now separating from one another." Puṇyānanda-nātha, *Kāma-kalā-vilāsa*, trans. Arthur Avalon [John Woodroffe] (Madras. Ganesh & Co., 1961), p. 15.

[3]Dance, of course, is not always and necessarily spontaneous activity. It is not always an activity that is random "fluttering." (See below, Chap. III, Sec. B.) Indeed, Śiva's dance has stately, majestic, ordered aspects about it. Dance is, nevertheless, a superfluous activity—an extra activity—that denies calculation and premeditation. Particularly when viewed as the "cause" of creation, creation appears as a spontaneous activity. Creation is an incidental by-product of Śiva's dancing, not the result of premeditation, careful planning, or brooding. The spontaneity, lightness, effortlessness of Śiva's dancing are quite clear in Śaivite iconography. See, for example, T. A. Gopinatha Rao, *Elements of Hindu Iconography* (2 vols., each in 2 parts; 2d ed.; New York: Paragon Book Reprint Corp., 1968), Vol. II, Part I, Pl. LVI. This particular bronze Naṭarāja from South India depicts a fluid grace that is clearly not mere fluttering. The kicking foot and bright smile, however, clearly convey the sense of effortless, spontaneous action.

fond of dancing. Thou art he that is always engaged in dancing. Thou art he that causes others to dance."[1] Once Śiva has created the world, he continues to dance with the world. Finally, in somewhat the same spirit in which a child destroys in delight the sand castle he has so laboriously created, the great dancing god destroys the world by means of his dance. The world, to continue the analogy, is simply his plaything. In the *Mahābhārata* again we read: "Thou art he who sports with the universe as his marble ball."[2] The impermanence of the world vis-à-vis Śiva, its status as his toy or reflex, is seen in the following delightful story. Śiva and Pārvatī were dallying on the slopes of the Himalayas when Pārvatī, in jest, placed her hands over Śiva's eyes. "The whole universe was at once submerged in cosmic darkness and all activity was suspended; sacrifices stopped and gods became quiescent."[3] Thereupon Śiva's third eye appeared in the middle of his forehead and the universe was restored

---

[1]*Mahābhārata*, Anuśāsana Parva XVII. 50; *The Mahabharata of Krishna-Dwaipayana*; trans. K. M. Ganguly; published by Pratap Chandra Roy (12 vols.; Calcutta: Oriental Publishing Co., n.d.), X, 86. In the *Ṛg-veda* Indra is also called a dancer, and his dancing appears to be related to creation in II. 22. 4 and X. 72. 6.

[2]*Mahābhārata*, Anuśāsana Parva XVII (X, 107).

[3]Rao, *Elements of Hindu Iconography*, II, Part I, 49. See *Mahābhārata*, Anuśāsana Parva CXL. 43-44 (XI, 293). See also *Brahma-vaivarta-purāṇa*, Kṛṣṇa Janma Khaṇḍa 36. 12 ("There is none wiser than Śiva who, by the mere twinkling of his eye, by dint of his celestial wisdom, can destroy and create death and time") and 41. 60 ("He is capable of destroying the entire creation by a mere twinkle of his eye"); *Brahma-Vaivarta Puranam*, Part I: *Brahma and Prakriti Khandas*; Part II: *Ganesa and Krishna Janma Khandas* trans. Rajendra Nath Sen (Allahabad: Sudhindra Nath Vasu, Part I, 1920; Part II, 1922), Part II, pp. 263 and 282, respectively. The verse numbers in the Sanskrit version do not always correspond to those in Sen's translation; the verse numbers given here are from the Sanskrit version: *Brahma-vaivarta-purāṇam*, Śrīmaddvaipāyanamuni (praṇītam) (Ānandāśramasanskrit-granthāvaliḥ, Granthāṇkaḥ 102; 2 vols., n.p.: Ānandāśramamudranalaya, 1935).

Another version of creation in Śaivite tradition suggests a playful theme. In the *Yoginīhṛdaya* Śiva is said to paint the "World-Picture on Himself with the Brush which is His Will." Quoted in John Woodroffe, *Śakti and Śākta: Essays and Addresses* (6th ed.; Madras: Ganesh & Co., 1965), p. 44. See also Natanānanda-nātha's commentary on vs. 1 of the *Kāma-kalā-vilāsa* (Puṇyānanda-nātha, p. 2).

to life. The universe, that is, is a gossamer thing that dies at the mere closing of Śiva's eye. And it is re-created upon the mere opening of the divine eye.

God's rhythmical dance of creation and his ongoing pulse in the preservation of the world were favorite themes of the poet Kabīr (1440-1518). The world is the playground of God, and everything in it keeps time with his dance.

> From day to night, from night to day the soul of the world is swinging, each living thing to this world-soul doth cling, swinging, swaying, swinging. Heaven and Earth, the air and the water, the Moon and the Sun as their course they run are swinging, swaying. And God, the highest God . . . Swinging, swaying, swinging.[1]

> Dance, my heart! dance to-day with joy.
> The strains of love fill the days and the nights with music, and the world is listening to its melodies:
> Mad with joy, life and death dance to the rhythm of this music. The hills and the sea and the earth dance. The world of man dances in laughter and tears.[2]

> Held by the cords of love, the swing of the Ocean of Joy sways to and fro; and a mighty sound breaks forth in song.
> See what a lotus blooms there without water! and Kabir says,
> 'My heart's bee drinks its nectar.'

---

[1]Paul Althaus, *Mystic Lyrics from the Indian Middle Ages,* trans. P. Althaus (London: George Allen & Unwin, 1928), p. 64. Kabīr's image of swinging is also seen in a Ṛg-vedic hymn to Varuṇa. The *ṛṣi* sings: "When Varuṇa and I embark together and urge our boat into the midst of the ocean, /We, when we ride o'er ridges of the waters, will swing within that swing and there be happy" ("ā yad ruhāva varuṇaś ca nāvam pra yat samudra īrayāva madhyam / adhi yad apāṁ snubhis carāva pra preṅkha [rocking, swaying, pitching] īṅkhayāvahai śubhe kam"). VII. 88. 3; *Hymns of the Ṛgveda,* trans. Ralph T. H. Griffith (2 vols.; 4th ed.; Varanasi: Chowkhamba Sanskrit Series Office, 1963), II, 84.

[2]Kabir, *One Hundred Poems of Kabir,* trans. Rabindranath Tagore and Evelyn Underhill (London: Macmillan & Co., 1967), song 32, pp. 38-39.

. . . .
Music is all around it, and there the heart partakes of
the joy of the Infinite Sea.
. . . .
Kabir says: 'It is the sport of the Unattainable One:
look within, and behold how the moonbeams of that
Hidden One shine in you.'

There falls the rhythmic beat of life and death:
Rapture wells forth, and all space is radiant with light.
There the Unstruck Music is sounded;
. . . .
There the drum beats, and the lover swings in play.
. . . .
There the whole sky is filled with sound, and there that
music is made without fingers and without strings;
. . . .
What a frenzy of ecstasy there is in every hour!
. . . .
Kabir says: 'There have I witnessed the sport of One
Bliss!'
. . . .
. . . . I am drunken with the sight of this All![1]

He is pure and indestructible,
His form is infinite and fathomless,
He dances in rapture, and waves of form arise from His
dance.[2]

The poet-saint conveys a vision in these songs that affirms that all is the activity of God. It is a positive vision. For the cycles and rhythms of nature, including death as well as life, are a joyful dance in which God and man participate together. Together they perpetuate the life-soul of the created order by dancing on and on.

The Bengali poet Rabindranath Tagore portrays a similar picture of creation. He speaks of the "waves of creation," a common image referred to above. "These undulations and vibrations, these risings and fallings, are not the erratic con-

[1] *Ibid.*, song 17, pp. 18-24.
[2] *Ibid.*, song 26, p. 33

tortions of disparate bodies, they are a rhythmic dance."[1] The tempo of this dance is the heartbeat of God that pulses through the created order. As such, God is inextricably caught up in His creation.

> This world-song is never for a moment separated from its singer. It is not fashioned from any outward material. It is his joy itself taking never-ending form. It is the great heart sending the tremor of its thrill over the sky.[2]

For Tagore the world was one great festival, saturated with the bliss of God.

> Light, my light, the world-filling light, the eye-kissing light, heart-sweetening light!
>
> Ah, the light dances, my darling, at the centre of my life; the light strikes, my darling, the cords of my love; the sky opens, the wind runs wild, laughter passes over the earth.
>
> The butterflies spread their sails on the sea of light. Lilies and jasmines surge up on the crest of the waves of light.
>
> The light is shattered into gold on every cloud, my darling, and it scatters gems in profusion.
>
> Mirth spreads from leaf to leaf, my darling, and gladness without measure. The heaven's river has drowned its banks and the flood of joy is abroad.[3]

Tagore frequently celebrated the mystery of man's intimate link to this great festival of divine light in terms almost reminiscent of a biologist. The circulating blood and the orbiting planets dance to the same music.

> The same stream of life that runs through my veins night and day runs through the world and dances in rhythmic measures.
>
> . . . .
>
> I feel my limbs are made glorious by the touch of this

---

[1]Rabindranath Tagore, *Sādhanā*: *The Realisation of Life* (New York: Macmillan & Co., 1913), p. 97.

[2]*Ibid.*, p. 143.

[3]Rabindranath Tagore, *Gitanjali* (*Song Offerings*), trans. R. Tagore (London: Macmillan & Co., 1967), song 57, pp. 52-53.

world of life. And my pride is from the life-throb of ages dancing in my blood this moment.[1]

Last night, in the silence which pervaded the darkness, I stood alone and heard the voice of the singer of eternal melodies. When I went to sleep I closed my eyes with this last thought in my mind, that even when I remain unconscious in slumber the dance of life will still go on in the hushed arena of my sleeping body, keeping step with the stars. The heart will throb, the blood will leap in the veins, and the millions of living atoms of my body will vibrate in tune with the note of the harp-string that thrills at the touch of the master.[2]

A consistent theme in these poems is the delight that God takes in the act of creating, and the delight that he takes in participating in the ongoing order he has created. The image is not one of an aloof God, brooding and then carefully shaping the universe according to some premeditated plan. The image is rather of a bounteous, blissful deity whose delight overflows to create a dancing world. Creation proceeds not from any necessity on God's part but as a means of expressing his overabundance. The outstanding characteristic of the created order in these poems is not its once-for-allness, its well-regulated nature, its steady march toward a predetermined end, its inviolable laws, but its throbbing rhythm. And the rhythm is not that of a lifeless clock, of a well-tuned machine, but of a human heart, of rushing blood. If we must ask the question why God creates the world in these passages from Tagore and Kabīr, we must answer that He creates the world for the sheer delight of it, for the purpose of aimless display, as a stage upon which he may revel.

B. Māyā

The songs of Kabīr and Tagore convey the image of man delighting in a dancing creation. Indeed, one might almost say they convey the image of man bewitched by God's creation. The idea of the world enticing and enchanting man suggests

---

[1]*Ibid.*, song 69, pp. 64-65.
[2]Tagore,, *Sādhanā*, p. 144.

the idea of *māyā*, a central theme in Indian religion and a theme that further illustrates the *līlā* of the gods.

Māyā is frequently interpreted and defined as illusion, as something that distracts and hinders man in his spiritual quest. In the philosophy of strict nondualism (*advaita*) all appearances of diversity and form (*nāma-rūpa*) are "caused" by (or are) *māyā* and are essentially illusory; *māyā* is simply appearance, having no real cause *or* effect. It is the result of superimposition, or it *is* superimposition (as when a rope is mistaken for a snake). As such, it has no definite ontological status. It is nothing more (or less) than ignorance, or the projection of that ignorance (*avidyā*). It has nothing to do with the One, the Absolute Brahman.[1]

Māyā may be seen from another point of view, however. Or, we might say that *māyā* has another aspect. For *māyā* is also the power of the Absolute, or the power of the gods. As the power of the gods *māyā* is more than simply a negative concept, more than simply illusion. In the *Ṛg-veda māyā* means power, or the ability of the gods to change form and to create. *Māyā* is the supernatural ability on the part of the gods to extend themselves. It is their ability in this hymn, for example, to cause rain:

> Imperial Kings, strong, Heroes, Lords of earth and heaven, Mitra and Varuṇa, ye ever active Ones,
> Ye wait on thunder with the many-tinted clouds, and by the Asura's magic power [*māyā*] cause Heaven to rain.[2]

In the following hymn *māyā* is clearly linked to creation, to Varuṇa's establishing the world:

> I will declare this mighty deed of magic [*māyā*], of glorious Varuṇa the Lord Immortal,
> Who standing in the firmament hath meted the earth out with the Sun as with a measure.
>
> None, verily, hath ever let or hindered this the most wise God's mighty deed of magic [*māyā*],

[1]M. Hiriyanna, *Outlines of Indian Philosophy* (London: George Allen & Unwin, 1932), pp. 351 ff.

[2]*Ṛg-veda* V. 63. 3 (I, 534).

Whereby with all their flood, the lucid rivers fill
not one sea wherein they pour their waters.[1]

These passages are not unique but typical of the use of the term *māyā* in vedic literature.[2] In its earliest context, then, *māyā* meant the wonderful skill of the gods.[3] This meaning or aspect of *māyā*, furthermore, persists throughout Indian religious history.[4] In the *Bhāgavata-purāṇa*, for example, the same idea is seen when the illusion of Viṣṇu is called "wonderful wealth [*māyāvaibhavamadbhutam*]."[5]

From the finite point of view, from man's place in the world, *māyā* may indeed appear as primarily illusion. For the extraordinary effect of the gods' will is overpowering and bewitching, incomprehensible. But this is not to say that *māyā* does not exist, that it belongs to a realm of nonbeing. *Māyā* is illusory in much the same way that a mask is illusory. A mask creates illusion because it disguises something, it changes something into something else or someone into some-

---

[1]*Ibid.* V. 85. 5-6 (I, 552).

[2]See also *Ṛg-veda* III. 53. 8 and VI. 47. 18, where Indra projects himself in various forms by means of his *māyā*, and I. 80. 7, where Indra defeats Vṛtra with his "surpassing power" (*māyā*).

[3]Several studies have been done on the concept of *māyā*, all of which, to some extent, recognize this "positive" aspect of *māyā* as wonderful skill, mysterious power, magic ability. See, for example, Paul David Devanandan, *The Concept of Māyā* (London: Lutterworth Press, 1950); Prabhu Dutt Shastri, *The Doctrine of Maya* (London: Luzac & Co., 1911); and Ruth Reyna, *The Concept of Māyā: From the Vedas to the 20th Century* (Bombay: Asia Publishing House, 1962). Probably the most careful study of *māyā* has been done by Jan Gonda: *Change and Continuity in Indian Religion* (The Hague: Mouton & Co., 1965), "Māyā," pp. 164-97. See also his *Four Studies in the Language of Veda* ('s-Gravenhage: Mouton & Co., (9,195 "The Original Sense and the Etymology of the Skt. *Māyā*," pp. 119-94.

[4]According to Gonda, in fact, this aspect of *māyā* is the dominant aspect of the idea and is never lost sight of even in Śaṅkara. *Māyā* as mere illusion, hallucination pure and simple, is only maintained, he insists, in the philosophy of Prakāśānanda (*ca.* 1600), an *advaita* Vedantist. *Change and Continuity*, pp. 185-86.

[5]*Bhāgavata-purāṇa* XII. 10. 40 (V, 47).

one else. Yet a mask is real in that it enables its wearer to extend himself, to diversify. And a mask may also enable a deity to present himself. The mask may become a vehicle for his epiphany. In a similar way *māyā* can be seen as the mask of the Absolute; it is the way in which the Absolute displays itself.

It is as a vehicle of the gods' display, as their means of revealing themselves, then, that *māyā* may be understood as the *līlā* of the gods. For *māyā* is their means of creating and sustaining the phenomenal order, and *māyā* is always mysterious, unpredictable, and bewitching. The gods are great *māyins*, great magicians, and the created order is the result of their "trickery." They have conjured the world into being, and they similarly conjure it out of existence. The world is their toy, or their puppet, and they delight in making it dance by pulling invisible strings. Rāmakṛṣṇa says of Kālī: "She is the supreme Mistress of the cosmic play, and all objects, animate and inanimate, dance by her will."[1] In the *Devī Bhāgavata* it is written: "As a magician makes the wooden dolls dance in his hands at his will, so this world-enchanting Māyā is making this world, moving and nonmoving, dance from Brahmā down to the blades of grass and all human beings."[2] In his *Vinaya-patrikā* Tulsī Dās says of the world and *māyā*:

> Its realm is like a set of chessmen, the entire company is made of wood:
> You, O king [*Rām*], created this game,—in the beginning it was not.[3]

Another frequent and apt analogy that is used to describe the gods' relationship to the phenomenal world through their *māyā* is the spider and its web. In the *Bhāgavata-purāṇa* we read: "Just as a spider hides itself in its cobwebs so thou assuming the form of Brahma and others hast been sporting with the Creation, Destruction and Preservation of the Uni-

---

[1]M., *Gospel of Ramakrishna*, p. 30.

[2]*Devī Bhāgavata* VI. 31. 30-31; *The Srimad Devi Bhagavatam*, trans. Swami Vijnanananda (Allahabad: Sudhindra Nath Vasu, 1922), p. 593.

[3]*Vinaya-patrikā* 246. 4; Tulsī Dās, *The Petition to Rām*: *Hindi Devotional Hymns of the Seventeenth Century*, trans. F. R. Allchin (London: George Allen & Unwin, 1966), p. 242.

verse."[1] The spider's web is organically produced out of the spider. By means of his web he extends and displays himself. In his web others are unwittingly trapped. His web is enchanting and ephemeral. He himself remains unaffected by it although controlling it. So it is with the gods and their *māyā*. The world is a gossamer thing spun out by the gods and capable of bewitching and trapping men. But, unlike the spider in the analogy, the world is not spun out by the gods in deadly earnest with the intention of entrapment. Rather, bewitchment follows from the nature of the creation itself, which is the result of supernatural, mysterious, magical power. The effect is magical because the creator is a magician.

The mysterious and magical qualities of *māyā* express well the independence of the gods. For *māyā* is independent of space and time. It is not subject to regular laws or predictable patterns.[2] It is enchanting, often topsy-turvy, and therefore playful. The world born of *māyā* is at once a stage created by the gods upon which they may strut, a toy with which they play, and a mirage through and by which they dazzle.

Māyā may also be understood as a kind of divine self-understanding, or inner self-dalliance. This is particularly clear when the power of *māyā*, the urge to create form and diversity, is identified with the *śakti* of the gods. In the Trika school of Kashmir Śaivism, *śakti* is understood as that principle by which Śiva is enabled to realize his own self. *Śakti* is a mirror, as it were, in which Śiva is able to enjoy his own bliss. This is to say that within the Godhead there is a play between potentiality and actuality, between enjoyer and enjoyed.[3] In the *Bhāgavata-purāṇa* this inner development is spoken of in terms of Puruṣa and Prakṛti:

[1] *Bhāgavata-purāṇa* II. 9. 26-27 (I, 126). See also Natanānanda-nātha's commentary to vs. 1 of the *Kāma-kalā-vilāsa* (Puṇyānanda-nātha, p. 2). Woodroffe, discussing the creation of the world vis-à-vis the rhythmic action of Ātman, suggests also the image of the tortoise, which extends and then withdraws its limbs back into itself. *Śakti and Śākta*, p. 376.

[2] In the *Devī Bhāgavata* the different and strange effects of *māyā* are said to be as unpredictable as in dreams. VI. 30. 38-39 (p. 591).

[3] Sudhendukumar Das, *Sakti or Divine Power* (Calcutta: University of Calcutta, 1934), p. 61. See also *Kāma-kalā-vilāsa* 2, in which *śakti* is called "the Pure Mirror in which Śiva experiences Himself" (Puṇyānanda-nātha, p. 6).

> That Purusha is manifest of itself, and along with it the universe is manifested. When that Prakṛti of subtle attributes endowed with the divine powers of the Lord Viṣṇu comes in sportive revel before that Puruṣa, he accepts her at pleasure.[1]

Tagore sees man's striving after God, the relationship of I and Thou, as a movement that takes place within the Godhead, a kind of game initiated and resolved by God.

> That I should make much of myself and turn it on all sides, thus casting coloured shadows on thy radiance—such is thy *māyā*.
>
> Thou settest a barrier in thine own being and then callest thy severed self in myriad notes. This thy self-separation has taken body in me.
>
> . . . .
>
> The great pageant of thee and me has overspread the sky. With the tune of thee and me all the air is vibrant, and all ages pass with the hiding and seeking of thee and me.[2]

By means of his *māyā* God creates a galaxy of forms out of himself, which causes an artificial division, the appearance of diversity within his essential unity. He creates a pageant, Tagore suggests, a circus of things. And his delight is in playing a game of hide-and-seek with himself, in creating diversity from unity and resolving diversity back into unity. The point of this process is no point at all. It is simply display, always leading back to the beginning. It is a game, almost a joke. And man is part of the game. Salvation or release depends upon learning how to play the game or laugh at the joke.

The first step in learning the game is the recognition that the phenomenal world, the bewildering world of flux and shadows, is really identical with the *śakti* of God. To play the game one must affirm, not deny, this world, for to deny it is to reject that which is shot through with divine power—to frown, as it were, at God's joke. This is the lesson, I think, of the left-handed Tantrics (*vāmācāras*). The notorious

---

[1] *Bhāgavata-purāṇa* III. 26. 3-4 (I, 119).

[2] Tagore, *Gitanjali*, song 71, pp. 66-67.

pañcatattva ritual is a means of affirming in a radical way the "nonserious" nature of the world. The world, it is affirmed, is not a problem but a delight. The world, all of it, is neither good nor evil, permanent nor impermanent, but God Himself (or Herself) playing. The *vīra*, the hero, is he who has come to know that as the world is simply the playground of God it has no power to bind. Heinrich Zimmer sees this point clearly.

> Let those who suffer from the toils of saṁsāra seek release: the perfect devotee does not suffer; for he can both visualize and experience life and the universe as the revelation of that Supreme Divine Force (*śakti*) with which he is in love, the all-comprehensive Divine Being in its cosmic aspect of playful, aimless display (*līlā*)—which precipitates pain as well as joy, but in its bliss transcends them both. He is filled with the holy madness of that "ecstatic love" (*prema*) which transmutes the world.[1]

In the following passage Zimmer speaks of the heroic method in which the devotee partakes of things that are considered particularly vile or unclean, such as meat, wine, and sexual intercourse (the five forbidden things, the *pañcatattva*):

> In this way he breaks within himself the tension of the "forbidden," and resolves everything in light; recognizing in everything the one Śakti which is the general support of the world, macrocosmic as well as microcosmic, the mother of the gods and elves, the weaver of the moon-dream

[1]Heinrich Zimmer, *Philosophies of India*, ed. Joseph Campbell (Cleveland: World Publishing Co., 1956), p. 571.

of history. Therewith comes release from the world-illusion—release through its full enjoyment or realization.[1]

It is not the "radical left" alone that appreciates the affirmative aspect of the world of flux. In the *Bhāgavata-purāṇa* Brahmā says to Kṛṣṇa:

> Who in the three worlds can penetrate into the inscrutable mystery? . . . For thou dost sport about, spreading the whole of thy delusive energy over all. In consequence of this, the whole universe, which is an embodiment of illusion and is like unto the dream itself, which has the appearance of gloominess, and is full of troubles and vexations, shines most happily and seems to be indestructible; for it has sprung from thee, who art eternal and ever delightful.[2]

Rāmakṛṣṇa also saw the world in this way and often urged his devotees to take on an affirmative attitude toward the phenomenal world.

> The jñani says, "This world is a 'framework of illusion.' " But he who is beyond both knowledge and ignorance describes it as a "mansion of mirth." He sees that it is God Himself who has become the universe, all living beings, and the twenty-four cosmic principles.[3]

And Rāmakṛṣṇa told M. (one of his devotees and the author of *The Gospel of Ramakrishna*): "How can one who is eternally perfect be afraid of the world? *He knows how to play his game.* An eternally perfect soul can even lead a worldly life if he desires."[4] He says of his own experience during his Tantric *sādhana*: "The whole world and everything in it appeared as the lila, the sport, of Shiva and Shakti."[5] And he often beseeched the Goddess to let him continue enjoying the carnival of her creation. "O Mother, let me remain in contact with

---

[1] *Ibid.*, p. 579. See also Woodroffe, *Śakti and Śākta*, p. 377.
[2] *Bhāgavata-purāṇa* X. 14. 21-22 (IV, 62).
[3] M., *Gospel of Ramakrishna,* p. 523.
[4] *Ibid.*, p. 689 (italics mine).
[5] *Ibid.*, p. 21.

men! Don't make me a dried-up ascetic. I want to enjoy Your sport in the world."[1]

The spiritual seeker is perfected when he learns to accept the world of flux as the play of God, when he learns to join in the play of God's phantasmagoric creation. The veil of *māyā* is not overcome by withdrawal, by shunning the world. The veil is overcome by tearing and ripping, by wrapping the veil around the self, as it were, and delighting in it. Commenting on this method of release vis-à-vis *māyā*, Mircea Eliade says:

> To tear the veil of *maya* and pierce the secret of cosmic illusion amounts primarily to understanding its character as "play"—that is to say free, spontaneous activity of the divine—and consequently to imitating the divine action and attaining liberty. The paradox of Indian thought is that the idea of liberty is so concealed by the idea of *maya*—that is of illusion and slavery—that it takes a long detour to find it. It is enough, however, to discover the deep meaning of *maya*—divine "play"—to be already on the way to deliverance.[2]

The lesson of the *śākta* devotee, then, is that the world is not such a serious and somber place after all. The world in all its flux and confusion is the sport of the gods, the dance of *śakti-māyā*. The coming and going of things, the birth and death of men and universes, is all a fantastic ballet, and every facet of the phenomenal world has a place in its choreography. From such an affirmative, almost radical, point of view the "dried-up ascetic" is a wallflower, refusing to participate in the cosmic dance. To put it another way, the puppet in the case of the withdrawn ascetic has had the audacity to cut his own strings. The *śākta* devotee would prefer to dance his way to heaven and leave the world echoing with his laughter or haunted by his secret smile.

[1] *Ibid.*, p. 66.

[2] Mircea Eliade, *Mephistopheles and the Androgyne: Studies in Religious Myth and Symbol*, trans. J. M. Cohen, pp. 36-37.

C. *The Great Goddess and the Play of Grace*

In the context of Indian religion the term *śakti* suggests much more than just the power of the gods or of a particular God. Śakti is a being, for many the greatest Being of all. She is called Durgā, Kālī, Mahāmāyā, and many other names. But she is the Great Goddess, or simply the Mother.

The myths of Kālī and Durgā illustrate particularly well the identification of the Goddess with the dynamic power, the *śakti*, of the gods. The Black One, Kālī, is commonly portrayed as dancing on the prostrate figure of Śiva. Her aspect is terrible; her whirling arms suggest the frantic merry-go-round of life. Rāmakṛṣṇa sings of her:

> Behold my Mother playing with Shiva, lost in an ecstasy of joy!
> Drunk with a draught of celestial wine, She reels, and yet She does not fall.
> Erect She stands on Shiva's bosom, and the earth trembles under Her tread;
> She and Her Lord are mad with frenzy, casting aside all fear and shame![1]

Śiva, the Absolute, is typically pictured lying deathly pale and still beneath her, self-contained potentiality. Kālī dances on his chest, tongue lolling, divine potential realized in the concreteness of the phenomenal world.[2] Her appearance suggests vitality, the liquid, tumultuous aspect of creation. And almost certainly there is a sword and a severed head held in two of her several hands, and a garland of skulls hangs around her neck. Her lolling red tongue suggests her all-consuming nature, her nature as the universal destroyer. For Kālī is the creation itself, a crazy, spinning top that reels along, carefully maintaining the balance between life and death. Quoting Rāmakṛṣṇa again:

---

[1] M., *Gospel of Ramakrishna*, pp. 494-95.

[2] Heinrich Zimmer, *Myths and Symbols of Indian Art and Civilization*, ed. Joseph Campbell. See Pls. LXVI-LXIX for typical representations of Kālī. To this day similar images may be seen by the thousands in Bengal during Kālī Pūjā.

O Mother Shyama, full of the waves of drunkenness divine !
Who knows how Thou dost sport in the world ?
Thy fun and frolic and Thy glances put to shame the god of love.
O Wielder of the sword ! O Thou of terrifying face !
The earth itself is shaken under Thy leaps and strides.[1]

The origin of the goddess Durgā illustrates just as clearly the identification of the Great Goddess with the *śakti* of God. At a time when the gods were threatened with extinction by a fearsome demon, they banded together and pooled their powers in the form of a great cloud. When the cloud condensed, Durgā appeared, many armed and lovely. The primordial power of the gods, their will and creativity, became embodied in the wonderful Durgā, who went forth and easily defeated the awful Mahiṣāsura, the buffalo demon.[2]

Unlike such great deities as Śiva and Viṣṇu, the Great Goddess rarely expresses herself in quietude or withdrawal from the world. Kālī and Durgā particularly seem constantly bent on frantic movement, the realizing of every potential that is hinted at in the sleeping Viṣṇu or the meditating Śiva. The Great Goddess is divine display embodied. Her immense yet apparently aimless energy is *māyā* itself, and so she is frequently called Mahāmāyā. She is as illusive as an elf and as tangible as the earth itself. She is unpredictable, difficult to know, but easy to serve. She is relative in that she is identified with flux and movement. But she is the Absolute relative. She is the essence of the flitting *līlā* of the gods. Her cosmic gamboling is totally free and tumultuous.[3]

---

[1]M., *Gospel of Ramakrishna*, p. 808.

[2]This story is told in the *Mārkaṇḍeya-purāṇa, Devī-māhātmya* 81-93; *The Mārkaṇḍeya Purāṇa*, trans. F. Eden Pargiter, pp. 465-523.

[3]As I write, it is impossible to ignore the sounds of the great Durgā Pūjā festival that each year in the early autumn resound throughout Calcutta. Durgā Pūjā is a time when cares are forgotten and the people give themselves up to merrymaking. Throughout the city *pūjā* tents, or *pandals*, are erected to shelter images of Durgā killing the great demon as he emerges from the carcass of the just-slain buffalo. For four days the countless *pandals* are centers of great activity. *Pūjā* itself centers around the reading of the Devi's exploits from the *purāṇas* and is always accompanied by the racket of drums, cymbals, and sometimes horns. During those times when the priest is not actually

In her many and varied forms the Goddess is probably the clearest manifestation of creation as divine *līlā*. Her restless nature is the very embodiment of *līlā*. Tulsī Dās sings of Pārvatī:

O nurse of moving and unmoving things,
  Mother, daughter of the upholding mountains,
By your grace Viranchi creates the world,
  Hari sustains it and Hara does destroy it;
In you is the evolving of the universe,
  in you is all its play,
And in you too is its dissolution,
  O Mother, daughter of the mountains.[1]

"This world, moving and unmoving," says the *Devī Bhāgavata*, "rolls in madness, overpowered by Her Mâyâ."[2] "This whole cosmos is always urged into activity by Her and thus goes rolling on and on incessantly."[3] The Goddess is so intimately associated with the creation of the world that, as in the case of Śiva mentioned above, the world vanishes when she blinks her eyes.[4]

Rāmakṛṣṇa often spoke of the dual aspect of the divine as the *nitya* and the *līlā*. The former is the Absolute—the formless, attributeless Brahman. The relative aspect of the divine—its

---

performing *pūjā*, loudspeakers tuned to peak volume keep up a constant din. Any music at all seems appropriate, film songs seeming to be most popular right now. The effect of Durgā Pūjā in Calcutta is, indeed, that of tumult. Work has stopped; everyone is out in the streets and enjoying a certain license. It seems that the drunken universe of the Goddess is being aptly celebrated. And while many Bengalis see the loudspeakers as a hopeless commercialization of the festival, their awful noise, I think, is necessary to pay adequate homage to the fantastic whirligig that is Calcutta. It seems the more traditional drums and cymbals simply can't produce the din that is necessary to celebrate Calcutta, this fantastic and tumultuous display of the Devi's *māyā* (September 28--October 2, 1968, Calcutta). See Chintaharan Chakravarti, *Tantras: Studies on Their Religion and Literature*, pp. 94-103, and Mahāmahopādhyāya Pandurang Vaman Kane, *History of Dharmaśāstra* (*Ancient and Mediaeval Religious and Civil Law in India*), Vol. V., Part I, pp. 154-87, for a description of Durgā Pūjā.

[1]Tulsī Dās *Kavitāvali* VII. 173; trans. F. R. Allchin, p. 199.

[2]*Devī Bhāgavata* IV. 13. 36-37 (p. 297).

[3]*Ibid.* IV. 20. 51 (p. 326).

[4]*Ibid.* IX. 9. 1 (p. 840). See also *Saundaryalaharī* 56; *The Saundaryalaharī: or, Flood of Beauty*, ed. and trans. W. Norman Brown, p. 70: "From the closing and opening of your eyes the earth is dissolved and created."

manifestation as man and particularly *śakti*, or the Goddess—Ramakṛṣṇa called *līlā*. To Rāmakṛṣṇa, it seems, *līlā* was the appropriate term to express the movement and ambiguity of the phenomenal world, of man's "moon-dream of history." The Goddess for Rāmakṛṣṇa definitely belonged to this realm of *līlā*. For the Goddess is eminently concrete. She is the abundant Mother who delights in coddling her devotee. And sometimes like a mother her love seems to fluctuate. She seems almost frivolous with her favors, blessing now one and now the other child. The world and its mistress are a game and a gamester, respectively, and so their realm in the scheme of things for Ramakṛṣṇa is appropriately called *līlā*.[1]

Within the relative aspect of the divine, within the Goddess herself, of course, there is also a dual aspect. She is the mother of all, on the one hand, and the destroyer of all, on the other. And this dual aspect points again to an erratic, almost capricious, aspect of the divine that is indicative of its playful aspect in Hinduism. This dual aspect is clearly common to other Indian gods. Śiva, for example, is the paradigm of the withdrawn *yogin*, on the one hand, and the mad dancer, on the other.[2] He is both the creator and the destroyer of the world. Among the Hindu gods, however, the dual aspect of the Great Goddess, especially Kālī, is the most strikingly polarized. The effect of this polarity is an overwhelming ambivalence vis-à-vis her devotees. In the *Devī-māhātmya* Durgā is saluted as both "the Night of the world's destruction, the Great Night, and the Night of delusion, terrible !"[3] and "gentle, *yea* more than gentle, exceedingly beautiful to those who are wholly gentle."[4] In the *Devī Bhāgavata* the Goddess is called "Horrible, Awful, That appearance looked terrific to the eyes, heart and mind."[5] In the next passage, however, the Goddess suddenly shows her compassionate aspect to reassure the gods who have become frightened of her:

---

[1]M., *Gospel of Ramakrishna*, p. 382.

[2]Wendy Doniger O'Flaherty has articulated several other polarities within the figure of Śiva, particularly the polarity of asceticism and sexuality. "Asceticism and Sexuality in the Mythology of Śiva," *History of Religions*, VIII, No. 4 (May, 1969), 300-337; IX, No. 1 (August, 1969), 1-41.

[3]*Mārkaṇḍeya-purāṇa* 81. 59 (p. 471).

[4]*Ibid.* 81. 62 (p. 471).

[5]*Devī Bhāgavata* VII. 33. 38 (p. 712).

> The World Mother, the Ocean of mercy, seeing the Devas terrified, withheld Her Fearful Cosmic Form and showed Her very beautiful appearance, pleasing to the whole world. Her body became soft and gentle. In one hand She held the noose, and in another She held the goad. The two other hands made signs to dispel all their fears and ready to grant the boons. Her eyes emitted rays of kindness; Her face was adorned with beautiful smiles.[1]

In the myth of Durgā in the *Devi-māhātmya* there is a passage that illustrates her two contrasting aspects in a delightful way. When she confronted the demons who were oppressing the world, she appeared so beautiful to them that they at once proposed marriage to her. She agreed to marry any one of them who could defeat her in battle. Once battle was joined, however, Durgā's aspect as Cāmuṇḍā, the awful one, came forth. The hideous shrew suddenly replaced the charming maid, and the demons shrank from her in horror.[2] And when this aspect of Durgā is celebrated on the second night of Durgā Pūjā, one senses the change in mood. Just before the animal sacrifice, which is performed in orthodox *śākta* families, the atmosphere loses its gaiety and the mood becomes tense. At that moment when Durgā is believed to have slain the buffalo demon, the animal (a goat or young buffalo) is beheaded and its still-twitching head offered to the Terrible One. At this point in the festival the Benign Mother remains temporarily in abeyance.[3]

The variety of ways in which the Goddess appeared to Rāmakṛṣṇa and the striking contrasts of these appearances, however, seem to be unsurpassable in their ambivalence. She appeared to him on one occasion, for example, as a little girl. "She came to me another day as a Mussalman girl six or seven years old. She had a tilak on her forehead and was naked.

---

[1] *Ibid.* VII. 33. 54-55 (pp. 713-14). Cf. *Mahānirvāṇa-tantra* XIII. 9-10 (p. 373), where Kālī's ferocious and benign aspects are similarly contrasted.

[2] See Zimmer, *Myths and Symbols*, Pl. LVII, for Durgā's horrible aspect.

[3] I saw this sacrifice performed on the Mahāṣṭami day of Durgā Pūjā at the home of Samaren Roy, an orthodox Śākta, in Calcutta on September 29, 1968. The actual sacrificial ritual is called the Sandhi Pūjā.

She walked with me, *joking and frisking like a child.*"[1] Here is a lovely image of the carefree, happy simplicity of the Goddess's unreserved enjoyment of man. So intimate was Rāmakṛṣṇa's love for her that she appeared to him as a child and joked with him. Compare with this image, then, the following vision he had of the Mother as divine *māyā*, the creator of the world:

> In this vision he saw a woman of exquisite beauty, about to become a mother, emerging from the Ganges and slowly approaching the Panchavati. Presently she gave birth to a child and began to nurse it tenderly. A moment later she assumed a terrible aspect, seized the child with her grim jaws, and crushed it. Swallowing it, she re-entered the waters of the Ganges.[2]

This great Being, so popular in India and especially in Bengal, is the mother of man. It is she who nurses him and protects him when he is desperate. But it is also she who suddenly seems to lash out at him capriciously and viciously. And it was precisely this inexplicable aspect of the divine that Rāmakṛṣṇa used to call the gods' play. Rāmakṛṣṇa is speaking to one of his disciples:

> Hari: "Why is there so much suffering in the world?"
>
> Master: "This world is the lila of God. It is like a game. In this game there are joy and sorrow, virtue and vice, knowledge and ignorance, good and evil. The game cannot continue if sin and suffering are altogethe eliminated from the creation."[3]

On another occasion a different disciple asked him a question in the same vein, and he, too, received the same kind of answer.

> Bhavanath (to the Master): "Sir, I have a question to ask. I don't quite understand the *Chandi* [the *Devi-māhātmya*]. It is written there that the Divine Mother kills all beings. What does that mean?"
>
> Master: "That is all Her lila, Her sportive pleasure."[4]

---

[1] M., *Gospel of Ramakrishna*, p. 175 (italics mine).
[2] *Ibid.*, pp. 21-22.
[3] *Ibid.*, p. 436.
[4] *Ibid.*, p. 768.

It was clear to Rāmakṛṣṇa that the Goddess in her grandeur surpasses man's comphrehension. To man, the mere toy of the Goddess, she appears uncontrollable, one could almost say an outlaw. For the Goddess is not bound by cause and effect, or by theological or moral laws. This was also seen by an earlier Bengali poet-saint, Rāmprasād, one of whose songs Rāmakṛṣṇa sings:

> Naked She roams the world, slaying Her demon foes,
> Or stands erect on Shiva's breast.
> Her feet upon Her Husband's form!
> What a strange wife She makes!
> My mother's play, declares Prasad, shatters all rules and laws.[1]

The gods' erratic, playful nature is also clearly manifest in the way they bestow their grace, how they seem to toy with each individual destiny. It is as if the ultimately serious business of salvation is some kind of divine game. "Just as kiddies play with a stick-horse, even so the Lord, only as a matter of play, submits Himself to those who are His own and acts with the fools otherwise, without however presenting Himself (before them)."[2] Rāmakṛṣṇa suggests that God has essentially the nature of a child who bestows his favors in a totally unpredictable, playful way:

> God has the nature of a child. A child is sitting with gems in the skirt of his cloth. Many a person passes by him along the road. Many of them pray to him for gems. But he hides the gems with his hands and says, turning his face, "No, I will not give any away." But another man comes along. He doesn't ask for the gems, and yet the child runs after him and offers him the gems, begging him to accept them.[3]

Tagore submits himself to the whims of God, to His play, as he calls it. He is willing to win or to lose. And one senses in Tagore that being part of the play is more important than

[1] *Ibid.*, p. 474.
[2] From the Karnatak poet Jagannāthadāsa (1727-1809); in A. P. Karmarkar and N. B. Kalamdani, *Mystic Teachings of the Haridasas of Karnataka*, p. 119.
[3] M., *Gospel of Ramakrishna*, p. 769.

whether one wins or loses. For in the play these opposites are transcended.

> If this be thy wish and if this be thy play, then take this fleeting emptiness of mine, paint it with colours, gild it with gold, float it on the wanton wind and spread it in varied wonders.
>
> And again when it shall be thy wish to end this play at night, I shall melt and vanish away in the dark, or it may be in a smile of the white morning, in a coolness of purity transparent.[1]

The Great Goddess, however, appears most often as the ringmaster of this bewildering carnival of grace, this game of hide-and-seek. The sage Vyāsa says to the Goddess, half in complaint and half in wonder:

> We think it is all sport with You to see our opinions different, rather contradictory, and it is You who got us involved in quarrels with each other and it is Your pleasure to witness how we fight against each other.
>
> O Sinless one! Châmunde! Were You not so fond to see our fight, how then, we being brothers are at war against each other. Certainly it is Your Divine Sport.[2]

The remarkable Rāmakṛṣṇa, again, clearly realized the playful aspect of the Goddess's grace. He pictures her here as taking delight in her human creation, in playing her game with him:

> Master: "The Divine Mother is always playful and sportive. This universe is Her play. She is selfwilled and must always have Her own way. She gives freedom to one out of a hundred thousand."
>
> A Brahmo Devotee: "But sir, if She likes, She can give freedom to all. Why, then, has She kept us bound to the world?"
>
> Master: "That is Her will. She wants to continue playing with Her created beings. In a game of hide-and-seek the running about soon stops if in the beginning all the

---

[1]Tagore, *Gitanjali*, song 80, pp. 74-75.
[2]*Devī Bhāgavata* IV. 15. 45-46 (p. 306).

> players touch the 'granny.' If all touch her, then how can the game go on? That displeases her. Her pleasure is in continuing the game."[1]

And when one of her playmates can win the game, can gain release, she is delighted. "Then the Divine Mother claps her hands in joy and exclaims, 'Bravo! There they go!' "[2]

The Great Goddess, then, illustrates the sportive aspect of the divine in three respects. She is the embodiment of the mighty and magical power of the gods, their *śakti*. As the *śakti* of the gods her nature is tumultuous, both creative and destructive, but totally free and unpredictable. She is the great enchantress. Second, the Goddess displays most clearly and dramatically the dual nature, the ambivalence, of the divine. She is at once the loving mother and the terrible fiend. She shatters all laws, alternately coddling and terrifying her devotees in the process. And, finally, presiding over the game of grace, the sport of salvation, she delights in man's feeble attempts and repeated failures and applauds his sometime triumphs.

D. *Divine Madness*

The anarchical, tumultuous aspect of the divine, so clearly expressed in several of the above passages, hints at something even deeper in the divine, something even more totally other, and something that also expresses the playful aspect of the gods. One senses, that is, that the gods are drunk, or maybe even mad. This eerie, somewhat frightening presence is reflected in the following passage from the *Agni-purāṇa*, a *mantra* to the wild man-lion *avatāra* of Viṣṇu:

> Om ksoum obesiance to Narasinha, who is effulgent with the light of ten thousand million suns, who is provided with teeth and claws hard and strong as the bolts of heaven, and who with his dreadful and dishevelled manes wildly dancing in storm, is manifest as blowing on a trumpet, whose unearthly peals have heaved up the one universal ocean of the millinim, the ocean madly, mightily, dashing rolling, dancing, with its sable energy of destruction over

[1] M., *Gospel of Ramakrishna*, p. 136.
[2] *Ibid.*, p. 436.

the space where the suns and constellations have been, in a weird dance of the ecstasy of death.[1]

There is madness hinted at, too, in the following invocation to Viṣṇu: "May the Almighty Lord. . .whose loud and violent laughter reverberates in the etherial space and causes miscarriage in the pregnant women,—protect me."[2] One feels that perhaps there is an insane being in control of things who is perpetrating a not-too-harmless joke upon man.

The two deities, however, that seem to have the strongest strains of madness are Śiva and the Great Goddess. Tulsī Dās says of Śiva: "This serpent-and skull-bearing god is playful, and on all sides of his house is a curtaining veil of hemp."[3] And he rather unambiguously calls Śiva "this monstrous lunatic" and "Master Simpleton."[4] Rao describes Rudra-Śiva during the purāṇic period in terms that I do not think are exaggerated:

> He laughs, sings and dances in ecstacy, and plays on a number of musical instruments; he leaps, gapes and weeps and makes others weep; speaks like a mad man or a drunkard, as also in sweet voice. . . .He dallies with the daughters and wives of the *rishis;* he has erect hair, looks obscene in his nakedness and has an excited look.[5]

There is in Śiva an aspect of primordial wildness, as his earlier name, Rudra (the howler, from the root *rud*), suggests. His untamed nature is overwhelming. He is a genuinely free spirit, bound by no rules. For madness, like play, is a release from duty and responsibility. Śiva the mad god is not bound by any of the restricting limits of the rather tedious sane world.

Another aspect of Śiva's madness is expressed in a poem by an anonymous Bengali poet, in which Umā explains to her mother why she cannot visit home more often:

> You forget me, Mother, and all that I endured with my mad husband. Bhōlā is ever laughing and weeping and

---

[1]*Agni-purāṇa* 63. 3; *Agni Purāṇam : A Prose English Translation,* trans. Manmatha Nāth Dutt Shastrī, I, 229.
[2]*Bhāgavata-purāṇa* VI. 8. 14 (II, 301).
[3]Tulsī Dās *Kavitāvalī* VII. 155 (p. 192).
[4]*Ibid.* VII. 158 (p. 192) and VII. 159 (p. 193).
[5]Rao, *Elements of Hindu Iconography,* II, Part I, 43.

knows no one save me. He is always eating hemp, and I must stay near him. I cannot keep from worrying and wondering if he is safe or if any harm has come to him.

I have to lift his food up to his mouth, or he would forget to eat. There is nothing left of me, I am spent with worrying about this madman. I put him at his ease and came away, and then what floods of tears I shed, Mother. For I was fearful lest he go off alone, and none is so careless of himself as he.[1]

Here is the image of a more sedate madness, of a drug-intoxicated god who is absent minded and unable to take care of himself. And in this tamer aspect of madness one also senses a playful theme. Śiva is irresponsible and careless. He is beyond the restrictions of the householder. He could not care less about behaving as a husband should. His actions sound aimless and senseless. He is as irresponsible and helpless as a child.

The Great Goddess is frequently described as drunken, which well she might be, for she embodies *māyā*, the effect of which is intoxicating. Śaṅkara sings of her:

> Ever are we protected by Her whose abode is the Kadamba forest,
>
> . . . .
>
> Whose cheeks are flushed with wine,
> Ever singing sweet songs; the playful one, dark as a cloud,
> Ever compassionate to all.[2]

Rāmakṛṣṇa puts the matter more directly when he says of Kālī: "She appears to be reeling under the spell of wine. But who would create this mad world unless under the influence of divine drunkenness?"[3]

In the *Bhāgavata-purāṇa* Kālī is described in a way that suggests she is more than simply intoxicated. She is described as

---

[1]Edward J. Thompson and Arthur Marshman Spencer, *Bengali Religious Lyrics, Śākta*, no. 98, p. 98.

[2]From *Tripurasundarīstotra* 3; *Hymns to the Goddess*, trans. Arthur and Ellen Avalon [John Woodroffe and Lady Woodroffe], pp. 162-63. See also the meditation *mantra* (*dhyāna mantra*) in *Śāradātilakatantram* 10. 71; *Shāradātilakatantram*, in Arthur Avalon (ed.), *Tantrik Texts*, XVI, Part I, 27.

[3]M., *Gospel of Ramakrishna*, p. 13.

becoming demonical in appearance and laughing as if to destroy the universe. She becomes drunk on blood and begins to dance and sing aloud. Then "she with her followers sported with the severed heads of the thieves as if they were wooden balls in sport."[1] This outrageous behavior is similarly described in the songs of Rāmprasād:

> This world, O Mother, is Thy madhouse! What can
> I say of all Thy virtues?
> Setting aside Thine elephant, Thou roamest alone on foot;
> Putting off Thy gems and pearls, O Self-willed Mother,
> Thou dost adorn Thy comely neck with a garland of human
> heads.
> Now Thou must rescue Ramprasad out of the forest of
> this world.[2]

> All this is a girl's madcap pleasure, in whose enchantment the three worlds swoon into forgetfulness. She is mad, her lord is mad, his two disciples are mad. Her beauty and her nature, her gestures and her thought, surpass all speech. If one takes her name, one's happiness flames into ashes, and the burning pain of poison comes into the throat.[3]

The insanity of the Devī is also strikingly portrayed in contemporary Bengali religious lithographs. I have before me, for example, an image of the Goddess in which she is shown dancing on the prostrate bodies of Kāma and his wife, Ratī. The Devī, wearing a garland of skulls, holds in one hand a bloodied sword and in the other her own severed head. Three jets of blood spurt from her severed neck; two jets are arching into the mouths of her female devotees, and the other is flowing into her own mouth.[4] A more insane being than this headless goddess is difficult to imagine.

---

[1]*Bhāgavata-purāṇa* V. 9. 18 (II, 195).

[2]As sung by Ramakrishna; M., *Gospel of Ramakrishna*, p. 516.

[3]Thompson and Spencer, no. 23, pp. 45-46. Other examples of Kālī's madness in the poems of Rāmprasād may be found in *Rama Prasada's Devotional Songs: The Cult of Shakti*, trans. Jadunath Sinha, pp. 75, 95, 98, 111, 150.

[4]This aspect of the goddess is one of ten forms (called *daśamahāvidyā*) that Satī took to frighten Śiva when he tried to prevent her from attending her father's sacrifice. Each form covered a direction of the cosmos, thus surrounding Śiva. This particular form is called the Chinnamastā, the severed-headed one. The story of this aspect is told in the *Nārada-pañcarātra*, and a

Finally, the following insane, rollicking poem sung by Surendra, a devotee of Rāmakṛṣṇa, will suffice to illustrate the madness of this peculiar divine couple, Śiva and Kālī:

> Crazy is my Father, crazy my Mother,
> And I, their son, am crazy too!
> Shyama [the dark one] is my Mother's name.
> My Father strikes His cheeks and makes a hollow sound:
> *Ba-ba-bom! Ba-ba-bom!*
> And my Mother, drunk and reeling,
> Falls across my Father's body!
> Shyama's streaming tresses hang in vast disorder;
> Bees are swarming numberless
> About Her crimson Lotus Feet.
> Listen, as She dances, how Her anklets ring![1]

It is difficult to think of a more fitting way in which to express the anarchical *līlā* of the gods. Their presence is so overwhelmingly eerie, their actions so weird and otherworldly, that they must certainly be mad. A mad god, a mad goddess. Indeed, a mad couple in whose hands tenuously rests the fate of this tumbling, spinning world. Here is a radical affirmation that the gods are totally other, completely free to behave according to no rule, law, or logic. In their madness they gambol, rollick, and laugh their way through the universe as unhampered as adolescents at play.

E. *Divine Comedy*

The image of Chinnamastā holding her own severed head in one hand and the sword with which she has decapitated herself in the other suggests another theme that expresses the *līlā* of the gods. It suggests the theme of divine self-enchantment or, in

---

detailed description of its appearance is given in the *dhyāna mantra* of Chinnamastā in the *Tantrasāra*, a major "textbook" of Tantrism, by the sixteenth-century Bengali theologian Kṛṣṇānanda Āgamavāgīśa. The modern lithographs are remarkably faithful to the *dhyāna mantra*, even to the point of picturing Kāma and Ratī copulating within the blossom of a lotus beneath the Devī. "Daśamahāvidyā," in Nāgendranāth Basu (ed.), *Viśvakoṣa*, VIII, 405-18. *Viśvakoṣa* is a Bengali encyclopedia. An illustration of the Chinnamastā can be found in Ajit Mookerjee, *Tantra Art: Its Philosophy and Physics*, Pl. LXV.

[1] M., *Gospel of Ramakrishna*, p. 961.

this extreme case, divine self-destruction. The headless goddess is the all-consuming goddess who has become so absorbed in her dance of destruction that she has destroyed herself.

This theme is delightfully illustrated in the *Brahma-vaivarta-purāṇa.* Śiva is approached by the demon Vṛka, who has performed strict austerities. Vṛka asks Śiva for a boon as a reward for his long and difficult exercises. Śiva asks Vṛka what boon he would like, and when Vṛka asks to be able to kill anyone simply by his touch, Śiva grants that boon. As soon as it has been given, Vṛka seeks to test his new power by touching Śiva him-self. Śiva, in panic, flees with Vṛka in pursuit. Coming to Kṛṣṇa, Śiva asks for protection, whereupon Kṛṣṇa, by means of his *māyā*, deludes Vṛka into touching his own head and killing himself.[1]

In the *Bhāgavata-purāṇa* another story is told that illustrates this theme vis-à-vis Śiva. When the gods have finished churning the cosmic ocean and have produced their precious heavenly nectar, the *asuras* appear on the scene and attempt to drink it. In order to dissuade them, Viṣṇu takes the form of a beautiful woman. The *asuras* are so enchanted by her appearance that they forget to drink the nectar, which is thus saved for the *devas.* Śiva, who has been elsewhere during this episode, arrives after Viṣṇu has reassumed his natural form. When Śiva is told about the effect of Viṣṇu's feminine appearance on the *asuras,* he begs Viṣṇu to show him this bewitching form. Viṣṇu obliges Śiva and again assumes the form of a beautiful woman. When he sees this form of Viṣṇu, the great ascetic Śiva is so totally enchanted that he begins to chase the woman through the forest. He is only brought back to his senses when Viṣṇu reappears in his masculine form.[2]

Śiva the destroyer, fleeing for his life from Vṛka, who seeks to kill the Great God with a power bestowed by the god himself, and Śiva, the detached, austere ascetic, madly chasing Viṣṇu in the guise of a woman in order to possess her, convey the image of a god who is not entirely in control, who is surprised by his own creation or by the results of his own decisions. One

---

[1] *Brahma-vaivarta-purāṇa,* Kṛṣṇa Janma Khaṇḍa 36. 22-41 (Part II, p. 260). The same story is told in the *Bhāgavata-purāṇa* X. 88. 18-40 (V, 123).
[2] *Bhāgavata-purāṇa* VIII. 12. 1-36 (III, 131-33).

senses that Śiva does not carefully consider his decisions, that they are spontaneous and often rebound upon him in a way that is as surprising to him as to anyone else. One senses, further, that there is a playful Spirit beyond even the great gods who is smiling all the while.

The god Brahmā also illustrates this theme of the divine comedy in Hinduism. One of Brahmā's most common epithets is "the Grandfather." And this is an appropriate name, as he often seems to behave as if he were a bit senile. In the *Mahābhārata*, for example, we find Brahmā brooding just after he has created the world. What is he brooding about? He is thinking of how he can destroy the world he has just created! And so he creates the goddess of death.[1] The Grandfather is also notorious for repeatedly endangering the world by granting boons to the demons. In the *Mahābhārata*, again, he bestows a boon on the female *asuras* Pulamā and Kalakā to the effect that their offspring will not be subject to destruction by the gods. Their children, as a result of this, bring the gods under bondage.[2] In the *Matsya-purāṇa* Brahmā grants the demon couple Vajrāṅga and Vārāṅgī the same boon, that their son will be destined to defeat the *devas*.[3] In the *Harivaṁśa* he grants the demon Hiraṇyakaśipu the double boon of being immune to the curses of *ṛṣis* and weapons of all kinds and of success in defeating the *devas*.[4] Finally, in the *Devī Bhāgavata* he grants two more demons the boon of subduing the *devas*, and the world is consequently once again thrown into chaos.[5] In many cases these demons have practiced severe austerities and built up much *tapas*. So they are justified in asking Brahmā for a boon. But the disastrous consequences of his granting these boons never seem to enter Brahmā's mind. The creator of the world, the grandfather of the gods, seems only incidentally concerned with the maintenance of his order. Brahmā, indeed, seems to be the *devas*' and the world's worst enemy. He plays the part of the crotchety old grandfather who delights in making trouble for

---

[1] *Mahābhārata*, Droṇa Parva LII. 38-39 (VI, 106).
[2] *Ibid.*, Vana Parva CLXXII (III, 363-66).
[3] *Matsya-purāṇa* 147. 10-19 (Part II, pp. 55-57).
[4] *Harivaṁśa*, Bhaviṣya Parva 37. 1-26 (pp. 915-16).
[5] *Devī Bhāgavata* V. 21. 24-58 (p. 427).

his offspring. It seems to amuse him to see the *devas* in trouble. The "old man's" sport is to make trouble for them.

Sometimes, too, he causes a good deal of trouble for himself. In the *Brahma-vaivarta-purāṇa* Brahmā says to Kāma, whom he has just created:

> I give you the following arrows or weapons *viz.*, enchanting, agitating, stupefying, maddening, fever-producing and sense-depriving. Please accept them and bewilder everybody. Child, by my boon, you will be irresistible.[1]

And who is Kāma's first victim? Why Brahmā himself, of course!

This theme of "involuntary creation," as Heinrich Zimmer calls it, is also seen in the *Devī Bhāgavata*.[2] While Viṣṇu is enjoying his cosmic slumber upon the serpent Ananta, two demons are created from the wax of his ears. When Viṣṇu awakes he is immediately confronted with the problem of subduing his own created beings, who are in the process of trying to overpower him.[3]

The story of creation in the *Kālikā-purāṇa*, however, seems to bear out this theme most consistently. Sitting in deep meditation, Brahmā decides to create. His first result is a surprise to him. She is a beautiful goddess, who stares about and laughs softly. Brahmā is thoroughly charmed by her. He is so charmed, in fact, that he begins to perspire, and from his perspiration various good and evil beings are spontaneously created. Later in the myth, Brahmā creates, to his own surprise, the god Kāma, who, as in the version above, is granted by Brahmā the boon of bewitching all beings and who chooses Brahmā as his first victim.[4] In each case Brahmā seems quite surprised by what he has created. His imagination has run wild, as it were, and has led him along paths he did not know existed. He seems unable to control either the nature of what he is creating or the actions

[1] *Brahma-vaivarta-purāṇa*, Kṛṣṇa Janma Khaṇḍa 35. 42 (Part II, p. 256).

[2] Heinrich Zimmer, *The King and the Corpse*: *Tales of the Soul's Conquest of Evil*, ed. Joseph Campbell, p. 257. Watts notes the same theme vis-à-vis *māyā*: "*Maya* also means art and miraculous power, the creation of an illusion so fabulous that it takes in its Creator. God himself is literally a-mazed at and in his own work." *Beyond Theology*, p. 20.

[3] *Devī Bhāgavata* I. 6-7 (pp. 19-25).

[4] Zimmer's synopsis, *The King and the Corpse*, pp. 240-48.

of those he has created. Zimmer comments on his creative process:

> And so it is that creation proceeds, according to this remarkable myth: by surprises, involuntary acts, and abrupt reversals. The creation of the world is not an accomplished work, completed within a certain span of time, but a process continuing throughout the course of history, refashioning the universe without cease, and pressing it on, every moment afresh. Like the human body, the cosmos is in part built up anew, every night, every day; by a process of unending regeneration it remains alive. But the manner of its growth is by abrupt occurences, crises, surprising events and even mortifying accidents. Everything is forever going wrong; and yet, that is precisely the circumstance by which the miraculous development comes to pass. The great entity jolts from crisis to crisis; that is the precarious, hair-raising manner of self-transport by which it moves.[1]

> Brahma, the Creator, broods the world of matter out of himself by spiritual means, by sinking into his own depth in a state of yogic meditation; but he cannot control or determine the apparitions that he then produces. They surprise, stun, and disconcert him.[2]

The next central event of this myth is the involvement of the aloof, ascetic Śiva, who up to this point has been greatly

---

[1] *Ibid.*, p. 251. This theme is seen in many other myths. In the *Kāmikāgama*, for example, Viṣṇu begins to destroy the world in his man-lion form after he has killed the demon Hiraṇyakaśipu. That is, Viṣṇu has incarnated himself in the form of a man-lion in order to relieve the burden of the earth, and then proceeds to destroy the earth. In the end, Śiva appears on the scene in his form as the Śarabha animal (a creature with two heads, two wings, eight lion legs, and long tail) and slays Viṣṇu the would-be redeemer gone wild. Cited in Rao, II, Part I, 172.

A similar story is told in the *Kālikā-purāṇa* 30. 1-42 and 31. 1-153. Only this time it is Viṣṇu in his boar *avatāra* that must be subdued. Having rescued the earth from the cosmic waters, Viṣṇu proceeds to rape Mother Earth. In distress, she cries for help, and Śiva appears in order to save her. Cited in O'Flaherty, "Asceticism and Sexuality," VIII, 311.

The myth of Jaladhara, finally, illustrates the same theme vis-à-vis Śiva. Jaladhara is born from the fire that issued from Śiva when he destroyed the castle of the three *asuras*. And after an involved plot it is Jaladhara who seeks to rape Pārvatī and who must be destroyed by Śiva, his own creator. The story is found in the *Śiva-purāṇa*, cited by Rao, *Elements of Hindu Iconography*, II, Part I, 188-90.

[2] Zimmer, *The King and the Corpse*, p. 261.

amused by Brahmā's discomfiture. The gods decide it is necessary to distract Śiva from his meditation, for without his active co-operation the creation cannot continue. They decide, therefore, that he must first take a wife, who will then involve him in the ongoing order of things. The mother of the universe, Kālī herself, is persuaded by Brahmā to help solve the problem. She condescends to become Satī, the daughter of the sage Dakṣa. While she is practicing austerities in the hope of impressing Śiva, his attention is momentarily caught by her, and for an instant a crack in his armor appears. At that instant Kāma pierces him with his arrows, and the Great God is immediately set on the rambunctious road of the continuing creation.[1]

A new Śiva appears, a being that Śiva himself most certainly never suspected was within himself. He has married Satī, and the two are living an idyllic life on a mountain peak.

> Shiva would gather wood flowers for Sati and place them in a wreath about her head; and when she then studied her features in the glass, he would step behind her, and in the mirror the two faces would be merged into one. He let down her night-dark hair, let it stir about and play, and then himself was also stirred to a rollicking play. He knotted it up, let it loose again; and convoluted himself endlessly in that occupation. Her pretty feet he painted with scarlet lac, in order to hold them, while doing so, in his hands. He whispered into her ear what he could just as well have spoken aloud, only to bring himself close to her face. And if he stepped away from her for a moment, as quickly as possible he hurried back. Wherever she turned herself to some task, he constantly followed with his eyes. By means of his arts he made himself invisible, then suddenly startled her with his embrace, and kept her dizzy and excited with fright. He set a spot of musk on her beautiful lotus-breast in the form of a sucking bee, then lifted off the necklaces of pearl and set them back again in some different arrangement, just to touch her lotus-softness. He drew the bracelets from her wrists and arms and opened the knots of her clothing, tied them again, and put back the ornaments. "Here is a

---

[1] *Ibid.*, pp. 266-75.

wasp," he said, "dark as you; that is why he is pursuing you . . . ." She turned to see, and he gathered up her breasts. Heaps of lotus blossoms and wood flowers he piled on top of her in the frolic of love, blooms that he had plucked for her delight. And wherever he walked, stood or reposed, he would not be happy for an instant without her . . . . He decked her whole person in chains of flowers and studied her; he joked and laughed and conversed with her; he lost himself in her, as a yogi in full self-collection submerges in the Self, there deliquescing totally.[1]

The great *sannyāsin* has discovered the joys of involvement, the bliss of enchantment. But he is soon plunged into great pain as a consequence, for Satī kills herself in pique when her father refuses to invite Śiva to his great sacrifice. Discovering her corpse, Śiva becomes delirious in grief, and Kāma wounds him again with several more arrows. Śiva calls to his wife repeatedly, and when she does not answer he falls on the ground and weeps. "Shiva lifted himself from the ground; he was blind with agony. He stopped, lifted the corpse to his shoulder, and, wandering madly, vaguely, without aim, headed eastward, babbling to himself crazily."[2]

Who would have believed such a course of events could have come about? Śiva, who looked on the enchantment of Brahmā with such amusement and disdain, who sat loftily on his mountain peak far removed from worldly involvement, has become hopelessly, inextricably involved in the world. A whole new dimension of his being has appeared.

This extraordinary myth declares that the gods are in danger of being enchanted by their own *māyā*. Within the depths of each god there are hidden recesses and dimensions that even they do not know are there. Brahmā is constantly surprised by his own creations, but, even more, he is then enchanted by them. "What has reposed within the God like a dream, self-enclosed and all-comprised, arises, steps into shapes, and variously confronts itself, to work effects upon itself. That is the continuous creation, that is the play of the world."[3]

---

[1]Zimmer's synopsis, *ibid.*, pp. 286-87.
[2]*Ibid.*, p. 301.
[3]*Ibid.*, p. 263.

Śiva, the immobile, immutable, placid model of the *yogin*, becomes a deeply caring husband who can absorb himself in his wife as completely as he has absorbed himself in withdrawn meditation. This Great God, too, who of all gods seems most aloof from the tumult of the world, becomes caught in the great play of *māyā*, the transcendent divine comedy. It is clear that there is an order even above the gods, and this order dictates that the gods themselves must become involved in the world play. And one senses that the Master or Mistress of this order is an eminently playful spirit who takes as much delight in playing a joke on the gods as the gods take in playing their jokes on man.

F. *The Heavenly Sporting Ground*

The nature of the Hindu gods is further revealed as playful when their heavenly *lokas*, or places, are described in the scriptures. Their *lokas*, whether mountains, valleys, forests, or infinite space, are frequently described as sporting grounds where the gods dally by themselves, with a consort, or with companions of various descriptions.

When the burden of the goddess Earth has become too great, she goes to Brahmā for help, and the *Brahma-vaivarta-purāṇa* contains a description of Brahmā's *loka*: "She saw that the effulgent god was ministered to by saints, adepts, etc. He was cheerfully witnessing at the time the dance of the heavenly prostitutes and listening to the song of the Gandharvas."[1]

In the *Devī Bhāgavata* Viṣṇu is described as sporting in Vaikuṇṭha after creation: "Thus the wheel of creation being started, the Great God Bhagavân Viṣṇu Achyuta remained in sport with Mahâ Lakṣmi in His own sphere Vaikuṇṭha."[2] The

---

[1]*Brahma-vaivarta-purāṇa,* Kṛṣṇa Janma Khaṇḍa 4. 4-5 (Part II, p. 107). The idea of a heavenly sporting ground appears to be quite ancient in the Indian tradition, although the most elaborate accounts are given in the purāṇic literature. See *Ṛg-veda* VII. 88, in which the *ṛṣi* recalls the time that he and Varuṇa sailed over the seas in a boat together, and *Chāndogya Upaniṣad* VIII. 12. 3, in which the spirit freed after death is described as entering heaven, where he "moves about, laughing, playing, rejoicing with women, chariots or relations, not remembering the appendage of this body." *The Principal Upaniṣads* (hereinafter cited as *Upaniṣads*), ed. and trans. S. Radhakrishnan, p. 509.

[2]*Devī Bhāgavata* III. 13. 27 (p. 172).

same scripture says: "Again you find Viṣṇu Bhagavân, full of youth, fond of the Leelâ [*līlā*], enjoying the company of Ramâ in Vaikuṇṭha."[1] In the *Bhāgavata-purāṇa* it is said that in Viṣṇu's heaven Lakṣmī is seen "moving in sprightly sport there."[2]

From the *Devī Bhāgavata* I quote one of several descriptions of the Great Goddess's *loka*. The sage Vyāsa is speaking:

> I told you before about the beautiful Maṇi Dvipa; that island is the place of sport to the Devi and very dear to Her. In that place Brahmâ, Viṣṇu, Mahâdeva were transformed into females; they afterwards became males and were engaged in their respective duties. That place is grand and splendid and is in the centre of the ocean of Nectar; the Devi Ambikâ assumes various forms there as She likes; and She sports there. To that Maṇi Dvîpa the auspicious Devi departed after She had been praised by the Gods, to that place where sports always the eternal Bhagavatî Bhuvaneśvari, the incarnate of Para Brahma.[3]

The haunts of Śiva, though, seem to be the most frequently and glowingly described in the Hindu scriptures. In the *Matsya-purāṇa* there is a description of Śiva's palace, where he has retired with Pārvatī shortly after their marriage:

> There, the Kinnaras were singing, the whole place was well scented and the peacocks were sporting, the cranes were throwing out their notes, the pillars of gems were dazzling with lustre, the parrots were sporting on the walls of lapis lazuli. At some places the ladies of Yakṣas were playing on lutes and sporting. The Kinnaras were constantly singing and dancing at various places; . . . at other places the pearls were reflecting on the floors made of gems; and Śuka birds thinking them to be pomegranates were striking them with their beaks. Within such a mansion, Śiva and Pârvatî began to play dice . . . both of them were engaged in play on a floor made of Indranila pearl.[4]

---

[1] *Ibid.* IV. 13. 22-24 (p. 296).
[2] *Bhāgavata-purāṇa* III. I5. 21 (I, 70-71).
[3] *Devī Bhāgavata* V. 20. 16-19 (p. 423).
[4] *Matsya-purāṇa* 154. 517-23 (Part II, p. 104).

In the *Mahābhārata* a forest beyond Mount Meru is described as Śiva's sporting ground:

> On the northern side of Meru is a delightful and excellent forest of *Karnikaras*, covered with the flowers of every season, and occupying a range of hills. There the illustrious *Pashupati* himself, the creator of all things, surrounded by his celestial attendants and accompanied by Uma, sporteth bearing a chain of *Karnikara* flowers (on his neck) reaching down to his feet, and blazing with radiance with his three eyes resembling three risen suns.[1]

Śiva's sylvan sporting ground is a place adorned by beautiful plants, where a variety of animals frolic. It seems a description of Eden before the Fall. Śiva is showing Pārvatī his sacred forest of Kāśi (Benares):

> Śiva said:—"O Dear! how nice is this garden! How beautiful! See this forest smiling with many kinds of flower clusters, creepers, . . . and various sweet-smelling flowers swarmed by the buzzing blackbees.
>
> In this forest, the sweet singing birds are throwing their melodious notes on the blooming lotuses; somewhere beautiful swans and enchanted blackbees are creating a bustle . . . somewhere . . . the creepers circling round the delicious flavoured mango trees are looking so beautiful;" . . .
>
> Somewhere the Vidyâdharas, Siddhas and Châraṇas were singing beautiful songs, somewhere the nymphs were dancing. . . .
>
> . . . somewhere were seen the beautiful trees embraced with creepers, somewhere the gamboling peacocks and the Yakṣas made a show of their strutting; somewhere cooed the pigeons . . . The peaks of the mountains where sports and amusements are held are being echoed by pigeons . . .
>
> . . . the perfume of Ambu and Kadamba flowers diffused a maddening smell all round.[2]

---

[1] *Mahābhārata*, Bhiṣma Parva VI. 24-26 (V, 15).

[2] *Matsya-purāṇa* 180. 24-41 (Part II, pp. 158-60). See also *Harivaṁśa* 264. 8-13 (p. 745) for a similar description of Śiva's playground.

Śiva is also, of course, the lord of the mountains. The Himalayas and Meru in particular are his favorite places. Indeed, Kālidāsa once referred to the eternal snows of the Himalayas as "Shiva's piled-up laughter."[1] In the *Mahābhārata* Kṛṣṇa and Arjuna sojourn to "that prince of mountains called Vrishadansa, and the great Mandara, abounding in Apsaras, and graced with the presence of the Kinnaras."[2] They see many seas, cities, towns, and mines of wealth. At the top of the mountain they find Śiva with Pārvatī. "And his attendants were engaged in singing and playing upon musical instruments, in laughing and dancing, in moving and stretching their hands, and in uttering loud shouts."[3]

The god of Kabīr also has a sporting ground, beyond the boundaries of even mythological geography, somewhere in ethereal space.

> All the gardens and groves and bowers are abounding with blossom; and the air breaks forth into ripples of joy.
> There the swan plays a wonderful game,
> There the Unstruck Music eddies around the Infinite One;
> There in the midst the Throne of the Unheld is shining, whereon the great Being sits—
> . . . .
> Only he knows it who has reached that region: it is other than all that is heard and said.
> No form, no body, no length, no breadth is seen there: how can I tell you that which it is ?[4]

The heavenly sporting ground is almost always a place where there is dancing, singing, and music. There, where the gods enjoy their leisure, these amusements abound. Śiva himself, of course, is a great dancer. In the *Śiva-pradoṣa-stotra* the preparation for his evening dance is described:

> Placing the Mother of the Three Worlds upon a golden throne, studded with precious gems, Shulapani dances on the

---

[1]Noted in Nirad C. Chaudhuri, *The Continent of Circe*, p. 161.
[2]*Mahābhārata*, Droṇa Parva LXXX. 32-33 (VI, 152).
[3]*Ibid.* LXXX. 41 (VI, 153).
[4]Kabir, *One Hundred Poems*, song 76, pp. 79-81.

heights of Kailasa, and all the gods gather around Him:

Sarasvati plays on the *vina*, Indra on the flute, Brahma holds the time-marking cymbals, Lakshmi begins a song, Vishnu plays on a drum, and all the gods stand round about:

Gandharvas, Yakshas, Patagas, Uragas, Siddhas, Sadhyas, Vidyadharas, Amaras, Apsarases, and all the beings dwelling in the three worlds assemble there to witness the celestial dance and hear the music of the divine choir at the hour of twilight.[1]

Śiva also performs the Nadanta dance of Naṭarāja in the heavenly hall of Cidambaram (or Tillai) at the center of the universe, while the assembly of gods looks on.[2] In the *Matsya-purāṇa* we find that Śiva also dances with *yoginīs*. The following is a description of a *tīrtha* (a place of pilgrimage): "Yoginīs reside there and they please themselves in the company of Yogis, and dance with Śiva."[3]

Kabīr especially mentions music in connection with the heavenly *loka* of God. For Kabīr it seems as if there can be no bliss without music.

> Where Spring, the lord of the seasons, reigneth, there the
> Unstruck Music sounds of itself,
> There the streams of light flow in all directions;
> Few are the men who can cross to that shore!
> There, where millions of Krishnas stand with hands folded,
> . . . .
> Where millions of Saraswatis, Goddess of Music, play on
> the vina.[4]

The gods, goddesses, and various beings who inhabit the heavenly world are commonly described as occupying themselves in amorous dalliance there. I have already quoted the delightful description of Śiva sporting with Satī on a mountain peak from the *Kālikā-purāṇa*.[5] There are many such descriptions.

---

[1]Quoted in Ananda K. Coomaraswamy, *The Dance of Shiva*: *Fourteen Indian Essays* p. 67.

[2]*Ibid.*, p. 68. This dance was first revealed by Śiva in the Taragam forest before the *ṛṣis*, after their submission to Śiva as related in the *Koyil Upapurāṇa*.

[3]*Matsya-purāṇa* 193. 72-73 (Part II, p. 193).

[4]Kabir, *One Hundred Poems*, song 15, pp. 15-16.

[5]See above, Chap. I, Sec. E, p. 36.

In the *Devī Bhāgavata* Nārada sees Nārāyaṇa in Vaikuṇṭha "playing in amorous movements with the daughter of the ocean, fully capable to give one delight and enjoyment."[1] The *Devî Bhāgavata* also describes four gardens where the gods live and take delight:

> There are . . . . four very lovely gardens named Nandana, Chaitrarath, Vaibhrâjaka, and Sarvatobhadra, very lovely, enchanting and pleasing to the delicate female sex and where the Devas enjoy the wealth and prosperity and their other Yogic powers. Here the Devas live always with numerous hordes of women and have their free amorous, dealings with them, to their heart's contents; and they hear the sweet songs sung by the Gandharbas and Kinnaras.[2]

The *Brahma-vaivarta-purāṇa* says simply of Śiva and Satī on Mount Kailāsa: "There they dallied merrily in various ways . . . . for a thousand years."[3] The same *purāṇa* says of Indra and Rambhā:

> Then both of them were excited to such a great extent that they could not distinguish the night from the day. Iṅdra then took her to the river called the Puspa-bhadra for recreation in the water. Iṅdra dallied merrily with her, partly on the land and partly on the water.[4]

But perhaps the most illustrative example of the erotic dalliance of the heavenly beings is the temple complex at Khajurāho. The temples there teem with gods and goddesses, *siddhas*, *apsarases*,

[1] *Devī Bhāgavata* VI. 28. 6 (p. 582).

[2] *Ibid.* VIII. 5. 21-23 (p. 751). A similar description may be found in the *Brahmayāmala*, in which the sage Vasiṣṭha is sent to the Himalayas by the Goddess to learn from Viṣṇu (in the form of Buddha) the rituals of the *vāmācārā*. Upon arriving in Mahācina (probably Tibet), Vasiṣṭha finds a land "inhabited by great adepts and thousands of beautiful young damsels whose hearts were gladdened with wine, and whose minds were blissful due to erotic sport (*vilāsa*). They were adorned with clothes which kindle the mood for dallianec (*śṛṅgārāveśa*) and the movement of their hips made their girdles tinkle with their little bells. Free of fear and prudishness, they enchanted the world. They surrounded Īśvara in the form of Buddha." Quoted in Agehananda Bharati, *The Tantric Tradition* p. 69.

[3] *Brahma-vaivarta-purāṇa,* Gaṇeśa Khaṇḍa 1. 22 (Part II, p. 1).

[4] *Ibid.* 20. 47-49 (Part II, p. 40).

and other heavenly beings, and the theme is frequently erotic. The figures are combined in a multitude of erotic poses, and the impression is of uninterrupted and unrestrained sensual dalliance.[1]

The heavenly sporting ground is also a place where children play. In fact, Śiva himself is described as a youth on Kailāsa in the *Devī Bhāgavata*:

> In the meanwhile Bhagavân Nârâyaṇa after consulting with the other Devas went with some Devas to the abode of Śankara in Kailâśa. They saw there that Śrī Bhagavân Śankara . . . was playing there attended always by the Pramathas and adorned with various ornaments like a youth, sixteen years old.[2]

In the *Mahābhārata* Indra comes to Śiva's abode and also sees him there as a youth. "And soon he saw, not far off from where he was, a handsome youth with a young lady seated on a throne placed on one of the peaks of the Himavat and playing at dice."[3] In a description of Kailāsa in the *Brahma-vaivarta-purāṇa* children attend Śiva:

> The houses teemed with gems, gold, and golden jars and were peopled by numberless Yakṣas with white chowries in their hands. They were also graced by the presence of lovely maidens decked with jewels of gem and playful and smiling children with toys in their hands.[4]

In the *Matsya-purāṇa* Śiva and Pārvatī adopt one of Śiva's attendants, a small child by the name of Vīrabhadra (or Viraka),

---

[1]See plates in Kanwar Lal, *The Cult of Desire: An Interpretation of Erotic Sculpture of India*, and *Immortal Khajuraho*; Francis Leeson, *Kama Shilpa*; and Eliky Zannas, *Khajurāho*.

[2]*Devī Bhāgavata* XI. 15. 58-59 (pp. 1094-95).

[3]*Mahābhārata*, Ādi Parva CXCIX. 17 (I, 417).

[4]*Brahma-vaivarta-purāṇa*, Gaṇeśa Khaṇḍa 41. 6-8 (Part II, p. 84). See also Pl. XC in Rao, II, Part I, facing 317. The scene depicted is the descent of Ganges (from Elephanta). Around the legs of Śiva and Pārvatī are two small children, *gaṇas* probably, who appear to be playing. In Pl. CVII (facing p. 350), part of a mural from Madura of Śiva and Pārvatī's wedding, playful children also surround the couple. One is playing a flute, another dances.

whose play was a source of constant amusement for the divine couple.

> Viraka was very fond of Divine singing and dancing and was, therefore, respected by the Gaṇeśvaras. Sometimes, he used to play in mountains, where lions roared; sometimes, he remained in the mines of jewels, sometimes, he played in Sâlatâla forest; sometimes, the pleasant-blooming Tamâla forest; sometimes, under the trees, sometimes, in waters full of lotuses and having a little mud; and sometimes, he used to remain in the pure auspicious lap of his mother. Thus he spent his time in childish pastimes. Sometime, like Śiva, Viraka the lord of Gaṇeśvaras used to sing with Vidyâdharas in the groves, with all paraphernalia and amusements.[1]

Finally, Tagore sings of a place beyond this world, a children's playground where adults do not venture:

> On the seashore of endless worlds children meet. The infinite sky is motionless overhead and the restless water is boistrous. On the seashore of endless worlds the children meet with shouts and dances.
>
> They build their houses with sand and they play with empty shells . . . . Children have their play on the seashore of worlds.
>
> They know not how to swim, they know not how to cast nets. Pearl fishers dive for pearls, merchants sail in their ships, while children gather pebbles and scatter them again. They seek not for hidden treasures, they know not how to cast nets.
>
> The sea surges up with laughter and pale gleams the smile of the sea beach. Death-dealing waves sing meaningless ballads to the children, even like a mother while rocking her baby's cradle. The sea plays with children, and pale gleams the smile of the sea beach.
>
> On the seashore of endless worlds children meet. Tempest roams in the pathless sky, ships get wrecked in the trackless

[1] *Matsya-purāṇa* 154. 572-77 (Part II, p. 107).

water, death is abroad and children play. On the seashore of endless worlds is the great meeting of children.[1]

In several of the above passages various species of heavenly beings have been mentioned. The *apsarases*, *siddhas*, *kinnaras*, and others always seem present in the heavenly sporting grounds of the gods. Indeed, their *raison d'être* seems to be the entertainment of the gods. They are practiced singers, musicians, dancers, and lovers. They adorn the *lokas* of the gods and lend these places an atmosphere of light-hearted gaiety, boistrous revel, and frivolity. They busy themselves entirely in sport and in amusing and praising the gods. In the *Mahābhārata* the *gandharvas* are described as voluptuous:

> And possessing slim waists and fair large hips, they began to perform various evolutions, shaking their deep bosoms, and casting their glances around, and exhibiting other attractive attitudes capable of stealing the hearts and resolutions and minds of the spectators.[2]

On the Maṇi Dvīpa, the heavenly island of the goddess Mahāmāyā, the Great Goddess is surrounded by her attendants. "They were dancing, singing on and playing with musical instruments and were gladly chanting hymns in praise of the Devi."[3] In the *Mahānirvāṇa-tantra* there is a description of Mount Kailāsa covered with flowers, fanned by gentle, perfumed breezes, "where cool groves resound with the sweet-voiced songs of troops of Apsarās," and "peopled by troops of Siddha, Cāraṇa, Gandharva, and Gāṇapatya."[4] In the *Mahābhārata* there is a description of a place called Subhūmika on the banks of the Sarasvatī where Brahmā lives and where heavenly beings of all kinds flock for sport :

> There many fair-complexioned *Apsaras*, of beautiful faces, are always engaged in sports of a pure character without any intermission. The gods and the *Gandharvas*, every

---

[1] Tagore, *Gitanjali*, song 60, pp. 54-55.
[2] *Mahābhārata*, Vana Parva XLIII. 31-32 (II, 99).
[3] *Devī Bhāgavata* III. 4. 12-13 (p. 128).
[4] *Mahānirvāṇa-tantra* 1. 1-5 (pp. 1-2).

> month . . . repair to that sacred *tirtha* which is the resort of Brahman himself. The *Gandharvas* and diverse tribes of Apsaras are to be seen there, O king, assembled together and passing the time as happily as they like. There the gods and the *Pitris* sport in joy, with sacred and auspicious flowers repeatedly rained over them, and all the creepers also were adorned with flowery loads.[1]

In the *Harivaṁśa* the *apsarases* and *gandharvas* are pictured as amusing Śiva and Umā on the banks of a river: "Once on a time Lord Bhava was sporting on the bank of a charming river. In that picturesque forest where all the seasons flourish the Gandharvas, with hundreds of Apsaras, were sporting on all sides." The *apsarases* make Umā laugh by various tricks and then assume the forms of Śiva and Umā and play. "There arose on all sides sounds of laughter and Bhava attained to an excess of delight."[2] In the *Matsya-purāṇa* it is said of the attendants of Śiva that "they indulge in various kinds of sports . . . and are addicted to singing, music and dancing."[3] And of course these beings are present at such glorious affairs as heavenly weddings, in this instance the wedding of Śiva and Pārvatī:

> The chief Gandharvas began to sing and the nymphs started dancing. The Gandharvas and the Kinnaras danced and sang exquisite music. The six seasons appeared incarnate to participate in the universal rejoicings and danced and sang. The sportive attendants of Śiva paused on the Himâlaya, after being exhausted by their pastime.[4]

These wonderful creatures, finally, take delight in welcoming righteous souls to heaven. In the *Mārkaṇḍeya-purāṇa* we read :

> What happens to righteous-doers, listen while I declare that. They take the holy course decreed by Yama. Bands of Gandharvas singing, bevies of Apsarases dancing, brilliant with various celestial garlands, bedecked with strings of

[1] *Mahābhārata*, Śalya Parva XXXVII. 2-5 (VII, 112).
[2] See *Harivaṁśa* 264. 6-12 (p. 745), esp. vs. 12.
[3] *Matsya-purāṇa* 154. 541 (Part II, p. 105).
[4] *Ibid*. 154. 491-93 (Part II, p. 103).

> pearls and anklets and *gay with* music, and heavenly chariots beyond compare go forth quickly *to them.*"[1]

These heavenly beings embody the atmosphere of *līlā* that pervades the countless descriptions of the heavenly sporting grounds in the Hindu scriptures. They are beings who flit about the throne of God, content to amuse indefinitely and dally aimlessly. E. B. Havell has written of the *apsarases* that "the lissom bodies of the pure spirits who know divine escstasy and heavenly bliss, float through space with the effortless ease of the winged denizens of the air."[2] And of the *siddhas* he has written:

> The pure ecstasy of the dance, the *joie de vivre* which lifts the body out of itself into the realms of heavenly bliss, is nowhere shown better in Indian art than in the portrayal of the demi-gods and goddesses, the *Siddhas* and *Siddhis* of the upper air, who hover round the summits of stupas or holy mountains and take part as messengers, dancers and musicians in divine ceremonials.[3]

In their heavenly spheres the gods are at ease. There they do not toil but amuse themselves endlessly. When the gods retreat to their *lokas* after creation, combat, or involvement in the affairs of the world, they sport there. Their *lokas* are pleasure palaces or sporting grounds that ring with the carefree sounds of laughter and song. Happy children, those truly accomplished players, sometimes live there. The gods surround themselves with heavenly nymphs accomplished in the arts of entertainment and pleasure. And there the gods dally with their consorts. It is entirely appropriate that the gods should do this, as they are great beings who transcend the workaday world of the human sphere. Their limitless capacity for amusement and dalliance expresses their transcendence. They seem insatiable, never tiring of this aimless sport. Unlike man, this is their "natural" condition. They are players, not workers and in play their essential nature as free, transcendent beings is expressed.

---

[1] *Mārkaṇḍeya-purāṇa* 10. 91-93 (pp. 68-69).

[2] E. B. Havell, *Himalayas in Indian Art*; quoted in Enakshi Bhavnani, *The Dance in India: The Origin and History* . . . p. 12.

[3] *Ibid.*, pp. 12-13.

G. *Combat as Play*

The Hindu scriptures, especially the *purāṇas*, frequently depict the world as being on the brink of disaster. Periodically a particularly powerful demon, or group of demons, gains the upper hand over the gods and brings the world under his tyranny. Inevitably, a hero or god comes forth to reclaim the universe for the gods, but at first glance the implication seems to be that the gods are not all-powerful, that their dominion is in constant danger from the *asuras*.

In the many battles that are described, however, there emerges a theme that suggests that the gods, after all, are never really in any danger, that the periodic resurgence of the demons is all a comedy in which the gods, because of their superior power or *jñāna*, will always have the last laugh. The theme that runs through this ever recurring struggle is that of combat as play on the part of the gods. At the height of battle, for example, the deity will laugh uproariously.

> Kali, the goddess, began to roar like a lioness in the battle-field; whereupon all the demons fainted. This goddess burst into a guffaw of horse-laugh again and again, cheerfully began to drink honey and danced frantically.[1]

Or the narrator of the story will suggest that all this business is simply done for the amusement of the deity, that the god is merely an actor on a stage. In the *Bhāgavata-purāṇa* we read: "O monarch ! Do thou observe that the incarnation of God on earth is like unto the appearance of the actors on the theatrical stage."[2] One gets the impression that the gods are really never in trouble at all, that they condescend to battle the demons simply because it is part of some cosmic script or because they enjoy it.

At the beginning of this chapter I quoted Kṛṣṇa's comment to Arjuna from the *Bhagavadgītā*, to the effect that, although Kṛṣṇa is entirely complete, still he continues to act. This theme is just as clear in the other *avatāras* of Viṣṇu. In almost

---

[1] *Brahma-vaivarta-purāṇa*, Prakṛti Khanda 19. 44-45 (Part I, p. 144).
[2] *Bhāgavata-purāṇa* XI. 31. 11 (V, 262).

every case we are told explicitly, or it is inferred, that Viṣṇu's *avatāras* are as much bent on amusing themselves as they are on saving the world.[1] A playful theme, for example, is clear in the opening passage of the *Matsya-purāṇa*:

> May the lotus feet of Bhava [Śiva], who shook the *diggajas* [the tusks of the ten elephants who support the corners of the universe] at the time of His dance, disperse all obstacles.
>
> May the words of Lord Viṣṇu, embodied in the Vedas and uttered by His Matsya-avâtara, in which incarnation, at the time of His sallying forth from the region of the pâtâla, the blow of His tail caused the seven seas to intermingle with the high heavens and then to fall down, spattering the earth, steal away all your evil![2]

One does not get the impression that Viṣṇu's fish *avatāra* is on his way toward a critical battle, a cosmic struggle. He "sallies forth" and by the mere flick of his tail churns up all the oceans. Viṣṇu's *avatāra-līlā* is more explicit in his boar incarnation. "In days of yore when the earth had gone down to the deeps, thou assumed the form of a mighty boar and setting up tremendous roars sportively raised the earth up with thy teeth and as easily as a mighty elephant would up-root a lotus stalk."[3] The demon Hiraṇyākṣa is clearly no match for the aggressive boar.

> As an elephant engaged in digging the earth in sport becomes coloured by red chalk and other minerals, so the Lord has his cheeks and mouth besmeared with the mire of the Asura's blood.
>
> O Vidura! When the Lord raised the Earth up on his tusks sporting like an elephant, His body assumed the dark blue hue like unto Tamala.[4]

This fantastic creature, Viṣṇu's boar *avatāra*, is obviously enjoying himself. This great boar who rescues the earth "with ease

---

[1]This was noted sometime ago by Helmuth von Glasenapp, *Madhva's Philosophie des Vishnu Glaubens*, III, 32 ff.

[2]*Matsya-purāṇa* 1. 1-2 (Part I, p. 1).

[3]*Bhāgavata-purāṇa* IV. 7. 46 (II, 37).

[4]*Ibid.* III. 13. 32-33 (I, 60-61).

as in sport,"[1] who raises the earth from the cosmic ocean "in a sportive revel,"[2] is never in serious trouble from his opponent. For the boar this is not combat but play. Viṣṇu's man-lion *avatāra*, Narasiṁha, seems equally amused by the cosmic struggle in which he is engaged. When he confronted the demon who was oppressing the gods, Narasiṁha "gave forth a loud shrill laughter, in consequence of the terrific sound of which the eyes of the Asura began to blink." [3]

The two popular human *avatāras* of Viṣṇu, Rāma and Kṛṣṇa, also reflect this playful theme. I have already mentioned Kṛṣṇa's statement to Arjuna in the *Bhagavadgītā*, and as I will deal with Kṛṣṇa in detail in the next chapter, I only wish to quote a short statement from the *Matsya-purāṇa* about him here. There it is written: "The lord of all, the Protector of the universe, manifested Himself as Śríkṛṣṇa for the purpose of His pastime."[4] The theme of play as combat in Viṣṇu's Rāma *avatāra*, while it is not nearly as explicit as in Kṛṣṇa, is nevertheless quite evident. In North India, for example, when the epic of Rāma is re-created in dramatic form, often by whole towns or villages, it is called Rām Līlā.[5] The implication is that Rāma's whole adventure was play for him, that he was essentially removed from the action as an actor on a stage. In Tulsī Dās's *Vinaya-patrikā* the poet addresses Rāma:

> Steadfast upholder of religion, Raghuvīr of unmatched strength of arms,
> Casting down earth's heavy load *of demons* in *mere* sport ![6]

Viṣṇu sometimes involves himself directly in combat, without resort to *avatāras*. The playful theme remains. "Then with his strength Hari began to grind the hundred dreadful faces of that demon [Suparṇa] with wild laughs like the grinding of fire."[7] In the *Viṣṇu-purāṇa*, Viṣṇu boasts: "They [the *asuras*]

---

[1]*Ibid.* III. 13. 47 (I, 62).
[2]*Ibid.* III. 20. 8 (I, 92).
[3]*Ibid.* VII. 8. 28 (III, 39).
[4]*Matsya-purāṇa* 47. 1 (Part I, p. 124).
[5]See Norvin Hein, "The Rām Lilā," in Milton Singer (ed.), *Traditional India: Structure and Change*, pp. 73-98.
[6]Tulsi Dās *Vinaya-patrikā* 44. 4 (*The Petition to Rām*, p. 111).
[7]*Harivaṁśa* 48. 47 (p. 211).

shall perish before the withering glance of mine eyes."[1] And in the *Bhāgavata-purāṇa* it is said of Viṣṇu : "The Wind of irresistible might is His gait (Movement) and the destruction of the Creatures is His play."[2]

The Goddess in her many forms is also a formidable warrior who enters combat with zest. She clearly enjoys it and rarely seems in any trouble. For her also it is simply a diversion.

> Without hurling any trident, axes, Śaktis, clubs, or any other weapons; merely by Thy mere will Thou canst kill; still for sports and for the good of all beings Thou incarnatest and fightest for the sake of Lîlâ.[3]

The *Brahma-vaivarta-purāṇa* says of the goddess Maṅgal-Caṇḍī : "By her mere breath, she can destroy the whole world. Fight with the demons for the preservation of the world is mere child's play to her."[4] In the *Devī Bhāgavata* the goddess Ambikā burns to ashes the demon Dhūmralocana simply by her shouts.[5] The most celebrated triumph of the Goddess—her defeat of Mahiṣāsura, the buffalo demon, and his band of fellow fiends—also expresses the playful nature of her combat. In her several forms the Goddess mocks the rabble enemy. "Śivadútī [Caṇḍī] uttered a loud inauspicious laugh. At those sounds the Asuras trembled."[6] When the demon Niśumbha stepped forward, "the goddess laughing aloud then struck off his head with her scymitar."[7] In her battle with Śumbha, "the supreme goddess in merest play broke the heavenly missiles that he discharged, with fierce shouts, ejaculations and other *sounds*."[8] During this battle "the goddess betrayed no exertion in her countenance."[9]

Faithful to the myth, Hindu iconography consistently portrays the Goddess during this battle as having a calm,

---

[1] *Viṣṇu-purāṇa* V. 1. 62 (p. 400).
[2] *Bhāgavata-purāṇa* II.. 1. 33 (I, 91).
[3] *Devī Bhāgavata* V. 22 32 (p. 431).
[4] *Brahma-vaivarta-purāṇa*, Prakṛti Khaṇḍa 1. 95 (Part I, p. 87).
[5] *Devī Bhāgavata* V. 25. 22 (p. 441).
[6] *Mārkaṇḍeya-purāṇa* 89. 21 (pp. 507-8).
[7] *Ibid.* 89. 34 (p. 508).
[8] *Ibid.* 90. 9 (p. 510).
[9] *Ibid.* 82. 49-50 (p. 476).

unconcerned expression. The images of Durgā killing the buffalo demon that are used in Durgā Pūjā in Bengal are striking in this respect. With very few exceptions Durgā's face shows no exertion. The horrible demon is emerging from the carcass of the slain buffalo and almost always shows signs of pain, horror, surprise, or strain. The Goddess stands or hovers above him, placid, often enigmatic, dealing him the deathblow. For her this titanic struggle is a game that she knows she will win. She is not really involved in the struggle. She is aloof, as an actor always remains somewhat aloof from the character he is portraying. Zimmer says, commenting on a Javanese image of Durgā slaying the demon:

> She has caught the demon by the hair and is about to deal the death-blow, the heroic stroke that is to save the world. But in the features of the great victress there is no trace of wrathful emotion; she is steeped in the serenity of eternal calm. Though the deed in time and space is bound to be accomplished, the expression on the countenance of the Goddess minimizes, indeed annihilates, its importance. For her the whole course of this universe, including her own apparition in the role of its rescuer, is but part of a cosmic dream. It is only a feature of the universal display of Māyā.[1]

Finally, the great Śiva illustrates the theme of combat as *līlā*, and this is expressed clearly in Śaivite iconography. In Rao's volume on Śiva in his *Elements of Hindu Iconography* there are two sets of plates in particular that show this. In Plates XXXVII and XXXVIII Śiva is shown attacking the fort of the three *asuras* who have made themselves inviolable to the assaults of the gods. The only condition whereby the fort can be destroyed is if one arrow can pierce it. These two plates show Śiva standing in a chariot and drawing his mighty bow, about to destroy the fort. His face, like Durgā's at the moment of her triumph, is impassive, placid. In both plates he seems entirely aloof from the action.

Plates LIII and LIV illustrate Śiva's defeat of Rāvaṇa, king of Laṅkā. Rāvaṇa in his travels came upon Śiva's mountain

[1]Zimmer, *Myths and Symbols*, pp. 196-97, commenting on Pl. LVIII.

home and despite the warnings of Śiva's dwarf guards entered the sacred compound where Śiva and Pārvatī were sporting. Not only did the audacious king violate the sacred ground, he proceeded to try to dislodge Śiva from his mountain top by shaking Kailāsa. The plates show Śiva's reaction, which was to crush the mountain down on Rāvaṇa with his big toe, making him a prisoner beneath the mountain. Śiva's face is again placid. Indeed, he is paying more attention to Pārvatī than to the crushing of his enemy.[1]

One more image of Śiva also illustrates his detachment from combat, his role as a player in a drama. It is a seventeenth-century icon illustrating Śiva's *tāṇḍava* dance, the vigorous, violent aspect of his dance. Śiva has just killed a demon who took the form of an elephant by causing him to dance till he died (itself a playful theme). Śiva has stripped the beast of its skin and has draped it over himself and is dancing wildly in victory. Within the skin of the elephant Śiva dances, arms and legs whirling. But his face, in sharp contrast to this, is calm.[2] In the midst of stormy circumstances or strife, the deity remains eternally unmoved.

Finally, there is a story alluded to by Kingsbury and Phillips that appears to be an embellishment of the story of the fort of the three *asuras* mentioned above and that epitomizes the combat-as-*līlā* theme. In this version the three *asuras* obtained by means of austerities three castles from Śiva, one gold, one silver, and the other iron. These forts flew through the air at the demons' will, and with their aerial castles the demons brought havoc to the countryside. Eventually the demons became so puffed up with pride that Śiva determined to punish them.

> Śiva mounted a chariot whose wheels were the sun and moon and whose seat was the earth. Brahmā was his charioteer, the four Vedas the horses, Mount Meru his bow, the ancient serpent Ādiśesha his bow-string, and Vishṇu his arrow. At sight of these preparations the gods became conceited,

[1]Rao, *Elements of Hindu Iconography*, Vol. II, Part I, Pls. XXXVII and XXXVIII and Pls. LIII and LIV.

[2]Zimmer, *Myths and Symbols*, pp. 172-73, discussion of Pl. XL. See also Rao, *Elements of Hindu Iconography*, Vol. II, Part I, Pls. XXX-XXXIII.

> thinking that Śiva could not destroy his enemies without them. Śiva knowing their thoughts simply laughed, and at that laugh the three castles were on the instant reduced to ashes.[1]

The combat-as-*līlā* theme suggests in a straightforward way that the gods are so powerful, so removed from the finite limitations of the human sphere, that for them the most monumental struggle is resolved effortlessly. They "sally forth," as the *Matsya-purāṇa* says, to play at battle with the demons. Actual combat is out of the question, for these great beings are all-powerful and unassailable. They merely condescend to go through the actions. They may appear to exert themselves — employing various weapons, dancing vigorously, and so on — but their placid faces reveal their internal calm, their detachment, their aloof superiority. For the gods it is all a game they know they will win. They involve themselves simply for their own amusement.

[1]F. Kingsbury and G. E. Phillips, *Hymns of the Tamil Śaivite Saints*, p. 7.

CHAPTER II

KṚṢṆA'S LĪLĀ

A. The Kṛṣṇas—Continuities and Discontinuities

Play as divine activity in India is nowhere more fully illustrated than in the god Kṛṣṇa. Among Indian gods he is certainly the most playful. His sport is more diverse, more sustained, and more unambiguous than the play of any of the deities mentioned so far. This entire chapter, therefore, will deal exclusively with Kṛṣṇa, the divine player *par excellence* of Indian religion.

Before discussing the play of Kṛṣṇa itself, however, I would like to comment on two matters concerning the history of Kṛṣṇa in order to put this chapter in the proper perspective. The first is the matter of Kṛṣṇa and the Kṛṣṇas, or the quite distinct aspects of Kṛṣṇa that emerge in the course of his long and illustrious history. I shall not discuss that history here, as it has already been done adequately by others.[1] And I shall not dwell at length on the various aspects of Kṛṣṇa, as these also have been pointed out by others.[2] I only wish to make it clear which Kṛṣṇa, or which aspect of Kṛṣṇa, I have in mind when I say that he is the most unambiguous example of *līlā* in Indian religion.

As will soon be apparent, the Kṛṣṇa that moves through this chapter is the cowherd boy of Vṛndāvana, whose story is told in the *Harivaṁśa*, *Viṣṇu-purāṇa*, *Bhāgavata-purāṇa*, *Brahmavaivarta-purāṇa*, and other places. It is primarily this youthful, carefree aspect of Kṛṣṇa that embodies so fully the play of the gods. This being is clearly a quite different figure from the Kṛṣṇa of the *Mahābhārata*. The epic Kṛṣṇa is a counselor, a politician (a

---

[1]For example, R. G. Bhandarkar, *Vaiṣṇavism, Śaivism and Minor Religious Systems*, and Hemchandra Raychaudhuri, *Materials for the Study of the Early History of the Vaishnava Sect*.

[2]See n. 1 above. See also William G. Archer, *The Loves of Krishna in Indian Painting and Poetry*, and Daniel H. H. Ingalls' Foreword to Milton Singer (ed.), *Krishna: Myths, Rites, and Attitudes*, p. i.

conniving one at that),[1] and a hero. He is thoroughly bound up in worldly affairs. The cowherd youth is removed from this kind of setting almost entirely. The Vṛndāvana Kṛṣṇa, further, is quite different from the Kṛṣṇa of Mathurā and Dvārakā. Even within the *Bhāgavata-purāṇa* itself, the contrast between Kṛṣṇa's early biography in Vrndāvana and his later life as king of Dvārakā is striking. In Vṛndāvana he is carefree, almost reckless. He frolics there continually. In Dvārakā he is married and has taken on the burdens of a kingdom, and his behavior reflects this. He no longer expresses the freedom of divine play so fully as in Vṛndāvana. When I speak of Kṛṣṇa in this chapter, then, I will be speaking of this cowherd youth of the *purāṇas*, the Kṛṣṇa who became the supreme Bhagavān in many parts of North India and remains to this day one of the most popular gods throughout India, if not the most popular.

The second matter I wish to mention is necessary, actually, to balance my first point. I do not want to give the impression that the cowherd Kṛṣṇa is an entirely separate being who has little or no connection with the "other Kṛṣṇas." In fact, I think more emphasis should be put upon the continuities that exist between these Kṛṣṇas than has sometimes been the case. The peculiar divisions of Kṛṣṇa's aspects that have been delineated in two recent books show by their differences that one aspect of Kṛṣṇa blends into another imperceptibly.[2] Important continuities exist even between the most disparate aspects

---

[1] Kṛṣṇa's deceit, trickery, and artifice in the context of the epic might be seen as consonant with his later character as a mischievous child and illicit lover. Kṛṣṇa's treachery might well reflect *upādhi*, "deception, deceit, guile," which is typical of divine activity in Hinduism, or *upāya*, divine or holy cunning. If Kṛṣṇa's actions are interpreted in this way, they might be seen as typically divine activities, rather than as indications of his human or heroic nature. See Joseph Campbell, *The Masks of God*: *Primitive Mythology*, pp. 55-57, and Watts, *Beyond Theology*, p. 55.

[2] Archer (*The Loves of Krishna*) speaks of three Kṛṣṇas, or aspects of Kṛṣṇa: the hero of the *Mahābhārata*, the cowherd of the *Bhāgavata-purāṇa*, and the prince of the *Bhāgavata-purāṇa*. Ingalls (see p. 56 n. 2) also speaks of three Kṛṣṇas, but they are a slightly different three: the chief of the Yādavas and hero of the epic, the god incarnate who instructs Arjuna in the *Bhagavadgtiā*, and the cowherd of Vṛndāvana. Ingalls, that is, adds the *avatāra* aspect of Kṛṣṇa and leaves out the purāṇic, royal aspect mentioned by Archer. Each of the four aspects obviously exists, but just which is properly separated from the other is clearly a matter of disagreement.

of Kṛṣṇa. So, for example, there are continuities discernible even between the epic hero and the cowherd youth.

The cowherd youth, for example, has a clearly defined cosmic aspect. He is a great god, if not the greatest of all gods. In the *Mahābhārata*, where Kṛṣṇa seems to be primarily a heroic figure, however, there are also some rather straightforward indications that he is a great god there too. While Archer sees only two examples of the cosmic aspect of Kṛṣṇa in the *Mahābhārata*,[1] and even goes so far as to say, "Except on the two occasions mentioned, Kṛṣṇa is apparently not recognized as God by others and does not himself claim this status,"[2] I find several other examples in the epic that clearly affirm his cosmic aspect.

Kṛṣṇa, for example, is obviously more than a hero in the following passages. Bhīṣma says of Kṛṣṇa in the Sabhā Parva that he "is the origin of the universe and that in which the universe is to dissolve. Indeed, this universe of mobile and immobile creatures hath sprung into existence from Krishna only."[3] Arjuna addresses Kṛṣṇa and clearly links him to Viṣṇu: "O thou of the Vrishni race, at the beginning of the *Yuga*, there sprang from thy lotus-like navel, Brahma himself, and lord of all mobile and immobile things, and whose is this entire universe !"[4] At the court of Dhṛtarāṣṭra, where he has come to negotiate peace on behalf of the Pāṇḍavas, Kṛṣṇa laughs at the stupidity and stubbornness of Duryodhana.

> Kesava . . . burst out into a loud laughter. And as the high-souled Sauri laughed, from his body, that resembled a blazing fire, issued myriads of gods, each of lightning effulgence, and not bigger than the thumb. And on his forehead appeared Brahman, and on his breast Rudra. And on his arms appeared the regents of the world, and from his mouth issued Agni.[5]

---

[1]Archer, *The Loves of Krishna*, p. 23. The two incidents are : (1) Kṛṣṇa's revelation to Arjuna in the course of his presentation of the *Bhagavadgītā* (11.9 ff.) and (2) Kṛṣṇa's miraculous help given to Draupadī in her distress, when the Kauravas are trying to strip her clothes from her after they have won her from the Pāṇḍavas in a gambling match (*Mahābhārata*, Sabhā Parva LXVIII. 41-48 [II, 144-45]).

[2]Archer, *The Loves of Krishna*, p. 24.

[3]*Mahābhārata*, Sabhā Parva XXXVIII. 23 (II, 88).

[4]*Ibid.*, Vana Parva XII. 38 (II, 30) and XII, *passim*.

[5]*Ibid.*, Udyoga Parva CXXXI. 4-6 (IV, 262).

During the great epic battle Kṛṣṇa creates a darkness that covers the battlefield at a point when the Kauravas seem to have the upper hand. Thinking night has fallen, they make easy targets of themselves, and the Pāṇḍavas are saved.[1] This is not the action of a mere hero. In the same *parva* Yudhiṣṭhira addresses Kṛṣṇa as follows :

> Through thy grace, O mighty-armed one, the universe became manifest . . . . Thou art the creator of all the worlds, thou art the Supreme Soul, and thou art immutable ! . . . Thou art the Supreme God, thou art the God of gods, and thou art Eternal . . . . Without beginning and without death, thou art Divine, the Creator of all the worlds, and immutable . . . . Thou art Supreme, the Ancient one, the Divine-Being, and that which is the Highest of the high.[2]

These passages (and others like them) indicate that perhaps the cosmic aspect of Kṛṣṇa was not such a late product after all.[3] It certainly seems clear from these passages that the cosmic aspect of the cowherd Kṛṣṇa is not unique to him, that the epic Kṛṣṇa also had this feature. It is of course true that the epic Kṛṣṇa does not consistently display cosmic features as does the Kṛṣṇa of the *Brahma-vaivarta-purāṇa*, for example, but he does move against a background of divinity, a background that breaks into the foreground rather more frequently than Archer, at least, suggests.

The nature of Kṛṣṇa, no doubt, changed noticeably between the epic and purāṇic periods, but certain striking continuities

---

[1]*Ibid.*, Droṇa Parva CXLVI. 60 ff. (VI, 321 ff.).

[2]*Ibid.* CXLIX. 18-21 (VI, 333).

[3]It could be argued that these passages and others like them (e.g., *ibid.*, Śānti Parva XLIV and XLVIII) are late additions to the epic, that they were inserted at a time after Kṛṣṇa had attained a more elevated, divine position. This has not been proven by Archer, nor to my knowledge by anyone else. Rather, it seems to me that as a gradual evolution from hero to divinity is assumed in the history of Kṛṣṇa, it is further assumed that these passages must be late. I think, however, that these passages could be used to show something quite different, that Kṛṣṇa was never simply a heroic figure, or at least that he was considered a great deity at a very early date.

should not be overlooked,[1] or simply dismissed as later interpolations simply because of an *a priori* assumption that an evolution from hero to god has taken place in the history of Kṛṣṇa. Essential features of the cowherd Kṛṣṇa, then, appear to me to be at least hinted at in the epic. The purāṇic Kṛṣṇa, and the Kṛṣṇa worshiped in the medieval *bhakti* cults of North India, however, brings to full bloom both the cosmic and the playful dimensions of the god. So it is this figure that will now be discussed in detail.

B. *The Frolicking Child and Adolescent God*

Among Hindu gods the purāṇic Kṛṣṇa is unique in that his birth, childhood, and youth are told in detail. Throughout

[1]Another striking continuity is suggested in the following passage: "Then, O Bharata, having consulted thus with each other, Partha and Govinda [Arjuna and Kṛṣṇa], with Yudhishthira's leave, set out, surrounded by friends. Reaching a fine spot (on the banks of the Yamuna) suitable for purposes of pleasure, overgrown with numerous tall trees and covered with several high mansions that made the place look like the celestial city and within which had been collected for Krishna and Partha numerous costly and well-flavoured viands and drinks and other articles of enjoyment and floral wreaths and various perfumes, the party entered without delay the inner apartments adorned with many precious gems of pure rays. Entering those apartments, everybody, O Bharata, began to sport, according to his pleasure. The women of the party, all of full rotund hips and deep bosoms and handsome eyes, and gait unsteady with wine began to sport there at the command of Krishna and Partha. Some amongst the women sported as they liked in the woods, some in the waters, and some within the mansions, as directed by Partha and Govinda. Draupadi and Subhadra [Kṛṣṇa's sister and Arjuna's wife], exhilarated with wine, began to give away unto the women so sporting, their costly robes and ornaments. And some amongst those women began to dance in joy, and some began to sing; and some amongst them began to laugh and jest, and some to drink excellent wines. Some began to obstruct one another's progress and some to fight with one another, and to discourse with one another in private. Those mansions and the woods, filled with the charming music of flutes and guitars and kettle-drums, became the scene of Prosperity personified" (*Mahābhārata*, Ādi Parva CCXXIV [I, 462-63]). This passage is remarkable, for it sounds as though it could have been taken directly from the tenth book of the *Bhāgavata-purāṇa*, where Kṛṣṇa's life in Vṛndāvana is described. The sylvan setting and the play with women immediately call to mind the cowherd Kṛṣṇa. However, there is strong evidence that this passage is an interpolation, or at least an embellishment of an authentic incident. In the critical edition of the *Mahābhārata*, for example, the episode is described only briefly. Ādi Parva CCXIV. 28 and Appendix I, 117, 1-22; *Mahābhārata* (Sanskrit), ed. Vishnu S. Sukthankar *et al.*

India, moreover, but especially in Bengal and North India, Kṛṣṇa is worshiped in the form of a child, and the image of Bāla Kṛṣṇa, the baby Kṛṣṇa, crawling on the ground with a ball of butter in his hand and head upturned, is commonly found in homes and temples. It is in the form of a child that Kṛṣṇa expresses the spontaneous, pure play of the divine. As a child, he is the expert player. For the very nature of a child is to play.

Just when the worship of the child Kṛṣṇa became popular is difficult to determine. The Sanskrit poet Bhāsa (A.D. 200-300) described the child Kṛṣṇa, so this part of his biography is obviously very ancient.[1] And in the songs of the South Indian Āḷvārs, sometime before A.D. 900, the baby god clearly had become the object of adoration. In a poem by Periyāḷvār we read:

> He rolls in the dust, so that the jewel on his brow keeps swinging, and his waist-bells tinkle! Oh, look at my son Govinda's play, big Moon, if thou hast eyes in thy face—and then be gone! My little one, precious to me as nectar, my blessing, is calling thee, pointing, pointing, with his little hands! O big Moon, if thou wishest to play with this little black one, hide not thyself in the clouds, but come rejoicing.[2]

In the *Harivaṁśa*, the *Viṣṇu-purāṇa*, and the *Bhāgavata-purāṇa* (probably written in that order from the sixth to tenth centuries A.D.) detailed accounts of Kṛṣṇa's life from his birth through his departure from Vṛndāvana are set forth. And in the *Bhāgavata-purāṇa* especially we begin to find his childhood and youth doted upon.

> O my child (King Parikshit) in course of time, *Rama* and *Krishna* began to crawl in Gokula placing the weight of their body on their hands and their knees. When they crawled speedily on the muddy pastures of Braja dragging their little feet, their *Nupuras* and *Bangles* made a pleasing tinkling sound. Delighted by hearing these sounds, they

[1] Sūrdās, *The Poems of Sūrdās*, trans. S. M. Pandey and N.H. Zide, p. 11.
[2] *Tirumoli* I. 1-2; in J. S. M. Hooper, *Hymns of the Alvars*, p. 37.

would sometimes follow men for a little distance. Then, as if terrified and bewildered, they would hastily come back to their mothers.[1]

With the blossoming of the Caitanya sect of Bengal and the Vallabha sect of the north, however, the importance of the child Kṛṣṇa became a vital aspect of the worship of Kṛṣṇa. While Kṛṣṇa as lover is more important than the child Kṛṣṇa in Bengal Vaiṣṇavism, the sect has several works that revel in describing the baby god. The entire first half of Jīva Gosvāmin's huge *Gopāla-campū* is devoted to Kṛṣṇa's childhood and boyhood. Each episode of Kṛṣṇa's childhood that is mentioned in the *Bhāgavata-purāṇa* is retold with further elaborations, and the author added several events himself. In Kṛṣṇadāsa Kavirāja's *Govinda-līlāmṛta* one day in the life of Kṛṣṇa is described. In the course of that day he appears as an infant, child, boy, and lover, for he is all things to all devotees. The Bengali *padāvalīs*, devotional songs, also dwell on the charms and antics of the child god. The Hindi poet Sūrdās (1478-1581), though, appears to have been particularly partial to the baby Kṛṣṇa. As a member of the Vallabha sect, in which the child Kṛṣṇa is central, Sūrdās composed over eight hundred poems on the childhood of Kṛṣṇa.[2]

The play of Kṛṣṇa as a child is of three varieties, each more or less associated with a stage in his maturation. As an infant his play is highly unstructured. He moves his arms and legs erratically, wants one thing or another, crawls around aimlessly in his mother's yard, and covers himself with dirt. As a child his play centers around his tricks, the most common of which is his repeated theft of butter from his mother and other women of Vṛndāvana. As a boy or adolescent his play is more varied. He plays games with his friends, teases the *gopīs*, imitates various animals, and gambols in the forest.

In the *Gopāla-campū* we read of the infants Kṛṣṇa and Balarāma (Kṛṣṇa's elder brother) playing in their parents' yard:

> Then Nanda's courtyard turned into Kṛṣṇa's and Balarāma's playground. They sported there in various ways,

[1] *Bhāgavata-purāṇa* X. 8. 21-22 (IV, 35).
[2] Sūrdās, *The Poems of Sūrdās*, p. 8.

moving their hands and feet and crawling around. Other little boys came there and joined Kṛṣṇa and Balarāma and had great pleasure . . . . "O Hari ! Glory to you and Balarāma. You please your mother when you play and crawl around. You're displaying your childhood sports, banishing suffering with your playful laughter. You kick your feet rhythmically and enjoy the sound of your foot bangles. You crawl around the courtyard for the sheer fun of it, ignoring the dirt and mud."[1]

The idea of God engrossed in child's play worries Sūrdās and causes concern among the lesser gods.

Holding his foot in his hand, Gopāl is sucking his toe.
He lies alone in his cradle absorbed in his happy play.
Śiva has started worrying and Brahmā has become thoughtful.
The Banyan tree has reached the level of the water of the sea.
Thinking that the clouds of Pralaya [cosmic disslolution] are gathering in the sky, the Dikpatis are rounding up their elephants.
Sages are fearful in their hearts, the earth is shaking and the serpent Śeṣa is spreading his hood in anxiety.
The folks in Braj do not know what is happening.
Sūrdās says that he knows what will happen and so is worried.[2]

God, as the baby Kṛṣṇa, is so absorbed in his own play that the world order has begun to run down. As this infant, God acts solely to amuse himself with no thought of the world and cares only to behave as he pleases. The infant god is that god who does not know work or responsibility, who passes his time in play.

The child Gopāla is dancing bewitchingly, and all the women of the Vraja are beating time with their hands and saying,

---

[1]Jīva Gosvāmin, *Śrī Śrī Gopāla-campū*, translated into Bengali by Rasabihāri Sāṁkhyatīrtha, pp. 386-87.

[2]Sūrdās, *The Poems of Sūrdās*, no. 22.

"Fine, O really fine!" Nanda, Sunanda, Yaśodā and Rohiṇī are joyfully looking at the child's face. The red corners of his eyes are tinged with collyrium, and he shows his teeth when smiling.[1]

> Looking like a child aged five years the Charmer (*i.e.*, Young Kṛṣṇa) is romping about in the courtyard. (There is) sweet milk and butter, (which he) eats, and with which he smears his face. Ah, the graceful swinging dance of the charming Gopāla . . . ! Quick are his steps, the girdle bells at his waist tinkle, and a garland of wild flowers . . hangs down (from his neck) . . . . Now he moves on tiptoe, and then he rolls on the ground: now he is gleeful, and then angry.[2]

> Kānh is joyfully crawling.
> In Nanda's golden yard, studded with jewels, he is moving to catch his own image.
> Looking at his shadow, sometimes he tries to grasp it with his hands.
> He laughs gleefully and his two baby teeth shine; he wants to seize the reflection.
> In the golden yard the shadows of hands and feet are cast together, putting forth a smile.
> Each hand and each foot and all his jewels combine in one, presenting a sight, as if a lotus flower were decorating the earth.
> Seeing the pleasant frolics of Kṛṣṇa, Yaśodā calls Nanda again and again.
> Then, hiding Kṛṣṇa in the folds of her clothes she starts suckling him, says Sūrdās.[3]

As a child, varying in age from five to ten, a new element is introduced into Kṛṣṇa's youthful sports. He is constantly disobeying his parents and becomes notorious throughout Vṛndā-

---

[1]From Vaṁśivadanadāsa (sixteenth century); in Sukumar Sen, *A History of Brajabuli Literature: Being a Study of the Vaisnava Lyric Poetry and Poets of Bengal*, p. 43.

[2]From Ghanarāma-dāsa (eighteenth century); *ibid.*, p. 273.

[3]Sūrdās, *The Poems of Sūrdās*, no. 28.

vana as a thief and prankster. His habit of stealing butter is a favorite theme of almost all those who dote on his childhood. In the *Bhāgavata-purāṇa*, where Kṛṣṇa seems first to have made his reputation as a butter thief, we read a catalogue of his pranks:

> Then the almighty Krishna accompanied by Balarama, began to sport with other boys of Braja of the same age with him, thus enhancing the joys of the women of Braja. The wives of the cow-herds seeing the beautiful boyish pranks of Krishna would go to his mother and say to her, Krishna untethers the calves untimely. And if some one out of anger says anything unto him, he laughs out. Inventing novel means of pilfering, Krishna steals away and drinks tasteful curd and milk. He distributes his drinks among the monkeys; and if they do not eat, he breaks the pot containing curd and milk. When he does not find anything in the household, being angry he goes away after having made the infants cry aloud. When these things such as milk, curd etc. are placed beyond the reach of his hands, he creates expedients by piling wooden seats and mortars, etc. Again, knowing these to be concealed in pots hanging in swings, he will strike holes into the pots. At times when the wives of the cow-herds would be occupied in the performance of household duties, he would finish his works of theft in dark rooms, making the jewels of his person to serve the purpose of lamps. He would perpetrate these and similar harmful acts. He would even pass urine and leave excretions in cleansed houses. In this way he commits vile deeds by thievish tricks, but when near thyself he lives like a very gentle boy.[1]

Sūrdās greatly elaborated on the theme of Kṛṣṇa's prankish nature and in the following poem describes the infamous butter thief confusing his own reflection with that of a fellow conspirator:

> Śyām went to the milkmaid's house.
> He looked all around him, and finding no one at the door
> he entered the house.

[1]*Bhāgavata-purāṇa* X. 8. 26-31 (IV, 35-36).

The milkmaid, when she knew of his arrival, hid herself.
Kṛṣṇa entered the empty house and sat down near the churning stick.
Seeing a pot full of butter he took some and started eating.
He beheld the reflection of his body in a jewelled pillar and he began to talk to it.
"It's the first day that I have come here to steal. You are such a good friend to have."
He himself eats and offers some to his reflection, and when the butter falls he asks, "What is the matter?
It is delicious. Why did you let it fall? If you like I will give you the whole pot.
It makes me happy to give you this. How do you feel about it?"
Hearing these words from his mouth the milkmaid of Braj bursts into laughter.
Sūrdās says, Kṛṣṇa ran away when he saw her face.[1]

In the *Gopāla-campū* Jīva Gosvāmin tells of Kṛṣṇa's constant attempts to foil his mother in order to play when and where he likes:

> Day by day the boys became increasingly clever at dodging their mothers. Their mothers repeatedly warned them not to stray, and the boys would pretend obedience, but as soon as their mothers were out of sight they would do what they wanted to do anyway, which was usually what their mothers had forbidden them to do. Though very young, they were extremely clever in hiding from their elders, and if discovered, would hide again where no one could find them.[2]

The exuberance of the children, their boundless energy, and their lively imaginations make them difficult, if not impossible, to control. Kṛṣṇa's foster father, Nanda, finds it increasingly impossible to manage his foster son in his ramblings with Balarāma.

---

[1]Sūrdās, *The Poems of Sūrdās*, no. 50.
[2]Jīva Gosvāmin, *Gopāla-campū*, p. 397.

> They thus sported there like boys. . . . While they sported there they appeared like the sun and moon in the sky possessed by each other's rays. Going every where, they, having arms like serpents, appeared like two proud young elephants covered with dust . . . . Sometimes they used to walk on knees and enter cow-sheds and used to sport there with their persons and hairs covered with cow-dung. Sometimes committing mischiefs to the inhabitants of Vraja those two boys used to create the delight of their sire with their laughing. . . . They grew exceedingly playful and naughty and used to walk all over Vraja. And Nanda could not (by any means) check them.[1]

What is striking in these passages is that Kṛṣṇa's pranks and wildness, his disdain for convention, are not apologized for. The authors obviously approve of his mischief and enjoy flaunting it and elaborating upon it. For as an illustration of divine sport, his pranks are perfectly in order.

Kṛṣṇa's pranks express an indifference to rules that typifies the behavior of children. The child's pranks and general misbehavior are not yet rebellion, as the child acts with little, if any, premeditation. The child has not yet assimilated social conventions and so is not yet limited by them. He behaves spontaneously, impetuously, without regard to "musts" and "oughts." The child seeks only to be amused and to amuse himself, and if such amusement means breaking parental or social rules, he goes right ahead and breaks them without hesitation. The child is free, that is, to express every impulse, to express his essential nature in every action. The theophany of the child Kṛṣṇa, then, expresses the nature of the divine as unconditioned. God, like the child (in this case, as a child), belongs to an other world that is not bound by social and moral convention, to a world where fulness and bounty make work superfluous. For the divine to become embodied as a child is eminently suitable, for they behave in similar ways. Each belongs to a joyous realm of energetic, aimless, erratic activity that is pointless yet significant: pointless, but at the same time imaginative and rich, and therefore creative. In play the mind

[1] *Harivaṁśa* 62. 3-12 (p. 265).

can go wild; the imagination is set free to conjure and conquer. With the world of necessity left behind, the imagination takes over, eagerly populating a world that knows no limits whatsoever. So it is with the play of children, and so it is with the activity of the gods. The child Kṛṣṇa is by no means a partial, lesser manifestation of the divine in India. He epitomizes the nature and activity of the divine.

When Kṛṣṇa reaches adolescence he becomes the leader of a frolicking band of cowherd boys. They spend most of their time in the forests of Vṛndāvana gamboling in imitation of animals and playing games among themselves. They are no longer tied to their parents and create a world of their own, where Kṛṣṇa leads their play.

> They raced with the shadows of running birds. . . . They climbed in the branches of trees with young monkeys . . . . And some plunged into the river with the jumping frogs. . . . Some laughed at their own reflections and jeered at the echo of their own voices.[1]

In the words of Jīva Gosvāmin they created a "din and bustle" and behaved like "wildmen, roaming about aimlessly."[2] This band of cowherd boys is rarely still, as to be still or quiet is not the nature of youth. Their bodies and minds overflow with energy and enthusiasm, and the natural outlet is boistrous play. The following passages show their play to be charged with this irrepressible restlessness:

> After going to the forest, some of the young cowherds, like young elephants freed from their chains, began to dance, sing, laugh, and do acrobatic feats, while others expressed their happiness by simply rolling on the ground. Some of the boys joked, and others indulged in sports of various kinds.[3]

With their heads as glossy black as the feathers of crows

---

[1] Jīva Gosvāmin, *Gopāla-campū*, pp. 583-84.
[2] *Ibid.*, pp. 541, 542.
[3] Kṛṣṇadāsa Kavirāja, *Govinda-līlāmṛta*, translated from Sanskrit into Bengali by Saccidānanda Gosvāmin Bhaktiratna of Navadvīp, Sixth Sarga, p. 242.

> (*Kakapaksha*), Krishna and Balarama would sport by running, jumping, leaping, striking their arms with their hands, and tugging one another and wrestling amongst themselves.[1]

As adolescents their play becomes more diverse and inventive. Competition, imitation, and dance are part of their daily play.

> O Monarch, at times when others would dance, both Krishna and Balarama would perform the parts of singers and players on musical instruments. They would then encourage them saying "well-done", "well-done", etc. Sometimes they would play with *bel*-fruit, and sometimes with *Kumbah* fruit, sometimes they would play the "Blind man's buff" and would engage themselves in other kinds of pastimes. Sometimes they would play with handfuls of *Amalaki* fruit. At other times again they would play imitating birds and beasts. Sometimes they would play leaping like frogs, and sometimes, by exchange [of] jokes and repartees. Sometimes, they would sport rocking and swinging; and sometimes they would play imitating the duties and functions of kings. Thus engaging themselves in these well-known pastimes, they sported in the rivers and lakes of the Brindabana, on its mountains and in their caverns, in groves and gardens and in lakes.[2]

The play of the adolescent is similar to the play of the child and is often indistinguishable from it. The variety and complexity may be compounded, but the same carefree spirit pervades both. What is noteworthy about Kṛṣṇa's adolescent play is its wildness. Some of the descriptions of Kṛṣṇa and his group of friends sound like descriptions of a pack of wild young animals. They caper and gambol through the forest, and even imitate and play with animals. Their play is frivolous and merry, rollicking and free. In the *Harivaṁśa* Kṛṣṇa's play is said to be "like fire in the cremation ground," leaping and flickering, erratic and vigorous.[3] The boastful, brash, and indomitable

---

[1] *Bhāgavata-purāṇa* X. 18. 9 (IV, 84).

[2] *Ibid.* X. 18. 10-16 (IV, 84).

[3] *Harivaṁśa* 77.35 (p. 324). A. K. Coomaraswamy, in fact, has suggested that the word *līlā* may derive from the root *lelay*, "to flare," "flicker," or "flame." And even if *līlā* does not derive from this root, the association of

spirit of Kṛṣṇa's play makes the world around him sparkle with aliveness. His youthful play lights up the world around him as a blazing fire lights up the darkness. The playful actions of Kṛṣṇa and his companions burst forth to tumble and romp like the wind in the trees, unpredictable and free. We have again a description of that other realm where things are as they were meant to be, where life goes on joyously and unhampered, where no thought is given, or need be given, to the future, where life is lived to the fullest every moment. Kṛṣṇa's playful realm is a description of a heavenly world of the gods and a description of divine activity that is anarchical in its freshness and tumult. The happy adolescent Kṛṣṇa expresses this facet of divine sport in a unique way among Hindu gods.

C. *Kṛṣṇa's Sport with Demons*

Vṛndāvana, while Kṛṣṇa is there, is a charmed place where the extraordinary is ordinary, where play and not work is the regular way of life. Only after Kṛṣṇa leaves this forest setting does he enter into the world of necessity and responsibility. He assumes the leadership of kingdoms and the lordship over thousands of wives. In Vṛndāvana, though, he behaves as he wishes. His life is play, and play is his life there. Even when the harsh world of jealousy and meanness tries to intervene in the form of demons sent by his uncle Kaṁsa, Kṛṣṇa's idyllic routine undergoes very little change. For the demons simply are no match for him, and he disposes of them as if it were all a game. For the cowherd boy the slaying of monstrous demons is an extension of his sport. Combat with them is all in a day's play, as it were. His scheming uncle Kaṁsa, who has been told that Kṛṣṇa will one day cause his death, repeatedly sends various fiends to Vṛndāvana to kill the boy, and each time Kṛṣṇa dispatches them with ease and playful imagination.

The first fiend to be sent is the demoness Pūtanā, who disguises herself as a lovely woman. She dotes upon the infant Kṛṣṇa and asks his mother if she can feed him from her own breasts. When Yaśodā allows her to do this, she poisons her

ideas is clear, he adds, as both fire and play suggest spontaneous, erratic movement. "Līlā," *Journal of the American Oriental Society*, LXI (1941), 99.

nipples and tries in this way to kill Kṛṣṇa. The poison, however, is not effective, and the baby Kṛṣṇa turns the tables on the demoness by sucking the life from her.[1] The demon Tṛṇāvarta is the next victim. Sent by Kaṁsa, he appears in the form of a tumultuous whirlwind and sweeps the baby Kṛṣṇa into the air. Kṛṣṇa, however, becomes so heavy that the demon is barely able to keep himself aloft. Finally, nearly exhausted from bearing the weight of the child, he tries to drop his burden. Kṛṣṇa, however, clings tenaciously to the demon's neck, and Tṛṇāvarta, exhausted, falls to the ground like a rock, shattering himself.[2] Kṛṣṇa defeats the demon Batāsura, in the guise of a calf, by hurling him by the tail into a tree.[3] When the demon Vakāsura, in the form of a huge crane, swallowed Kṛṣṇa, the boy became so hot that the giant bird was forced to spit him out. Then Kṛṣṇa attacked the demon and "easily tore it into pieces like a twig."[4] Aghāsura, the younger brother of Pūtanā and Batāsura, assumes the form of a huge snake. Lying on the ground he opens his mouth, which covers the earth and reaches the sky. His fangs look like mountain peaks. The cowherd boys, mistaking the fiend for the presiding deity of Vṛndāvana, fearlessly enter its mouth and are swallowed up. Kṛṣṇa rescues his friends by allowing the snake to swallow him also and then, once inside, increasing his size so the creature is torn apart from within.[5] The demon Dhenuka, in the form of a giant ass, is killed by Balarāma. When Dhenuka's relatives come to the forest to avenge his death, they are handled easily by the two brothers.

> Then Krishna and Balarama with perfect ease caught hold of these assaulting asses by their hind legs, and struck them against the palm trees. Then the ground of the forest was covered over with palm-fruits, palm twigs and the dead bodies of the Daityas (Dhenuka and his relatives) and resembled the beautiful firmament covered over with clouds.[6]

---

[1] *Bhāgavata-purāṇa* X. 6. 4-10 (IV, 25-28).
[2] *Ibid.* X. 7. 20-29 (IV, 31-32).
[3] *Ibid.* X. 11. 41-43 (IV, 46-47).
[4] *Ibid.* X. 11. 48-51 (IV, 47).
[5] *Ibid.* X. 12. 13-32 (IV, 49-51).
[6] *Ibid.* X. 15. 36-38 (IV, 70-71).

It is interesting to note that even the ground littered with the corpses of dead asses is not allowed to detract from the idyllic nature of Vṛndāvana. The sight of them, the author notes rather improbably, is as lovely as the cloud-filled sky! And the chopped-up corpse of the hag Pūtanā, when burned by the people of Vṛndāvana, gives off the sweet odor of sandal wood, as the fiend was redeemed simply by her physical contact with Kṛṣṇa.[1] To return to Kṛṣṇa's catalogue of conquests: The petulant Indra is humbled when he sends a torrential rainstorm on Vṛndāvana to chastise the cowherds for neglecting him, and Kṛṣṇa protects the people by holding aloft Mount Govardhana as a huge umbrella with his little finger for seven days.[2] The demon Ariṣṭa, disguised as a bull who shakes the earth with his strides, is no match for the cowherd boy.

> Kṛṣṇa stirred not from his post, but, smiling in sport and derision, awaited the near approach of the bull, when he seized him as an alligator would have done, and held him firmly by the horns, whilst he pressed his sides with his knees.[3]

And so Ariṣṭa is crushed to death. The *asura* Keśī, in the form of a mighty horse, whose speed is as swift as the mind, and whose thunderous neighs terrify the worlds, is simply tossed at a distance by Kṛṣṇa. Regaining his senses, the stubborn Keśī attacks again. This time Kṛṣṇa thrusts his arm into the demon's mouth and then increases its size until the demon chokes to death.[4]

The theme of combat as play persists after Kṛṣṇa leaves Vṛndāvana. The mad elephant Kubalayāpīḍa and the huge wrestlers Cāṇūra and Muṣṭika, sponsored by Kaṁsa in a tournament, are effortlessly defeated by Kṛṣṇa and Balarāma. The powerful blows of Cāṇūra on Kṛṣṇa's chest are said to have fallen like flower garlands on an elephant.[5] When Kṛṣṇa abducts Rukmiṇī, her brother Rukmin pursues Kṛṣṇa with his army. And "Kṛṣṇa destroyed with his discus, as if in sport, the host of Rukmin, with all its horse, and elephants, and foot, and

[1] *Ibid.* X. 6. 34 (IV, 28).
[2] *Ibid.* X. 25. 1-23 (IV, 108-10).
[3] *Viṣṇu-purāṇa* V. 14. 10-11 (p. 427).
[4] *Bhāgavata-purāṇa* X. 37. 1-8 (IV, 150-51).
[5] *Ibid.* X. 44. 1-22 (IV, 183-84).

chariots."[1] And in a battle with Śiva, Kṛṣṇa becomes victorious when he forces Śiva to yawn.[2]

But Kṛṣṇa's nature as a sporting warrior is most apparent in Vṛndāvana during his youth. And his sportive conquests are epitomized by his combat with the deadly, many-headed serpent Kālīya, who has poisoned the waters of the Kālindī and killed many cows. Kṛṣṇa climbs into a tree on the river-bank and then leaps into the poisonous waters, where he begins to bait the serpent by swimming and playing there. The enraged Kālīya emerges from his lair beneath the waters, and the combat begins. Kālīya seems to get the upper hand at first and grips Kṛṣṇa in his coils. But Kṛṣṇa is only humoring him and soon defeats him in the following playful way:

> Like unto the foremost of birds, Garuda,—Krishna moved in sport round this serpent, who was licking the two ends of his mouth with his divided fangs, and whose eyes were very terrible and emitting fiery venom. The serpent also moved, watching for an opportunity to bite him. Thus when the strength of the serpent failed in consequence of those movements, Krishna (the Prime Purusha) bending the serpent's raised neck ascended on his broad hood.
>
> Then Krishna, the master of all kinds of dancing, began to dance on the hood of that serpent, having his lotus-like feet rendered reddish by the lustre of the many jewels on the serpent's head. Thereupon, seeing him ready to dance, the wives of the Gandharvas, Siddhas, Sages, Charanas and Celestials, suddenly approached him playing out of delight on *Mridangas*, *Panavas*, *Anakas* and other musical instruments, and singing and praising him with presents of flowers, etc. The chastiser of the wicked, Krishna, trampled underneath the tread of his feet, the erect hoods of the hundred-headed serpent, that was moving in spite of his gradual failing of strength. Then profusely vomiting blood from his mouth and nose, the serpent Kaliya lost all consciousness. Again and again the serpent, breathing audibly out of wrath and shedding venom from his eyes, lifted his hoods, but again and

[1] *Viṣṇu-purāṇa* V. 26. 10 (p. 454).
[2] *Ibid.* V. 33. 24-25 (p. 468).

> again, dancing and striking by his feet, Krishna pressed them . . . down. Thereupon he was worshipped with flowers like unto the ancient Male Being (Parama Purusha).[1]

The body of the serpent having been smashed by Kṛṣṇa's dancing, Kālīya finally admits defeat and seeks refuge in Kṛṣṇa's mercy. Kṛṣṇa, at the pleading of Kālīya's wives, grants him his life and sends him away to an island in the ocean.

The mighty Kṛṣṇa, in the form of a child and youth, is obviously invincible, and his contests with demons and fiends never pose any real threat to him. Kṛṣṇa does not exert any measurable strength in these battles but toys with his enemies. "Powerful demons appeared now and then to create disturbances in the boys' games and He [Kṛṣṇa] killed them in various playful methods which only added to the pleasure of His playmates."[2] For the cowherd boy these battles are another form of his *lilā*, a mere diversion. They are imaginative and playful. He scampers about the forests of Vṛndāvana with his friends, carefree and reckless, and when a demon makes its appearance, the scampering does not stop but continues right through the combat. The great player is not distracted from his play.

D. *The Most Relishable One*

One of the most striking features of the cowherd Kṛṣṇa is his fantastic beauty. While beauty itself is not necessarily playful, the physical attractiveness of Kṛṣṇa and its centrality in his myths and cult is a fitting concomitant to his sportive nature. For beauty, like play, is an end in itself. It strives for nothing, achieves nothing. It is apart from the instrumental world of necessity. It belongs to that other world of abundance. It is part of a world of effortless grace, an ornamental thing that justifies itself by simply being, and so like play belongs appropriately to the divine sphere.

Kṛṣṇa is beauty itself—his appearance alone transcends the world of the ordinary. His every characteristic, furthermore, is the most relishable. In the language of Sanskrit poetics,

---

[1]*Bhāgavata-purāṇa* X. 16. 26-30 (IV, 75-76).
[2]Srimat Bhakti Vilas Tirtha Goswami Maharaj, *Sri Chaitanya's Concept of Theistic Vedanta,* p. 57.

where aesthetic beauty (*rasa*) is tasted (not simply enjoyed), his taste is the sweetest.[1] His speech is the most melodious and irresistible and his conversation the wittiest.

> The speech of the Lord is sweet too. And it is full of much sweet humour. But the mischief that it does is unspeakable.
> For it enters by force the ears of all the maidens of the world.
> And by the cord of its sweetness it ties them all. And it pulls them so hard that the ears can hardly stand it.[2]

Even his smell is delicious. One day in the forest when Kṛṣṇa became separated from his cowherd companions, they found him without difficulty simply by following his fragrant, irresistible odor. "Then like bees attracted by the fragrance of flowers, they by the fragrance of Kṛṣṇa were attracted, and ran toward him in groups and touched him."[3]

Another essential characteristic of Kṛṣṇa's beauty is his youthfulness. In Bengal Vaiṣṇavism it is stated that Kṛṣṇa reveals himself most fully in Vṛndāvana, where he is always a youth.[4] In Vṛndāvana itself, moreover, he appeared in three different bodies, or stages of growth: the child body, the *pauganda* body (the body between the fifth and the tenth year), and the *kiśore* body (the body in the prime of youth, from ten to fifteen years of age). While each body is eternal, ever present in eternal Vṛndāvana, the *kiśore* body is the best.[5] And it is in this form,

[1]Kṛṣṇadāsa Kavirāja, *Śrī Śrī Caitanya-caritāmṛta* (Bengali), Madhya-līlā 2. 30; Krishnadasa Kaviraja Goswamin, *Sri Sri Chaitanya Charitamrita*, trans. Nagendra Kumar Ray, p. 30. English translations are from Ray unless otherwise indicated.

[2]*Ibid.*, Antya-līlā 15.18 (p. 261). The Great Goddess's beauty is also frequently extolled in minute detail, as in *Śāradātilakatantram* 8. 74-88 and 24. 102 (p. 57), in which the origin of Śiva's third eye is explained as follows: "Shiva not satisfied with looking at and admiring Her with two yese created in the excess of his adoration a third eye on his forehead the more fully to see the, beauty of Her thighs." See also *Saundaryalaharī* 13, where it is said that even a glimpse of her beauty turns old men into irresistible youth.

[3]Jiva Gosvāmin, *Gopāla-campū*, p. 582.

[4]Sushil Kumar De, *Early History of the Vaisnava Faith and Movement in Bengal from Sanskrit and Bengali Sources*, p. 347.

[5]Rūpa Gosvāmin, *Bhakti-rasāmṛta-sindhu*, Eastern Division: Fourth Wave, *śloka* 1, Viśvanātha Cakravartin's commentary; Rūpa Gosvāmi, *Bhakti-rasāmṛta-sindhuḥ*, Vol. I, trans. Tridaṇḍi Swāmi Bhakti Hṛdaya Bon Mahārāj p. 374.

as an adolescent or youth, that he is extolled as the most relishable thing. It is in this sparkling, carefree form that he becomes the great lover of the *gopis*, the irresistible exhilarator and inebriator. A few examples of the many passages that praise his beauty will illustrate the importance of Kṛṣṇa's appearance in his mythology and cult.

> The light of Lord Krisṇa is circular and vies with millions of suns. The Yogis, adepts and gods adore this light. But the Vaiṣṇavas adore the indescribable, lovely image of Krisṇa located in the centre of this light. He is blue like a new cloud; his eyes are like lotuses; his face is as graceful as the autumnal full Moon; his lips are like *bimbas*; the row of his teeth shames the pearls. A gentle smile plays on his lips. He holds a flute in his hands . . . . He is clad in yellow dress.[1]

> He had a smiling and cheerful appearance . . . ; his hands held the merry lotus meant for joy and the flute; his image harboured the sportive grace of ten millions of Cupids.[2]

In a poem by Mīrābāī Kṛṣṇa is described in similar terms :

> Live in my eyes, Nandalal.
> Your peacock crown, and fish-shaped earrings,
> And the red tilak on your forehead are beautiful.
> Your figure is charming, your face is dark, and your eyes
> are large.
> On your lips there is a flute
> And a garland of jasmine adorns your chest.
> Mirabai says, the Lord is a giver of joy to the pious
> And the protector of the poor.[3]

In the *Caitanya-caritāmṛta* even the nails of Kṛṣṇa are extolled.

> And the white nails in the hands of the Lord are also like so many moons. As the Lord blows His flute there, little

---

[1] *Brahma-vaivarta-purāṇa*, Brahma Khaṇḍa 21. 32 ff. (Part I, p. 65).

[2] *Ibid.*, Kṛṣṇa Janma Khaṇḍa 27. 220-21 (Part II, p. 228).

[3] Mīrābāī, "Poems from Mīrābāī," trans. S. M. Pandey and Norman H. Zide, *pada* 3, p. 2.

moons dance upon the holes of the flute. They appear as
if the tune proceeds not from the flute but from these beautiful nails of the Lord.

And the nails of His feet are also like moons. They also seem
to dance as the Lord walks and the tinkling sounds proceeding from the nupur (ornaments adorning the feet) appear
to be songs sung by the moonlike nails.[1]

Finally, from a Bengali song, we read a typical description of
the *dhīralalita* lover, the lover "who is in the prime of youth,
artful, humorous, careless":[2]

That prince of gallant lovers, dressed as a great dancer, is
standing at his ease under a *nīpa* tree by the bank of the
Daughter of the Sun (Yamunā). The loveliness of his
complexion surpasses that of a mirror made of pure emerald.
Every item of his person is a riot of love. The oval of his
face is (as beautiful) as the round of the moon. Earrings
decorate his ears. Under the arches of the eyebrows that
are the veritable bows of the god of love dance his eyes like
a pair of hopping *khañjana* birds. The sweetness of the notes
of the flute at his lips that resemble buds of *bāndhulī* flower
has intoxicated my heart. On his crest shivers the lovely
peacock's feather in slight breeze. So says Yadunandana
in a way that is ambrosiac to the ear : "He has stolen everything, both body and soul."[3]

So it is that in almost every Vaiṣṇava-Kṛṣṇa work, be it
devotional, poetic, or theological, Kṛṣṇa's physical appearance
is doted upon. And the ultimate goal of all devotees is actually
to see Kṛṣṇa in a vision while living or to dwell with him in
heavenly Vṛndāvana after death. The attitude of the devotee
should be like that of the *gopī* who cursed the creator for having
given her eyelids that prevented her seeing Kṛṣṇa constantly.[4]

---

[1]Kṛṣṇadāsa Kavirāja *Caitanya-caritāmṛta*, Madhya-lilā 21. 107 (p. 535).
Cf. praise of the Devi's beauty, top to bottom, head to toe, in *Saundaryalaharī*
52-94 (pp. 68-84).

[2]Krishnadas [Charuchandra Guha], *Krishna of Vrindabana*, p. 275.

[3]From Yadunandana-dāsa (ii) (seventeenth century); in S. Sen, *Brajabuli
Literature*, p. 182.

[4]Kṛṣṇadāsa Kavirāja *Caitanya-caritāmṛta*, Madhya-lilā 21. 112 (p. 534).

E. *The Divine Lover and His Carnival of Joy*

This charming, youthful god who entrances all by his beauty is the hero of the love-*līlā* of Vṛndāvana, the central episode of the Kṛṣṇa cult. Other gods in Hinduism indulge in erotic sports and amorous diversions, as has been mentioned, but Kṛṣṇa stands supreme among the gods as the Divine Lover. As the lover *par excellence* Kṛṣṇa expresses in its every facet the playful nature of love and love-making.

Kṛṣṇa's activity as a lover can be considered of two general types: in relation to Rādhā alone or to a particular *gopī* and in relation to the *gopīs* as a group. The first type is more personal and complex, involving a wide range of moods and situations. The latter type is in general uniformly described in the various texts. It is riotous, festive, at times rollicking.

A consistent feature of Rādhā and Kṛṣṇa's love, and indeed of love in general, is that it takes place in a world apart, in an ideal world that shuns the ordinary world.[1] Their love takes place in a magic circle, as it were, where everything they see, do, and are is transformed. It is from this general point of view that love participates in the world of play, which also takes place in another realm under special conditions and at special times. Within the love relationship itself, however, playful themes

[1]Although Rādhā is known quite early in Indian literature, her central position in Vaiṣṇava myth and cult came much later. She is mentioned in the Prakrit work *Gāhāsattasaī*, attributed to Hāla and probably written before the seventh century A.D. (Sūrdās, "The Poetry of Sūrdās," p. 12). But she did not become popular in Sanskrit poetry until the eleventh and twelfth centuries. (S. Sen, *Brajabuli Literature*, p. 485, has a list of Sanskrit plays that deal with Rādhā at about this time.) If Rādhā was known to the author of the *Bhāgavata-purāṇa*, written sometime around A.D. 900 (J. N. Farquhar, *An Outline of the Religious Literature of India*, p. 32), he chose not to mention her, even though Kṛṣṇa's dalliance with the *gopīs* is central there. Her acceptance by the Vaiṣṇavas seems to have taken place, therefore, sometime between the composition of the *Bhāgavata-purāṇa* and Jayadeva's *Gītāgovinda*, written near the end of the twelfth century in Bengal. In this work the sole theme is the love between Rādhā and Kṛṣṇa. Nimbārka seems to have been the first well-known religious leader to regard Rādhā as central to his cult (thirteenth century). For a discussion of the origin and development of the Rādhā cult, and particularly its history in Bengal, see S. C. Mukherji, *A Study of Vaiṣṇavism in Ancient and Medieval Bengal—upto the Advent of Chaitanya (Based on Archaeological & Literary Data)*, Appendix A, pp. 183 ff.

abound, and these are clearly portrayed, and even emphasized, in the love of Rādhā and Kṛṣṇa that is described in Vaiṣṇava scriptures and songs.

The awakening of love, or the mood of first love (*pūrva-rāga*), is pervaded with a comic theme in which Rādhā shows a curious mixture of the girl and the woman, of curiosity and shyness. She is not yet a woman and no longer a girl. She is a flutter of girlish giggles at one moment and pensive the next. She is a favorite subject of Vaiṣṇava poets.

> Now (the pupils of) her eyes follow the corners (*i.e.*, she gives a side-long glance), and now again she fills up (the hem of) her skirt with dust (*i.e.*, trails the hem of her garment on the ground). Now she smiles, exposing the dazzling white of her teeth, and then she (bashfully) covers up her lips with (the hem of) her *sari*. The young girl is on the meeting ground of childhood and youthfulness: one cannot judge which is more prevailing (*literally*, which is the older and which the younger). Finding her breasts budding slightly she now covers them up with her *sari*, but in the next moment she has forgotten all about it. Now she runs forward with a start, and then immediately she walks in a slow gait.[1]

According to the classification of heroines in Sanskrit poetics she is known as *navala-anaṅgā*, newly excited, and she is one "who plays, speaks, and laughs sportively as children do and wins her husband with her dalliance."[2] Her näiveté, girlish boldness, and womanly modesty combine to create an irresistible charm that is at once endearing and amusing.

> The girl and the woman
> bound in one being:
> the girl puts up her hair,
> the woman lets it
> fall to cover her breasts;
> the girl reveals her arms,

---

[1]From Vidyà-vallabha; in S. Sen, *Brajabuli Literature,* p. 165.

[2]From Keśav Dās (1580-1601) *Rasikapriyā* (Hindi); in M. S. Randhawa, *Kangra Paintings on Love*, p. 35.

her long legs, innocently bold;
the woman wraps her shawl modestly about her,
her open glance a little veiled.
Restless feet, a blush on the young breasts,
hint at her heart's disquiet:
behind her closed eyes
Kāma awakes, born in imagination, the god.

Vidyāpati says, O Krishna, bridegroom,
be patient, she will be brought to you.[1]

Another playful theme in this early stage of love is Rādhā's coyness, both unpremeditated and strategic. A girl friend has brought her to Kṛṣṇa, and she is about to be left alone with him.

Fingering the border of her friend's sari, nervous and afraid,
sitting tensely on the edge of Krishna's couch,

as her friend left she too looked to go
but in desire Krishna blocked her way.

He was infatuated, she bewildered;
he was clever, and she naive.

He put out his hand to touch her; she quickly pushed it away.
He looked into her face, her eyes filled with tears.

He held her forcefully, she trembled violently
and hid her face from his kisses behind the edge of her sari.

Then she lay down, frightened, beautiful as a doll;
he hovered like a bee round a lotus in a painting.

Govinda-dāsa says, Because of this,
drowned in the well of her beauty,
Krishna's lust was changed.[2]

---

[1]Edward C. Dimock and Denise Levertov (trans.), *In Praise of Krishna : Songs from the Bengali*, p. 7.
[2]*Ibid.*, p. 11.

Here Rādhā's coyness is genuine. She has consented to meet Kṛṣṇa alone but at the crucial moment offers herself hesitantly, clinging to her friend to the last moment. In the following poem, however, her go-between advises her to employ coyness as a strategy in the game of love:

> First, you will decorate your hairs and besmear (sandal)
> paste (over your body). Then you will paint your
> unsteady eyes with collyrium.
> You will go with all your limbs covered with cloth. You
> will remain at a distance so that he may become
> (very much) desirous (of meeting) you.
> O damsel, first you will manifest (signs of) bashfulness,
> and with your side-glances you will arouse Cupid.
> You will cover (one half of) your breasts and expose the
> other half. Every moment you will make the knot
> in the lower garment tighter.
> You will show anger and then exhibit some love (for him).
> You will preserve the sentiment so that he may come
> again and again.
> O damsel, what further instructions in the science of love
> shall I give you?
> Cupid himself will become the guide and will tell you
> everything, Vidyapati says.[1]

The nature of love, or, more exactly, courtship, as a game is clear here. Coyness and mock resistance heighten the suspense about who will "win." It is a ploy by which Rādhā elicits Kṛṣṇa's feelings for her before she has actually offered herself. It is a means of forcing Kṛṣṇa to declare himself first.

The consummation of the love relationship, the physical, sexual aspect of it, also has a playful theme about it and so is in fact appropriately called love play. From a strictly appetitive point of view, of course, the sexual act is an act of necessity, fulfilling one of man's strongest and most persistent needs. But from a romantic or ideal point of view, or indeed from any point of view other than the physiological, there is a sportive quality to the sexual act. Again, it is not instrumental behavior but

[1]Vidyapati, *The Songs of Vidyapati*, trans. Subhadra Jha, no. 62, p. 63.

intrinsically satisfying activity that is an end in itself, and as such it is frequently called dalliance, which suggests an aimless, useless kind of action. The flavor of the following poem, for example, is not that of lust but of playful dalliance, and it is typical of Bengali songs on Rādhā and Kṛṣṇa's love :

> The bodies of the two, when they saw each other, bristled up in joy, and the pains of the previous night's separation subsided. Rāī (Rādhikā) swam in the sea of bliss to the extent she suffered from the fever of separation. They two looked into and kissed each other's face: in joy they disported at will. It was a pleasurable night and the moon was shining: the cuckoo, wild with joy, was singing; beautiful flowers were all in bloom; and a southern breeze was blowing. The garden house was all aglow. Rādhā and Mādhava were in playful sport: seeing it Narottamadāsa is in exhilaration.[1]

The love play of Rādhā and Kṛṣṇa, furthermore, is pervaded with mock quarrels and fits of temper that heighten the sense of frivolity that surrounds their dalliance. The following passage from the *Brahma-vaivarta-purāṇa* is a good example of this:

> The expert Krisṇa playfully denuded Râdhâ of her dress and ornaments; and Râdhâ denuded him of his crest and apparel. As both were expert in the game, no harm accrued to any of them. Krisṇa took away the looking-glass of gem from her hands; and she snatched away from him his melodious flute. Râdhâ enchanted the mind of Krisṇa and Krisṇa charmed her heart. When this fight of love was over, the crooked eyed Râdhâ returned to him his flute; and Krisṇa returned to her the looking-glass and the lotus used as a toy to play with, fastened her chignon, and marked her forehead with vermillion.[2]

At times one or the other will have a fit of pique and feign indifference toward the other. In this poem Rādhā is speaking to Kṛṣṇa's messenger, an old woman, and scowls at the necessity of Kṛṣṇa's using a go-between:

---

[1] From Narottama-dâsa; in S. Sen, *Brajabuli Literature*, p. 100.
[2] *Brahma-vaivarta-purāṇa*, Kṛṣṇa Janma Khaṇḍa 15. 151-58 (Part II, p. 159).

From the time our eyes first met
our longing grew.
He was not only the desirer, I not only the desired:
passion ground our hearts together in its mortar.
Friend, do not forget to recall to Krishna
how it was with us then.
Then we required no messenger, sought
only each other's lips for our love.
It was the god of love himself who united us,
he of the five arrows . . .
But now my lordly lover has learned new manners,
now he sends *you*, herald of his indifference!
So, with anger like a king's, increasing,
sings the poet Rāmānanda Rāy.[1]

And in this poem Rādhā's pique has reached the point where in her sulking she mocks his entreaties and sends him on his way peremptorily:

The marks of fingernails are on your breast
and my heart burns.
Kohl of someone's eyes upon your lips
darkens my face.
I am awake all night;
your eyes are red.
So why do you entreat me, Kān,
saying that you and I have but one heart?
You come with choking voice
while I want to weep.
"Only our bodies are apart."
But mine is light,
and yours is dark.
Go home, then,
says Govinda-dāsa.[2]

The reconciliations that follow such quarrels and fits of pique frequently have a comic theme and often show the previous anger to have been false.

---

[1]Dimock and Levertov (trans.), *In Praise of Krishna*, p. 41.
[2]*Ibid.*, p. 45.

Having come, *Madhava* opened the door of the room
in which *Radha* was resting.
In her anger on account of drowsiness, she looked with a
suppressed smile at (him; her face) looked as if a
half of the moon had risen (above in the sky).
Radha began to bewail and speak to *Madhava*.
Who, in youth, beauty, accomplishment or in any other
quality, is superior to me? Who is the girl who is
more accomplished than myself?
"I delayed at *Mathura*." Then why did you not send a
messenger?
"There I met some traders and fell asleep." Your mind
is fickle: it is not steady: you do not assume gravity.
She cast her side-glances and with a little smile (she said)
your body is black even within. Vidyapati says.[1]

In the following passage from the *Rasikapriyā* Rādhā brings about reconciliation on her own initiative in a devious and delightful way:

> Rādhā came smilingly to Kṛishṇa and sang him a tale of love. She then asked him to explain to her the meaning of some of the sequences of the story: the simultaneous partaking by the lovers of the nectar of each other's mouths, and of other parts of the body which in consequence suffered amorous injuries by nails and teeth. Enclosing him in an embrace, she also asked him, on an oath, what mode of embracing the lovers in the tale had adopted. Thus did Rādhā herself make up her quarrel with her lover today.[2]

The love between these two is also full of laughing and joking, which surrounds the relationship with a cheerful air. "In that charming garden by the Yamunā there blew the South breeze, and they both were joking and talking intimately, and amusing each other."[3] This lighter theme dominates their love to the almost total exclusion of the brooding, oppressive aspects of love. The bitterness of recrimination, guilt, and hurt

[1]Vidyapati, *The Songs of Vidyapati*, no. 220, p. 223.
[2]In Randhawa, *Kangra Paintings on Love*, p. 95.
[3]From Devakīnandana-dāsa; in S. Sen, *Brajabuli Literature*, p. 49.

is never allowed to color the relationship. It is as if genuine love had nothing to do with the world of nastiness and jealousy. In the magic circle things are always light and cheerful, almost frothy. Anger and pique are brief, and the lovers never permanently injure each other.

The lovers' dialogue also underlines the light, playful nature of their relationship. Kṛṣṇa especially is made to embody the model of the clever, sporting young man whose forte is humorous conversation. The dramas portraying Kṛṣṇa written by the Bengal Vaiṣṇava school illustrate this well. While the dramas frequently resort to homilies on the superiority of *bhakti*, they take delight in portraying Kṛṣṇa as a witty hero who spends his time amusing his friends with jokes and teasing and playing tricks on the *gopīs*. One of his favorite pastimes is to pose as a landowner or toll-collector in order to meddle in the affairs of the *gopīs*. In the *Gopāla-campū* of Jīva Gosvāmin he pretends to be a great landowner and demands to know what the women of Vraja are doing on his property. They reply, recognizing his disguise, that they are goddesses of the forest (*banadevatā*) and that he should take care to treat them politely.[1] At another time he poses as a toll-collector and demands a payment from the *gopīs* before they are permitted to cross the river.[2] The dialogue that dominates this, and most other dramas of the same genre, is ornate and frivolous and is particularly fond of *double entendre*. In a play by Rūpa Gosvāmin, *Dāna-keli-kaumudī*, one of the *gopīs*, Lalitā, has refused to bow down to Kṛṣṇa, who is posing as the king of Vṛndāvana. She gives as her excuse the fact that she is observing a vow and that she has been instructed only to bow before *brāhmans*. Arjun, one of Kṛṣṇa's friends, says that it is all right for her to bow before the "king," as he is also observing a vow. "What kind of vow is he observing?" asks Lalitā. Kṛṣṇa, smiling, replies: "My vow is to give clothes to countless *brāhmans* who are not capable of buying clothes for themselves."[3] Another meaning of the vow, however, is that he has vowed to cut the lip-covering of these countless young

---

[1]Jīva Gosvāmin, *Gopāla-campū*, pp. 1590-91.
[2]*Ibid.*, pp. 1952-56.
[3]Rūpa Gosvāmin, *Dāna-keli-kaumudī*, translated into Bengali by Rāmanārāyaṇa Vidyāratna, p. 53.

women.[1] What should also be noted about these dramas is that they are written by devotees of the sect, in many cases by the foremost theologians of the sect. So they are in no way meant to mock or caricature Kṛṣṇa.

The playful, amusing nature of Rādhā and Kṛṣṇa's love, then, functions to keep it far removed from the harsh world of work and worrisome duty. And within the enchanted realm of their love each finds a new freedom, particularly Rādhā. This is as it should be, for within a love relationship man's deepest feelings can finally be expressed. His longings and secret dreams are cherished here, and in fact they no longer seem so frivolous to the sensitive lover.

> Lovely Rādhā was seated on (Kṛṣṇa's) lap. The two (lovers) were engrossed in each other's fresh youthfulness. Madly in love the Two (were) in mutual embrace, (and this looked) as if a golden creeper had entwined a *tamāla* tree. Their eyes were unsteady for the ecstasy of love, as if a pair of *khañjana* birds were hopping about. Their loveliness was reflected on each other's eyes, looking at which the moon disappeared from the sky. The two golden cups (*i.e.* Rādhā's breasts) were covered up by the hands (of Kṛṣṇa). Laughing they talked of their secret feelings. Their mutual love was fully known to each other, and both were appreciative lovers. So says Vāsudeva.[2]

And in the following poem of Vidyāpati the bondage of love is called a net, but within that net Rādhā finds her freedom :

As I near the bed,
He smiles and gazes.
Flower-arrows fill the world.
The sport of love,
Its glow and luxuries
Are indescribable, O friend,

[1]The double meaning centers around the words *oṣṭhādhara*, which can mean clothes generally, or clothes of the lips or face (*oṣṭha*, lips, covering), and *khaṇḍanarūpa*, which can mean to get rid of, to give, or to cut (*khaṇḍana*, give, cut).

[2]From Vāsudeva-dāsa; in S. Sen, *Brajabuli Literature*, pp. 365-66.

And when I yield myself,
His joy is endless.

Freeing my skirt,
He snatches at my garland.
My downcast mind
Is freed of frontiers,
Though my life is held
In the net of his love.
He drinks my lips.
With heart so thrilled,
He takes my clothes away.
I lose my body
At his touch
And long to check
But grant his love.

Says Vidyāpati:
Sweet as honey
Is the talk of a girl in love.[1]

The flood of emotions that overcomes the lover, whether in the presence of the beloved or not, is also treated in a playful way in the Rādhā-Kṛṣna literature. The poets delight in depicting Rādhā's distracted frame of mind, her rapidly changing moods, or her hopelessly obvious behavior that is meant to be discreet. In the *Rasikapriyā*, under a discussion of external indications of love, Keśav Dās speaks of *vibhrama-bhāva*, or flutter. As an example of this, he describes Rādhā upon hearing Kṛṣṇa's flute. She puts her necklace around her waist, her earrings on her hands, and generally loses control of her senses. And when Kṛṣṇa sees Rādhā he drops the betel in his hands and inadvertently begins to chew on a lotus.[2] In the following passage Kṛṣṇa's effect on the *gopīs* is extraordinary in its variety:

When Kṛṣna suddenly appeared among the smiling, joking women, they were simultaneously possessed by feelings of

[1]Vidyāpati, *Love Songs of Vidyāpati*, trans. Deben Bhattacharya, ed. W. G. Archer, no. 68, p. 107.
[2]Randhawa, *Kangra Paintings on Love*, p. 56.

respect, delusion, wonder, pride, shame, shamelessness, fear, adoration, jubilence, wishfulness, and so on, and thus overcome with these mixed emotions they became strangely silent.[1]

The height of emotion is reached when the lovers become totally immersed in each other. Shame is completely forgotten, and they behave with abandon, as if in a frenzy or intoxicated. In this state they are far removed from all else, completely enclosed in their own special circle. And there they are free to behave in any way they choose. In this poem Rādhā loses all inhibitions and takes the dominant part in the love-making:

> Her massive locks are dishevelled. She is the goddess of amorous sport, embodied and incarnate. Their passionate love is excessive. So the girl behaves as a man . . . . Her vase-shaped breasts are turned upside down, as if the god of love is pouring out the nectar of love. Over them the hands of the dearest (lover) have been placed, as if (a pair of) *cakravākas* are sitting over (a pair of) lotuses. Bangles and bells at her girdle are jingling, as if the band of joy has been struck by the company of the god of love.[2]

In the next poem the sight of Kṛṣṇa is sufficient for Rādhā to lose all her modesty. And everywhere she sees nothing but Kṛṣṇa, so immersed in him is she.

> After seeing him the eyes fled off (the face): it seemed as if the lotus, having discarded the sun was running away.
> The moon and the lily met each other. I could hide the expression of love with a trick.
> O lady, I saw *Madhava* today. Having forsaken its gravity my bashfulness vanished away.
> The knot in the lower garment became loose and fell on the ground. I was hiding my body under my body.

---

[1]Jīva Gosvāmin, *Gopāla-campū*, p. 728.

[2]From Kavirañjana (Vidyāpati ii) (late sixteenth century); in S. Sen, *Brajabuli Literature*, pp. 145-46.

> Even my own heart seemed to be of another person. In all directions I saw *Kṛṣṇa* and *Kṛṣṇa* alone. Vidyapati says.[1]

The lovers in this condition are so absorbed in each other, so apart from the regular world, that they can barely cope with normal life. The following is a description of Rādhā's frenzy (called *unmāda daśā*) from the *Rasikapriyā*:

> She stares as if startled; her heart beats heavily and seeing her own shadow she loses herself in thought. Her answers are irrelevant to the questions asked of her; in separation she has become an altogether changed person. . . . Thus deranged, she is now indifferent to her veil, her garments and her ornaments.[2]

Here Kṛṣṇa's frenzy is described, and he is obviously as hopelessly affected as Rādhā. One of Rādha's friends is speaking to her shortly after having seen Kṛṣṇa:

> With tearful eyes and dazed mind he gazes all around, then stares fixedly, and then walks away hurriedly. He keeps brooding with agitated mind and fever in his body. Sometimes he weeps and sometimes laughs. Fear-stricken and agitated in my mind, I have come to tell you of his condition. He is talking so incoherently that I fear lest the secret of his love for you may not be disclosed.[3]

Finally, the realm of Rādhā and Kṛṣṇa's love dalliance is a world of joy. Their love is a celebration that enables them to enter completely that extraordinary, other world of the divine where everything is resolved in bliss. Rādhā sings:

> The moon has shone upon me,
> the face of my beloved.
> O night of joy !

---

[1]Vidyapati, *The Songs of Vidyapati*, no. 66, p. 67.
[2]From Keśav Dās *Rasikapriyā*; in Randhawa, *Kangra Painttings on Love*, p. 112.
[3]*Ibid.*, p. 117.

Joy permeates all things.
My life: joy,
my youth: fulfillment.

Today my house is again
home,
today my body is
my body.
The god
of destiny smiled on me.
No more doubt.

Let the nightingales sing, then,
let there be myriad
rising moons, let Kāma's
five arrows become five thousand
and the south wind

softly, softly blow:
for now my body has meaning
in the presence of my beloved.

Vidyāpati says, Your luck is great;
may this return of love be blessed.[1]

The joy of the loving couple is also the joy of the *gopis* of Vṛndāvana. Turning to the second type of Kṛṣṇa's amorous dalliance, we find the emphasis is upon Kṛṣṇa as the ringmaster of a festival of love. He instigates it, leads it, enjoys it, and is by far the best at it. By means of his flute he beckons the women of Vṛndāvana to that separate world of his where intoxication and abandon, joy and rollicking sport reign supreme. The *Brahma-vaivarta-purāṇa* takes special delight in describing Kṛṣṇa's sports with hundreds of *gopis* in the forests of Vṛndāvana:

> Some of the cow herdesses . . . out of fun forcibly took away the flute from the hands of Lord Krisṇa. Then they pulled his yellow dress. Some passionate girl denuded

[1]Dimock and Levertov (trans.), *In Praise of Krishna*, p. 66.

him of his clothes, took away his yellow garment and then in jest returned it to him . . . . Some cowherdess intentionally showed to him her smiling lunar face full of glances, rising breast and delicate waist . . . . Some pulled his crest and attached to it the plumage of peacock. Others adorned the crest with wreaths of flowers, others fanned and tended the lord of their lives with white chowries . . . . Some danced and sang with Krisṇa in the centre; others forcibly caused him to dance. Krisṇa also out of fun, dragged the clothes of some milk-maid, made her naked and then returned the clothes to her.[1]

The sport of Kṛṣṇa with the *gopis* is so enchanting that even the gods assemble to watch and are filled with emotion.

In that war of love, the cloth tied round their waist, their chignon and small bells slipped and their lovely garment and toilet was ruffled. Then the prince of the witty embraced them in nine ways, kissed them in eight ways and co-habited with them in sixteen ways. The most licentious Hari embraced each limb of the milk-maids with each of the members of his body . . . . When this game of Râsa in its sphere was in full swing, the gods with their wives and attendants mounted the golden car and assembled in the heavens. The sight of the sports sent a thrill of emotion across their bodies and afflicted them with darts of Cupid.[2]

The *Govinda-lilāmṛta* is as explicit as the *Brahma-vaivarta-purāṇa* in describing Kṛṣṇa's participation in erotic dalliance with the *gopis*:

Kṛṣṇa danced around among the *gopis*, looking them over. He kissed some of them on the cheeks and lips, looked lustfully at others, and fondled the breasts of others, leaving nail marks on them. In that game of *rāsa* he enjoyed sexual intercourse with Rādhā and other *gopis*, and thus had intercourse with himself.[3]

---

[1]*Brahma-vaivarta-purāṇa*, Kṛṣṇa Janma Khaṇḍa 28. 84-93 (Part II, p. 232).

[2]*Ibid.* 28. 107-13 (Part II, pp. 232-33).

[3]Kṛṣṇadāsa Kavirāja, *Govinda-līlāmṛta*, p. 1281.

The last phrase in this passage suggests a Bengal Vaiṣṇava doctrine to the effect that the *gopīs* are really Kṛṣṇa's own *śaktis* and that in dalliance with them he is actually playing with himself. Another passage from the *Govinda-līlāmṛta* hints at the same thing by comparing Kṛṣṇa's sport with the *gopīs* to a boy playing with his own image in a mirror:

> In this way Kṛṣṇa made the fair ladies of Vraja sing and dance, and they also made him dance and sing, which he did wonderfully. He praised them, and they praised him. He played just like a boy playing with his own reflection.[1]

The idea of God making love to himself, being enchanted by his own beauty, and being amused by his own talents is a thoroughly playful one. I shall return to it below when I discuss the playful themes in Vaiṣṇava-Kṛṣṇa theology. Here I wish only to emphasize the carnival aspect of Kṛṣṇa's sport with the *gopīs*. The boistrous frolic of Kṛṣṇa and the *gopīs* continues in the waters of the Jumna.

> Kriṣṇa . . . sprinkeld Râdhâ's body with water. Râdhâ also poured three handfuls of water on the body of the passionate Krisṇa. Hari snatched away the cloth of Râdhâ . . . . Then he tore her wreath and loosened her chignon . . . . Then Krisṇa after having displayed the abashed, naked Râdhâ to the cowherdesses threw her again at a distance into the water. Râdhâ got up in haste from the water, seized Krisṇa by force, took away his flute in anger, cast it at a distance, snatched his yellow garment, tore the wreath of wild flowers and sprinkled water on him again and again . . . . In this way the imaginary forms of the Lord merrily played with the cowherdesses on the coasts of the Yamunâ and within the water. After the play was over, the naked Lord and Râdhâ both came to the coast and demanded their clothes from one another.[2]

As a male elephant in rut, after sporting with female elephants, goes to a river for rest, so Kṛṣṇa too, after dancing

[1] *Ibid.*

[2] *Brahma-vaivarta-purāṇa,* Kṛṣṇa Janma Khaṇḍa 28. 128-41 (Part II, pp. 233-34).

excessively with the *gopīs*, . . . began to sport in the waters of the Jumna. Drawing the tired *gopīs* by the hand, he immersed himself in the water and with great fun began to sport in the water. Sometimes with one, sometimes with five or six at a time, and sometimes with all the *gopīs*, Kṛṣṇa, in separate groups (being omnipresent), began mock fights in the water[1]

In the atmosphere of the carnival, normal laws, moral as well as civil, are suspended. It is a time when behavior can be spontaneous and without regret. The carnival is an anarchical celebration where the normal world has no place at all. And this is the world of Kṛṣṇa. His world is a sporting ground where nothing is done from necessity or custom. There all activity is free and indulgent.

The spring festival of Holī, which is associated with Kṛṣṇa, is in many respects a carnival, and in later Vaiṣṇava poetry Kṛṣṇa himself is depicted as celebrating it with the *gopīs* in Vṛndāvana. This is entirely appropriate, as his romps with the *gopīs* recall the Holī festival even though it is not specifically mentioned. So in this eighteenth-century poem Kṛṣṇa is shown leading the Holī play with the women of Vṛndāvana:

> In the Hori [Holī] sport drums are joyfully sounding, "dig dig thai thīyā." The Youth and the Girl, together with their female friends, are sporting on the bank of the Daughter of the Sun (*i.e.*, the Yamunā): it is the delightful Spring, the lord of the seasons, and with it (there is also) the lord of Rati (*i.e.*, the god of love). They (*i.e.*, Kṛṣṇa and the *Gopīs*) are throwing (at each other), through instruments, liquid *ghusṛṇa*, *cubaka* and sandal-paste in profuse quantity. Their rose-coloured garments and girdles are become dishevelled and loosened: drops of perspiration, due to (this) physical exertion, are falling away from their persons. (Various musical instruments such as) *vīṇā* (lute), *muraja* (drum), *svara* and *upāṅga* are being played upon: "drimiki drimiki drimi," the *mṛdaṅga* (drum) is sounding: quicker in steps than the *khañjana* bird, they are dancing in

---

[1] Kṛṣṇadāsa Kavirāja, *Govinda-līlāmṛta*, pp. 1294-95.

> superb poses. The *Gopīs* are singing in *gamaka* the melodies *Gaurī*, *Gurjjarī*, *Rāmakelī*, *Subhagā*, *Sohinī*, *Suhaï*, and *Sahānī*: (they are floating) in the waves of music. The maidens have fallen in bevies, and in their midst the Moon of Gokula (*i.e.*, Kṛṣṇa) stands resplendent.[1]

The great intoxicator himself, finally, also becomes intoxicated by drinking wine and indulging his passion.

> Then Kṛṣṇa stood between each pair of women [by multiplying himself]. Joking and laughing with them he kissed them on the lips, biting them and putting fruit mixed with honey in their mouths.... Then Kṛṣṇa became intoxicated with *kandarpa* [a kind of wine, also the name of the god of love and sexual passion] and *madya* wine. He took Rādhā into a bower furnished with wonderful beds by the riverbank. Rādhā, too, flared up under the same intoxicating drinks.[2]

The comic themes that run through Kṛṣṇa's love for Rādhā and the festival nature of his dalliance with the *gopis* portray a vision of the divine that is essentially playful. Kṛṣṇa moves in a realm of love and love-making, a realm where all those who enter it are freed from bondage to the ordinary, freed to behave imaginatively and spontaneously. The erotic aspect of this other world is not degrading but life-affirming. Erotic dalliance shuns the world of taboos and lives for the moment. It is an ovation to all that is vigorous and full of joy. The young god Kṛṣṇa is an unrepentant reveler stirring his lover and the *gopīs* to frenzy, exciting in them feelings and possibilities they did not know existed. In the world of the great lover Kṛṣṇa they expand themselves, they plumb depths and reach heights of emotion that are impossible within the humdrum world of habitual action. They leave behind the ordinary and participate in the extraordinary. Under the influence of the intoxicating and intoxicated god they lose their inhibitions and revel in playful freedom.

[1]From Govardhana-dāsa; in S. Sen, *Brajabuli Literature*, p. 287.

[2]Kṛṣṇadāsa Kavirāja, *Govinda-līlāmṛta*, p. 1288.

F. *The Call of Kṛṣṇa's Flute*

Kṛṣṇa's flute is an extension of his beauty. Not only is it the most beautiful sound imaginable, it imparts the essence of Kṛṣṇa's intoxicating nature. While Kṛṣṇa is also adept at singing, it is the sound of his flute, not his voice, that echoes throughout Vṛndāvana, beckoning all to join him in the forest.

The flute is perhaps the simplest of musical instruments, a mere hollow stick, and permits Kṛṣṇa to express himself through it with a minimum of adulteration. The flute gives forth a clear, pure, simple sound that can be both intensely melancholy and entrancingly sprightly. In either mood, haunting or haughty, its clear notes sound as if they come from a world beyond the din of the ordinary.[1] Amid the sounds of the humdrum world the flute, especially Kṛṣṇa's flute, is sweet and pure, prancing along to nowhere in particular. It comes from and belongs to that world of abundance and bliss that Kṛṣṇa rules.

---

[1]The following anecdote makes the same point, and although it reminds Ortega y Gasset of the god Pan, it bears striking similarities to Kṛṣṇa and his flute. Ortega y Gasset is reminiscing about his childhood and a circus he once attended. "A clown would stroll in with his livid, floured face, seat himself on the railing, and produce from his bulky pocket a flute which he began to play. At once the ringmaster appeared and intimated to him that here one could not play. The clown, unperturbed, stalked over to another place and started again. But now the ringmaster walked up angrily and snatched his melodious toy from him. The clown remained unshaken in face of such misfortune. He waited till the ringmaster was gone, and plunging his hand into his fathomless pocket produced another flute and from it another melody. But alas, inexorably, here came the ringmaster again, and again dispoiled him of his flute. Now the clown's pocket turned into an inexhaustible magic box from which proceeded, one after another, new musical instruments of all kinds, clear and gay or sweet and melancholy. The music overruled the veto of destiny and filled the entire space, imparting to all of us with its impetuous, invincible bounty a feeling of exultation, as though a torrent of strange energies had sprung from the dauntless melody the clown blew on his flute as he sat on the railing of the circus. Later I thought of this clown of the flute as a grotesque modern form of the great god Pan of the forest whom the Greeks worshipped as the symbol of cosmic vitality—serene, goatfooted Pan who plays the sacred syrinx in the sinking dusk and with its magic sound evokes an echo in all things: leaves and fountains shiver, the stars begin to tremble, and the shaggy goats dance at the edge of the grove." José Ortega y Gasset, *Toward a Philosophy of History*, pp. 20-21.

The sound of Kṛṣṇa's flute, though, is more than a melody. It is a summons, a call to come to him. From a theological point of view it calls the souls of men back to their Creator.

The lute stands for the attractive power of Kṛṣṇa . . . . It is a part of Divine Sport that he unfolds himself into diversity involving the plurality of individual souls. But it is a part of the same Sport that he calls the souls back to his own self.[1]

The nature of the call, consistent with the nature of Kṛṣṇa, is irresistibly charming. In this poem its enchanting sound is called the "All-pervading Net," from which no one or no thing is immune :

". . . The pipe (he plays on) is by nature contrary, and it is known to all the world by the name of the 'All-pervading Net': at the guidance of Kānu it is wantonly cruel, and it is a veritable enchanting maze for girls. Neither faults nor virtues does it count; nor does it respect time or duty." The Lord of Rāya Vasanta is an enchanter: can there be in him any consideration for others?[2]

The call of Kṛṣṇa's flute is anarchical, breaking down and mocking resistance. And the best way to convey its entrancing nature is to give some examples of its effect upon those who hear it. The Vaiṣṇava scriptures and poems delight in describing the effect of Kṛṣṇa's flute on the *gopis*, who are all married women but are powerless to resist its call. The famous passage from the *Bhāgavata-purāṇa* expresses this well:

Beholding the friend of the lilies (moon) rise in his full splendour on the sky, and shine like the countenance of (Lakshmi), red like fresh saffron, and also seeing the groves flooded and variegated with the soft lustre of the moon, Krishna melodiously sang with his flute in a manner so as to captivate the hearts of women with beautiful eyes.

---

[1]Siddheśvara Bhaṭṭācārya, *The Philosophy of the Srīmad-Bhāgavata*, Vol. I: *Metaphysics*; Vol., II: *Religion* I, 116.

[2]From Rāya Vasanta (sixteenth century); in S. Sen, *Brajabuli Literature*, p. 142.

Having heard that music capable of exciting desire, the damsels of Braja had their heart enslaved by Krishna. Without apprising one another of their respective intentions, they (the *Gopees*) hastened to the place where their darling was. Their ear-rings dangled on account of their haste. Some damsels who had been milking their cows, started anxiously leaving the milking half-done. Some went away leaving the milk they had been boiling over fire, without waiting for its boiling. Others again flew to him (Krishna) without even taking down, from the hearth, the preparation of wheat they had been baking. Some had been distributing eatables among her family members, some had been suckling their babies, some had been serving their husbands, some had been taking their meals, some had been toileting with cosmetics, some had been cleansing their persons and some had been painting their eyes with collyrium. All those *Gopees*, leaving their respective business and duties unfinished flew to Krishna their garments and ornaments having fallen off from their persons in consequence of their great hurry.[1]

In the *Gītāgovinda* the effect of Kṛṣṇa's flute is described as being similarly bewitching.

> Hear the maddening flute-born melody
> Of the Enemy of Madhu dance
> On the air; it captivates the free
> Maidens with its magic spell in trance.[2]

The Bengali poet Govindadāsa (sixteenth century), finally, describes the helpless *gopīs* all aflutter when they hear Kṛṣṇa's flute and recalls the passage from the *Bhāgavata-purāṇa*:

(It is) an autumnal moon; a soft wind (is blowing); the woodland is saturated with the perfume of flowers; *mallikā*, *mālati*, and *yūthī* flowers (are) in bloom, (and they are) deceiving the bees. On seeing such beauty of the night Śyāma, intoxicated with the charm of love, (begins) to

[1] *Bhāgavata-purāṇa* X. 29. 3-7 (IV, 119-20).
[2] *Gītāgovinda* 11. 20. 3; Jayadeva, *The Song of Divine Love* (*Gita-Govinda*), trans. Duncan Greenlees, p. 74.

play the fifth note (*pañcama tāna*) that steals the hearts of chaste girls. The *Gopīs* hear it and they are filled with love. Mentally they offer themselves (to Kṛṣṇa) and run to the place from where issues the passionate music of the flute. They forget their home: they forget their body. (Some have) painted with collyrium only single eyes; some girls' single arms only are decked with bracelets; and some have only single earrings dangling. The knots of their girdles have become loosened. The maidens are rushing on with speed; their clothes and girdles are slipping away (from their person), and their top-knots, becoming loose, dangle at their back. Then the friends meet, but they cannot take any notice of each other on the way. In this manner they came to the Moon of Gokula (*i.e.*, Kṛṣṇa). So sings Govindadāsa.[1]

The flute's effect on Rādhā is even more tumultuous and alarming and another favourite theme of Vaiṣṇava writers. In a poem by the seventeenth-century Bengali poet Vraja-kiśora Rādhā is so distracted by the flute that she cannot dress herself properly :

> Rādhā was dressing herself (for going out) when the flute sounded, and it did not stop. (Rādhā's) heart was overwhelmed with love: she lost control over her actions. Her heavy tresses, already done, she combs (again): she ties the wreath of flowers round her leg; she has lost all consideration. Her feet she paints with collyrium, and her eyes with red-dye. She pushed *nāga-latā* into the cavities of her ears. The girdle she puts on her neck, the necklace round her waist: the anklets she fastens round her wrists and wristlets round her ankles. Being thus intoxicated (as it were), Rāï walks quickly away. Why indeed does not the cruel way end soon? Vraja-kiśora says: the path ended (at last) and reaching Nidhuvana Rāï raised a cry of joy.[2]

In the following two poems the effect of the flute is violent in its intensity. Rādhā is "thrust to the ground" and speaks of women being dragged by their hair to the forest.

---

[1]From Govindadāsa Kavirāja; in S. Sen, *Brajabuli Literature,* p. 125.
[2]From Vraja-kiśora; *ibid.*, pp. 417-18.

At the first note of his flute
down came the lion gate of reverence for elders,
down came the door of *dharma*,
my guarded treasure of modesty lost,
I was thrust to the ground as if by a thunderbolt.
Ah, yes, his dark body
poised in the *tribhanga* pose[1]
shot the arrow that pierced me;
no more honor, my family
lost to me,
my home at Vraja
lost to me.
Only my life is left—and my life too
is a breath that is leaving me.

So says Jagadānanda-dāsa.[2]

How can I describe his relentless flute,
which pulls virtuous women from their homes
and drags them by their hair to Shyām
as thirst and hunger pull the doe to the snare?
Chaste ladies forget their lords,
wise men forget their wisdom,
and clinging vines shake loose from their trees,
hearing that music.

Chandidāsa says, Kālā the puppetmaster leads the dance.[3]

The call of Kṛṣṇa's flute cares nothing for this world and its moral and social laws. It comes crashing in upon man and

[1]*Tribhanga*=thrice bent. This is Kṛṣṇa's most famous pose, in which he is bent at the waist, at the neck, and at the knee, with one leg crossed over the other. It is a very graceful posture and is typical of Kṛṣṇa the "dandy." The pose may be seen in any book dealing with the Kṛṣṇa legend in Kangra painting. It may also be seen in Rao, *Elements of Hindu Iconography*, Vol. II, Part I, Pl. CVIII. Only here it is Śiva who is being depicted. The image looks exactly like Kṛṣṇa. However, the figure leans casually against a bull (Śiva's bull Nandi) and carries no flute. In all other respects, though, Śiva is depicted as a beautiful young "dandy" in this icon.

[2]Dimock and Levertov (trans.), *In Praise of Krishna*, p. 28.

[3]*Ibid.*, p. 29.

cannot be denied. It comes from another world where this-worldly morality and conduct have no place. Nothing in this world is able to keep Rādhā or the *gopīs* from answering its call.[1] The world the flute calls them to is the one described above, a world of ravishing beauty, boistrous carnival, and rollicking play that makes the ordinary world look pale, unexciting, and wearisome in comparison.

Even the gods cannot ignore the sound of Kṛṣṇa's flute. Their heavenly abodes seem dull compared to Kṛṣṇa's luscious Vṛndāvana, and so when Kṛṣṇa plays his flute the celestials are irresistibly drawn also. The heavenly maidens "lose all patience and become senseless";[2] the gods "hearing those harmonious cadences lose all consciousness [and] bend their necks and concentrate their hearts, to catch the music all the better."[3]

> The sound of the Lord's flute suddenly diffused all over;
> it astounded the clouds; it struck wonder into the hearts

---

[1]The debate that took place in Bengal Vaiṣṇavism concerning whether Rādhā and the *gopīs* were Kṛṣṇa's wives (*svakīyā*) or the wives of others (*parakīyā*) serves to underline this point. In the *Bhāgavata-purāṇa* it is rather clear that the *gopīs* were the wives of others, but this did not deter Rūpa and Jiva Gosvāmin from trying to prove that the opposite was the case. Their argument is primarily theological and revolves around the idea that as the *gopīs* and Rādhā are really manifestations of Kṛṣṇa's *svarūpa-śakti* they are *svakīyā*, not *parakīyā*, to him. Rūpa even went so far as to portray a regular marriage between Rādhā and Kṛṣṇa in the tenth act of his play *Lalitā-mādhava* (translated into Bengali by Satyendranāth Basu, pp. 575-87). Despite the weighty authority of these theologians, however, the *parakīyā* doctrine eventually won out. Indeed, the *svakīyā* doctrine was never really accepted at all, as the great majority of the cult's works testify. The matter was formally and decisively settled when in the eighteenth century a debate in Bengal was arranged between advocates of the two positions. The proponents of the *parakīyā* doctrine, led by Rādhāmohana-ṭhākura, were triumphant, and the *parakīyā* doctrine was firmly established as orthodox. The dominance and eventual triumph of the *parakīyā* doctrine emphasizes the revolutionary otherness of that world to which Kṛṣṇa's flute calls the *gopīs*. By answering its call they leave conventional morality behind to revel illicitly with Kṛṣṇa, their lover. For a discussion of the *parakīyā* doctrine and its place in Bengal Vaiṣṇavism, see Edward C. Dimock, *The Place of the Hidden Moon*: *Erotic Mysticism in the Vaiṣṇava-sahajiyā Cult of Bengal*, esp. pp. 200-215.

[2]*Bhāgavata-purāṇa* X. 21. 12 (IV, 94).

[3]*Ibid.* X. 35. 14-15 (IV, 144).

of *Tumburu* and other *Gandharvas*; it cried halt to the hearts of Sananda and other sages deep in their meditation. It astonished the Lord Brahma, augmented the holy exultation of the king *Vali*. And last not the least of all, it made the head of the Ananta, king of the serpents, whirl in loving delusion, yea it penetrated deep into the very bottom of the whole creation.[1]

The sweet tune that the flute produces is sublime and powerful. It spreads like lightning in all directions. It penetrates into the creation and reaches the highest heaven known as Vaikuntha.

From the heaven known as Vaikuntha it re-acts with a terrific atomic force and penetrates into all ears in the creation and enchants all.[2]

The sound of Kṛṣṇa's flute is no earthly sound. Its vibrations fill the heavens and distract even the gods from their usual activities. Even nature cannot remain unaffected. When he plays his flute the river and reeds from which the flute grew weep tears of delight.[3] When the clouds hear his flute, they hover over him to provide shade and shower him with drops of fresh water.[4] Rivers slow down when they hear his flute and grow lotuses for him.[5] The deer in the forest "stand at the distance with their ears erect, holding a mouthful of grass by their teeth, like things painted or asleep" when they hear Kṛṣṇa's flute.[6] The whole creation can concentrate on nothing but its sound.

When my Black One put the flute to his lips the ecstasy of the sages was disturbed. The cars of the gods stopped when they heard it and the wives of the gods became like pictures. The planets and the stars did not leave their constellation; they were tied up to the sound. Joy overflowed to hear

---

[1]Rūpa Gosvāmin *Vidagdha-mādhava* I. 39; quoted in Kṛṣṇadāsa Kavirāja *Caitanya-caritāmṛta*, Antya-līlā 1 (p. 23).
[2]Kṛṣṇadāsa Kavirāja *Caitanya-caritāmṛta*, Madhya-līlā 21. 119 (p. 538).
[3]*Bhāgavata-purāṇa* X. 21. 12-15 (IV, 93).
[4]*Ibid.* X. 21. 16 (IV, 94).
[5]*Ibid.* X. 21. 15 (IV, 94).
[6]*Ibid.* X. 35. 4-5 (IV, 143).

it and the immovables of water and earth moved. The movement of the movable and the immovable was reversed to hear the song produced by the Venu (flute). Stones began to throw up springs and the divine singers were charmed with the sweet songs. Hearing this the birds and the beasts became still and forgot their food and did not drink milk and the birds lost patience. The trees and creepers became restless and they gave out new leaves. The trees and the leaves of which were restless, became anxious to be near (him). Those, which had the buds as the horripilation of joy began to shed tears of love. Hearing it the restless wind became tired and water of the river could not move.[1]

Even Kṛṣṇa himself is not immune to the sound of his flute. In this poem by Sūrdās we are reminded of the theme of the self-intoxicated god, whose conjurings result in self-enchantment:

The flute has done her work.
She plunders for herself, depriving us of the nectar of
  Hari's lips.
Nanda's son [Kṛṣṇa] is under the influence of her music.
  She has cast her spell over him.
The living and the non-living, the moving and the unmoving, and even the God of Love are spellbound.
She disturbed all, even those not easily distracted.
The milkmaid says that the Lord, the crown of the wise,
  has fallen into her hands.[2]

By means of his flute, Kṛṣṇa fills himself and the universe with bliss. He distracts everyone and everything from normal activity and enchants them to revel in ecstasy. His flute sends shudders of delight to the very foundations of the world. Natural laws fall away as rocks and trees respond to his call and stars wander from their courses. The sound of his flute puts an abrupt end to man's mechanical, habitual activity as well as to

[1]From Sūrdās' *Sūrsāgar*; in Janardan Misra, *The Religious Poetry of Surdas*, pp. 107-8.
[2]Sūrdās, *The Poems of Sūrdās*, no. 60.

the predictable movements of nature. His music explodes upon the world and society insisting that all else be forgotten. It is time, it proclaims, to join his symphony of joy, to frolic in the forest, to scamper in play, to realize every dream that one has ever dreamed in his world of infinite possibility. Kṛṣṇa's flute incites the world to dance, to lose itself in superfluous rhythms. It invites man to return to that carefree, playful world of his youth. It asks nothing but surrender to its frenzied tune and enthusiastic participation in its magic world. Kṛṣṇa is the master magician, ruling over a fairyland, and his wand is his flute.

G. *Bhagavān—the Ocean of Bliss*

The centrality of sport in Kṛṣṇa's purāṇic biography is clear, and the theologians and philosophers of his cult have not sought to minimize it. While this study is not concerned with Vaiṣṇava theology per se, it is important to discuss a few theological themes in order to fully appreciate Kṛṣṇa's sportive nature.

As a background to these themes it is necessary, first of all, to mention three ideas that form the basis of Vaiṣṇava theology.[1] The first doctrine is that Kṛṣṇa is not an *avatāra* but the *avatārin*, the Absolute God who is the source of all *avatāras*.[2] Just when this change in status took place is not certain, but by the time of Vallabhācārya and Caitanya it was clearly the devotional, if not the theological, fact. In the *Brahma-vaivarta-purāṇa*, of uncertain, but probably recent, authorship,[3] Kṛṣṇa's supreme place

[1]When I use the term 'Vaiṣṇava theology," I am referring primarily to the systems of North India, beginning with Nimbārka and including Vallabhācārya and the six Gosvāmins of Vṛndāvana. The Gosvāmins were scholar-devotees of Caitanya who were sent to Vṛndāvana by Caitanya to codify the philosophy of the cult. The six are: Raghunātha-dāsa, Raghunātha Bhaṭṭa, Gopāla Bhaṭṭa, Sanātana, Rūpa, and Jīva Gosvāmin.

[2]This is obviously not the case in the *Harivaṁśa* or the *Viṣṇu-purāṇa*, where Kṛṣṇa is called "a part of a part of the supreme" (V. 1 [p. 395]). Nor is it absolutely clear in the *Bhāgavata-purāṇa*. There Kṛṣṇa is listed as the nineteenth *avatāra* of Viṣṇu (I. 3. 23 [I, 10]), and the context of his incarnation is that of rescuing the world from the tyranny of Kaṁsa. The *purāṇa* does say, however, that "the incarnation of Sri-Krishna is identical with the Lord Himself [*Kṛṣṇas-tu svayaṃ bhagavān*]" (I. 3. 28 [I, 11]), which somewhat muddies the issue.

[3]Farquhar thinks it is a product of the Nimbārka school, tenth to eleventh centuries (*Religious Literature of India*, pp. 240, 271, 376); De is not willing to

is unambiguously established. In a wink of his eye, Brahmā falls and the universes dissolve,[1] while Mahā-Viṣṇu, who holds a universe in every pore of his skin, is only one-sixteenth part of Kṛṣṇa.[2] In Rūpa Gosvāmin's *Laghu-bhāgavatāmṛta* and Jīva Gosvāmin's *Śrikṛṣṇa-saṁdarbha*, two fundamental philosophical works of the Bengal Vaiṣṇavas written during the sixteenth century, this doctrine is stated unequivocally.[3] Kṛṣṇa's biography, then, is not to be understood as that of an *avatāra* who comes to rescue the world from *adharma*. Rather, it is to be understood as the complete and essential manifestation of what is usually unmanifest, the revelation of the Absolute in his essential and complete form.

The second idea that is important as background is the centrality of the *Bhāgavata-purāṇa*, and particularly the tenth book, in which the story of Kṛṣṇa is told. In Bengal Vaiṣṇavism there is no higher philosophical authority, and the *Bhāgavata-purāṇa* is held to be the essence of the *upaniṣads* and *vedas*. S. K. De says of its place: "The Bengal school . . . proceeds almost entirely on an explication of the *Bhāgavata Purāṇa*."[4] The fact of the matter is, then, that the highest God, the Absolute, is revealed as a cowherd boy who sports with cowherd boys and girls in the sylvan setting of Vṛndāvana.

The third idea I wish to mention as background is the superiority of Bhagavān to Brahman. This idea is as old as *bhakti* itself and was philosophically canonized as early as Rāmānuja. The object of the devotee's passionate service is not the attributeless, aloof Brahman of the *advaita* school. The devotee's object, rather, is God as infinitely qualified, infinitely blessed, the Lord Bhagavān. In Bengal Vaiṣṇava theology God is one

guess which sect produced it but says it was probably contemporaneous with Jayadeva, end of the twelfth century (*Vaisnava Faith and Movement*, p. 11); and F. S. Growse suggests that the Bengal Gosvāmins of Vṛndāvana may have composed it in the sixteenth century (*Mathura*: *A District Memoir* [N.p.: North-Western Provinces and Oudh Government Press, 1883], p. 75).

[1] *Brahma-vaivarta-purāṇa*, Prakṛti Khaṇḍa 7. 77 (Part I, p. 107).

[2] *Ibid.*, Kṛṣṇa Janma Khaṇḍa 5. 110 (Part II, p. 117).

[3] Rūpa Gosvāmin, *Laghu-bhāgavatāmṛta*, translated into Bengali by Śrī Pran Gopan Gosvāmin, ed. Śrī Balai Cand Gosvāmin, pp. 66, 73; Jīva Gosvāmin, *Śrikṛṣṇa-saṁdarbha*, translated into Bengali by Śrī Pran Gopan Gosvāmin, throughout, but esp. pp. 44-47, 61-66, 71.

[4] De, *Vaisnava Faith and Movement*, p. 227.

but has a threefold aspect: Bhagavān, Paramātman, and Brahman. Paramātman is God in relation to nature (*prakṛti*) and spirit (*jiva*), Brahman is unqualified and, therefore, never expressed, while Bhagavān is infinitely qualified and infinitely perfect and is considered the best aspect of all.[1] And Kṛṣṇa, finally, is identical with Bhagavān.

With these basic ideas in mind, I would now like to mention a few doctrines that underline Kṛṣṇa's sportive nature. A central theological point in Vaiṣṇava-Kṛṣṇa thought is that the essential nature of the Absolute is bliss (*ānanda*). Indeed, the Lord is an ocean of bliss, and as such he is the most relishable thing, in which every devotee longs to be immersed. So it is that Kṛṣṇa's beauty is infinite and attracts all beings. And so it is that his actions are the result of the overflowing of bliss. Vis-à-vis the idea of creation this means that the creative activity of God is sport.

> The motive which prompts the Absolute Being—all whose wishes are fulfilled and who is perfect in himself—to the creation of the wonderful world is not the attainment of any object to Himself or others, but simply sport, play. We see in ordinary life how when a man is in ecstatic joy, the joy tends to overflow itself—to stream forth, and ultimately produces some sort of act in the shape of merry sportive dance and song independent of any motive of attaining any object whatsoever.[2]

Indeed, all actions of Kṛṣṇa are consistently referred to as *līlā*, as he is completely self-satisfied and acts from no discernable motive. His actions proceed only from bliss. As such they shine forth, or overflow endlessly and aimlessly, unpredictably.

> Divine Sport is the expression of the majestic independence of the Absolute, and so, it refuses to be conditioned by time and space or to be cast into a specific pattern. It bristles with infinite variety that baffles prediction or description of any kind.[3]

---

[1]See De's discussion of Jiva Gosvāmin's *Bhagavat-saṁdarbha*, *ibid.*, pp. 472-80, for a concise treatment of this theological system.

[2]Girindra Narayan Mallik, *The Philosophy of Vaiṣṇava Religion*, p. 222.

[3]Bhaṭṭācārya, *The Philosophy of the Srimad-Bhāgavata*, I, 46.

God pulsates into action, as it were, with no motive whatsoever. By acting he displays his bliss and distributes and infuses it into the created order and created beings; that, undoubtedly, is sufficient "explanation" for all his activity. So Kṛṣṇa's aimless frolics in Vṛndāvana epitomize his nature as all-blissful and all-playful. Their very pointlessness, their complete separation from the world of the pragmatic, makes them essentially divine.

The doctrine of *māyā* in Vaiṣṇava-Kṛṣna theology further points up God's sportive, or fickle, nature. According to Vaiṣṇava philosophy, and nearly all Hindu philosophy as well, God is entirely complete. In his completeness, furthermore, he is self-contained unity. Why, then, should there be a phenomenal world and beings who are different, or appear to be different, from God? Why is God not content to remain One? Why does the Absolute create artificial barriers within himself?[1] The Vaiṣṇavas answer these questions by saying that God diversifies simply in order to amuse himself. The creation of the world is his sport, as has already been mentioned. It is created for no other reason than to express his boundless energy and bliss. In answer to the question why God should be many:

> The *Bhāgavata* [*purāṇa*] answers the logical mind by resorting to a position which is primarily alogical. According to the *Bhāgavata*, the perpetual realisation of its blissful nature makes the Absolute perpetually charged with free creativity. It is the spontaneous overflow of the Absolute to realise itself in all kinds of ideal possibilities.[2]

A further question is posed, however, when one considers the nature (or apparent nature) of the world, and particularly of man within the world. That is, why, if God created man as his playmate, as it were, from the overflow of his bliss, is man

[1]For the strict nondualists, of course, God does indeed remain one, the appearance of a separate, phenomenal world and beings being just that, an appearance due to illusion, *māyā*. This neat solution, however, is not acceptable to the Vaiṣṇavas, as they insist upon maintaining a semblance of duality in order to give devotion ontological meaning. On the other hand, the Vaiṣṇavas are reluctant to admit that there exists anything apart from God, so none of the Vaiṣṇava philosophers, with the exception of Madhva, declares himself a thorough dualist.

[2]Bhaṭṭācārya, *The Philosophy of the Śrīmad-Bhāgavata*, I, 45.

estranged from him? If man has been created by him, and partakes of his nature, why does man act consistently as if he were indifferent to God? The Vaiṣṇava theologians proclaim, on the one hand, that *jīvas*, the eternal souls of men, are godlike in nature and that their natural *dharma*, their *svadharma*, is to revel in his bliss. On the other hand, the philosophers admit that with certain notable exceptions men do not enjoy God's bliss. The "explanation" for this ambiguous situation is that God, by means of his *yoga-māyā*, has cast a spell over them whereby they do not remember their essential nature and natural proclivities.[1] The Absolute, that is, creates *jīvas* so that they may revel with him in bliss, and he with them, and then, as if to thwart his own scheme, casts a spell over them so that they cannot, without great difficulty, realize the *telos* of their creation. While it is not expressly stated in Vaiṣṇava theology, I suspect that this inscrutable business is simply another way of stating the drama of the play of grace, only in rather complicated terms. It is as if God takes great delight in baffling and misleading man, only bringing man to His feet after He has forced man to pass through an artificial barrier, a nightmare of tumult and pain.

The ultimate theological interpretation of Kṛṣṇa's Vṛndā-vana-*lilā*, especially his play with Rādhā and the *gopīs*, involves resort to another self-created, artificial barrier within the Absolute. Within the Godhead there exist several *śaktis*, the three most important of which are: *svarūpa-*, *jīva-*, and *māyā-śaktis*. And within the *svarūpa-śakti* (the essential *śakti*) there are three more *śaktis*: *samdhinī* (identified with *sat*), *samvit* (identified with *cit*), and *hlādinī* (identified with *ānanda*, although including also *sat* and *cit*). By means of his *jīva-* and *māyā-śaktis* God creates man and the world, respectively, which, as has been suggested above, involves the theme of self-amusement. By means of his *svarūpa-śakti*, however, a real divine comedy is set in motion and perpetuated. While the world and man are of God and therefore godlike, they are decidedly not equal to, or the same as, God. They are finite and estranged. The creations of his *svarūpa-śakti*, however, are essentially the same as God, as they move entirely within his essential selfhood. And

---

[1] Surendranath Dasgupta, *A History of Indian Philosophy*, Vol. IV: *Indian Pluralism*, pp. 16, 21.

what are the creations of his *svarūpa-śakti*? They are the people of Vṛndāvana, especially the *gopīs*, and particularly Rādhā. The theological interpretation as to the origin of Rādhā and the *gopīs* is important, for it declares that not just Kṛṣṇa alone but Kṛṣṇa surrounded by the population and paraphernalia of Vṛndāvana is the essential form of the Godhead. The whole sport of Vṛndāvana, then, is understood as taking place *within the Godhead constantly*. It is an eternal inner dalliance.[1]

The gradations within the *svarūpa-śakti* serve to further underline the Godhead as playful to the core. The most essential aspect of the essential *śakti* is the *hlādinī-śakti*, which is pure bliss. And the *hlādinī-śakti* is identical with Rādhā.[2] Because this is the case, Kṛṣṇa is referred to as the *rasika*, the enjoyer.

> God, who is Infinite Joy and Pure self-consciousness, brings into play an eternally manifested energy of his, so that He may feel that Joy which He is Himself and at the same time make all other beings feel it. This is called the Exhilarating Energy (*Hladini sakti*).[3]

Kṛṣṇa's most excellent attribute, bliss, his most intrinsic and highest selfhood, the *hlādinī-śakti*, is nothing else but Rādhā. The Absolute, then, is an eternal love relationship between God and Himself that is played out eternally with all its humor and tenderness, pique and reconciliation.

The centrality of the *hlādinī-śakti* and Rādhā's identification with it underscore dramatically the sublimation of lordship to bliss in the Godhead. In Vṛndāvana, which is God's most perfect revelation, Kṛṣṇa's lordship is in almost total abeyance.[4] In Vṛndāvana Kṛṣṇa is a son, companion, and lover. Here he does not dictate his will, govern from a throne, or behave in

---

[1]Mallik, *The Philosophy of Vaiṣṇava Religion*, pp. 128-29.

[2]Prabodhānanda Sarasvatī, *Ānanda-vṛdāvana-campū* (Bengali), p. 120. Rādhā was also identified with the *śakti* of Kṛṣṇa by Nimbārka and Vallabha. De, *Vaisnava Faith and Movement*, p. 7.

[3]Krishnadas, *Krishna of Vrindabana*, p. 445.

[4]This explains why in Bengal Vaiṣṇavism the two-armed form of Kṛṣṇa is considered superior to the four-armed or many-armed forms. The four-armed form suggests power and majesty, an aloofness that is not consistent with God's essential nature as bliss.

a lordly or mighty way. His sole occupation is to revel in bliss, to frisk about as if intoxicated. While lordship and awesome power certainly belong to the Godhead, its most essential nature is to infuse and taste bliss in the intimacy of love.[1]

Kṛṣṇa's sport in Vṛndāvana—his sport with the *gopīs* and Rādhā, who are but extensions of his *svarūpa-śakti*—suggests again the theme of divine self-enchantment. The eternal love relationship that takes place within the *hlādinī-śakti* between Rādhā and Kṛṣṇa is divine self-enchantment infinitely exalted. And divine self-enchantment is precisely the *raison d'être* of Caitanya's life in the context of Bengal Vaiṣṇava theology. In the *Caitanya-caritāmṛta* Kṛṣṇa muses about his own beauty:

> My grace and loveliness are wonderful, complete and beyond measure.
> There is no one in the three worlds who can completely fathom it,
> No one, that is, but Rādhā alone,
> Who tastes my sweetness continually by the strength of her love.
> Her love is like a stainless mirror.
> And though her love is pure and unblemished, it continues to grow.
> My loveliness is perfect and so cannot increase;
> But in front of this clear mirror it takes on various new forms.
> My loveliness floods Rādhā, and her love floods me;
> Our love expands continuously, never stopping for a moment.

---

[1]A story in the *Bhaktamāl*, the Hindu book of saints, illustrates this well. A devotee named Bhabuk Brāhman lived in Vṛndāvana and worshiped Kṛṣṇa in the form of a child. He treated the god as his own son, feeding him, disciplining him, and playing with him. One day, however, the devotee was possessed by the thought that the image he worshiped as his own son was actually the supreme God and suddenly had feelings of awe and servitude toward him. He lost his feeling of parental affection for Kṛṣṇa and prayed to him, blessing his majesty and power. As soon as this happened, Kṛṣṇa disappeared, reprimanding Bhabuk Brāhman for his loss of love for God as a child. With the appearance of distance between the devotee and Kṛṣṇa came the disappearance of the god. From Nābha Dās, *Bhaktamāl*, translated from Hindi into Bengali by Kṛṣṇadās Babaji, ed. Upendranāth Mukherji, pp. 143-44.

And so my loveliness blooms anew in the presence of Rādhā.
Our love overflows and is enjoyed by our devotees, who taste it according to their capacity.
Seeing my own beauty in this foremost of mirrors,
I am tempted to taste it myself.
So I begin to consider a way to do this,
And desire to be identified with Rādhā.[1]

Wishing to embrace himself, craving his own beauty, Kṛṣṇa incarnates himself as both Rādhā and Kṛṣṇa in one body, that of Caitanya.[2] Caitanya's outward appearance, his fair, golden complexion, is taken to be that of Rādhā, while inside he is Kṛṣṇa. In the person of Caitanya, Kṛṣṇa has wrapped Rādhā about himself, clothed himself in her. Caitanya is the essence of Godhead locked in permanent embrace. "Sri Chaitanya is that aspect of Krishna who seeks Himself as Radha intoxicated with his surpassing divine beauty in the manner and role of Sri Radha."[3] Kṛṣṇa's embodiment in Caitanya is not didactic or moral. He has not appeared to teach, preach, or rescue the world from tyranny. He has become embodied as Caitanya solely to revel in his own irresistible beauty.

There is one more doctrine that emphasizes the importance of *līlā* vis-à-vis the Godhead that I would like to note. It concerns the eternality of Vṛndāvana. I mentioned above that Vṛndāvana's population and general paraphernalia were the creations of Kṛṣṇa's *svarūpa-śakti*. That is, they are part of the essential Godhead.[4] What this means is that the sport of

---

[1]Kṛṣṇadāsa Kavirāja *Caitanya-caritāmṛta,* Ādi-līlā 4. 120-27; my translation.

[2]*Ibid.* 6. 93-95 (p. 95). While this idea was not promulgated by the Gosvāmin theologians of Vṛndāvana, who were consistently and strangely silent on the significance of Caitanya for both theology and devotion, it appears soon after their time, in Kṛṣṇadāsa Kavirāja's *Caitanya-caritāmṛta.* And Kṛṣṇadāsa was a disciple of Sanātana Gosvāmin and was specifically commissioned to write this biography of Caitanya by the theologians of Vṛndāvana themselves. The doctrine may have originated in Bengal among Caitanya's Navadvip companions and disciples and, in any case, very soon was accepted by the entire cult. See De's discussion of the problem in *Vaisnava Faith and Movement,* pp. 423-45.

[3]Sambidananda Das, *Sri Chaitanya Mahaprabhu* (English), p. 221.

[4]Jīva Gosvāmin, *Śrīkṛṣṇa-saṁdarbha,* pp. 328-41.

Kṛṣṇa in Vṛndāvana is not something that happened once and for all. His life as set forth in the *Bhāgavata-purāṇa* is not to be understood as having taken place once upon a time only. His life as set forth there, particularly his life at Vṛndāvana, is both a description of an earthly manifestation *and* the eternal movement within the essence of the Godhead.[1] This fantastic and delightful interpretation is theologically explained by resort to the doctrine of Kṛṣṇa's manifest (*prākṛta*) and unmanifest (*aprākṛta*) *līlās*.[2] According to this doctrine Kṛṣṇa's earthly sport in Vṛndāvana was simply a making manifest of what is ordinarily unmanifest. Or, to put it the other way, Gokula (the name of Vṛndāvana and its surrounding area) has been translated into Goloka (Kṛṣṇa's eternal realm, even above Viṣṇu's heaven, Vaikuṇṭha).

> By the Bhagavat's inscrutable power (*acintya-prabhāva*), therefore, his highest Paradise, which is situated beyond all the Lokas, also exists on the phenomenal earth. The terrestrial Goloka or Vṛndāvana is thus not essentially different but really identical with the celestial Goloka or Vṛndāvana, and the Lord Kṛṣṇa exists eternally in both places with the same retinue.[3]

Kṛṣṇa's childhood, adolescence, and love for Rādhā and the *gopīs* are forever taking place in the paradise of Goloka. Each aspect of his biography, every incident, is therefore eternal.[4]

---

[1]S. K. De, *Bengal's Contribution to Sanskrit Literature and Studies in Bengal, Vaisnavism,* p. 114.

[2]For a discussion of this see Rādhāgovinda Nāth, *Śrī Śrī Caitanya-caritāmṛta Bhūmika* (Bengali), pp. 200-201.

[3]De, *Vaisnava Faith and Movement,* p. 334.

[4]This idea is also seen in the texts of the Vallabhācāryas. "The sacred Brindavana and Syam are eternal. Radha and the women of Braj also are eternal. . . The happiness in the bowers is eternal and the gust of three kinds of wind also is eternal. Where Vasanta (Spring) also lives eternally and there is always pleasure and no sorrow. There the cuckoos and the parrots always make noise and the prepossessing beauty of the Lord like Kama is eternal. In the forest on the branches flowers of many kinds bloom up and the intoxicated black bees hum eternally. The beauty of the new leaves in the forest is unique, where many maidens enjoy in the company of Hari. The female cuckoo makes her cooing audible. The woman is pleased when she hears it." From Sūrdās's *Sūrsāgar*; Misra, *The Religious Poetry of Surdas,* pp. 114-15.

Within the Godhead his sport is constantly taking place, and this sport is identical with the sport described in the *Bhāgavata-purāṇa*, except that in Goloka it is unmanifest. The Godhead then, is not restful, silent, and still in its essence but constantly and restlessly moving in ecstatic play.

These various theological ideas, then, do not dilute the significance of Kṛṣṇa's sport. Rather, they nourish and magnify it. Kṛṣṇa's aimless, blissful play in Vṛndāvana is not dismissed as an inconsequential preparation for his later victory over Kaṁsa, the mission he was ostensibly sent to perform in the *Harivaṁśa*, *Viṣṇu-purāṇa*, and *Bhāgavata-purāṇa*. His life among the cowherds is not an idle sidelight of his career but the epitomy of it, his fullest revelation. The beautiful adolescent player is not a freakish manifestation of the Absolute but the Absolute himself in his essential form.

H. Vṛndāvana—Kṛṣṇa's Playground

It will be clear from what has already been said about Vṛndāvana that it is the heavenly sporting ground *par excellence*. Although Vṛndāvana is considered simply the temporary home of Kṛṣṇa during his youth in the *Harivaṁśa*, *Viṣṇu-purāṇa*, and *Bhāgavata-purāṇa*, by the time of the *Brahma-vaivarta-purāṇa* it has become identified with the highest heaven.

> Within the spherical light . . . of that mighty corporeal Being [Kṛṣṇa], there exists a region called the Goloka, or the Cow-world, quadrangular, covert and expanded over an area of 9 lakh crores of miles. This region is very lovely and round like the Moon, built with precious gems and suspended on the void by the will of God, without any support. It is situate 50 crores of Yojans above the Vaikuṇṭha. It is full of cows, cow-herds, cow-herdesses and Kalpa-trees, teems with celestial cows which fulfil all desire, is decorated with the sphere of the Rāsa . . . and encompassed by the wilderness of Vrindâ-Vanâ. It is surrounded by the river Virajâ, decorated by the hundred summits of the Śata-Sringa mountains and ornamented with millions of hermitages possessing countless mansions.[1]

[1] *Brahma-vaivarta-purāṇa*, Brahma Khaṇḍa 28. 40-46 (Part I, p. 79.)

Just as Kṛṣṇa in the form of the beautiful, adolescent cowherd came to attain the supreme position as the highest god, Bhagavān, so his earthly sporting ground, the humble Vṛndāvana, came to attain the place as the highest heaven. Beyond Śiva's Kailāsa, beyond mighty Viṣṇu's heavenly Vaikuṇṭha, beyond the reach of the imagination, suspended in space by the will of Kṛṣṇa, is the highest heaven, and it is nothing else but the idyllic forest town of Vṛndāvana unabashedly magnified.

Because Kṛṣṇa's heavenly sporting ground is identical with the scene of his earthly life as a youth, it goes without saying that all the sports described so far in this chapter continue there also, only eternally. In that high heaven Kṛṣṇa plays as a child, steals butter, romps with his young friends, plays his flute, and dallies with the *gopis*. What happens in earthly Vṛndāvana is simply a reflection of what happens continually in heavenly Vṛndāvana.[1] It will be unnecessary at this point, therefore, to discuss most of the playful activities that take place in Kṛṣṇa's heaven, as they are simply repetitions of what has already been discussed. There are, however, a few themes that have not been mentioned that further emphasize Vṛndāvana's place as the heavenly sporting ground *par excellence*.

While Vṛndāvana is not noted for its teeming bands of *apsarases*, *siddhas*, and *gandharvas*, as are many of those other heavens described earlier, it is crowded with thousands of young cowherd boys and girls who fulfil the same functions. While the gods and other heavenly beings appear in Vṛndāvana on certain occasions, to watch and applaud Kṛṣṇa's fight with demons, to watch his *rāsa* dance with the *gopis*, or in answer to his flute, it is the *gopas* and *gopis* who are the main guardians of Kṛṣṇa's sport. It is they who are primarily responsible for maintaining it and participating in it. They sing, dance, play, and revel in erotic dalliance just as the heavenly nymphs do. In fact,

[1]Because of this it is often difficult to be sure which Vṛndāvana is being described when reading Vaiṣṇava texts, and I shall make no attempt to distinguish between the two, as, in fact, no distinction exists at all in the minds of many Vaiṣṇava-Kṛṣṇa devotees. To add to the confusion, there is a third Vṛndāvana that should be delineated: the present town of Vṛndāvana (located in Uttar Pradesh), where Kṛṣṇa no longer lives, or manifests himself, but where he still presides.

these humble people portrayed in the *purāṇas are* heavenly nymphs in Kṛṣṇa's heaven.

> Then Kṛṣṇa sang various songs in differing styles and began to dance with the playful women of Vraja. When he and Rādhā began to dance, Lalitā and other *sakhis* [female friends and companions of Rādhā and Kṛṣṇa] began to sing, Chitra and other *sakhis* kept time with the dance by clapping their hands, and Brinda and other *sakhis* stood as onlookers to judge the merits of the songs and dances. While Kṛṣṇa and several of the women danced, the rest surrounded them like a covering screen and sang poetic verses accompanied by harps, gongs, and other instruments. The sounds of harps, gongs, flutes, drums, and voice were in rhythmic harmony with the slow movements of the dancers' feet, bodies, hands, and eyes there in that playground with Kṛṣṇa.[1]

In the early Vaiṣṇava *purāṇas* the *gopīs* are portrayed as rustic women who live in the country, tend cows, and churn butter. In later Vaiṣṇava-Kṛṣṇa literature, such as the *Brahmavaivarta-purāṇa* and the *Govinda-līlāmṛta*, however, most of their rough edges have been polished. They are first and foremost Kṛṣṇa's playmates, and their primary function is to amuse him and be amused by him. As such they have become accomplished concubines who excel at singing and dancing.

> The women who had been playing harps and flutes now began to sing and provided the background music for the dance, and those women who had been playing the drums joined the dancers and danced with delight. When these women became overcome by the dance and song, their carefully arranged hair began to fall loose, and their carefully tied clothes began to slip. Kṛṣṇa stopped dancing and retied them properly. Then the singing women, using all the musical scales, sang a great variety of wonderful songs. They sang in pure and mixed *rāga* and sang thousands of tunes in both the classical and popular styles. In that dancing place their songs, accompanied by gongs,

[1]Kṛṣṇadāsa Kavirāja, *Govinda-līlāmṛta*, pp. 1261-62.

> sounded like the deep rumbling of the clouds in the rainy season . . . . The male dancer was Kṛṣṇa and the female dancers were the fair women of Vraja. The sounds that came from their bangles reached the peak of musical accomplishment. As they danced the women continued to sing, their hands made gestures expressing their moods, their lotus feet beat in rhythm, their necks and waists trembled in dance, and their eyes moved back and forth as they glanced at Kṛṣṇa. Their happiness at being near Kṛṣṇa was reflected in his face, and thus they were further inspired. The beautiful women of Vraja could make sounds that usually could not be made except with musical instruments.[1]

In the *Brahma-vaivarta-purāṇa* the husbands and children of the *gopīs* are rarely mentioned. The *gopīs* never work but spend all their time accompanying Rādhā to her trysting place, entertaining Kṛṣṇa, or romping with Kṛṣṇa all over his heaven.

> The milk-maids having wantonly played with Hari in the sphere of the Râsâ played with him again on different occasions and in different places, in some lovely solitary place, in a grove of flowers, on the coast of a river, in the cave of a mountain, in a crematorium, in the forest of the holy fig tree, in the Vrindâvana, in the pleasing forest of the Kadam, in the forest of Nim.[2]

The *gopīs* stage plays and prove themselves to be accomplished actresses. And they particularly enjoy imitating Rādhā and Kṛṣṇa.

> Some of the girls with pitchers on their head were dancing. Some of them were dressed as males and others played the parts of heroines courted by the above males. Some assumed the form of Râdhâ: and others, of Krishṇa. Some mixed freely with others. Some were embracing their companions: others were playing.[3]

---

[1]*Ibid.*, pp. 1270-71.

[2]*Brahma-vaivarta-purāṇa*, Kṛṣṇa Janma Khaṇḍa 28. 159-63 (Part II, pp. 234-35).

[3]*Ibid.* 4. 79-81 (Part II, p. 113). See also *Bhāgavata-purāṇa* X. 30. 15-23

Although the *gopis* do not fly through the air like the celestial *apsarases* and *siddhas*, they are in almost every other respect just like them. In these late Vaiṣṇava-Kṛṣṇa passages they are no longer simple country women faithfully carrying out their domestic routines. They are talented and impish playmates of Kṛṣṇa adorning his heaven with grace and beauty.

Another feature of Vṛndāvana that heightens its nature as a sporting ground is the popularity of dancing there. This has already been seen in many of the passages cited earlier, but I would like to comment specifically on Kṛṣṇa as a dancer and on the importance of dance in his realm. Kṛṣṇa dances rhythmically when he plays in his mother's courtyard as a child, he dances in the forest with his young companions, he defeats the serpent Kāliya by dancing on his head, he dances with Rādhā, and he dances collectively with the *gopis* in the *rāsa* dance. Through his dancing Kṛṣṇa expresses in another way his exquisite charm and grace. In the *purāṇas* and later Vaiṣṇava-Kṛṣṇa texts he no longer retains any of the sharp, caustic features of the epic counselor and politician. His bearing is not impressive in its nobility but gentle in its beauty. His figure is lithe and his movements fluid. And he displays this grace constantly in dance, in superfluous motion.

> Syama, who delights in the sport of *Rāsa*, and who is a young prince, (is dancing) in the company of young damsels. He is moving in quick steps to charming music. He dances in charming steps and with delightful movements of the body. Lutes and other musical instruments are being played to accompaniment. Drums (*mṛdaṅga*) are raising a beautiful note—*tā tā*, *thai thai thai*. Kānu raises a charming music with his lovely anklets, and he is singing a fine melody in proper beats and harmony.[1]

> To-day the damsel and her swain take delight in novel ways. What can I say? they are altogether exquisite in every limb; sporting together with arms about each other's neck and cheek to cheek, by such delicious contact making a

(IV, 125-27), where the *gopīs* imitate the actions of Kṛṣṇa, but not in such a theatrical way.

[1]From Śivarāma-dāsa; in S. Sen, *Brajabuli Literature*, p. 178.

circle of wanton delight. As they dance, the dark swain and the fair damsel, pipe and drum and cymbal blend in sweet concert with the tinkling of the bangles on her wrists and anklets and the girdle round her waist.[1]

As the embodiment of grace and joy Kṛṣṇa's every gesture and movement is rhythmic and harmonious. In the *Dāna-keli-kaumudi* he is described as "coming down from the top of the mountain dancing all the while" to meet the *gopis*.[2] Indeed, some Vaiṣṇava writers have said that the movements of all inhabitants of Vṛndāvana are so graceful that they are dancelike and their voices so melodious that their speech is like song. "Pleasing song is the natural speech of the people there, and their natural gait is dance."[3] In Goloka "talk is music and ordinary movement is fascinating Dance!"[4] In the heavenly sporting ground ordinary things such as walking and speaking lose their pragmatic nature altogether and become dance and song. For this is where Kṛṣṇa is. And where Kṛṣṇa is, nothing is ordinary, nothing is harsh, nothing is graceless.

I should like to comment on just one more theme vis-à-vis Vṛndāvana as Kṛṣṇa's heavenly sporting ground. Vṛndāvana is particularly special because of its natural beauty, which is exquisite and which Vaiṣṇava writers seem never to tire of describing. Indeed, lengthy tracts have been written for the sole purpose of praising its virtues and proving it to be the supreme paradise. Prabodhānanda Sarasvatī was particularly fond of describing Vṛndāvana[5] and set himself the task of writing ten thousand verses on this single theme.[6]

---

[1]From Hari Vans, *Caurāsi Pada* (Hindi); in Growse, *Mathura*, pp. 214-15.

[2]Rūpa Gosvāmin, *Dāna-keli-kaumudī*, p. 48.

[3]Kṛṣṇadāsa Kavirāja, *Caitanya-caritāmṛta*, Madhya-lila 14. 211; my translation.

[4]Rūpa Gosvāmin, *Bhakti-rasāmṛta-sindhu*, Eastern Division: Second Wave, *śloka* 237, Mukundadāsa Gosvāmin's commentary (I, 234).

[5]His identification is not certain, but he most likely lived in the sixteenth century and may have been acquainted with the Gosvāmins of Vṛndāvana. It has been suggested that he was Gopāla Bhaṭṭa's *guru*, or perhaps his uncle, although De doubts this. *Vaisnava Faith and Movement*, pp. 132-33.

[6]*Ibid.*, p. 653. He did not accomplish his goal but did complete 1,871 verses.

> I have been enchanted by the flora of Vṛndāvana, strangely beautiful, varied trees and creepers bearing flowers and fruits; by the twitterings and songs of strangely beautiful peacocks, cuckoos, parrots, and other birds, their songs maddened by bliss; by green bowers beautified by the presence of enamoring lakes, rivers, and mountains. The golden fields of Vṛndāvana have also captured me. The earth of Vṛndāvana is made of transparent and variegated stones and gems, its trees and creepers laden with flowers and fruits diffusing bliss of pure consciousness, the birds expressing the sweetest songs of the *Sāma-veda* through their twitterings, the rivers and other water-containing places full of *rasa* of pure consciousness; let my mind ponder on them. The leaves are like emeralds, the flowers are like diamonds, the buds are like pearls, the sprouts are like rubies, the juicy fruits are also like rubies, and the trees of Vṛndāvana stand picturesquely with perpetually-honey-shedding flowers on them, and the flowers are bedecked with circular big black bees that look like shining blue gems upon them.[1]

And on and on. In Vṛndāvana nature itself seems to revel in bliss, intoxicated by Kṛṣṇa and his carnival of joy. In Vṛndāvana the extremes of heat and cold are not known. During the time of the insufferable summer heat, spring continues to reign in the forest town.[2] In Kṛṣṇa's heaven naturally hostile animals are friendly to each other.[3] And, finally, in Vṛndāvana no one knows old age or death.

> Vrindavana, the abode of his love-games, is beyond description; it is self-luminous, and consists in love and joy. There happiness reigns, and in that land of infinite bliss there is no old age, nor death nor pain. There the relishful love-games of Krishna go on without cease.[4]

Kṛṣṇa is eternally young in Vṛndāvana, and so are all of its

---

[1]Prabodhānanda Sarasvati, *Vṛndāvana-mahimāmṛta*, translated into Bengali by Haridās Babaji, Part II, pp. 1-2.
[2]*Bhāgavata-purāṇa* X. 18. 3 (IV, 83).
[3]*Ibid.* X. 13. 60 (IV, 57-58).
[4]Krishnadas, *Krishna of Vrindabana*, p. 596.

inhabitants. Nature does not wear them down but constantly expresses her joy through youthful vigor. The wheel of life and death does not revolve in Kṛṣṇa's heaven. It has permanently stopped to revel in life alone, stupified in trance, as it were, by Kṛṣṇa's bewitching presence.

J. "*Without Kṛṣṇa There Is No Song*"

Kṛṣṇa's long history is nearly as old as Hinduism itself, and over the centuries he has been many things to many people. He has been a counselor, companion, politician, teacher, preacher, king, and the Absolute God. But it was as a humble cowherd boy that he was destined to gain his immense popularity and fame. From Kṛṣṇa's long and detailed history, from his elaborate purāṇic biography, it is striking that the medieval *bhakti* cults of the north (those of Nimbārka, Vallabha, and Caitanya) have focused on Kṛṣṇa's superfluous life as a youth in Vṛndāvana to the almost total exclusion of the rest of his history and biography. In these cults his idyllic life there has been bracketed, as it were, and extolled as his most complete manifestation. His sojourn in Vṛndāvana has in effect been taken from its biographical context and made into the be-all and end-all of his manifestation. His later biography is seen as an insignificant epilogue compared to his life in Vṛndāvana. Dvārakā is not important as the seat of his kingly rule and courtly life. It is primarily a synonym for his absence when Rādhā and the *gopīs* sing their threnodies of love in separation. In attempting to understand why the most frivolous and apparently inconsequential chapter of Kṛṣṇa's biography has been fastened upon as the most meaningful by the medieval *bhakti* cults, I would refer to a popular Bengali saying: "Without Kṛṣṇa there is no song" ("kānu binā gīta nāhi").

In the teeming Hindu pantheon there are several gods who excel at making the world whirl in the maddening rhythms of creation, maintenance, and destruction. There are gods whose heavens are merry sporting grounds, whose days are spent in amorous dalliance with dancing *apsarases* and singing *gandharvas*. There are intoxicated and intoxicating gods who seem insane in their tumultuous, reckless adventures. There are great magicians among the gods who conjure up dizzying creations to amsue themselves and stupify others. There are beautiful gods and goddesses, gods who sing and laugh and dance. There are many gods who play.

But "without Kṛṣṇa," the Bengali verse says, "there is no song." For of all the Hindu gods Kṛṣṇa expresses most completely all that is beautiful, graceful, and enticing in the other world of the divine. He embodies all those things that are extra in life, all those luxuries and characteristics that are not necessary to life but without which life would not be worth living. He is witty, gay, careless, accomplished at dancing, singing, and playing the flute. He is loved with abandon and loves with abandon. And he is beautiful, surpassingly beautiful. He is irresistibly and bewitchingly charming. All that he does is done with effortless grace and harmony. And though he is an immensely powerful being, he is not haughty or proud, he is not vindictive or jealous. He does not live in a palace; he does not sit in majesty upon a throne. His heavenly court is held in the glades and bowers of Vṛndāvana, where he sports as an equal with lowly cowherd women or plays with cowherd boys. His appearance is not mighty but almost rustic. He always smiles and never frowns. He is young, eternally young. He runs, jumps, scampers, and bounds through the forest in a constant display of irrepressible vitality and enthusiasm. His entire life at Vṛndāvana "accomplishes" nothing. It is quite frivolous. His essential qualities as a cowherd youth are not those that would lend themselves to an orderly, pious routine in the normal, pragmatic world. His essential qualities are "mere" adornments. His beauty, humor, artistic talent, and playful spirit are ornamental and meant only for aimless display. And it is precisely these extra qualities, his ornamental nature, that set him apart from the world of the ordinary and express the essence of the divine world of the other. He is the embodiment of all that is implied in the word *līlā*: light, almost aerial activity, boistrous revel, frivolity, spontaneity, and freedom.

In Vṛndāvana Kṛṣṇa's life is a continuous song, a melodious, harmonious symphony of beauty, grace, and joy. Here God plays, losing himself in ecstatic, spontaneous revel. Here life is a celebration, not a duty. Here life does not grind along but scampers in dance and rejoices in song. All that makes life in the pragmatic world endurable is to be found here. This is the other world of the divine, from which beauty and luxurious bounty and freedom proceed. Here the bondage of necessity does not exist. Kṛṣṇa is here, filling the world with the melody of his flute. And those who have heard it say: "Without Kṛṣṇa there is no song."

CHAPTER III

PLAY AS AN EXPRESSION OF MAN'S RELIGIOUS ACTIVITY

A. *Play as an Expression of Cult*

In Hinduism the play of the gods in its abundance and variety shows that play is an appropriate means of expressing the otherness of the divine sphere. The spontaneous and superfluous nature of play is eminently appropriate to express the freedom of the gods, who are entirely self-satisfied and complete. Play, indeed, seems a particularly divine activity, as it is the opposite of work, and the gods by their nature have no need to work at all. Although it is a logical contradiction to say so, it seems as if it is almost necessary for the gods to play. While it is true that play that is not voluntary is not play at all, nevertheless the gods have no needs or desires, which leaves them only to exert themselves in superfluous, aimless activity, which is so well done in play.

I should like now to consider the relationship of play to religion from a different point of view, from the point of view of man's expression of the religious in cult. In this section I shall concentrate on the place of play within cult in an attempt to see to what extent play is also an expression of man's religious activity: to show to what extent, if any, the play of the gods is reflected in cult and to what extent different kinds of play or playlike activities are important to cult.

Before actually treating the place of play in Hindu cult, however, I should like to discuss play from a strictly theoretical point of view. For some time the positive relationship of play to cult has been recognized, and it has even been suggested that all cult and cultic activities belong essentially to the play sphere. Before investigating the Kṛṣṇa cult and the place of play in it, it is relevant to review and evaluate certain arguments and definitions that have led to this remarkable conclusion. For it is necessary in trying to understand the importance of play in cult to have clearly in mind both a precise definition of play and a clear understanding of the central element or *raison d'être* of cult. And a discussion of those authors who have already dealt with the problem will help in clarifying both of the concepts and the relationship between them.

It is impossible to discuss the play concept theoretically without acknowledging the work of Johan Huizinga. Before him the place of play in culture and cult was barely considered. After him almost all work done on the problem has been in reaction to his work. His work still stands as the most creative and comprehensive treatment of the play element in culture, and with a few modifications his definition of play and its place in culture is still accepted. A brief review and evaluation of Huizinga's work and the responses to his ideas, then, seem the obvious preliminaries to any attempt to understand properly the nature of play and its place in cult.

In his definition of play Huizinga delineates five formal characteristics. The outstanding feature of play, he says, is its primal, irreducible nature. It is activity that is done as an end in itself; it is completely voluntary. One plays simply to play. Second, play is superfluous, nonutilitarian. It is useless activity, a "waste of time." Third, play takes place outside "ordinary life," and according to Huizinga it is "not serious," although it may absorb the player completely. Fourth, play proceeds in an orderly way within its own limits of space and time in accordance with its own rules. And, fifth, as play tends to surround itself with secrecy and emphasizes its otherness from ordinary life, it may lead to cohesive social groups.[1]

While Huizinga lists only these five characteristics in his formal definition of play, he suggests three other characteristics later on that are crucial to his argument for the place of play in cult. He adds that play is commonly pervaded with a sense of make-believe, or pretending.[2] Second, in play there operates a process that he calls "actualization by representation," by which he means an imaginative process whereby worlds are created by imitative actions or symbolic representation.[3] And, third, play is characterized by a joyous mood.[4]

---

[1]J. Huizinga, *Homo Ludens: A Study of the Play-Element in Culture*, pp. 1-13 (first published 1938).
[2]*Ibid.*, p. 22.
[3]*Ibid.*, p. 14.
[4]*Ibid.*, pp. 20-21.

For the moment let us allow this definition of play to stand, for it is upon these characteristics that Huizinga builds his argument for the centrality of play to cult. I shall evaluate his definition after considering his ideas and some critical responses to it.

There are five main points of similarity between play and cultic activity that Huizinga delineates. Probably the most obvious one is the fact that both play and cult take place in a world apart, in circumstances that separate them from an ordinary sphere. Play takes place in a realm that is removed from the world of necessity. It is a special world where things are done simply for enjoyment. Cultic activities take place in a sacred or holy place that is removed from the profane world. This similarity is particularly clear when play takes the form of a game and when cultic activity takes the form of a ritual or ceremony. In each case the act of separation or isolation from the ordinary world is quite formal and precise temporally and spacially. Huizinga says:

> We found that one of the most important characteristics of play was its spatial separation from ordinary life. A closed space is marked out for it, either materially or ideally, hedged off from the everyday surroundings. Inside this space the play proceeds, inside it the rules obtain. Now, the marking out of some sacred spot is also the primary characteristic of every sacred act. This requirement of isolation for ritual, including magic and law, is much more than merely spatial and temporal. Nearly all rites of consecration and initiation entail a certain artificial seclusion for the performers and those to be initiated. Whenever it is a question of taking a vow or being received into an Order or confraternity, or of oaths and secret societies, in one way or another there is always such a delimitation of room for play. The magician, the augur, the sacrificer begins his work by circumscribing his sacred space. Sacrament and mystery presuppose a hallowed spot.
>
> Formally speaking, there is no distinction whatever between marking out a space for a sacred purpose and marking it out for purposes of sheer play. The turf, the tennis-court,

> the chessboard and pavement-hopscotch cannot formally be distinguished from the temple or the magic circle.[1]

With some qualifications (which I shall discuss below in evaluating Huizinga's theory), the spatial and temporal similarity Huizinga mentions is incontestable. Formally, both play and cult are characterized by being set apart in tmie and space. They each involve, in his words, a "*stepping out of* common reality into a higher order."[2]

A second similarity between play and cultic acivity, Huizinga says, follows from this. The fact of stepping out of the real world entails the creation actually or mentally of another world. A common element in play, that is, is what Huizinga calls "actualization by representation."[3] In play the imagination is called upon to make a world, either in imitation of the real world or totally different from it. This may be done actually, by imitation, or figuratively by use of symbols. Now in cultic activity this "actualization by representation" also operates. Being isolated from the ordinary, profane world, the sacred world is created actually, by imitation and reiteration, or figuratively by symbolic rituals and ceremonies. In both play and cult something out of the ordinary or in imitation of the ordinary is represented and thereby actualized.

The importance of the imagination, the importance of conjuring other worlds into being that characterizes play and cultic activity, suggests a third similarity. In order to move in these worlds, indeed, even to enter them at all, Huizinga says, involves an element of pretending or make-believe, a suspension of disbelief. In play there is the awareness of things not being real, of moving in a world that is in some sense imaginative. To enter the play sphere and to play within it requires a wilful acceptance of the rule that for the time being the unreal and fantastic will become present. Those who do not accept this rule or who cannot effect within themselves this transformation are "spoilsports" who will not or cannot play.[4] In cultic activity also, Huizinga says, a certain "leap" is required, a willingness

[1]*Ibid.*, pp. 19-20.
[2]*Ibid.*, p. 13.
[3]*Ibid.*, p. 14.
[4]*Ibid.*, p. 23.

to pretend for a time that what is imaginatively created, or what is summoned by imitation, reiteration, or invocation, becomes actual. Now the element of make-believe that pervades the world of play with a sense of things being "not real," or not ordinary, with a sense of things being done simply for enjoyment, may lead the player to an attitude of earnestness, in which he becomes so completely absorbed in his play that he experiences rapture, in which he is overwhelmed or seized, as it were, by something in the play world he has himself conjured up or willingly accepted as real for the sake of play. The same process may take place in cultic activity. The participant enters the sphere of the sacred by temporarily suspending his disbelief, by leaping into a world of the fantastic. And here the suspension of disbelief, the feeling of make-believe, may also lead to absolute earnestness and rapture. The spirit of "let's pretend" may lead to frenzied possession or seizure in which the entire being becomes gripped by those things that were originally make-believe, "not real."[1]

The fourth similarity Huizinga delineates between play and cult concerns the mood of play, which is exuberant, exhilarating, and joyful. This mood is also the mood of the religious celebration and festival, which, he says, is common to most cultic activities.

> Consecration, sacrifices, sacred dances and contests, performances, mysteries—all are comprehended within the act of celebrating a festival. The rites may be bloody, the probations of the young men awaiting initiation may be cruel, the masks may be terrifying, but the whole thing has a festal nature. Ordinary life is at a standstill. Banquets, junketings and all kinds of wanton revels are going on all the time the feast lasts. Whether we think of the Ancient Greek festivities or the African religions to-day we can hardly draw any sharp line between the festival mood in general and the holy frenzy surrounding the central mystery.[2]

The festive mood that characterizes play and the religious celebration stems from the primacy of both, Huizinga says. Both

---

[1]*Ibid.*, pp. 16-17, 23.
[2]*Ibid.*, p. 21.

are done for no discernible, pragmatic purpose. They are done as ends in themselves. In play and in the religious festival man enters with the sole intent of indulging in exuberance and exultation—his only intent is to rejoice.[1]

A final point of similarity, according to Huizinga, stems from the fact that in play order and secrecy are central. Rules, though they may be completely arbitrary in play, must be obeyed absolutely, or the play cannot continue. "All play has its rules. They determine what 'holds' in the temporary world circumscribed by play. The rules of a game are absolutely binding and allow no doubt."[2] The apartness of play, furthermore, tends to secrecy and the feeling that the players are special, different from the people of the ordinary world. The mutual observance of special rules and the secrecy with which play is often performed, then, tend to form cohesive units that may lead to social groupings. In this sense play is socially productive, creating controlled, disciplined, cohesive groups within a society that lend that society order. The order of the playground may be transferred to the real world. This is also the case with cultic activity, particularly "secret societies," where extraordinary rules are imposed and obeyed that create an internal order and cohesion that may come to be imposed upon society.

For Huizinga the similarities between play and cult indicate that for cult play is not only central but essential. Play, he argues, is anterior to culture and therefore must have come before cult. And, furthermore, he argues that it is *in play* that man discovers the sacred.

> In the form and function of play, itself an independent entity which is senseless and irrational, man's consciousness that he is embedded in a sacred order of things finds its first, highest, and holiest expression. Gradually the significance of a sacred act permeates the playing. Ritual grafts itself upon it; but the primary thing is and remains play.[3]

On the whole, the reaction to Huizinga's work has been positive. Joseph Campbell, while he does not evaluate Huizinga's

---

[1] *Ibid.*
[2] *Ibid.*, p. 11.
[3] *Ibid.*, pp. 17-18.

theory critically, agrees that the isolation of the sacred sphere and the element of make-believe in cultic activity indicate the centrality of play in cult. Of the mythological and cultic sphere he says:

> There has been a shift of view from the logic of the normal secular sphere, where things are understood to be distinct from one another, to a theatrical or play sphere, where they are accepted for what they are *experienced* as being and the logic is that of "make-believe"—"as if."[1]

Campbell also agrees with Huizinga that the mood of festivals and celebrations is thoroughly playful. "The spirit of the festival, the holiday, the holy day of the religious ceremonial, requires that the normal attitude toward the cares of the world should have been temporarily set aside in favor of a particular mood of dressing up."[2] The world of play, he says, opens up possibilities that are inconceivable in the ordinary world—in the play sphere the extraordinary is present. And so the spirit of play is that within which cultic activity can best proceed.

> From the position of secular man (Homo sapiens), that is to say, we are to enter the play sphere of the festival, acquiescing in a game of belief, where fun, joy, and rapture rule in ascending series. The laws of life in time and space—economics, politics, and even morality—will thereupon dissolve. Whereafter, re-created by that return to paradise before the Fall, before the knowledge of good and evil, right and wrong, true and false, belief and disbelief, we are to carry the point of view and spirit of man the player (Homo ludens) back into life; as in the play of children, where, undaunted by the banal actualities of life's meager possibilities, the spontaneous impulse of the spirit to identify itself with something other than itself for the sheer delight of play, transubstantiates the world—in which, actually, after all, things are not quite as real or permanent, terrible, important, or logical as they seem.[3]

---

[1]Campbell, *Primitive Mythology*, pp. 21-22.
[2]*Ibid.*, p. 25.
[3]*Ibid.*, pp. 28-29.

For Campbell play is not simply a waste of time, a denial of reality, mere frivolity. It is an activity or a state in which man is freed to move toward ultimate realities. "The play state and the rapturous seizures sometimes deriving from it represent, therefore, a step rather *toward* than away from the ineluctable truth."[1]

Campbell, then, does not actually admit that cult can be reduced to play, as Huizinga does, but he does suggest that cult moves typically and naturally in the play sphere, that in cult man the thinker is replaced by man the player.

Adolf Jensen has also responded affirmatively to Huizinga's ideas concerning the importance of play to cult. Indeed, he has even gone so far as to say:

> I believe that ethnology can accept Huizinga's ideas without the slightest hesitation. The most sacred acts are play. Play is "a contest *for* something or a representation *of* something" . . . . These are the two basic aspects under which we may describe cultic acts in terms of play.[2]

Formally, Jensen agrees, cultic activity strives for something—an "other" world, the sacred world, the mythical realm, the Real sphere—and is a representation of something, the ultimately real models of the sacred sphere, and therefore may be called play. The process common to play, "actualization by representation," is particularly important in cult, he says, because it enables man to make the sacred order present. Jensen also emphasizes the fact that cultic activity is purpose free, an end in itself. In this respect it is similar to play, which Huizinga defines as superfluous activity.

> The relationship between a cult and reality must under no circumstances be confused with an explanatory purpose. Man's *Ergriffenheit* [seizure] by "cosmic phenomena" and other realities, his representations of them in human transformations, his cognitive awareness of a world order and its enactment in the form of a human order, all this is no less

---

[1]*Ibid.*, p. 28.

[2]Adolf E. Jensen, *Myth and Cult among Primitive Peoples*, trans. Marianna Tax Choldin and Wolfgang Weissleder, p. 49.

> purpose-free than the performance of a modern stage play. It partakes of the same freedom of action which Huizinga saw as an essential criterion of play. At the same time, it shares with it a measure of bondage, if we take account of the compulsion inherent in man's representational nature.[1]

The extent of Jensen's agreement with Huizinga is difficult to assess, for, as in the case of Campbell, he does not say exactly to what extent play is a necessary vehicle for cult, although he does deny Huizinga's statement that play is always anterior to cult and that cult must therefore arise from and in play.[2] He seems to agree with Huizinga that all cultic activity is play but does not explain whether this is a necessary relationship or an accidental similarity arising from the fact that play employs techniques that are congenial to cult and shares with cultic activity a certain superfluousness. Jensen does, however, make some pointed criticisms of Huizinga's theory, and his criticisms will be a suitable beginning to my own evaluation of the problem.

If Huizinga states that all cult is play, the converse of this is clearly not the case. All play is not cultic activity. Cultic activity, therefore, appears to be a special kind of play. Indeed, Huizinga himself calls cult *sacred* play, which implies that cult cannot be understood as *mere* play. He says: "Passing now from children's games to the sacred performances in archaic culture we find that there is more of a mental element 'at play' in the latter, though it is excessively difficult to define."[3] This additional "mental element," which Huizinga does not define, is the basis for an important qualification of Huizinga's theory, according to Jensen. Jensen says that the crucial difference between play and sacred play, or between play and cultic activity, is the latter's direct relationship to, and participation in, a mythical or sacred order. As distinct from ordinary play, in cult

> there is a deeper and more fundamental relationship to reality; . . . a special psychological state is indicated, a spirit

[1] *Ibid.*, pp. 55-56.

[2] *Ibid.*, p. 64. Here Jensen goes to considerable length to show how some games originated in cult and are a product of cult.

[3] Huizinga, *Homo Ludens*, p. 14.

> of celebration and solemnity without which the creative process would be unthinkable. . . . cult is not just any order re-enacted but the true order, the order under which man lives and which shapes his image of reality.[1]

Jensen uses the term *Ergriffenheit* (seizure) as descriptive of these distinctive characteristics of cult.

> "To be seized" means (even in common usage) to experience a psychological state that lifts man out of the customary. It is a festive sense which is to a certain extent characteristic of man in the creative moments of his life. "To be seized" points toward a reality oriented toward man. Frobenius said that man was seized by the essence of things. One might say that at an inspired moment in time man won a deeper knowledge and had revealed to him the order of reality—that which is divine in things.[2]

I agree with Jensen that the additional "mental element" Huizinga mentions in sacred acts indicates more than simply a superficial difference between ordinary play and cultic activity. However, I do not think the term *Ergriffenheit* is the most satisfactory term to underline the difference. The "festive sense" and the "psychological state that lifts man out of the customary . . . in . . . creative moments" that characterize seizure are just as clear in ordinary play. Without reference to context or agency *Ergriffenheit* is primarily a neutral process—neither sacred nor profane. It is often seen in children's games and dramatic performances. The child or the actor is just as prone to rapture, to the seizure of "other" forces, as is the participant in cult. Imitation may also become participation in either children's games or dramatic performances. Indeed, it may even be more common in these phenomena than it is in cultic activity. The distinction between play and sacred play is a more qualitative difference, one that involves content rather than technique. Jensen says that it is more creative than ordinary play, but again I think that he underestimates the creativity of play (or overestimates the creativity of cult). While it is true that myth

---

[1] Jensen, *Myth and Cult*, p. 53.
[2] *Ibid.*

and cult are eminently creative at their inception, as Jensen says, and reveal the true order of things, and while it is also true that this creativity is not necessarily diminished due to repetition and imitation, cult almost inevitably reaches the state where the patterns it imitates and re-creates are as readymade as those children seek to imitate in their play. It is also true that in play children are highly creative, discovering and conquering reality, becoming seized by reality, in a way that is impossible outside the play sphere. In play the child may cease to be a child—he may imagine things and participate in things that are new and startling to him.

The difference between ordinary play and sacred play does, indeed, lie in the fact that cult always moves in relation to *the* true order, the *real* order of things, as Jensen says. Cult always keeps in the foreground a vertical referent, as it were, that points to a transcendent sphere that is basic to man's place in the world. I think, however, that Jensen goes on to confuse the distinction between play and cult when he insists that cultic activity, or sacred play alone, is characterized by seizure and creativity. Ordinary play, too, exhibits these features. The crucial distinction is one of content. Cult proceeds in relationship to an ultimate order, an order that has final and authoritative meaning that extends beyond the boundaries of any particular circumstance of time and place. The "other" order of cult is not just any order but the ultimately real order, and because this is so its authority is not limited to a particular ritual or ceremony but includes birth, marriage, death, and man's place in the world generally. It is the standard by which a man may be ultimately measured and judged.

It is undeniable that there are striking similarities between play and cultic activity. But if we begin by delineating the most essential nature of each, the similarities become formal and not necessary. The *raison d'être* (if we may use that term at all vis-à-vis play) of play is diversion, amusement, enjoyment. Play is done for the fun of it. Play is fun, and when it ceases to be fun it ceases to be play and becomes work. If we keep this basic fact of play in mind, much unnecessary confusion will be avoided. In comparing play to cult it is notable that, among the five similarities he lists, Huizinga only once suggests an affinity on this basis, namely, that in religious festivals and celebrations there is a mood of rejoicing, of enjoyment, of fun.[1] And I disagree that the great majority of cultic activities can be subsumed under feasts and celebrations, as he does. Clearly "consecrations, sacrifices, sacred dances and contests, performances, mysteries" may have their festive aspects; the mood may be that of a feast, and "banquets, junketings and all kinds of wanton revels" may be "going on all the time the feast lasts." But it takes little imagination to think of many examples of cultic activity that can only be called celebrations or festivals by an impossible stretch of the imagination. The cultic rituals surrounding death are frequently celebrational, no doubt, but it is stretching a point to suggest that funerals and rites associated with death are characteristically festive. The same is true of initiation. In many archaic societies the initiation of the young is the occasion for carnival and banqueting. But is this the central theme of the initiation? The central fact is the introduction of the young into a sacred order, or at least a new order. The motif of death to an old or profane order and rebirth in a new one is central. This may be understood in the context of, or as an occasion for, a festival, but often it is not. The relationship is not necessary even if it may be typical.

If the *raison d'être* of play is fun, then what is the essential nature of cult, and to what extent is it dependent upon or similar to play? The central fact of cultic activity is affirmation, imitation, repetition, actualization of, or participation in a sacred order. All cultic activity is done with reference to a sacred sphere that is considered the true or ultimately real order. The *raison d'être* of cult is to have this world or in some way to participate in or commune with it. It is man's attempt to relate himself to the transcendent order of the gods, or the "Other." Now to what extent can this activity be called play ? At first glance it would appear that such activity would have no relationship to play, as cultic activity is not primarily done for

[1]C. Kerenyi emphasizes precisely this aspect of religion as central when discussing Greek and Roman materials. It is feast and celebration that are central to religion, he suggests, not play per se. The above criticism would also apply to this theory, of course. *The Religion of the Greeks and Romans*, trans. Christopher Holme, chap. ii, "The Feast," pp. 49-92.

diversion, amusement, or enjoyment, simply for fun. But as Huizinga has pointed out there are striking similarities upon closer observation. The question is, do any of these similarities indicate a necessary connection? Do any of the similarities he mentions point to an essential relationship, or do these similarities simply constitute a formal resemblance?

Let us look briefly at each of the similarities. Play and cult, Huizinga says, each takes place in isolation, outside the normal sphere of reality. They are both hedged off from the ordinary world. Now to what extent is isolation a necessary characteristic of either cult or play? If isolation is not necessary to either, then it cannot constitute a necessary relationship between the two. While isolation is typical of both play and cult, I disagree that it is necessary to either. The highly energetic and unstructured play of animals and small children in which they run, jump, and scamper about spontaneously is set off from the normal world in no clear-cut way. In this type of play "a closed space is marked out for it" neither "materially [n]or ideally." It is not isolated, nor is it orderly, Huizinga's fifth point of similarity between cult and play. Indeed, it is so disorderly that it borders on the anarchical. Nor is isolation absolutely necessary for cultic activity. While cultic activity does often proceed by first marking itself off from the profane sphere, there are examples of religious behavior that may be called cultic that do not require this. I have in mind those cults that require participants to wander alone in the forest or bush, often with the aim of having a visionary or mystical experience. Among archaic cults there are examples of this among the North American Indians. In the "high" religions there are other examples of cultic activities that do not require either material or ideal isolation. While most religious orders or societies are isolated from the profane world, their members often perform mandatory cultic activities in the world, for example, begging, charity, and teaching. While the attitude inculcated may often be that of "being in but not of the world," suggesting an ideal isolation, the separation is not physical or temporal in the way that Huizinga suggests.

The second similarity Huizinga mentions is that of "actualization by representation." Again, while this is very often a common characteristic of both play and cult, I think it can be shown that it is necessary to neither. The highly unstructured, rollicking play of animals and children, again, can continue without representing anything. In fact, actualization by representation is limited to those types of play that employ imitation, common enough in children's play and dramatic performances but missing in certain competitive games, particularly sports. Cult also is not always limited to imitative activity. While imagination and reiteration are central to most archaic cults, there are examples among the high religions of cultic activity that proceeds without reiteration or imitation. The meditation of the Zen Buddhist, the Catholic confession, and the Protestant sermon may proceed without imitation or reiteration of primordial or sacred history. In many cases, while sacred history may be the context or the original cause of a given cultic activity, there is no overt attempt to recall this event actually or symbolically.

The third similarity Huizinga delineates is the centrality of make-believe in play and cult. Again, there are examples of play in which this element is missing. Highly structured games such as chess, gambling, and athletic contests are not characterized by an element of make-believe. As for cult, I do not agree with Huizinga's estimate of the centrality of make-believe in the attitude of the participants. He says:

> As far as I know, ethnologists and anthropologists concur in the opinion that the mental attitude in which the great religious feasts of savages are celebrated and witnessed is not one of complete illusion. There is an underlying consciousness of things "not being real."[1]

Now the extent to which the participant in, or the witness of, a sacred ritual completely loses the feeling of self and becomes identified with what he is imitating or reiterating is exceedingly difficult to define. For that matter, to what extent can we say that children always maintain a feeling of make-believe, however latent, when they pretend to be something or someone else in their play? What is notable about both play and cultic activity is that make-believe may lead to rapture or seizure in which the attitude of just pretending falls into abeyance, if it

[1]Huizinga, *Homo Ludens*, p. 22.

does not disappear altogether. In his imaginary fight with demons or monsters the child may suddenly become terrified. The demon may become quite real. The actor in cult may be seized by a model he is imitating or may frighten an observer with his appearance to the extent that the amusement or make-believe falls away. But whether or not the feeling of make-believe ever entirely vanishes in either play or cult, we must answer the question of how this mental attitude functions in each. In play the invitation "let's pretend" is a summons to diversion, amusement, and fun. Rapture or seizure is not the aim of children's play. Rapture is an accidental result of complete involvement. Indeed, rapture or seizure, especially if it results in fright or terror, will quickly end the play. In cult this is not the case. In cult it seems that the state of rapture or seizure, the possession of the "other mind" that enables the participant to enter completely into the realm of the gods, is sought after and cherished. If the attitude of pretending falls away, if the sense of things being done for fun disappears, that is of no consequence; indeed, it is desirable, for fun is not the primary aim of cult, while the actual presence of the true order is.

Huizinga's fourth point of similarity, the importance of the festive mood in play and cult, I have already discussed. His fifth point, I think, is probably the least significant. Play and cult, he says, are both characterized by order and secrecy, which may lead to the formation of social groups. In the first place, neither play nor cult is necessarily secret. While the isolation of both may lead to a sense of comradeship or even mission, this is not true of many types of play and cult that involve the public or the entire community. And while the secrecy of certain types of play groups or cult groups may lead to social organization, this is a secondary phenomenon that cannot be shown to be a necessary development of isolation. Nor is play necessarily characterized by order. When Huizinga says of play that "it creates order, *is* order,"[1] he must not have had in mind the anarchical play of animals and children whose wild gambolings often appear to be the opposite of orderliness. And while cult may be more orderly than many types of unstructured play, the religious festival and carnival are often characterized by chaos,

[1]*Ibid.*, p. 10.

tumult, and anarchy that purposely subvert the normal order of things.

Another similarity between play and cult, not specifically delineated by Huizinga, but noted by Jensen, should be considered before making a final judgment on the necessary relationship between play and cult. Huizinga notes in his definition of play that it is superfluous, nonutilitarian activity. Jensen makes the same point vis-à-vis cult by saying that cult is as purpose free as play. While it is quite clear that Huizinga is correct in defining play as nonproductive, superfluous activity, I do not think that cultic activity can be consistently characterized in this way. When Jensen speaks of cult as purpose free he is speaking about it in the context of *Ergriffenheit,* during that primal time when sacred realities were first revealed to man, or when these realities are again revealed by repetition. He also says that imitation and reiteration of these realities are as purpose free as a stage play. It is clear that much cultic activity is done as an end in itself, that it bears little or no relationship to the pragmatic world and only seeks communion or participation in the sacred. There are many cases, however, in which cultic activity is done as a means to an end: to bring rain, thwart an enemy, or nourish crops. It was once fashionable to distinguish genuine religion from spurious religion, or magic, by using this criterion of ends and means. Those cultic activities that operate as a means to an end, with some ulterior motive apparent, were felt to smack of magic, while those rituals and ceremonies that are ends in themselves, that are characterized by praise, thanksgiving, and submission, were felt to be more genuine or superior types of religion. In Jensen's scheme there is an echo of this approach. He distinguishes between cult in its primal and secondary stages, the latter being in what he calls a state of application in which the original sacred reality has lost its primal impact and presence and in which cultic activity is done as a means to an end. While Jensen does not say that cult in its state of application is some kind of spurious religion or magic, he does imply that it has lost its original *raison d'être.* Jensen's distinction is useful, and I agree that the process he describes is a common one. But I do not agree that means and ends is a workable or justifiable criterion when trying to determine whether cult has reached the state of application. I agree with

Jensen's distinction and also with his estimate of the primal *raison d'être* of cult, but I do not think that it is possible to characterize a ritual done with an ulterior motive as necessarily an example of cult in the state of application. Plentiful rain, good crops, health, long life, or protection from enemies or persecution can naturally be felt to be brought about or in some way influenced by the ultimately meaningful sphere of the sacred without diminishing the reality or presence of that sphere. I do not agree that this pragmatic or utilitarian connection, which seems obvious in many rituals, necessarily implies degeneration. It may very well imply, on the contrary, an enhancement of the sacred realm by admitting its power and control over these matters. But even cult in the state of application is still cult. It is still activity that is done vis-à-vis a vertical referent (no matter how vaguely remembered or understood) without which the ritual would not be effective. Cult, then, is not necessarily purpose free and may take place within a pragmatic context. Indeed, it may be felt to be the most productive activity of which man is capable.

My purpose has been to show that cult cannot be reduced to play, as Huizinga has suggested it can be. I have tried to show that there is no necessary relationship between the two despite the fact of the striking similarities that exist between them. It is clear, I think, that each represents an irreducible phenomenon in its own right. The similarities between play and cult, then, must be explained, not in terms that postulate the growth of one from the other, but by the appropriateness of one as a means of expressing the other. The place of play in cult should be seen, not in terms of the former being the necessary substratum of the latter, but rather as a common means of expression for cult.

The ultimate question to be answered in this argument is to what extent play can be understood to be the *raison d'être* of cult. While the sacred sphere may be dramatically "played out" in cult, while cultic activity often expresses itself in superfluous festivity and isolation, the distinction between cultic activity and play is unmistakable. To mention only the minimum difference, the distinction is between ordinary play and sacred play. As opposed to ordinary play, cultic activity, or sacred play, is always characterized by that "additional mental element," by the fact that it is activity done vis-à-vis a transcendent realm. If reference to a sacred sphere were to disappear, the activity would cease to be cultic.

If the relationship between play and cult cannot be shown to be necessary, the similarities between the two, in particular the evident importance of play in cult, should indicate to the historian of religions that play can reveal much about the nature of cult and religion. If I cannot admit with Huizinga that in essence cultic activity is born from and continues in play, I do think that play, or activities that share common characteristics with play, have an important place in cult. While cult may exist apart from play, it finds play a congenial vehicle for its expression, and the techniques of play peculiarly appropriate to its ends.

I should like, then, to approach the matter of the centrality of play to cult by discussing the *raison d'être* of cult and the appropriateness of play to its ends and means. In the first place, as Huizinga, Campbell, and Jensen have said, cult represents a stepping out of, or from, one order into another. While this may not necessarily always be the case, it follows from the nature of cult that this should be so. The central fact of cult is man's relationship to a sacred sphere or transcendent order. In cult man does not seek participation in just any order or reality, furthermore, but in *the* real or ultimate order. And it is entirely appropriate that he should seek to heighten the significance of his actions vis-à-vis this order by a certain isolation. In cult man carries out those activities that are felt to be the most meaningful of all, and as such they are accorded special care, which usually includes a definite isolation, both spacially and temporally, from his other activities. The point is that cult may proceed without marking out special boundaries in space and time but that it is a perfectly appropriate thing to do given the *raison d'être* of cult. What is of primary importance in cult is not the isolation itself but the nature of the activity that suggests that isolation is appropriate.

"Actualization by representation" and make-believe, and their importance to cult, should also be understood from this point of view. In his relationship to the other world of the sacred, man seeks to make that world as present as possible, to have that world so that he may participate in it. This may be done in a variety of ways, but a particularly appropriate means is by imitation and reiteration of divine models. Just as a child imitates models from the real or imaginary world and makes them present in his play, so man in cult actualizes the sphere of the sacred by imitating and reiterating it. What is important to keep in mind, however, is that in cult the imitation and reiteration are done as a means to an end—as a means of achieving a relationship to the transcendent order of the gods.

The mood of cult, which, as Huizinga says, is often festive and celebrational, also follows naturally from the essential nature of cult, and not necessarily from the fact that cult arises from and in play. When man enters the sacred sphere he explodes the confines of the ordinary world, he participates in transcendence and enjoys comparative freedom vis-à-vis the profane order. The sacred realm is almost always characterized by wholeness, bounty, and perfection. It is a realm that is lustrous compared to the ordinary world. It seems perfectly appropriate that man should express himself within this sphere by rejoicing and celebration, indeed, by playing joyously, by behaving in a spontaneous, uninhibited way.

The tendency to secrecy and the strict adherence to rules sometimes seen in cult can be understood, again, from the point of view of their appropriateness to cult itself. Just as there is a tendency to perform cultic activity in isolation because of its special nature, so there may be a tendency to perform cultic activities in secret, to insure against interference from the profane world, which may be felt to be inimical to the sacred sphere. The observance of special rules follows naturally from the fact that in the sacred sphere things are no longer ordinary but extraordinary. The rules and assumptions of the profane world often are felt to be irrelevent, superseded by the often radically different assumptions and rules of the sacred order. It is quite logical that in *the* true order, or the transcendent realm of the gods, the old rules should in some way be altered or abolished. Finally, the fact that cultic activity is often superfluous and nonproductive is seen by the fact that participation in the divine sphere is self-satisfying. To participate in its fulness, to recognize one's place vis-à-vis a transcendent order, to rejoice in its bounty, is fulfilling in itself.

Huizinga has argued that insofar as cult shares so many similarities with play, and insofar as play is a primal, irreducible phenomenon that must have preceded culture, cult must have arisen from play and continues in play. It is my position that the *raison d'être* of cult, man's affirmation of and participation in a transcendent order, is just as primal and irreducible as play. Huizinga explains the similarity of play and cult by saying that cult arose from and in play. I have tried to show that the similarity arises from the nature of cult itself, which finds a natural means of expression in play and play techniques. In fact, cult may exist and proceed apart from play, but it finds in play full and appropriate expression.

There are a few more comments I should like to make about the definition of play that has taken shape so far. Huizinga's definition is by and large acceptable to me. However, in the process of showing that there is no necessary relationship between cult and play, I have called into question the universality of several of his formal characteristics of play. Some of his characteristics, that is, do not apply to all types of play and therefore cannot be considered necessary features of play. All play, for example, does not take place in isolation, within the context of make-believe, or in secrecy according to rules. It is difficult, nevertheless, to fault Huizinga on his comprehensive definition, as the phenomenon of play covers a bewildering variety of activities. I think, however, that if in his definition of play Huizinga had insisted on giving primary importance to the fact that play is done for amusement, for the fun of it, he would not have been led to make his conclusion about the origin and development of cult in play. Play, as I understand it, must always be approached with this primary characteristic in mind. It is the basic fact of play. Huizinga's conclusion that cult derives from and proceeds in play, and therefore may be reduced to play, stems partially from his losing sight of this basic element of play and his emphasis upon common, but nevertheless subsidiary, characteristics of play.

There is one more important matter that Huizinga's definition neglects. There is discernible among the varied activities that are called play a polarity between unstructured and structured play. The wild gambolings of animals and children proceed with a lawless vigor, while a chess game is played out within the confines of complex and binding rules. Yet both are correctly included under the category of play. Roger Caillois has recognized this polarity and insists that it is basic to any typology of play.[1] He refers to unstructured play as *paidia* and says that it is characterized by "an almost indivisible principle, common to diversion, turbulence, free improvisation, and carefree gaiety . . . It manifests a kind of uncontrolled fantasy."[2] Play that is more structured and hedged with rules he calls *ludus*. Moving from one pole to the other "there is a growing tendency to bind it [*paidia*] with arbitrary, imperative, and purposely tedious conventions."[3] The polarity between anarchy and order is clear in play and should be underlined, as it helps avoid confusion between the primary and secondary characteristics of play. Huizinga, for example, sees rules, order, secrecy, and isolation as basic characteristics of play. However, the anarchical play of children—*paidia*, play in its elemental form—is rarely characterized by secrecy and isolation, and never by rules and order. This does not mean, of course, that rules and order are not typical characteristics of certain types of play. It does mean though, that neither rules nor lack of rules should be taken to be a primary characteristic of play.

Huizinga's definition of play, then, is sound insofar as it delineates the most common characteristics of play. He fails, however, to distinguish between primary and secondary characteristics. And this is partially a result of ignoring the important polarity between unstructured and structured play. His conclusion that man's "first, highest, and holiest expression" of the sacred arises from and continues in play results from insisting upon the primacy of typical but not essential features of play, and also from the fact that he nowhere discusses the *raison d'être* of cult. Huizinga may, indeed, be right when he says that in play man "discovers" the sacred. In many instances the freedom and imagination inherent in playing enable man to transcend the ordinary, to participate in the extraordinary. It is also apparent, however, that when man participates in the sacred, when he experiences the fulness of the world of the gods, *then* does he yearn to play, to express his essential nature in superfluous, joyous activity. Play and cult both imply freedom—a

[1]Roger Caillois, *Man, Play, and Games,* trans. Meyer Barash.
[2]*Ibid.,* p. 13.
[3]*Ibid.*

release from the ordinary and the limitations of the finite. So it is not surprising that one should become a means of expressing the other. But Huizinga distorts the essential nature of both play and cult when he postulates the necessary origin of cult in play. The relationship is more accurately defined if we insist on the irreducible nature of both play and cult and explain the similarities between the two in terms of play being an appropriate form or vehicle of cult, or a means of expressing man's awareness of having exploded the limitations of the profane world.

B. *Play as a Technique of Release—the "Other Mind" in Indian Art*

When we move from the divine to the human sphere in Hinduism, it is striking that the wild, tumultuous play of the gods is only occasionally reflected in cult. The type of play that is central to cult is a more structured type of activity. In Caillois's terminology we move from *paidia* to *ludus* when we move from the play of the gods to the play of man in Hindu cult. The play of the gods is rarely hedged with rules. As they are by nature self-satisfied, they are free to act spontaneously and freely. Their actions are not determined by necessity or desire. The gods are by their very nature great players. Man, on the other hand, is a creature who is bound by limitations and desires, who is by nature a worker rather than a player. Man is not suited by his nature to prance off in aimless display as the gods are. He is bound by his nature to satisfy various needs and desires through work. This distinction between the natures of the divine and human is helpful, I think, in understanding the place and type of play in the two spheres. It suggests that for the gods play is a typical activity, while for man it is extraordinary—a special kind of activity that defies his basic nature as a creature in bondage to work.

Because Indian dance-drama and artistic theory serve to emphasize the extraordinary character of play in the human sphere, and because the *bhakti* cults have taken over and presuppose certain theories and techniques of Indian dance-drama and art, it will be helpful to consider them briefly as background to my discussion of play in the *bhakti* cults proper. In the tradition concerning the origin of classical Indian dance-drama there is a passage that mentions the distinction between the divine nature as free and playful and the human as bound and that suggests a point of view from which we may understand the importance of play and especially structured play in Hindu cult. At the end of the *kṛta yuga* the *dānavas*, *gandharvas*, *yakṣas*, *rākṣasas*, and *lokapālas* approached Brahmā and asked him to establish a pastime that could be enjoyed by all classes and castes, a fifth *veda* that even the *śūdras* could enjoy. Brahmā agreed to do this and so formed the "Nāṭya-veda," which he transmitted to Bharata and his hundred sons. The *Nāṭya-śāstra* of Bharata, revealed by Brahmā, consists primarily of detailed descriptions of how each emotion and mood should be expressed by various *mudrās* and postures. Very little freedom is given the actor in expressing any emotion according to his own inclinations. Only by imitating exactly the directions of the *Nāṭya-śāstra* can a particular emotion be truly conveyed. The necessity for human actors to imitate the movements and postures exactly as revealed, and the necessity for not acting impulsively or spontaneously, is explained in the *Nāṭya-śāstra* as follows:

> All the activities of the gods, whether in house or garden, spring from a natural disposition of the mind, but all activities of men result from the conscious working of the will; therefore it is that the details of the actions to be done by men must be carefully prescribed.[1]

Dance-drama is a type of play; it is superfluous activity meant for amusement. And the implication of the above passage is that prior to Brahmā's revelation it was entirely the province of the gods. The implication also is that the grace, harmony, and beauty of the dance-drama can only be achieved by man if he persistently holds in check his own impulses and stubbornly patterns his every movement on those revealed by Brahmā. Left to his own devices, man is an awkward, graceless being. We can say that according to the *Nāṭya-śāstra* man must learn to play; he must control his natural inclinations in order to play and behave gracefully as the gods do. The superior actor by constant control may participate in the activities of the gods. That is, if he succeeds in following the models set forth in the

[1]Nandikeshvara, *The Mirror of Gesture. Being the Abhinaya Darpaṇa of Nandikeshvara*, trans. A. K. Coomaraswamy and Gopala K. Duggirala, p. 3.

Nāṭya-śāstra perfectly, his actions appear spontaneous and graceful, while in fact this appearance is the result of great self-control.

> The perfect actor has the same complete and calm command of gesture that the puppet showman has over the movements of his puppets; the exhibition of his art is altogether independent of his own emotional condition. . . . Excellent acting wears the air of perfect spontaneity, but that is the art which conceals art.[1]

It was suggested above that certain types of play may be used in cult as a means toward participating in the divine sphere. The passage from the *Nāṭya-śāstra* suggests the same thing. By strictly imitating models one can approximate the actions of the gods. By playacting one can deny the bondage of action done "from the conscious working of the will." In this sense play, or playacting, may be used as a technique whereby one can gain release from the wheel of cause and effect. The accomplished actor is able to detach himself completely from the actions he is performing, to enjoy his own acting as a spectator. His bodily movements, facial expressions, and speech do not reflect his personal inclinations or individual emotions. His actions belong to the "other" world of grace and perfection, the world revealed by the gods. The actor's being becomes transparent, allowing the character he is portraying to reveal itself through him. And insofar as the actor completely identifies himself with the actions he is imitating, insofar as he may become overwhelmed or seized by his model, he comes to participate in the state of being called the "other mind" (*anyamānas*).[2] The one who experiences this state of being finds liberation, release from the finite limitations of the human sphere. His movements are no longer jerky and abrupt but fluid and easy.

The actor's art, then, may become a vehicle for release, and the techniques he uses may be compared to the *sādhana* of the *yogin*. The "other mind" of the one who loses himself in his model and the techniques employed to achieve this state, while they are clearly not the same as *samādhi* and the discipline

---

[1] *Ibid.*, p. 4.

[2] Beryl De Zoete, *The Other Mind: A Study of Dance in South India*, p. 13.

of *yoga*, have not been unjustifiably compared to them. Coomaraswamy says:

> The arts are not for our instruction, but for our delight, and this delight is something more than pleasure, it is the godlike ecstasy of liberation from the restless activity of the mind and senses which are the veils of all reality, transparent only when we are at peace with ourselves. . . . And for this reason Tiruvenkatacari does not hesitate to compare the actor's or dancer's art with the practice of Yoga. The secret of all art is self-forgetfulness.[1]

Another author on the subject agrees with this estimate of the arts as efficacious.

> Acting, in the true sense of the term as understood in India, is not mere impersonation, however clever or illusionistic the effect. The actor is compared to a *yogi*, meaning thereby that he is one who treads the path of *yoga* (union) or mental concentration, whereby the subject and the object, the worshipper and the worshipped, the actor and the acted become one.[2]

The discipline of the actor, I think, may be compared to that of the *yogin* insofar as the actor, like the *yogin*, seeks to remove himself from the limitations of the human realm by controlling his own impulses and emotions and seeking to act and be beside himself, as it were, in complete control of his every action and thought. But whether or not the parallel with *yoga* is completely justified, the point remains that the technique of the actor is employed as a means of attaining an impersonal state of release, and this is the point that I wish to emphasize.

The function of drama and acting as a means of release is clearly articulated in the case of Kathakaḷi, the dance-drama of Keraḷa and the Malabār Coast. Kathakaḷi itself is carried out in a ritualistic, almost cultic, context, the stage representing the cosmos and the dramatic material being almost exclusively mythological.

---

[1]Nandikeshvara, *The Mirror of Gesture*, p. 9.

[2]K. Bharatha Iyer, *Kathakali*: *The Sacred Dance-Drama of Malabar*, p. 26.

Kathakaḷi is conducted like a ritual and everything connected with it is invested with religious significance. Kathakaḷi actors have a tradition concerning the stage which gives it a highly symbolic significance. The stage represents the world that has come into being in space by the primal act of the Creator. The thick blazing wick of the oil lamp set towards the stage and the thinner one facing the audience symbolise the sun and the moon. . . . The curtain is *rajani* or *tamas* (the darkness that divides). Behind it a couple of dancers execute an invocative dance called *Tōḍayaṃ*. They stand for *Māya* and *Sakti*. The dancers remain unseen by the spectators, just as these forces work beyond the ken of human perception; their activities represent *lila*, the endless play of cosmic forces. There is no background for the stage, for life emerges from the dark, unknown void and there can be no background to the sport of the gods which transcends time and space. In this endless process of the advent of gods and mythological heroes, there is only an un-veiling or falling off of the veils that obstruct vision.[1]

The techniques of the actors, and the transformations that take place as a result of their ability, however, are my main concern. The actors, first of all, are trained from childhood by a *guru* to become adequate vehicles for displaying the sport of the gods. They are particularly schooled in how to imitate perfectly various moods according to revealed models and to keep in abeyance their own emotions and impulses. Elaborate masks and make-up, which are believed to be exact replicas of the faces of the gods and heroes, further reduce any individual characteristics of the actor from interfering with his aim of portraying a divine model. Through vigorous and long practice the Kathakaḷi actor eventually achieves the kind of control over his body that a *yogin* achieves over his. And, like the *yogin*, he becomes, in the words of one author on the subject, endowed with "super-human qualities, mental and physical."[2] After saluting the lamp and praying, the actor

gains a new grandeur and stature and his transformation

[1] *Ibid.*, pp. 23-24.
[2] *Ibid.*, p. 42.

> into a mythological hero is complete. He is that and no longer himself and he steps out in an "elevated mood." The actors no longer walk in the usual way but with heavy stamping steps, expressing an accentuated rhythmical tension; this is so both when they come out of the green-room and return to it from the stage. The several stylized manners of walking, even the position of the feet which touch the ground with their outer edge only, suggest super-worldly origin.[1]

According to another observer the actors are "like creatures who walk the earth as guests, though possessing also other means of motion."[2]

It is of course difficult to say to what extent an actor imitating a model actually becomes identified with that model. The intention of Kathakaḷi, and particularly the actors, however, is quite clear. It is to make present the mythology and the mythological figures upon which Kathakaḷi is based. And this is accomplished by "dehumanizing" the actors, as it were. The actors strive to submerge themselves in the character they are portraying, to let that character use their bodies, to become transparent in order to let that character reveal itself through them. They do this by carefully performing every action in a prescribed way, in a way that has been revealed by the gods and in many cases is in imitation of the gods. The nature of the prescribed *mudrās* and the fantastic masks results in the portrayal of characters that move and behave in extraordinary ways. The actors hold in control or overcome the merely human aspects of their being by patterning every movement on their extraordinary models, and in the process they become extraordinary beings themselves. Carl Jung has observed Kathakaḷi, and his remarks are pertinent.

> It is not the world of the senses, the body, colour and sound, or human passions, which are born anew in transfigured form through the creative power of the Indian soul; but it seems as if there were an "underworld" or an "overworld" of a

[1] *Ibid.*, p. 53.
[2] G. Boner, *Story Plays in Living Tradition*; quoted *ibid.*, p. 53 n.

metaphysical nature, out of which strange forms emerge into the familiar earthly world. If one observes closely the tremendously impressive impersonation of the gods, performed by the Southern Indian Kathakali dancers, there is not a single natural gesture to be seen. Everything is bizarre, both sub-human and super-human. The dancer-gods do not walk like people—they glide; they do not seem to think with their heads—but with their hands. Even the human faces disappear behind artistic blue enamelled masks. Our known world offers nothing which can be compared to such grotesque grandeur. When watching one of these spectacles one is transported into a world of dreams, for that is the only place where we might conceivably meet anything similar. The representations of the Kathakali dancers, or those depicted in the temple pictures, are, however, no nocturnal phantasms. They are tensely dynamic figures, logically constructed with the finest details, or as if they had grown organically.[1]

The realm of the gods, the *līlā* of the gods, is made present in Kathakaḷi. And it is made present by means of dramatic representation, particularly playacting. Indian dance-drama as exemplified by Kathakaḷi demonstrates clearly that playacting may be used as a technique of release, a means of submerging the limitations of the human by imitating transcendent models. This type of play, at first, is quite different from the sport of the gods. It is highly structured, it must be learned, and it requires great self-control. It is, nevertheless, play. It is nonproductive activity, it is done for amusement, it is removed from the ordinary world. Insofar as it is rigidly bound to follow prescribed models, however, it lacks the freedom of other types of play. There is very little room at all for spontaneity. On the contrary, the actors' impulses must be carefully controlled. But what is striking about this play, or playacting, is that it may, and often does, lead to freedom in release. When the actor succeeds in becoming beside himself, his actions cease to be his own and become those of the character he is portraying. When,

[1] C. G. Jung, "On the Psychology of Eastern Meditation," trans. Carol Baumann, in K. Bharatha Iyer (ed.), *Art and Thought*, p. 169.

and if, this happens the actor ceases to imitate and begins to participate in the realm of the "other." In his "elevated mood" his actions cease to be the result of "the conscious working of the will" and begin to "spring from a natural disposition of mind." His actions become effortless and graceful, not stilted or studied. In Indian dance-drama the actor begins by engaging in a highly structured type of play that aims at achieving a state in which his acting becomes natural and free, indeed, in which his acting ceases to be acting and becomes participation. The movement is from *ludus* to *paidia*, from highly ordered play to spontaneous, effortless movement.

What is true for the actor is also true for the audience in Indian dance-drama, and, indeed, for the connoisseur of Indian art generally. Just as the actor may achieve the state of the "other mind," so the witness to his performance may achieve a state that is similarly transcendent. The aim of Indian art generally, whether it be drama, poetry, painting or music, is to create *rasa*, usually translated as "sentiment." The root, or basic stuff, from which *rasa* is created is *bhāva*, "emotion." According to Sanskrit poetic theory there are eight or nine dominant emotions (*sthāyi-bhāvas*): love (*rati*), mirth (*hāsa*), sorrow (*śoka*), anger (*krodha*), energy (*utsāha*), fear (*bhaya*), disgust (*jugupsā*), and wonder (*vismaya*). A ninth, namely, self-disparagement (*nirveda*), is included by some theorists. Each of these *bhāvas* has its corresponding *rasa*: the erotic (*śṛṅgāra*), comic (*hāsya*), pathetic (*karuṇa*), furious (*raudra*), heroic (*vīra*), terrible (*bhayānaka*), disgustful (*bibhatsa*), marvelous (*adbhuta*), and quietistic (*śānta*). The basic aim of Indian art is to transform a particular *bhāva* into a corresponding *rasa*. This is done by setting a dominant mood by means of portraying the appropriate excitants (*vibhāvas*), ensuants (*anubhāvas*), and accessories (*vyabhicāri-bhāvas*).

The *bhāvas* are essentially individual or particular, and it is not the purpose of Indian art to portray a particular individual's anger, love, or wonder. Indian art, rather, seeks to make present anger, love, or wonder generically—as a universal sentiment. Poetry, for example, does not strive to depict the emotional feelings of a particular character in a given situation but tries, by means of various particulars to be sure, to create a context of mood from which the universal sentiment of love or anger may be relished by the connoisseur. Thus a poem or play about the love of Rāma and Sītā, while it may go to great length describing or portraying the situations and particulars of the love between these two, seeks by so doing to create a mood that will give rise to the rasa of *śṛṅgāra*.

Rasa, unlike *bhāva*, is impersonal—it is not dependent upon, but may arise from, individual emotions. It does not presuppose personal circumstances; it does not arise necessarily from biographical or historical situations. It is not associated with pain or pleasure, which imply personal circumstances and emotion. A particular *rasa* may be relished or experienced quite apart from the individual's personal emotion. A connoisseur, for example, may relish the sentiment of the pathetic manifest in the mood of a particular poem or drama without himself having the emotion of sorrow. The overriding experience of every *rasa*, whether of the comic or the terrible, is joy—a joy that stems from relishing an impersonal, universal sentiment that transcends individual particularity.

> The resulting relish, therefore, is neither pain nor pleasure in the natural sense, which is found in the ordinary emotions of life associated with personal interests. . . , a relish dissociated from all such interests, consisting of pure joy free from the contact of everything else perceived but itself. Put another way, an ordinary emotion (*bhāva*) may be pleasurable or painful; but a poetic sentiment (*rasa*), transcending the limitations of the personal attitude, is lifted above such pain and pleasure into pure joy, the essence of which is its relish itself.
>
> The artistic attitude is thus given as different from the naturalistic and closely akin to but not identical with the philosophic. It is like the state of the soul serenely contemplating the absolute (*brahmāsvāda*), with the difference that the state of detachment is not so complete or permanent. The artistic attitude is thus recognised as entirely spiritual. But the idealised artistic creation affords only a temporary release from the ills of life by enabling one to transcend, for the moment, personal relations or practical interests; it restores equanimity of mind (*viśrānti*) by leading one away, for the time being, from the natural world and offering another in its place. It is an attitude of pure bliss, detached

spiritual contemplation (*citsvabhāva saṃvid*), similar to but not the same as the state of true enlightenment.[1]

Viśvanātha in his *Sāhitya-darpaṇa* says of *rasāsvādana*, the experience of tasting *rasa* :

> It is pure, indivisible, self-manifested, compounded equally of joy and consciousness, free of admixture with any other perception, the very twin brother of mystic experience (*Brahmasvadana sahodarah*), and the very life of it is supersensuous (*lokottara*) wonder.[2]

The audience, the reader—the connoisseur of art—then, may also participate in a condition similar to the actor's state of the "other mind." Artistic creation, whether it be dramatic, musical, or poetic, can serve as a vehicle of transcendence to anyone who has the capacity to relish, or taste, the particular dominant mood impersonally, as a universal sentiment.

> This blissful condition [*rasāsvādana*] reproduced in the reader by the idealised creation of poetry is given as almost equivalent to the philosophical *ānanda*. In explaining that it affords an escape from the natural world by replacing it with an imaginative world, Sanskrit theorists rightly emphasise that, even from the reader's point of view, *the function of art is that of the deliverer.*[3]

Indian artistic theory affirms that within the realm of amusement, within the imaginative worlds of drama, music, poetry, and painting, man may find not only diversion and enjoyment but a certain transcendence, a release from bondage to the personal and emotional circumstances of his particular biography. Whereas in other traditions this function of art may be called "an escape from reality," or "a flight of fancy," and implicitly denigrated, in the context of Indian art the experience of *rasa* is considered precious and likened to the spiritual bliss (*ānanda*) of union with Brahman. Drama and art generally have the ability to draw man out of himself, as it were, to effect in him a

[1]S. K. De, *Sanskrit Poetics as a Study of Aesthetic*, pp. 12-13.
[2]Quoted in Coomaraswamy, *The Dance of Shiva*, p. 41.
[3]De, *Sanskrit Poetics as a Study of Aesthetic*, p. 69 (italics mine).

forgetfulness of self that enables him to transcend the condition of acting or feeling according to "the conscious working of the will." The key to experiencing *rasa*, as in the case of the actor and the "other mind," is self-forgetfulness, the ability to suspend one's involvement in the strictly personal. To taste *rasa* requires, as the *Bhagavadgitā* would say, to act without regard for fruits. It requires the ability to transcend the ordinary and enter the imaginary, to revel in the superfluous.

C. *Becoming Kṛṣṇa's Lover*

In Bengal Vaiṣṇavism man's relationship to god is understood within the context of drama and is nurtured by means of dramatic technique. The drama depicted is that of the purāṇic Kṛṣṇa, with particular emphasis upon his love for the *gopis* and Rādhā, and dramatic technique is employed as a means of enabling the devotee to participate in the drama by becoming a companion of Kṛṣṇa.

Bengal Vaiṣṇavism is not unique in conceiving of a transcendent order in dramatic terms, as a sphere to be reiterated and dramatically re-created. Bengal Vaiṣṇavism, however, has consciously and deliberately conceived man's relationship to Kṛṣṇa within the context of classical dramatic theory, for the structure of drama and dramatic theory was a particularly congenial mode for expressing and realizing man's relationship to god. In Bengal Vaiṣṇavism the highly articulated theory of aesthetics and drama that had come to be established over the centuries was transplanted to the realm of cult almost without change. In Bengal Vaiṣṇava cult the biography of Kṛṣṇa as revealed in the *purāṇas*, particularly the *Bhāgavata-purāṇa*, and in other sources is conceived of as continually taking place in dramatic form. The devotee, in this case, becomes the artistic connoisseur. And like the artistic connoisseur the devotee seeks to experience *rasa* as a result of the dramatic display that is continually taking place in a transcendental realm. In this peculiar context, however, *rasa* is of a new and different sort—it is the experience of *bhakti-rasa*. And unlike the aesthetic sentiment of *rasāsvādana*, *bhakti-rasa* is not a temporary state but a permanent condition that transforms the devotee into a heavenly being.[1]

Within the context of cult Kṛṣṇa is understood to be the ideal hero, indeed the only hero, having to a superlative degree all those attributes necessary to the hero of classical Indian drama.[2] He is pleasant, powerful, youthful, a good speaker, reserved, clever, and everything else appropriate to a hero.[3] Rādhā is the ideal heroine and likewise is portrayed as possessing all essential qualities of the classical heroine.[4] In the context of cult, the devotee is put in the position of responding to a dramatic performance, of which Kṛṣṇa is the hero and Rādhā the heroine. And like the aesthetic connoisseur his aim is to have the experience of *rasa*, which in this case is called *bhakti-rasa*, a pure, all-pervading sentiment of selfless love toward Kṛṣṇa, a sentiment possessed by Kṛṣṇa's companions and epitomized by the *gopīs* and Rādhā.

Because *bhakti* is considered a *rasa*, it is also considered impersonal, as in aesthetic theory. This requires of the devotee, therefore, a certain impersonalization. He is required, as is

---

[1]For a discussion of the alterations made in classic aesthetic theory by the Bengal Vaiṣṇava theorists, see Sushil Kumar De, *History of Sanskrit Poetics*, Vol. II: *Systems and Theories*, pp. 335 ff.

[2]Kṛṣṇa was not always seen as the ideal, sophisticated hero in Bengal. In a Bengali drama of the fourteenth or fifteenth century, *Śrīkṛṣṇakīrttana* by Baḍu Caṇḍīdāsa, for example, he is depicted as "utterly unscrupulous and seduces Rādhā with the cunning and credulity of a village lout." Mukherji, *Vaiṣṇavism in Ancient and Medieval Bengal*, p. 132.

[3]See Rūpa Gosvāmin, *Ujjvala-nīlamaṇi*, translated into Bengali by Rāmanārāyaṇa Vidyāratna, ed. Rasabihāri Sāṁkhyatīrtha, pp. 8-9, for a detailed list of such characteristics.

[4]Kṛṣṇa is more than simply the ideal hero in Bengal Vaiṣṇava cult, of course. He is the source of all *rasa*; indeed, he is *rasa* itself. This idea, actually, is quite ancient in India and precedes any clearly developed theory of aesthetics. In the *upaniṣads* Brahman is identified with *rasa*, which in the *upaniṣads* is regarded as the essence of all beauty and similar to *ānanda*, bliss. In *Taittirīya-upaniṣad* II. 7. 1 it is said: "He that is self-acting, He is *rasa* itself. Getting that *rasa* one is possessed by *ānanda*. And He makes others taste *ānanda*." The significance of this is that Kṛṣṇa, as the ideal hero, is more than simply the vehicle, or means, for conveying the mood through which *rasa* may be tasted. He controls that flow and is identical with it. In this sense it is possible to speak of grace, to speak of Kṛṣṇa bestowing *bhakti* upon a devotee while still ma intaining the position of the hero in the drama.

the aesthetic connoisseur, to lose himself in the mood of the drama, to resist involving his own personal desires and emotions. Before he can soar to the heights of all-consuming love for Kṛṣṇa he must forget himself, disassociate himself from those particular circumstances and feelings that make him unique. *Bhakti*, like *rasa* with which it is identified, is not understood to be a feeling or emotion that belongs to the realm of the sensual, that can be "felt," that can come and go according to various circumstances of mood, that can ever belong to particular individuals. *Bhakti*, like *rasa*, seems to be a thing in itself, an essence that exists apart from any individual but that can be experienced by individuals once they have divested themselves of individuality. In Bengal Vaiṣṇava devotional theory a particularly successful means of experiencing *bhakti* is by employing the methods of the actor in classical dance-drama. The effectiveness of the actor's method derives from the fact that he must discipline himself to forget or control his own emotions and reactions in order to let the character he is portraying appear through him. By playacting the devotee seeks to lose his identity by accommodating the identity of another. The devotee, like the actor, seeks to play a role and, like the actor in classical dance-drama, seeks to play it well and effectively by so completely identifying with the role that he loses himself, or forgets himself.

In Bengal Vaiṣṇava cult the roles available to the devotee are necessarily limited by the dramatic material available, which is the biography of Kṛṣṇa as set forth in the *purāṇas* and other sources. In fact, the roles considered appropriate to the devotee are all patterned on the various companions of Kṛṣṇa found throughout his biography in Vṛndāvana. The types of roles, therefore, are limited by the types of companions he had there and are considered to consist of four main types: servant, friend, parent, and lover. As far as experiencing *bhakti-rasa* is concerned, these are the four main *bhāvas*, or *sthāyi-bhāvas*, within which, or from which, *bhakti* may arise. While the devotional theorists of the cult admit that there are other *sthāyi-bhāvas* (eight or nine are generally admitted following classical theory), these four alone are relevant in the context of the great Kṛṣṇa drama.[1]

[1]It is clear that these four *bhāvas* do not correspond in any clear way to the *sthāyī-bhāvas* of classical aesthetic theory. Indeed, only two, those of the

All four are perhaps understood best from the point of view of classical aesthetic theory as modifications of one *rasa*, the erotic, *śṛṅgāra*. Although they are spoken of as being four different *sthāhyi-bhāvas* or *rasas*, they all fall under the category of love. They are all expressions of the general *bhāva* of *rati* and the *rasa* of *śṛṅgāra*.[1] In fact, it is fair to say that, within Bengal Vaiṣṇavism, devotion in the form of *bhakti* is consistently understood to be love of one kind or another. Wonder and awe, for example, are almost dismissed as worthy expressions of devotion. The attitude of the servant, therefore, is by far the most inferior of the four *bhāva-rasas*, for it lacks the intimacy of real love and has elements of fear that imply an impersonal distance between Kṛṣṇa and his devotees. The attitude of the lover, on the other hand, is the superior of the four because it implies great intimacy with the divine. While the attitude of the lover is considered the best, it is important that the devotee choose the mood that is appropriate to him. With the help of his *guru* the devotee should choose to imitate a role that suits his devotional and emotional proclivities.[2] The idea of imitating roles, of seeking

---

servant (*dāsya*) and the lover (*mādhurya*), can be said to correspond to the classical formulation. *Dāsya* corresponds to the *bhāva* of *nirveda* and the *rasa* of *śānta*, while *mādhurya* corresponds to the *bhāva* of *rati* and the *rasa* of *śṛṅgāra*. In fact, of course, the whole devotional system is suspect according to classical theory, where no experience vis-à-vis a transcendent reality such as Kṛṣṇa or Brahman is admitted to the possible basic emotions or sentiments. See De, *History of Sanskrit Poetics*, II, 350-51.

[1]It is clear that in the biography of Kṛṣṇa there were some individuals who responded to him negatively. There were those who were jealous of or antagonistic toward him. And it has even been argued in the cult whether Kṛṣṇa's enemies gained release by being possessed by negative *bhāvas* and *rasas* such as anger-fury and fear-terror. Jīva Gosvāmin is of the opinion that even negative *bhāvas* may be efficacious. Of Pūtanā, who tried to poison Kṛṣṇa with her nipples and later gained release, he says: "Take this paradigm: by simulating the role of a nurse Pūtanā gained her liberation. . . . Pūtanā, the killer of infants, the blood-thirsty one, though she gave her milk to Kṛṣṇa with feelings of revenge and enmity, yet was released" (*Bhakti-saṁdarbha* [Bengali], ed. Bhakti Vilās Tīrtha Mahārāj, *śloka*, 312, p. 348). He also mentions the case of Śiśupāla and other kings, who were enemies of Kṛṣṇa but gained release because their thoughts were constantly occupied with him (*śloka* 321, p. 355).

[1]Rūpa Gosvāmin, *Bhakti-rasāmṛta-sindhu*, Eastern Division: Second Wave, *śloka* 296, Jīva Gosvāmin's commentary (I, 307). See also Kṛṣṇadāsa Kavirāja *Caitanya-caritāmṛta*, Madhya-līlā 22. 91 (p. 563).

to become like Kṛṣṇa's companions, is called the royal doctrine, *rājatattva*, in Bengal Vaiṣṇavism but is more commonly known as *rāgānugā bhakti*.

Rāgānugā bhakti was first articulated in a theoretical way in the *Bhakti-rasāmṛta-sindhu* of Rūpa Gosvāmin, one of the six scholarly devotees personally chosen by Caitanya to formulate the theology and philosophy of the sect at Vṛndāvana in the sixteenth century. According to Rūpa there are two principal types of devotion: *vaidhī* and *rāgānugā*. The first type follows scriptural injunctions and involves primarily outward actions, such as service to a *guru*; respect for cows, *brāhmans*, and Vaiṣṇavas; refusal to associate with non-Vaiṣṇavas; and pilgrimage to Vaiṣṇava holy places.[1] Through *vaidhī bhakti* the devotee seeks to obtain and nourish a basic faith in Kṛṣṇa. He seeks to follow the injunctions of the scriptures, which teach submission to Kṛṣṇa. This type of devotion, however, is considered limited and mechanical, as it is induced by external forms. It is conditional insofar as it is "based upon the fear of transgression; and as fear enters as an element in guiding devotional practices, this method must be regarded as somewhat formal and mechanical."[2]

A more excellent type of devotion derives from an inward feeling of greed for Kṛṣṇa on the part of the devotee. When there arises spontaneously within the devotee a yearning for Kṛṣṇa, the need for following scriptural injunctions becomes irrelevant, and a new and higher path becomes appropriate for channeling his devotion. This new path is called *rāgānugā*. It is based upon the devotion displayed by Kṛṣṇa's companions in Vṛndāvana, which was of an intense, spontaneous type. Their devotion to him is called *rāgātmikā bhakti*, and devotion that seeks to pattern itself upon it is called *rāgānugā bhakti*. "Bhakti that is distinctly and uniquely and spontaneously manifest in the Brajavāsīs [inhabitants of Vraja, Vṛndāvana] is called *Rāgātmikā Bhakti*, and Bhakti that arises in the wake of this *Rāgātmikā Bhakti* is called *Rāgānugā Bhakti*."[3]

[1] There are usually sixty-four such actions listed in Bengal Vaiṣṇava literature. See Gopāla Bhaṭṭa *Hari-bhakti-vilāsa* 1. 40 and 4. 144.

[2] De, *Vaisnava Faith and Movement*, p. 373.

[3] Rūpa Gosvāmin, *Bhakti-rasāmṛta-sindhu*, Eastern Division: Second Wave, *śloka* 270 (I, 268).

Having passed beyond the need for following the injunctions of the scriptures, the devotee's *bhakti* now follows "in the wake of" the devotion of Kṛṣṇa's companions. Indeed, the devotee seeks to pattern his feelings for Kṛṣṇa on those of the inhabitants of Vṛndāvana. He seeks to become a lover of Kṛṣṇa by expressing his love in the context of one of the four *sthāyi-bhāvas* mentioned above.[1] He seeks to become, or have the attitude of, a servant, friend, parent, or lover of Kṛṣṇa. He does this by the constant exercise of his imagination, by remembering constantly the life of Kṛṣṇa and particularly the role of Kṛṣṇa's companions. He seeks to make the *līlā* of Kṛṣṇa actually happen within himself, within the realm of his imagination. He tries to live entirely within a transcendent world that is conjured up constantly by remembering and imagination.[2] He imagines himself to be actually a participant in that transcendent sport of Kṛṣṇa, to be taking on the identity of one of Kṛṣṇa's companions. *Rāgānugā*

> consists of devoted meditation or recollection (*smaraṇa*) of Kṛṣṇa and his dear ones (*preṣṭha*), and living either physically or mentally in Vraja, as a Sādhaka or as a Siddha, following the ways of Vraja-loka (*vraja-lokānusārataḥ*) with a desire to realise the same state of feeling (*tadbhāva-lipsā*). One desirous of this way of realisation will adopt the particular Bhāva (e.g. Rādhā-bhāva, Sakhī-bhāva, etc.) of the particular favourite of Kṛṣṇa according to his or her Līlā, Veśa and Svabhāva, and live in the ecstasy of that vicarious enjoyment.[3]

> It is only in a spiritual *siddha-deha* . . . in any one of the Four *Sthāyi-bhāvas* that the soul progresses in *Rāgānugā Bhakti*. When this happens, the individual then contemplates mentally in the stage of Rāgānugā Bhakti a spiritual body *as a Gopī*, more technically a *Mañjarī*, with a particular *name*, conception of her *form and beauty*, her particular *age*, her *costumes*, her specialised *service or seva*, her *grove* or *Kuñja* where she receives and serves the Divine Couple, special

[1]Kṛṣṇadāsa Kavirāja *Caitanya-caritāmṛta*, Madhya-līlā 22. 92 (p. 564).
[2]*Ibid*. 22. 90 (p. 563).
[3]De, *Vaisnava Faith and Movement*, p. 176.

> *bhāva* such as *madhyā* or *dhīra-madhyā*, etc., the special characteristics of her Beloved as *Nāyaka*.[1]

The devotee seeks to involve himself completely in the ongoing drama of Kṛṣṇa by identifying himself with one or another of its participants. In effect, the devotee seeks to replace the ordinary world with the imaginative world of Kṛṣṇa and his companions. While remaining physically in the ordinary world, he seeks to remove himself from it by constantly remembering the transcendental world of Kṛṣṇa and imagining himself to be a part of that world. With the help of scriptural descriptions he tries to conjure up a world that is as real and immediate to him as the ordinary world in which he normally lives. This technique of devotion is playful insofar as it involves both play-acting and the use of the imagination.

While certain external actions may accompany *rāgānugā*, such as living in Vṛndāvana, this devotional technique takes place almost entirely within the heart and imagination of the devotee. An immediate goal on the part of the devotee is to acquire a spiritual body, a *siddha* body that is in no way attached to the physical world. While this body theoretically may be either male or female, it is almost always spoken of as female. Narottama-dāsa, one of the leading figures of the cult in the seventeenth century, elaborated Rūpa Gosvāmin's theory of *rāgānugā* and put great emphasis upon the cultivation of a spiritual body. And it is interesting to note that when he speaks of *rāgānugā* he almost always speaks in terms of having the spiritual body of a *mañjarī* (a female friend of the *gopīs*) or a *gopī*.

> This is my opinion about the way of worship in tune with *rāga*. And this message is the essence of the *Vedas*, a great guide to men. Be a follower of the *sakhīs*, and acquire a divine body like theirs in Vraja. In this way quench the thirst of your mind.[2]

The great emphasis in Bengal Vaiṣṇavism upon becoming a

---

[1]Rūpa Gosvāmin, *Bhakti-rasāmṛta-sindhu*, Eastern Division: Second Wave, *śloka* 295, translator's note (I, 306).

[2]Narottama-dāsa, *Prema-bhakti-candrikā* (Bengali), ed. Rādhika Nāth Śarma, p. 73.

female friend (*sakhi*) of Kṛṣṇa, a *gopī*, or a female creates a
curious situation. Emotionally and mentally, within the devotee's imaginary world, he seeks constantly to identify himself
with the *gopīs*. Externally, however, he is encouraged to behave
as, and appear like, an ascetic. This dual role is more clearly
elaborated in another work by Narottama-dāsa, which has been
referred to as a "manual for ascetics."[1] The devotee is encouraged to dress outwardly like an ascetic and live the austere,
detached life of a *yogin*. But within he is to imagine himself
cavorting with Kṛṣṇa as a female. He is even to imagine that
his *guru* is a *gopī* and to serve him as such.

> According to the advice of their *gurus* who are in a state of
> *siddha* as *sakhīs* of Kṛṣṇa, those who follow the way of *rāga*
> must be their *gurus'* serving maids in their *sādhana*. The
> *sādhakas*, imagining themselves as *gopī* women, decorated with
> the garlands and dresses given to them by the grace of Rādhā,
> and thus appearing enchantingly beautiful to Kṛṣṇa, should
> take themselves to be the companions of such *sakhīs* as Lalitā
> and others, and then following their advice and command
> should do service to Rādhā and Kṛṣṇa. This mental act
> of identification should be followed by making up in every
> way, with coloring, dress, ornaments, way of living, playful
> habits, and so on in tune with the *sādhaka*'s object of identi-
> fication, and according to that identification personal rela-
> tionships with others should also be determined . . . . Creating
> imaginatively this divine body on the mental plane, the
> *sādhaka* should imaginatively recollect the *līlā* of Rādhā and
> Kṛṣṇa, every moment of the day and night, and this is the true
> *sādhana* of the *sādhaka*.[2]

One of the most important factors in *rāgānugā* is imaginative
recollection (*smaraṇa*). The devotee of Kṛṣṇa in Bengal Vaiṣṇavism is, in outward appearance, much the same as ascetics of
other *sampradāyas*. The central fact of his *sādhana*, however, is
an inward playacting. Like ascetics of other orders he seeks to
shun the ordinary world, to become detached from it. His

[1]Melville Kennedy, *The Chaitanya Movement: A Study of Vaishnavism of Bengal*, p. 166.
[2]Narottama-dāsa, *Vairāgya-nirṇaya* (Bengali), pp. 11-12.

technique, however, is not negative. The emphasis is not upon denying the world of the senses but upon acquiring by imagination a different, transcendent world. The Bengal Vaiṣṇava devotee does not seek to still his mind but to stir it by imagination. In *yoga* the *sādhaka* attains *samādhi* by immobilizing his mind and intellect—by stopping the imaginative process. In Bengal Vaiṣṇavism the devotee attains *samādhi* by ceaselessly imagining himself to be a female companion of Kṛṣṇa.[1] Like the actor in classical dance-drama he attains a state of mind that is "other" by identifying himself with another being. He loses himself in an imaginary world by assuming the identity of an imaginary character. When his imaginary world comes to completely dominate his life he achieves a state in which he is beside himself, outside himself. Through imagination, by means of "the alchemy of 'as if,'" the devotee transcends the ordinary world and enters the transcendent world of Kṛṣṇa.

In discussing the technique of the classical actor in India I emphasized the fact that he must rigidly follow prescribed models in order to excel, in order to give his art the appearance of spontaneity. In the *Nāṭya-śāstra* it was explained that man habitually behaves according to "the conscious working of the will." It was also noted, however, that when the actor loses himself in the role he is portraying he acquires a state of mind known as *anyamānas*, the "other mind," in which his actions, in fact, do become spontaneous, like those of the gods. The technique of *rāgānugā*, similarly, demands of the devotee that he follow prescribed models. He is not free to express his devotional love for Kṛṣṇa spontaneously, according to his own emotions and desires. He is instructed, rather, to pattern his devotion on the companions of Kṛṣṇa. It is understood that only insofar as he can identify with Kṛṣṇa's companions, "through years of constant practice," can he attain *bhakti-rasa*.[2] *Rāgānugā*, however, is not understood to be slavish imitation only. At a certain point, when the devotee begins to feel a strong identification with the model he is imitating, he is encouraged to behave freely within the confines of the character he is portraying. His aim,

---

[1]Narottama-dāsa, *Prema-bhakti-candrikā*, p. 44.

[2]De, *Vaisnava Faith and Movement*, p. 178.

in fact, is to have imitation become actual participation. S. K. De says of *rāgānugā*:

> It is governed by no mechanical Śāstric rules whatever, even if they are not necessarily discarded; it follows the natural inclination of the heart, and depends entirely upon one's own emotional capacity of devotion. The devotee by his ardent meditation not only seeks to visualise and make the whole Vṛndāvana-līlā of Kṛṣṇa live before him, but he enters into it imaginatively, and by playing the part of a beloved of Kṛṣṇa, he experiences vicariously the passionate feelings which are so vividly pictured in the literature.[1]

The centrality of conceiving of Kṛṣṇa's biography in terms of an ongoing drama and the importance of playacting in the cult are illustrated by two other phenomena that I would like to mention before discussing the importance of other types of play in the cult. Bengal Vaiṣṇavism is noted for its lovely devotional poetry. The love of Rādhā and Kṛṣṇa—indeed, almost every aspect of Kṛṣṇa's biography—is celebrated in thousands of poems that are cherished by the sect. Consistent with aesthetic theory, each poem is written in a particular *bhāva* with the intention of evoking in the reader or audience the experience or state of *bhakti-rasa*. And when sung or read in devotional context, usually *kīrtan*, the poems are sung in consistent groups. That is, several poems in the same mood are sung rather than several poems in different moods. In extraordinary circumstances, when *kīrtan* may last all night, the entire biography of Kṛṣṇa may be delivered in poetic song, in which case all varieties of moods will be presented in the course of reiterating his biography. In content the poems deal with Kṛṣṇa's life and in effect reproduce a dramatic context in which the audience or participants in *kīrtan* may experience *bhakti-rasa*. But the poems are also vehicles for dramatic participation for the poet himself, and by extension for the reader, too, as is clearly seen by the poet's signature line, or *bhanita*. For the poet's signature line frequently illustrates that the poet himself has taken one role or another vis-à-vis the scene he is describing. In descriptions of

---

[1]*Ibid.*, p. 177.

the child Kṛṣṇa, for example, the poet will often write about the anxiety of Yaśodā, Kṛṣṇa's foster mother, as she contemplates the possible dangers to the child when he follows the cows to pasture. In a typical poem Kṛṣṇa begs his mother to let him follow the older boys to the forest with the cows. She responds to his plea by saying: "How can those tender feet keep pace / With the restless calves in the forest?" and then begins to weep and falls down in a faint. The poet's signature line is: "Vipradāsa Ghoṣ says, 'How can the mother bear it / If one goes to the pasture at such a tender age?' "[1] The poet speaks from the point of view of a parent, from the point of view of *vātsalya-rasa*, the mood in which the poem is written. In the following poem the author's degree of participation is even more marked. Yaśodā is speaking and pleads with Kṛṣṇa to be careful when out tending the cows:

Life of my life, O Blue Jewel!
Promise you would not run before the cows.

Let the cows graze near and play on your flute
So that I may hear it from the house.

Valāi will go in front of you with the others on the left
Śrīdama and Sudama should be behind you.
Be right in their midst and never stray away.
The pasture-ground is full of dangers.

Eat when you are hungry and watch your steps.
The path is full of keen-edged *kuśa*,
And promise on my head, Kānu,
That you will not listen to anyone
And stay away from the full-grown cows.

[*Bhanita*] Listen to the entreaties of your mother.
Stay in shade, protected from the sun.
Take Jādavendra [the author] with you to carry your shoes.
He will help you to put them on when necessary.[2]

---

[1]From Khagendranath Mitra *et al.* (eds.), *Vaiṣṇava-padāvalī* (Calcutta: University of Calcutta, 1952), no. 16; in Edward C. Dimock and Roushan Jahan, "Bengali Vaisnava Lyrics: A Reader for Advanced Students," no. 8.

[2]From Mitra *et al.* (eds.), *Vaiṣṇava-padāvalī*, no. 17; in Dimock and Jahan, "Bengali Vaisnava Lyrics," no. 9.

Many poems describe the entreaties of either Kṛṣṇa or Rādhā to the other delivered by messengers—entreaties to meet at a given rendezvous or, more often, to give up stubborn pride and return the love of the sender. In this poem Kṛṣṇa's messenger is pleading with Rādhā:

Shining one, golden as the *champa* flower,
the god of fate has given your radiance to you
in sacred offering.
Fortunate one, blessed and golden one,
his dark body shall wed with yours.
Waste nothing of the light of youth,
go quickly to him.

[Signature line] *And Lochana* [the author], *entreating, says, if you go you save the life of Shyām* [Kṛṣṇa].[1]

The poet speaks from the position of the messenger herself, breaking into the scene directly to plead himself with Rādhā to go to Kṛṣṇa. The *bhāva* of this poem is *sākhya-bhāva*, that of friendship to either Rādhā or Kṛṣṇa, and probably the most popular within the cult. Concerning this particular *bhāva* it is notable that, while it may be relished from the male point of view, it is almost always relished from the feminine, as indicated above in my discussion of *rāgānugā*. There is no clear indication in the above poem that Locana-dāsa speaks as a female, although the messenger in any love affair is invariably a woman. In the following poem, however, the feminine *sākhya-bhāva* is clearly adopted by the poet himself.

When they had made love
she lay in his arms in the *kunja* grove.
Suddenly she called his name
and wept—as if she burned in the fire of
separation.
The god was in her *anchal*
but she looked afar for it!
—Where has he gone? Where has my love gone?
O why has he left me alone?

[1]Dimock and Levertov (trans.), *In Praise of Krishna*, p. 38.

And she writhed on the ground in despair,
only her pain kept her from fainting.
Krishna was astonished
and could not speak.

[Signature line of Govindadāsa, a male] *Taking* her *beloved friend by the hand, Govinda-dāsa led her* [Rādhā] *softly away.*[1]

In the process of creating this scene the poet has entered into the action himself, taking on the role of a female friend or confidante of Rādhā. Seeing her despair, the poet steps in directly to offer her comfort as a confidential girlfriend, though the poet himself is not, in fact, a woman.[2]

The signature lines of many poems show that the Vaiṣṇava poets were not reluctant to identify with Rādhā, although the works of the Gosvāmins say this particular stage of *mādhurya-bhāva* is extremely difficult to attain, and among the orthodox Vaiṣṇavas of the present-day cult it is held to be virtually impossible. In a poem by Yadunātha-dāsa, in which Rādhā declares that she cares nothing about the scandalous talk that surrounds her love for Kṛṣṇa, the poet's *bhanita* reads: "Yadunātha-dāsa (identifying himself with Rādhā) says, 'This is the desire of my heart. If there will be, throughout the world, scandalous talk in connection of (myself and) Kṛṣṇa, let that be so.' "[3] In another poem, where Rādhā speaks of the hardships she has had to overcome in order to meet Kṛṣṇa—rain, darkness, snakes, etc.—and declares that these are nothing due to her great love, the poet Govindadāsa ends with: "*I no longer count the pain of coming here, says Govinda-dāsa.*"[4] In a charming poem by Caṇḍīdāsa, Rādhā has become violently upset on account

---

[1]*Ibid.*, p. 23 (emphasis mine).

[2]An indication of how commonly Vaiṣṇava poets identified with females is seen in the following passage from Sukumar Sen, who is arguing the sex of the Vaiṣṇava poet Mādhavī-dāsa. Sen says of those who blithely consider the poet a female: "But the theorists forget that Mādhavī was a devout Vaiṣṇava, and it is the esoteric practice of Vaiṣṇavas to think themselves as women, friends and attendants of Rādhā, and as a matter of fact many Vaiṣṇava (male) poets have subscribed themselves as 'dāsī.' " *Brajabuli Literature*, p. 58.

[3]*Ibid.*, p 471.

[4]Dimock andLevertov (trans.), *In Praise of Krishna*, p. 21.

of her love for Kṛṣṇa. She threatens to commit suicide by drowning in the sea,

> with this last wish:
> that I be born again as Nanda's son [Kṛṣṇa]
> and you [Kṛṣṇa] as Rādhā.
> Then, after loving you, I shall abandon you.
> I shall stand beneath the *kadamba* tree;
> I shall stand in the *tribhanga* pose and play my flute
> as you go to draw water.
> And when you hear the flute you will be enchanted,
> simple girl.
>
> [*Bhanita*] *Chandidāsa says, Then you will know how love can burn.*[1]

In another poem the author describes Rādhā's increasing anger at the thought of Kṛṣṇa's sending a messenger instead of coming to her himself. And, as in the preceding poem, the author shares Rādhā's feeling in his signature line. Rādhā speaks to the messenger whom Kṛṣṇa has sent:

> From the time our eyes first met
> our longing grew.
> He was not only the desirer, I not only the desired:
> passion ground our hearts together in its mortar.
> Friend, do not forget to recall to Krishna
> how it was with us then.
> *Then* we required no messenger, sought
> only each other's lips for our love.
> It was the god of love himself who united us,
> he of the five arrows . . .
> But now my lordly lover has learned new manners,
> now he sends you, herald of his indifference.
>
> [Signature line] *So, with anger like a king's, increasing, sings the poet Rāmānanda Rāy.*[2]

The device of the *bhanita* in these poems clearly shows that

---

[1] *Ibid.*, p. 32.
[2] *Ibid.*, p. 41.

Bengal Vaiṣṇava poetry is more than simply descriptive. The signature lines consistently shift one's point of reference from that of observer to that of participant. By speaking from the point of view of one of the participants, the signature lines give the poetry a dimension of intimacy that is missing in simple, descriptive prose or poetry. This device, furthermore, is not, in my opinion, a simple literary technique. It is perfectly consistent with the theory of *bhāva-rasa* and *rāgānugā* discussed above. The poet, quite simply, imagines himself present at the scene he is describing, and often goes to the extreme of identifying himself with one or another of the protagonists, speaking from that point of view in his signature line. I agree with Edward Dimock's estimate of the degree to which the poets were emotionally or devotionally involved in their poetry. He says:

> In their *bhanitas* (signature lines), they speak directly to the couple, and perhaps offer their comments and suggestions to them. Nor is this mere convention. *Bhāva* is a term which is usually rendered "emotion," but in Vaiṣṇava context it means far more. It signifies such depth of emotion that one's personality is changed. That a *pada*-writer, for example, will be so moved by his vision of the Divine that he will partake of it; that he will feel so much passionate love for Kṛṣṇa that he becomes Rādhā, as Kṛṣṇa's lover. It is a characteristic not only of the *pada*-writers. It is true of Vaiṣṇavas as a whole, and to the present day.[1]

The other phenomenon that illustrates the centrality of conceiving of Kṛṣṇa's biography in terms of an ongoing drama in Bengal Vaiṣṇavism is the belief that Caitanya himself was a reincarnation of Kṛṣṇa (and Rādhā). Caitanya's biography is full of incidents that are obviously patterned on Kṛṣṇa's biography, and he was undoubtedly identified with Kṛṣṇa and Rādhā even before his death in 1533. A natural concomitant to this belief is the belief that Caitanya's companions represent Kṛṣṇa's Vṛndāvana retinue, that his companions and most other prominent Bengal Vaiṣṇavas are reincarnations of Kṛṣṇa's

---

[1]Edward C. Dimock, Jr., "The Place of Gauracandrikā in Bengali Vaiṣṇava Lyrics," *Journal of the American Oriental Society*, LXXVIII (July September, 1958), 154.

companions (usually his female companions). As the conviction grew that Caitanya's life was a reiteration of Kṛṣṇa's, that, indeed, Caitanya was Kṛṣṇa himself, it was assumed that Caitanya's companions were also part of the great Kṛṣṇa drama. As early as the sixteenth century Kavi-karṇapūra wrote detailed works delineating the correspondences between Kṛṣṇa's companions and Caitanya's. In his *Kṛṣṇagaṇoddeśa-dipikā* he enumerated Kṛṣṇa's companions, and in his *Gauragaṇoddeśa-dīpikā* he listed which companions of Caitanya they had become in this age.[1] In the following passage, for example, he tells who the six Gosvāmins were among Kṛṣṇa's retinue:

> Formerly, she who was Rūpamañjarī in Vraja has appeared manifested as Rūpa Gosvāmin now. She who was a dear friend of Rūpamañjarī, called Ratimañjarī, also had another name, Labangamañjarī; according to some scholars, she now has become a constant companion of Caitanya and everybody's object of worship as Sanātana, the crown jewel of ascetics, due to the result of action indwelling in her. He who is famous as the manifestation of Śrī Mallbangamañjarī, and now resides in Vṛndāvana, his name is Śivānanda Cakravartin. She who was Anangamañjarī is now Gopāla Bhaṭṭa, but there are some who call Gopāla Bhaṭṭa the manifestation of Gunamañjarī. She who was formerly Ragamañjarī now lives as Raghunātha Bhaṭṭa in a cottage near the tank called Rādhikakunda (near Vṛndāvana). The former name of Raghunātha-dāsa was Rasamañjarī. Some call him Ratimañjarī, who was also called Bhānumati.[2]

In the context of *rāgānugā*, given the importance of imitating and attempting to participate actively in the drama of Kṛṣṇa by means of creative remembrance, this peculiar doctrine is quite understandable. Great devotees, those who have taken the royal way of *rāgānugā* in their devotion, became identified

---

[1]De dates the *Gauragaṇoddeśa-dīpikā* around 1576 and the *Kṛṣṇagaṇoddeśa-dīpikā* about the same time. *Vaisnava Faith and Movement,* p. 44 n.

[2]Kavi-karṇapūra, *Gauragaṇoddeśa-dīpikā,* translated into Bengali by Rāmanārāyaṇa Vidyāratna, ed. Ramdev Misra, *ślokas* 180-86, pp. 48-49. See also Kṛṣṇadāsa Kavirāja *Caitanya-caritāmṛta,* Antya-līlā 6. 8-10 (p. 117), for other such correspondences.

with one or another of Kṛṣṇa's companions. The ongoing drama of Kṛṣṇa takes place here and now, whenever such devotees attain success in their *sādhana.* It is but a logical extension of this doctrine to postulate a complete correspondence between the respective retinues of Kṛṣṇa and Caitanya. Very simply the drama is being played out again in this world; the unmanifest *līlā* has once again become manifest. Kṛṣṇa has become Caitanya, and Kṛṣṇa's companions have become Caitanya's companions. From both a devotional and a historical point of view the importance of this is that genuine devotion is always manifested vis-à-vis the great ongoing drama of Kṛṣṇa and his companions, that intense *bhakti* is always patterned upon and participates in the ultimate expression of *bhakti*—the devotion of Kṛṣṇa's associates (particularly the *gopis*) to him. The very unlikely comparisons that Kavi-karṇapūra postulates between, for example, the withdrawn, ascetic scholars of Vṛndāvana and the carefree *gopī* women only underline the importance of this idea. Such great devotees as the Gosvāmins, despite the fact that they bear no resemblance to cowherd women, *must* in some way be related to these paradigms of devotion, for the Gosvāmins' devotion is only significant vis-à-vis the reality of Kṛṣṇa's ongoing drama and their participation in it.

The importance of playacting as a technique of devotion to Kṛṣṇa is also apparent outside orthodox Bengal Vaiṣṇavism: in other Vaiṣṇava-Kṛṣṇa *sampradāyas* and in certain heterodox Bengal Vaiṣṇava sects. The Rādhāvallabhīs, founded in the sixteenth century by Harivaṁśa, used to dress as women (presumably as *gopīs*) at their ceremonies as a matter of course.[1] The much maligned practices of the Vallabhācāryas of West India may also be understood, I think, in the context of playacting as a means of participating in the ongoing drama of Kṛṣṇa and the *gopīs*. The leaders of this sect, founded by Vallabha in the late fifteenth century, claim the title of Mahārāja Gosāinji (or Gausvāmis), "great lord of the cows," a name that often refers to Kṛṣṇa, and are said to be the descendents of Vallabha. An important feature of devotion among the Vallabhas is the Rās Līlā, or the Rās Maṇḍalī, in which the devotees seek "to re-enact the scenes of the mythological story of Kṛṣṇa's amorous

[1]Charles Eliot, *Hinduism and Buddhism: An Historical Sketch*, II. 251.

sporting with the *gopis* by the waters and in the woods of Mathurā."[1] During these celebrations the Mahārājas take the part of Kṛṣṇa.[2] In fact, the Mahārājas and the devotees of the sect are understood to be reincarnations of Kṛṣṇa and the *gopis*, respectively, quite apart from those times when the Vṛndāvana-*līlā* is reiterated, so the celebration of Rās Līlā is really nothing extraordinary for the sect. The texts of the sect make it clear that the Mahārājas are incarnations of Kṛṣṇa and that all members of the sect are *gopis*.

> The descendent of Vallabha is the amorous Káná,
> Enamoured, he has made [us], in the roads of Vraj.
> See, sisters, the full moon-like face,
> With his sharp eyes my heart he has enticed and attracted
> . . . .
> A descendent of Vallabha is the amorous Káná,
> The sound of the jingling of [his] toe-rings has deprived me of my heart.
> The very personification of God you are.[3]

The devotees of the sect are said to be manifestations of two *gopis*, Priyā and Candravatī, who once argued with Krsna and were cursed to fall from heaven. They fell to earth at the city of Champāraṇya, the birthplace of Vallabha. Krsna, in the form of Vallabha, then appeared there to redeem them.[4] In the persons of the Mahārājas of the Vallabha sect, furthermore, Kṛṣṇa continually descends to earth to redeem devotees in the same way that he redeemed Priyā and Candravatī. In the theology of the sect, that is, all devotees are understood to be *gopis* who are temporarily estranged from heavenly Vṛndāvana.

> Multitudes are daily descending, one after the other, in the persons of the followers of the sect, to secure whose recovery to the heavenly abode the successive generations of

---

[1]D. Mackichan, "Vallabha, Vallabhāchārya," in James Hastings (ed.), *Encyclopaedia of Religion and Ethics*, XII, 583.

[2]Karsandas Mulji, *History of the Sect of Mahārājas, or Vallabhāchāryas, in Western India*, p. 131.

[3]From a poem of the sect cited *ibid.*, pp. 111-12.

[4]This story may be a variant of a myth found in the *Brahma-vaivarta-purāṇa*, in which Kṛṣṇa himself is cursed to fall from heaven by Rādhā. To make his stay on earth as enjoyable as possible, his entire retinue descends with him. Kṛṣṇa Janma Khaṇḍa 3 (Part II, p. 104 ff.).

> Vallabhácharya are born as incarnations of the god Krishṇa. They redeem their followers by sending them to Gouloka, where the disciple, if a male, is changed into a female, who obtains the everlasting happiness of living in sexual intercourse with Krishṇa in the heavens.[1]

In practice the female devotees of the sect were reputed to sustain adulterous affairs with the Mahārājas in imitation of the *gopis*. This practice brought about furious condemnation of the sect and culminated in the famous libel trial in Bombay during the middle of the nineteenth century. A witness at that trial said:

> I was aware that the females of my sect believed the Mahárájás to be incarnations of Krishna, and that as the gopis obtained salvation by falling in love with Krishna, our females were bent upon adulterous love towards the Mahárájás.[2]

While the attitude or role of a *gopi* is predominant in this sect, the centrality of the child Kṛṣṇa also results in the devotees acting as parents or friends toward Kṛṣṇa.

> The followers of these Mahárájas have usually in their houses an image of Krishṇa and a small book or wooden case containing portraits of Krishṇa in various attitudes, as well as of Vallabhácharya and some of his descendents, which they worship after the morning ablutions and bath. The image represents a young child, and the worship consists in playing before it with toys and childish trifles.[3]

The Vaiṣṇavas of the Kanarese area, the Haridāsīs of the fifteenth to the eighteenth centuries, also assumed particular roles vis-à-vis Kṛṣṇa and Rādhā, but they invariably maintained a discreet distance between themselves and their deity by preferring the attitudes of mother, father, or brother rather than lover.[4]

The worshipers of Rāma also recognize the efficacy of adoring

---

[1]Mulji, *History of the Mahārājas*, p. 79.

[2]*Ibid.*, Appendix, "Specimens of the Evidence and the Judgment in the Libel Case," p. 17.

[3]*Ibid.*, p. 123.

[4]Karmarkar and Kalamdani, *Mystic Teachings*, pp. 128-29.

Rāma by means of one or another devotional sentiment.[1] In Rāma worship, however, all sentiments are subordinate to the servile.

The erotic sentiment is present in a definitely subsidiary role, as exemplified by the section of the story leading up to the marriage of Sītā and Rāma. So too is the parental sentiment present in the part of the narrative relating to the childhood of Rāma. But the dominant sentiment for the devotee of Rāma is the servile (*Dāsya*).[2]

At about the same time that the Vallabhācāryas were being publicly condemned in Bombay, another group, most likely direct descendents of the orthodox Bengal Vaiṣṇavas, was becoming popular in Calcutta. The members of this group believed themselves to be *gopis* (a common-enough belief among orthodox Vaiṣṇavas) and dressed the part. Unlike the orthodox Bengal Vaiṣṇavas, who condemn such practices, this group, called the Sakhī-bhāvaks, dressed as women in imitation of the *gopis* as a regular part of their devotional *sādhana*. Some of the members, particularly those who went to live at Vṛndāvana, wore feminine dress throughout their lives.[3] The members of the sect took the names of one or another of the fourteen chief *gopis* and were known among the other members of the group by those names.

From time to time, especially on the twelfth day of the full moon, they would meet in the house of one of the group of

[1]Priyā Dās in his commentary on the *Bhaktamāl* mentions precisely those five sentiments listed in Bengal Vaiṣṇavism: *śānta*, *dāsya*, *sākhya*, *vātsalya*, and *śṛṅgāra*. Tulsī Dās, *The Petition to Rām*, p. 57.

[2]*Ibid.*, pp. 58-59. Kane, however, says that the erotic sentiment did become central for the Rāma cult. The cult of Rāma, he says, "culminated in an erotic mysticism about Rāma and Sitā also. The devotees of this mystic cult have to consider themselves as brides of Rāma or the female friends of Sītā, they are supposed to seek Lord Rāma's favour through Sītā, who graciously intercedes with the Lord for the devotees" (*History of Dharmaśāstra*, V, Part II, 980). Unfortunately, Kane does not indicate specifically which sect of the Rāma cult he is referring to, nor when and where they were popular, nor if they produced any texts adoring Rāma in this mode. To my knowledge, the erotic sentiment was never (and is not now) central to the Rāma cult.

[3]Aksoy Kumar Dutta, *Bhāratbarser-upāsak-sampradāya* (Bengali), I, 229.

the subsect. Dressing themselves as females they served Kṛṣṇa as *sakhīs*, and to satisfy their "husband" they used to sing songs about the love of Rādhā and Kṛṣṇa. All those dressed up as *sakhīs* used to divide themselves into two teams, one belonging to the party of Rādhā, the other one to that of Kṛṣṇa, and used to carry on a kind of singing duel consisting of questions and answers, repartees, jokes, and counter-jokes that ended in singing the praises of both Rādhā and Kṛṣṇa and the glories of their mutual love. This performance used to send the participants into heights of ecstasy.[1]

It is understandable that the practice of dressing as *gopis* would eventually appear in the worship of Kṛṣṇa given the fact that so much emphasis is placed upon becoming a *gopi* mentally in the orthodox tradition in Bengal. It is not clear why the orthodox themselves condemn this practice, as it seems a logical extension of *rāgānugā*, but most likely it is to avoid ridicule and misinterpretation by outsiders. In any event, the practice no longer seems to exist in Bengal today.

Another sect, at one time quite popular in Bengal, but now very rare, that might be considered a heterodox sect vis-à-vis the orthodox Vaiṣṇavas employed even more overt means in order to participate in the drama of Rādhā and Kṛṣṇa's love. These were the Vaiṣṇava Sahajiyās. While the Vaiṣṇava Sahajiyās were clearly influenced to a great degree by the orthodox Bengal Vaiṣṇavas, they were also in the tradition of the Buddhist Sahajiyās and Tantrism proper. Their *sādhana* obviously is based on Tantric theory in which, through means of the body and its subtle centers, the *sādhaka* seeks to unify two opposite principles: Śiva and Śakti in Hindu Tantrism and Prajñā and Upāya in Buddhist Tantrism.[2] The Vaiṣṇava Sahajiyās of Bengal, however, departed from Tantric tradition (which usually tends to be Śaivite) by introducing Rādhā and Kṛṣṇa as personifications of the two opposite principles. *Sādhana* for this sect meant the union of Rādhā and Kṛṣṇa. And, as in Tantric tradition, the Sahajiyās held that this union could be achieved in two ways: individually or with the help of another,

[1]*Ibid.*, pp. 230-31.
[2]Shashibhusan Dasgupta, *Obscure Religious Cults*, pp. 120-22.

invariably female, partner. In the former case, in which the Tantric *sādhaka* seeks to unite two subtle forces within his own body, the *kuṇḍalinī* (the female force in Hindu Tantrism pictured as a coiled serpent located beneath the genitals) is identified with Rādhā. When the *sādhaka* succeeds in arousing the *kuṇḍalinī* in traditional Hindu Tantrism, it is believed to rise to the head and unite with Śiva or a corresponding male power or principle. A Vaiṣṇava Sahajiyā text in discussing this aspect of *sādhana*, however, speaks not of the rising *kuṇḍalinī* but of Rādhā awakening and going out to meet Kṛṣṇa for a tryst.[1] When *sādhana* involves an assistant, however, the theme of playacting, which is my primary concern here, becomes clear. Like the orthodox Bengal Vaiṣṇavas, the Sahajiyās believe that the love sport of Rādhā and Kṛṣṇa takes place eternally.

> But they further held that the eternal concrete spiritual type manifested itself not only in the historical personages of Rādhā and Kṛṣṇa, but that it reveals itself in actual men and women themselves. Every man has within him the spiritual essence of Kṛṣṇa, which is his Svarūpa (real nature) associated with his lower existence, which is his physical form of Rūpa, and exactly in the same way every woman possesses within her a lower self associated with her physical existence, which is her Rūpa,—but within this Rūpa resides the Svarūpa of the woman, which is her ultimate nature as Rādhā. It is none but Kṛṣṇa and Rādhā who reside within men and women, and it is this Kṛṣṇa and this Rādhā that are making dalliance as men and women.[2]

The belief is typically Tantric insofar as the macrocosm is reflected in the microcosm. And the method of *sādhana* is also that sometimes used in left-handed Tantrism. Having fully realized his nature as Kṛṣṇa, the *sādhaka* employs a woman with whom he undertakes ritual sexual intercourse, the woman, of course,

[1] Kamalā-kānta's *Sādhaka-rañjana* (nineteenth century); cited *ibid.*, p. 129.

[2] *Ibid.*, pp. 127-28. It is interesting to note that this idea is also mentioned in Kṛṣṇadāsa Kavirāja's *Caitanya-caritāmṛta*, in which Kṛṣṇa is said to make his own body present in that of the pure devotee. Antya-līlā 4. 183-84 (p. 94).

representing Rādhā.[1] The woman (called a *nāyikā*) must fulfil various qualifications, among which are that she be *parakiyā* to the *sādhaka* (belonging to another) and that she be a married woman. Both of these qualifications, of course, are in imitation of Rādhā, who during her love affair with Kṛṣṇa in Vṛndāvana was married to another.[2] The aim of this *sādhana* is to enjoy *sahaja*, the sublime essence of the cosmos that is eternally generated by the union of Rādhā and Kṛṣṇa in eternal Vṛndāvana (Nitya-Vṛndāvana).[3]

In orthodox Bengal Vaiṣṇavism the centrality of attaining *sakhī-bhāva*, the importance of realizing the devotional attitude of a *gopi*, is clear. The possibility of relishing Kṛṣṇa-*bhāva*, of imitating and becoming identified with Kṛṣṇa, however, is denied. Among the orthodox the devotee's devotional attitude is always vis-à-vis Kṛṣṇa and never of Kṛṣṇa. The Sahajiyās, on the other hand, by admitting the essential "Kṛṣṇahood" of all men and the essential "Rādhāhood" of all women, emphasize the necessity of the devotee to take part in the ongoing drama of Kṛṣṇa as the hero (or the heroine) himself (or herself).

We have perhaps come a long way from the theory of *rāgānugā* expounded by Rūpa Gosvāmin. According to Rūpa and other orthodox scholars the primary emphasis in this type of devotion is psychological or mental. With a minimum of outward props the devotee is encouraged to create an imaginary world in which he may identify himself with one or another of Kṛṣṇa's companions (but never with Kṛṣṇa himself). The Rādhāvallabhīs, Vallabhācāryas, and Sakhī-bhāvaks all emphasize the importance of becoming Kṛṣṇa's lover or companion but introduce outward props to facilitate the procedure. The Sahajiyās go even further. Their participation in the drama of Rādhā and Kṛṣṇa is physical. Their identification with

[1] There is perhaps another playful theme apparent in the fact that in Tantric ritual sexual intercourse the *sādhaka* never experiences a sexual climax. The purpose of this is to save the *semen virile*, in fact, to channel it to the mind. As a result of this practice, the *sādhaka* is playing at sexual intercourse. He is not entirely involved in it but uses it for his own ends. He is, as it were, beside himself.

[2] For a description of this ritual, see Dimock, *The Place of the Hidden Moon*, pp. 235-45. For a description of the ideal *nāyikā*, see *ibid.*, pp. 215-21.

[3] Dasgupta, *Obscure Religious Cults*, p. 131.

Kṛṣṇa (and Rādhā) is much more than mental or psychological; it is physiological as well. This is particularly clear when the *kuṇḍalinī* of traditional Tantrism is understood to be Rādhā. Within the *sādhaka's* body, physically within him in subtle form, dwell both Rādhā and Kṛṣṇa.

The centrality of role-playing or playacting, however, remains clear in all the examples mentioned above. In each case an important aspect of devotion or *sādhana* is the assumption of a new identity (in the case of the Sahajiyās the discovery of one's true identity). The aim of devotion in each case is identification with a participant in the ongoing drama of Kṛṣṇa. The assumption is that the most appropriate mode for expressing genuine devotion is by participation in the Kṛṣṇa drama, by becoming part of that drama and losing one's original identity. This, of course, is precisely the aim of the actor in classical Indian dance-drama, and it is also a basic element in games of make-believe. As in the realm of classical Indian acting and the world of make-believe, there is, as Huizinga has said, a stepping out of common reality into another realm.

While it is clear that playacting or role-playing and the necessary element of make-believe involved in this are central to Bengal Vaiṣṇavism and the other sects I have mentioned, it is stretching the case to suggest that cult can be reduced to this element, as Huizinga implies in his argument. In my opinion it is clear that *rāgānugā* and other forms of playacting discussed above are primarily vehicles for devotion, a means of directing devotion that is already present in the devotee. The basic fact of cult remains man's devotion to Kṛṣṇa and not the means by which this is expressed.

D. The Frenzy of Devotion: Kīrtan and Holī

The mainstay of Bengal Vaiṣṇava devotion, particularly for lay devotees, is *kīrtan*. The word *kīrtan* means praise, but in Bengal it refers specifically to congregational singing in praise of Kṛṣṇa.[1] Traditionally, Caitanya is said to have introduced

[1]Basically, there are two types of *kirtan*: *nāmakirtan*, in which the name of God is sung over and over ("Hare Kṛṣṇa, Hare Kṛṣṇa, Kṛṣṇa, Kṛṣṇa, Hare, Hare. Hare Rāma, Hare Rāma, Rāma, Rāma, Hare, Hare"), and *līlākīrtan*, in which the deeds (*līlā*) of Kṛṣṇa are celebrated in song. *Kīrtan* may also

kīrtan as a unique way of acquiring and expressing *bhakti*. However, there are clear indications in Bengal Vaiṣṇava literature itself that *kīrtan* was known in Bengal before Caitanya made it popular. In the *Caitanya-bhāgavata* of Vṛndāvana-dāsa, for example, the author describes daily *kīrtan* as taking place at the home of Advaitācārya, later to become a companion of Caitanya.

> In the afternoon all Kṛṣṇa devotees come and gather at Advaita's place. As soon as Mukunda [a great singer from Chittagong] sings about Kṛṣṇa, there is no one who is not beside himself, and many fall to the ground in a swoon. Some weep, some laugh, some dance, and some roll on the ground and cannot manage to keep their clothes on. Some with shouts jump, clapping their hands and beating their thighs, and some go and do obeisance at the feet of Mukunda.[1]

Until Caitanya popularized *kīrtan* as a means of devotion, however, it was not typical of Vaiṣṇavism in Bengal, and there are even indications that it was frowned upon by the orthodox.[2] *Kīrtan* became so popular during the lifetime of Caitanya and the century following, though, that the following saying became well known in Bengal: "All shaven-headed merchants became *kīrtan*-singers, and they melted everything of metal and made cymbals out of it."[3]

In regard to the question of the importance of play and play techniques in cult, *kīrtan* is important in at least two respects. In the first place, it is frequently the occasion for overt identification with Kṛṣṇa's companions, usually the *gopīs*, and therefore

---

be categorized according to the circumstances in which it takes place. *Saṁkīrtan* refers to any group singing in praise of Kṛṣṇa, and *nagarkirtan* refers to street processions in which songs of praise are sung. In either case, *nāmakīrtan* or *līlākīrtan* may be sung. Jatindra Ramanuja, "Kirtan," *Bhāratokoṣa* (a Bengali encyclopedia), II, 338-39.

[1] Vṛndāvana-dāsa, *Caitanya-bhāgavata* (Bengali), ed. Bhaktisiddhānta Gosvāmin Thakur, Ādi Khaṇḍa 9. 23-26, p. 212.

[2] See, for example, Kṛṣṇadāsa Kavirāja *Caitanya-caritāmṛta*, Ādi-līlā 17. 196-204 (p. 204), where the orthodox *brāhmans* of Navadvīp complain to the Muslim ruler of the city that Caitanya and his followers are disgracing Hinduism by their noisy and emotional antics.

[3] Quoted in Khagendranāth Mitra, *Kīrtan* (Bengali), p. 20.

represents an outlet or means of expressing the type of role-playing I have discussed above. As mentioned above, *kirtan* is the occasion for singing the poems (*padāvālis*) of the Vaiṣṇava poets. Consistent with aesthetic theory, the poems are sung in groups according to the same theme. The same *bhāva*, that is, is elaborated and repeated so that it may be relished by the devotees. A common feature of *kirtan*, consequently, is the "seizure" or "possession" of the participants by the *bhāva* being sung. For example, if the theme of a particular *kirtan* is Kṛṣṇa's departure from Vṛndāvana and Rādhā's resultant woe (the theme of love-in-separation), the participants may cry in anguish and weep. Or when Kṛṣṇa's play with the *gopis*, particularly his circular dance with them, is described, some devotees will stand up and dance in circles as the *gopis* did with Kṛṣṇa.[1] Like the poets in their *bhanitas*, the participants in *kirtan* may come to take an active and immediate role in the action being described. In Vaiṣṇava literature Caitanya is frequently described as doing this.[2] In *lilākirtan* the ongoing drama of Kṛṣṇa is made present, and the devotee's response is consistent with the theory of *rāgānugā*, which encourages devotees to participate actively in the drama.[3]

Kirtan demonstrates the relationship between play and cult in another respect, for it almost invariably results in ecstatic frenzy, a characteristic of the more abandoned types of play. Such frenzy is one of the outstanding features of Bengal Vaiṣṇa-

---

[1]Dimock and Levertov (trans.), *In Praise of Krishna*, p. xiii.

[2]For example, Kṛṣṇadāsa Kavirāja *Caitanya-caritāmṛta*, Madhya-līlā 14. 220 (p. 333).

[3]There is a certain amount of identification with Kṛṣṇa's companions, particularly the *gopīs*, in the *bhajanas* of South India. Like *kīrtan*, *bhajanas* are communal song festivals in praise of Kṛṣṇa in which particular aspects of his biography are celebrated. See Milton Singer, "The Rādhā Krishna *Bhajanas* of Madras City," in Singer (ed.), *Krishna*, pp. 95-96, 98-99. See esp. p. 130, where one devotee explains the efficacy of imitating the *gopīs*. *Kīrtan* (*bhajana* or *katha*) was also popular during the time of Rāmdās in West India. Professional singers, known as *kīrtankar*, used to roam from village to village singing in praise of Rāma and Kṛṣṇa. Rāmdās himself is said to have preached through the medium of *kīrtan*, which "held a high place in his esteem" (Wilbur S. Deming, *Ramdas and the Ramdasis*, pp. 10, 98). The performance of *kīrtan* was important in the devotion of the Haridāsīs of Karnatak as well (Karmarkar and Kalamdani, *Mystic Teachings*, p. 40).

vism. Speaking of the sixteenth and seventeenth centuries, when Vaiṣṇavism was most popular in Bengal, one author says: "For two centuries the Bengali people sang, danced, and passed out in an ecstatic trance."[1] The history of the sect is full of descriptions of shrieking, swooning, intoxicated devotees. The *Caitanya-bhāgavata* describes the wild behavior of Haridās, a companion of Caitanya, as he sings *kirtan*:

> Haridās used to walk along the banks of the Ganges, roaming about playfully, singing loudly the name of Kṛṣṇa. Absolutely unattached to worldly pleasures, the name of Kṛṣṇa was always on his lips. Not for a second did he stop saying the name of Govinda, and due to the *rasa* of *bhakti* he expressed different emotions and assumed different aspects. Sometimes he danced all alone, sometimes he roared like a mad lion. Sometimes he wept loudly, sometimes he laughed loudly. Sometimes he shouted in a thundering voice. Sometimes he lay on the ground senseless . . . . Shedding tears, raising of body hairs, laughter, swooning, sweating, all these body signs of Kṛṣṇa devotion were there.[2]

In the *Bhāgavata-purāṇa* there is another pertinent passage that indicates the importance of frenzy to devotion.

> Save by the erection of hairs, through emotion, the melted state of the mind and drops of tears begotten by joy, how can devotion be known? . . . . Whoever has a suppressed voice, whose heart melts away, whoever weeps again and again, who sometimes laughs and sings aloud shamelessly, and dances, such a devotee of mine purifies the three worlds.[3]

These passages are significant in that they state clearly that such signs of ecstasy as crying, swooning, horripilation, sweating, and laughing are "body signs of Kṛṣṇa devotion."[4] The greatest

---

[1] J. C. Ghosh, *Bengali Literature*, p. 24.

[2] Vṛndāvana-dāsa *Caitanya-bhāgavata*, Ādi Khaṇḍa 16. 22-29, p. 340.

[3] *Bhāgavata-purāṇa* XI. 14. 24 (V, 189).

[4] There are also signs that devotion to Śiva manifests itself in frenzy. From a poem of the Tamil Śaivite saint Māṇikka Vāchakar, who lived in the ninth and tenth centuries, for example, we read: "Thrills and trembles my frame; /

devotees of Kṛṣṇa are not necessarily great scholars or ascetics. Almost all the famous devotees of Kṛṣṇa, particularly in Bengal, were men who were prone to ecstasy. Many delightful passages depict aged, ascetic men suddenly losing their dignity and behaving like madmen or children. During the Jagannāth Car Festival in Purī, where Caitanya lived during the latter part of his life, Caitanya and his companions once sang *kīrtan* and played in the waters of the temple-garden tanks. This passage from the *Caitanya-caritāmṛta* describes a scene, which must have been unusual indeed, of shaven-headed ascetics frolicking with each other in the water:

> They began the water fight in pairs.
> Now one would win, and then another, as the Lord looked on.
> Advaita played the water game with Nityānanda,
> And when he was defeated, scolded him.
> Vidyānidhi played with Svarūpa,
> While Gupta [Murari Gupta] played with Datta [Mukunda Datta].
> Śrībasa played with Gadādhar,
> And Rāghava-pandit played with Vakreśvara.
> Sārvabhauma and Rāmānandarāy played together,
> And both of them lost their gravity and became childlike.[1]

The *Caitanya-bhāgavata* comments specifically on the childish nature of Caitanya's devotees when they were singing *kīrtan*:

> When those devotees sang *kīrtan* they became overwhelmed by bliss, and like children became restless and prankish. Many of them were grave, old men with perfect manners, full of civility, perfect "gentlemen." But now they were childlike. Such is the strange and wonderful power of devotion to Viṣṇu.[2]

The *Caitanya-caritāmṛta* says on the same subject: "And sometimes they cried out in joy. Sometimes they bowed down in

---

Hands are lifted on high; Here at Thy fragrant feet; / Sobbing and weeping I cry." Kingsbury and Phillips, *Hymns of the Tamil Śaivite Saints*, p. 89.

[1]Kṛṣṇadāsa Kavirāja *Caitanya-caritāmṛta*, Madhya-līlā 14. 76-80; my translation.

[2]Vṛndāvana-dāsa *Caitanya-bhāgavata*, Madhya Khaṇḍa 13. 330-31, p. 666.

humility. Sometimes they were fickle like children and sometimes again they showed various motions of their limbs."[1]

Caitanya himself, although he is sometimes pictured as a great scholar and logician,[2] was primarily a love-intoxicated madman who frequently fell into trances, danced for hours, laughed, wept, and sang in praise of Kṛṣṇa. This ecstatic frenzy, more than anything else, characterized Caitanya and seemed to set him apart as a peculiarly holy man.

> And the body of the Lord was filled with joy. And now he was in a stupor, now he shook, now his colours changed and then again the whole body of the Lord began to sweat. And there was a change in the voice of the Lord and tears constantly flowed from his eyes. And the Lord laughed and wept, danced and sang and he ran this way and that. And the very next moment again he fell down senseless to the ground.[3]

To this day Vaiṣṇavas in Bengal are characterized by their emotional frenzy, which may be seen almost invariably whenever *kirtan* is performed. While there is no rigid pattern that is followed in the performance of *kirtan*, the participants almost always sing a song or two in praise of Caitanya (*gauracandrikās*) before they begin to sing of Kṛṣṇa. No matter what the pattern, though, whether it consists primarily of singing *nāmakirtan* or *lilākirtan*, there comes a point when some, if not all, of the participants will stand up and begin to dance. Such dancing usually consists simply of rocking or hopping from one foot to another or jumping up and down in time to the music. Some participants will raise their arms high above their heads or clap their hands to the music. It is common for the whole *kirtan* party, including the musicians, to get up and dance as they play their instruments or clap their hands. Old men do not seem the least bit inhibited and are frequently active participants in this dancing, which builds to a crescendo of sound and movement. I

[1]Kṛṣṇadāsa Kavirāja *Caitanya-caritāmṛta*, Madhya-lilā 25. 59 (p. 642).

[2]This is particularly clear in his theological and philosophical discussions with Rāmānandarāy (Kṛṣṇadāsa Kavirāja *Caitanya-caritāmṛta*, Madhya-lilā 8 [pp. 142-82] and Sārvabhauma *ibid.* 6 [pp. 97-126]).

[3]*Ibid.* 2. 62 (p. 36).

have even seen such dancing and shouting-singing during a Vaiṣṇava car procession of the Gauḍīya Maṭh in Calcutta. A flamboyant chariot carrying the images of Rādhā, Kṛṣna, and Caitanya was pulled along the main streets of South Calcutta by several hundred devotees. Between the two lines of devotees who were pulling the car, ten or twelve devotees danced, sang, played their instruments, shouted, clapped their hands, and raised their arms above their head in typical Vaiṣṇava fashion. The entire scene could have been taken from the *Caitanya-caritāmṛta*, where *nagarkīrtan* (processional *kīrtan*) is frequently described in Navadvīp and Purī.

In *kīrtan* the singing of Kṛṣṇa's name and the retelling of his deeds are associated with ecstatic frenzy. In *kīrtan*, when the devotee remembers Kṛṣṇa in songs of praise, there comes about an almost predictable turbulence of emotion. The mood of *kīrtan*, because of this, can be described as festive and celebrational, as taking place within the context of excitement. Huizinga, in the process of arguing his case for man's discovery of the sacred in play, noted that the context of religious festivals is frequently celebrational, that the *raison d'être* of such festivals is the simple expression of joy in celebration.

Kīrtan is a good example of a cultic activity that seems to have as its primary aim ecstatic celebration. The enthusiasm and intoxication of the Bengal Vaiṣṇavas, however, cannot be properly understood without regard to their all-important referent, Kṛṣṇa himself. For the *bhakti* that is so emotionally expressed in *kīrtan* is also described elsewhere, in the madness of emotions that exist between Rādhā and Kṛṣṇa. The divine couple intoxicate and incite each other, they swoon and sweat, they are overcome by powerful emotions that cause their bodies to tremble uncontrollably. Speaking of Bengal Vaiṣṇava literature generally, J. C. Ghosh says :

> The terms most frequently met in the Padas and in Vaiṣṇava literature generally are those denoting the ecstasy, even the madness, of love; such as *rasollās* [ecstasy of *rasa*], *premonmād* [love mad], *divyonmād* [divine madness], *preme pāgal* [love mad], and *preme mātuārā* [intoxicated by love]. The poets betray a particular delight in using these expressions, and they

are only too ready to put Kṛṣṇa and Rādhā, particularly the latter, into a frenzied, trance-like state.[1]

The emotional fervor of the Bengal Vaiṣṇavas during *kīrtan* is not simply self-induced ecstasy, celebration as an end in itself. The weeping, laughing, swooning, and shouting are a reflection of what is taken to be the paradigm of genuine devotion, Rādhā's love for Kṛṣṇa. Vis-à-vis the Lord Kṛṣṇa such frenzy is certainly appropriate. For Kṛṣṇa is frequently called (and described as) *modana* and *madana*, the exhilarator and inebriator. His irresistible beauty and charm devastate the veneer of man's civility and orderly habit by breaking in upon his inmost being and releasing a torrent of emotions and turning wise old men into shrieking madmen or playful children. Under the influence of the exhilarator man can only respond in frenzy. Like Rādhā and the *gopīs*, he is torn away from familiar routines and circumstances and drawn to the revel of god's sport with man in the bowers of Vṛndāvana. And like Rādhā he is ravished there.

For the Vaiṣṇavas of Bengal the festive joy of celebration is not the necessary context in which man is enabled to discover the sacred. Rather, their frenzy is to be understood as a perfectly appropriate response to the "other" world of Kṛṣṇa, which incites man to frenzy and madness. In the context of Bengal Vaiṣṇavism, where Rādhā's turbulent emotions are extolled as the epitomy of *bhakti*, man's most appropriate expression of devotion is understandably turbulent too. And, like Rādhā's emotion, the emotion of the devotee is never adequately understood without reference to Kṛṣṇa, toward whom, and in response to whom, such emotions are directed.

The association of Kṛṣṇa with festive joy is also apparent in the Holī festival. This festival as it exists today in India is the result of a long history during which several festivals or customs became amalgamated. The original Holī festival was concerned with agriculture and seems to have featured a sacrifice of some kind, perhaps human. Such a festival does not seem to have been part of the vedic milieu. The first reference to the Holī festival in Sanskrit is found in Jaimini's *Pūrvamīmāṁsā*, *Śābarabhāṣya*, where he says that the origin of the festival is lost in

1. Ghcsh, *Bengali Literature*, p. 62.

antiquity. And it is among the tribal people of India that the agricultural and sacrificial aspects of Holī are the strongest.[1] Two festivals that originally were not a part of Holī were incorporated with it some time after the third century A.D. and account for two popular characteristics of the festival as it is celebrated today. A festival called Vasanta or Suvasantaka is mentioned in the third century A.D. by Vâtsāyana, and, as described in a drama named *Ratnāvali* in the seventh century, featured the throwing of colored powder and water. This festival was quite popular until the eleventh century but then seems to have died out as an independent celebration,[2] no doubt as it came to be identified with Holī. A second festival, the worship of Madana and Ratī, the god of love and his wife, featured a certain amount of sexual license and obscene speech. This festival is no longer celebrated, but, again, sexual license and obscene speech are now characteristic of Holī in many places.[3] Finally, a swing festival, whose origin is not clear, became associated with Holī. It seems that originally the swing festival did not involve the swinging of images, but by the eleventh century it was the custom to swing Rādhā and Kṛṣṇa (or more uncommonly Śiva and Pārvatī or Madana and Ratī) at this festival. Sometime before the sixteenth century the date of this festival was changed from the month of Caitra to the full-moon day of Phālgun and thus corresponds to the Holī festival.[4]

The festival as it exists today, then, consists of four main elements. (1) In almost all areas the festival begins with a huge bonfire, the ashes of which are often felt to fertilize the soil. In most cases a human effigy is burned, although in some places an animal is sacrificed. In most cases the bonfire is said to represent the burning of the demoness Holī, or Holikā, the sister or aunt of Prahlāda. According to the story, Prahlāda refused to curse the Lord on the order of his demon father Harnākas

[1]For example the Khands of Orissa, the Gonds, the Oraons, and the Nagas all betray a clear agricultural connection in their celebrations of Holi. In each case the ashes of the bonfire are felt to make the soil fertile, a sheep is sacrificed in the fire, and a certain amount of sexual license is tolerated. See Nirmal Kumar Bose, *Cultural Anthropology*, "The Spring Festival of India," pp. 89-91.

[2]*Ibid.*, pp. 92-93.

[3]*Ibid.*, p. 93.

[4]*Ibid.*, pp. 95-96.

(the purāṇic Hiraṇyakaśipu) and was consequently tortured. As this had no effect, Harnākas decided to burn Prahlāda. Holikā was told to sit in the midst of the fire and hold Prahlāda. She was assured that she would be fireproofed by her devotion to Harnākas. The reverse, of course, was the case. Holikā was consumed, and Prahlāda went unscathed. The fire is also said to represent the burning of Pūtanā, the demoness who suckled the infant Kṛṣṇa in an attempt to poison him. After she was killed by Kṛṣṇa she was chopped up and burned by the people of Vṛndāvana. In some parts of Bengal, the effigy is simply referred to as the "old woman."[1] (2) The day following the bonfire, which is always held at night, is a day of festivity, almost of rebellion. It is a day when members of the low castes can abuse those of the upper castes both physically and verbally without fear of retaliation. Women become bolder and attack men on the streets. Both sexes use abusive and obscene language in some areas, and some sexual license is permitted in some areas. Marriott notes that the entire social structure seems about to come apart. Roles are reversed and "an order precisely inverse to the social and ritual principles of routine life" emerges.[2] (3) Perhaps the most distinctive feature of Holī is the throwing of colored powder and water. Groups of young men roam the streets and pelt or soak anybody in sight. Women, too, take part in this, often attacking en masse a poor, unsuspecting man. In the villages cow dung and urine as well as almost anything else are thrown at people. (4) The day is also called the Dol ("swing") festival. On this day the images of Rādhā and Kṛṣṇa are placed on a swing and ceremonially swung and sprinkled with colored powder.

What is important for this study is that Kṛṣṇa has come to be identified with the Holī festival. The association is twofold: the celebration of the Dol festival on Holī day and the more general association of Kṛṣṇa with the festival of Holī in all its revelry. It is difficult to say which association took place first (the association of Dol with Holī or Kṛṣṇa's association with

---

[1] *Ibid.*, p. 118. See also McKim Marriott, "The Feast of Love," in Singer (ed.), *Krishna*, p. 200.

[2] Marriott, "The Feast of Love," p. 210. Cf. Chakravarti, *Tantras*, p. 100, for parallels in the Durgā Pūjā festival: obscene language, cursing, and throwing of mud and dust.

the revelry of Holī) and whether one led to the other. What is clear, though, is that originally Kṛṣṇa had nothing to do with Holī (nor did any other Hindu deity). The *purāṇas*, although they mention the Dol festival, do not connect Kṛṣṇa or the swing festival with Holī. Kṛṣṇa's association with Holī in both respects seems to have taken place sometime before or during the sixteenth century. The first clear reference to this connection is made by Rūpa Gosvāmin in his *Stava-mālā*.[1] What is important for this discussion, however, is the association itself. For what is striking about the Holī festival today is the clear association of the Divine Player *par excellence* with India's most rollicking festival.

The swinging of Rādhā and Kṛṣṇa on Holī day may at first seem out of character with the rest of the festival. The swinging is actually quite ceremonial, as is the application of colored powder to the images. However, the act of swinging itself suggests a playful theme. Swinging is a useless, pointless activity, and as such it represents an appropriate symbol of both divine *līlā* and the play of the universe generally. Rādhā and Kṛṣṇa live eternally in the heavenly sporting ground of Vṛndāvana surrounded by an entourage of thousands of *gopas* and *gopīs*. Their sole activity is to revel in each other's bliss, to sport endlessly with their companions. Their swinging suggests a continuous, pointless, hypnotic yet exhilarating activity that is done simply for amusement.

The image of swinging is also reminiscent of the superfluous rhythms of the universe, the pointless cycles that are often understood to be the expressions of the aimless display of the gods. The poet Kabīr was particularly fond of this image and often spoke of the universe and everything in it as swinging to and fro.

> Held by the cords of love, the swing of the Ocean of Joy sways to and fro.[2]

---

[1]Rūpa Gosvāmin, *Stava-mālā*, collected by Jiva Gosvāmin, ed. Baladeva Vidyābhūṣaṇa, translated into Bengali by Rāmanārāyaṇa Vidyāratna. See section called Gītāvalī, pp. 632-98, on the Dol festival. The fact that Rūpa Gosvāmin may have been the first one to associate Holī with Kṛṣṇa might indicate that the logical context for such an association was that of Bengal Vaiṣṇavism, where such a high premium is placed upon ecstatic frenzy.

[2]Kabir, *One Hundred Poems*, song 17, ppl. 8-19.

Between the poles of the conscious and the unconscious,
there has the mind made a swing:
Thereon hang all beings and all worlds, and that swing
never ceases its sway.[1]

Hang up the swing of love to-day!
Hang the body and the mind between the arms of the
Beloved, in the ecstacy of love's joy.[2]

The image is used effectively by Kabīr in these passages both cosmically and emotionally. The cycles of the world and nature are repeated endlessly, rising and falling, apparently aimless in their eternal repetition. But these cycles generate joy and music; they are exhilarating in their energetic display. It is as if the world were on a swing, propelled, perhaps, by a smiling god. Or, possibly, the god himself is swinging, and the world is contained within him.

The image of swinging is also an appropriate expression of love. In Bengal Vaiṣṇavism it is no exaggeration to say that the world revolves around and is propelled by the love of Rādhā and Kṛṣṇa. The *telos* of the cosmos and of every individual biography is to revel in the bliss of love for Kṛṣṇa. The world is a stage for this love affair, and every individual is created to take part in it. The to-and-fro motion of swinging can symbolize both the movement between love in union and love in separation and the movement from aversion to greed for Kṛṣṇa on the part of men. The constant motion of the swing suggests the restless, ever changing moods of love. The exhilaration of the motion suggests the frenzy of love.

Kṛṣṇa's association with the Holī festival, however, goes beyond the swinging of his image on that day. He is considered the Lord of Holī, the one who originated the festival and taught men how to play it. Marriott, for example, was told: "It is a *līlā*—a divine sport of Lord Krishna!" "Lord Krishna taught us the way of love, and so we celebrate Holī in this manner."[3] If we look at Holī from the point of view of its being Kṛṣṇa's festival, several of its distinctive features take on an added signi-

[1] *Ibid.*, song 16, p. 16.
[2] *Ibid.*, song 100, p. 105.
[3] Marriott, "The Feast of Love," pp. 201, 204-5.

ficance. Holī becomes that time when Kṛṣṇa again calls men away from their stilted, habitual routines and incites them to play like children. The revelry of Holī becomes the play of Kṛṣṇa with the cowherd boys and girls.[1] Holī takes place in spring when life gushes forth in a riot of vigor and color, and we are reminded that in Vṛndāvana it is perpetual spring and that there nature is constantly excited by the sound of Kṛṣṇa's flute and by his very appearance.[2] The breakdown of certain social structures during Holī is clearly reflected in Kṛṣṇa's love for the *gopis*. This tumultuous love tore the *gopis* away from their homes and husbands and was consummated illicitly in the forest. The over-all atmosphere of Holī is one of playful abandon. And it is precisely in the context of playful abandon that Kṛṣṇa met the *gopīs*, in which he meets all men through the emotional frenzy of *bhakti*.

As it is celebrated today, then, Holī is Kṛṣṇa's festival. It provides an occasion during which men are free to play with Kṛṣṇa. And it is an occasion, furthermore, during which the kind of frenzy that is seen in *kīrtan* is also displayed. This is particularly clear in descriptions of the famous Vaiṣṇava festival at Kheturi in Bengal (now Bangladesh), where Holī was celebrated immediately after an extended session of *kīrtan*. During the Holī festivities (called *phāgu*, literally, "the colored powder," in the following passages) the participants are repeatedly overcome with *ānanda prema*, the bliss of love, and become ecstatic, just as they did during *kīrtan*.

> Śrīnivās got things started. Bringing containers of colored powder, he began to throw it at everyone with great zest . . . Śrī Achuta and Gopāla—great lovers of the Lord—Śrīpati, Śrīnidhi, Jadu—all great devotees—Śrī Raghunandana and other favorites of the Lord, all became possessed by *prema* while playing Holī. In great delight, some of the devotees put colored powder on the beautiful body of the Gaura image [the fair one, Caitanya, one of the six images installed

---

[1] Marriott's description of boys playing Holī is pertinent. "Boys of all ages were heaving dust into the air, hurling old shoes at each other, laughing and cavorting 'like Krishna's cowherd companions.'" *Ibid.*, p. 202.

[2] See above, Chap. II, Secs. F and H.

earlier in the festival] and couldn't take their eyes from the Lord's face and stood gazing at it . . . . Other devotees put powder on Vrajamohan [the charmer of Vraja, Kṛṣṇa, another of the six images] and were so overwhelmed by the rising flood of bliss that they couldn't keep quiet. Others put colored powder on the images of Rādhā and Kṛṣṇa and remained there gazing on their beauty and charm, expressing their ecstatic moods in various gestures. Other devotees, in playful fun, put colored powder on the image of Rādhākānta [the charmer, or darling, of Rādhā, that is, Kṛṣṇa] and with gleeful minds began to smile mischievously.[1]

All the Vaiṣṇava leaders took colored powder and began to throw it at the image of Caitanya, and laughed under the spell of love. Some threw powder at the images of Rādhākānta and Vallavakānta and began to talk about the dalliance of Kṛṣṇa and Rādhā with great pleasure. Other devotees, full of fun, threw powder at the dual image of Rādhā and Kṛṣṇa and put some more on the image of Vrajamohan . . . After playing Holī with the Lord, they began to play it among themselves, beside themselves with emotion. Some, in great excitement, recited verses describing the Lord's festival of Holī. Some sang about the *līlā* of Navadvīp, and some about the *līlā* of Vṛndāvana. Others went about playing on drums, some danced, some chased others with colored powder in their hands. All of them became self-forgetful, as if mad, and, catching each other smeared each other with colored powder. Thousands of people played Holī everywhere. They made colored powder fly all around so it flew up and covered the sky.[2]

The Holī festival as described in these passages illustrates dramatically that the relationship between Kṛṣṇa and his devotees is one of playful abandon. During Holī the devotees play not only among themselves but with Kṛṣṇa (and Caitanya).

---

[1]Narahari Cakravartin, *Bhakti-ratnākara* (Bengali), ed. Rāmanārāyaṇa Vidyāratna, pp. 649-50. I have not been able to determine the exact date of this festival, but it took place some time shortly after Caitanya's death in 1533.

[2]Narahari-dāsa, *Narottama-vilāsa* (Bengali), ed. Rāmanārāyaṇa Vidyāratna, pp. 162-63.

They shower his image with colored powder and "smile mischievously" at him. The devotees are *gopīs* or *gopas*, and the whole scene is reminiscent of Kṛṣṇa's sport in Vṛndāvana. In this atmoshphere of play they experience the bliss of *bhakti*. The devotees come to Kṛṣṇa in play and serve him in play.[1]

While Holī was not originally associated with Kṛṣṇa, the context of tumult that it creates provided an eminently appropriate stage for Kṛṣṇa's play with his devotees. The atmosphere of Holī is one in which emotions run wild. It is a carnival day on which men can give the lie to the stilted barriers of custom and habit and frolic like children.[2] During Holī there is an atmosphere of rebellion, in which men may become susceptible to their urge to run off prancing and dancing. During Holī it is as if some playful god has intoxicated men, freeing them to act as they wish instead of as they ought. The Bengal Vaiṣṇavas, no doubt, recognized this god as their own. In the tumult of Holī they heard the bewitching call of Kṛṣṇa's flute and made the day an occasion for playing with their Lord. Holī became a day on which devotees, like the *gopīs*, could express the joy of their love for Kṛṣṇa in playful revel.

E. *Bhakti, an Ovation of Bliss*

In discussing the relationship of play to cult earlier, it was noted that very often cultic activities, like play, are nonutilitarian. Huizinga emphasized the centrality of celebration in cult, while Jensen noted that cultic activities are frequently purpose free. The tradition of *bhakti* in Hinduism emphatically stresses the nonutilitarian nature of devotion while also emphasizing the celebrational aspect of serving God. It will be pertinent, therefore, to examine to what extent *bhakti* can be called play, or to what extent *bhakti* can illumine the relationship between play and cult.

---

[1]It is interesting to note that Caitanya's traditional birth date is said to have fallen on the full-moon night of Phālgun, thus corresponding to Holī. This is a particularly appropriate date for the saint whose entire life is described as *līlā*. Kṛṣṇadāsa Kavirāja *Caitanya-caritāmṛta*, Ādi-līlā 13. 18-19 (p. 156).

[2]The festivities held in honor of Kṛṣṇa's birthday are also characterized by playful abandon, playacting, and general pandemonium. See the description of this celebration in E. M. Forster, *A Passage to India*, pp. 283-90.

In the *Bhagavadgītā* we are told that the key to salvation is acting with indifference. If one acts without desire, without regard to the consequences of one's actions, he can gain freedom from the wheel of *karma* and *rebirth*. No matter what a man's *dharma* may be, even if he is from the lowest caste, he can find release through performing his duty disinterestedly. And *bhakti*, we are told further, represents a means to this end. Men of all castes can achieve indifference to the consequences of their actions if they offer all their actions as a sacrifice to Viṣṇu, if they offer all they are and do to him as the Lord.

> Whatever thou doest, whatever thou eatest,
> Whatever thou offerest in oblation or givest,
> Whatever austerity thou performest, son of Kuntī [Arjuna],
> That do as an offering to Me.

> Thus from what have good and evil fruits
> Thou shalt be freed, (namely) from the bonds of action;
> Thy soul disciplined in the discipline of renunciation,
> Freed, thou shalt go to Me.[1]

In the *Bhagavadgītā* the author has presented man with an alternative to the paths of works (*karma-mārga*) and knowledge (*jñāna-mārga*). Man can seek and gain release by whole-hearted devotion to the Lord Viṣṇu. However, this alternative by no means disregards the other two paths. The *Gītā* does not counsel man to give up either the path of works or the path of knowledge. On the contrary, the originality and brilliance of the *Gītā* lies in the fact that it brings about a synthesis. According to the *Gītā* it is not necessary for man to live outside society in order to find salvation. No matter what a man's situation in society may be, no matter how lowly his *dharma*, he can find release by offering his actions to Viṣṇu as a sacrifice. Nowhere in the *Gītā* is man advised to give up his inherited *dharma*. He is told that even if he performs his *dharma* poorly, it is better than doing another's *dharma* well.

> Better one's own duty, (tho) imperfect,
> Than another's duty well performed;

---

[1] *Bhagavadgītā* 9. 27-28 (p. 49).

Better death in (doing) one's own duty;
Another's duty brings danger.[1]

The *Gītā* does not supply man with a new *dharma*, with a new set of actions. It does not bring into question the ethical or spiritual values of highly structured society. The *Gītā*, rather, provides a new formula that is efficacious in any social circumstance. "Do your duty, but do it without regard to consequence. Do your duty without desire, as a sacrifice to the Lord." For the *Gītā* the religious man is he who has transcended cause and effect, who acts without desire, who has lost himself in devotion to Viṣṇu, but who, nevertheless, remains in society, faithful to his inherited social responsibilities.

The nature of *bhakti* as typified by Arjuna in the *Gītā* deserves comment, as it is quite different from the devotion of the medieval *bhakti* cults and again points up the rather conservative bias of the *Gītā*. When Kṛṣṇa reveals himself as the almighty Viṣṇu, Arjuna is struck with wonder and bows down in awe before him.

Making a reverent gesture, trembling, the Diademed (Arjuna)
Made obeisance and spoke yet again to Kṛṣṇa,
Stammering, greatly affrighted, bowing down.[2]

Arjuna is so frightened that he asks Kṛṣṇa to again take on his former appearance:

Having seen what was never seen before, I am thrilled,
And (at the same time) my heart is shaken with fear;
Show me, O God, that same form of Thine (as before)!
Be merciful, Lord of Gods, Abode of the World![3]

The relationship between God and his devotee in the *Gītā* is that between a lord and his servant. The mighty, epic hero Arjuna trembles in fright before the majesty of God and cannot withstand a direct vision of the divine. Throughout the tenth and eleventh chapters of the *Gītā* the majesty of Viṣṇu is extolled. In his terrible, awesome power he completely dominates the

[1] *Ibid.* 3. 35 (p. 21).
[2] *Ibid.* 11. 35 (p. 58).
[3] *Ibid.* 11. 45 (p. 60).

divine-human relationship. There is only one attitude appropriate to man vis-à-vis Viṣṇu in the *Gītā*, and that is humility.

For a period of several centuries after the *Gītā* was written there seems to have been a decline in the religion of *bhakti*. At least no significant texts have survived to indicate that *bhakti* was popular or widespread during this time. Between the seventh and tenth centuries A.D., however, there was a powerful resurgence of *bhakti* in South India. The type of *bhakti* that appeared in the south as typified by the Tamil saints indicates that the tenor of *bhakti* had undergone important changes. In the poetry of these saints *bhakti* is not expressed primarily as awe and respect but as ecstatic love.

> Into my vile body of flesh
> you came, as though it were a temple of gold,
> and soothed me wholly and saved me,
> O Lord of Grace, O Gem Most pure.
> Sorrow and birth and death and illusion
> you took from me, and set me free.
> O Bliss! O Light! I have taken refuge in you,
> and never can I be parted from you.[1]

It was in the south also that *bhakti* took on many of its characteristically "protestant" features. The Tamil saints came from all castes, and several rejected outright "the religion of the priest, ritual, and book," consciously rebelling against such "establishment" virtues as wealth and caste *dharma*.[2] This is especially clear in the iconoclastic poetry of the Vīraśaivas, written between the tenth and thirteenth centuries.

> They plunge
> wherever they see water.
>
> They circumambulate
> every tree they see.

---

[1]Māṇikka Vāchakar; quoted in A. L. Basham, *The Wonder That Was India: A Survey of the Culture of the Indian Sub-continent before the Coming of the Muslims*, p. 331.

[2]A. K. Ramanujan, "Medieval 'Protestant' Movements."

How can they know you
O Lord
who adore
waters that run dry
trees that wither ?[1]

In a brahmin house
where they feed the fire
as a god

when the fire goes wild
and burns the house

they splash on it
the water of the gutter
and the dust of the street,

beat their breasts
and call the crowd.

These men then forget their worship
and scold their fire,
O lord of the meeting rivers ![2]

The pot is a god. The winnowing
fan is a god. The stone in the
street is a god. The comb is a
god. The bushel is a god and the
spouted cup is a god.

---

[1]Basavaṇṇa (twelfth-century founder of the Liṅgāyata-sampradāya); in A. K. Ramanujan (trans.), *Speaking of Śiva*, p. 85. Basavaṇṇa's poems have also been translated into English in Basavaṇṇa, *Vacanas of Basavaṇṇa*, ed. H. Deveerappa, trans. L. M. A. Menezes and S. M. Angadi. The above poem is no. 579 in this collection, p. 189.

[2]Basavaṇṇa; in Ramanujan (trans.), *Speaking of Śiva*, p. 85; also in *Vacanas*, no. 584, p. 191. The epithet "Lord of the meeting rivers" (*kūḍala-saṅgama* in Kannada) refers to Śiva, specifically to the sacred place where the rivers Kṛṣṇa and Malaprabha meet. There is a Liṅga temple there called Kūḍala-saṅgama, and it was in this temple, or at this place, that Basavaṇṇa was initiated by his Śaivite *guru*. *Vacanas*, pp. 459-60.

Gods, gods, there are so many
there's no place left
for a foot.

There is only
one god. He is our Lord
of the Meeting Rivers.[1]

Even traditional good works are shunned in the poems of these saints. True devotion, according to Allama, has nothing at all to do with social virtues. While carrying out one's social *dharma* is not necessarily condemned, one feels that it is strictly beside the point.

Feed the poor
tell the truth
make water-places
for the thirsty
and build tanks for a town—

you may then go to heaven
after death, but you'll get nowhere
near the truth of Our Lord.

And the man who knows Our Lord,
he gets no results.[2]

In the *Bhagavadgītā* devotion takes place within the given social structure. In the *bhakti* revival of the south, however, devotion and traditional *dharma* come into conflict. The fervent devotion of the South Indian saints frequently ignores or condemns the status quo and sounds a note of religious rebellion. Another of the Liṅgāyata saints, Mahādeviyakka, a woman, found it impossible, for example, to reconcile her love for Śiva with her love for home and husband.

I have Māyā for mother-in-law;
the world for father-in-law;
three brothers-in-law, like tigers;

[1]Basavaṇṇa; in Ramanujan (trans.), *Speaking of Siva*, p. 84; also in *Vavcanas*, no. 561, p. 182.
[2]Allama; in Ramanujan (trans.), *Speaking of Siva*, p. 167.

and the husband's thoughts
are full of laughing women:
no god, this man.

And I cannot cross the sister-in-law.

But I will
give this wench the slip
and go cuckold my husband with Hara, my Lord.

My mind is my maid:
by her kindness, I join
my Lord,
my utterly beautiful Lord
from the mountain-peaks,
my lord white as jasmine,
and I will make Him
my good husband.[1]

The same poet describes her relationship with God in vividly sexual terms, as the meeting of a lover with her beloved:

Climbing over the bed
you came to my hand,
glinting and shining.
Dazzled in that blaze,
body, mind and vision stilled,
lost in the pouring pleasure
of mating with Śiva,
swinging and joining
in the play of love,
devoted, shameless,
I shall lie with you,
Cannamallikarjuna.[2]

These poems typify the tenor of the *bhakti* movement in the south and suggest the mood that the *bhakti* movements of the north were to assume. Vis-à-vis the type of *bhakti* that is reveal-

[1]Mahādeviyakka; in Ramanujan (trans.), *Speaking of Śiva*, p. 141.
[2]Mahādeviyakka; from A. K. Ramanujan's unpublished translations of Vīraśaiva (Liṅgāyata) poetry.

ed in the *Bhagavadgītā*, there are two important changes that have come about. Intense emotion and often abandon are central elements in the poems.[1] In comparison to these South Indian saints, the *bhakti* of the *Gītā* seems a bit staid and passionless. In part, perhaps, this intense emotion follows from the nature of the God who is worshiped. In the *Gītā* Viṣṇu was revealed in all his majesty and caused Arjuna to tremble before him. In the poems of these Tamil and Kannada Śaivite saints God is primarily a person, often a lover. The relationship is not necessarily between equals, but it is far more intimate than the *bhakti* of the *Gītā*. The second important change is the devotee's relationship or attitude toward society. The Kannada saints often show contempt for established religion and tradition. *Bhakti* for them has nothing to do with habit or custom. It takes place outside the status quo, and in some cases we are told that the true devotee cannot serve God and society at the same time. The *Gītā* taught man to live in society but to maintain an attitude of disinterestedness. For the new *bhakti* the possibility of man living in but not of the world is brought into question and at times is rejected outright.

It might be expected that the radical attitudes of the South Indian saints would be toned down, that a more congenial attitude vis-à-vis society might eventually come about. When the *bhakti* movement blossomed in North India in the fifteenth and sixteenth centuries, however, the radical attitudes of the earlier movement were not diminished. Indeed, they almost became canonized. This is seen quite clearly in two phenomena that were central to the North Indian *bhakti* movements: the efficacy of chanting the name of God and the importance of the *gopīs* as models of devotional excellence.[2]

In the *Bhakti-ratnāvalī* of Viṣṇu Purī, which is based on *ślokas* from the *Bhāgavata-purāṇa*, speaking the name of God is said to absolve all sins.

---

[1]See also *Bhāgavata-purāṇa*, of probably southern origin, XI. 14. 23-24 (V, 189).

[2]Although the *gopīs* made their appearance in the *Bhāgavata-purāṇa*, which was probably a product of South Indian *bhakti*, they only became paradigms for devotion in the north. For the origin and date of the *Bhāgavata-purāṇa*, see Thomas J. Hopkins, "The Social Teachings of the *Bhāgavata Purāṇa*," Singer (ed.), *Krishna*, pp. 3-6.

> The thief, the wine-drinker, the betrayer of his friend, the killer of a Brahman, the polluter of the bed of his *Guru*, the killer of a woman and of a cow, a regicide, a patricide, and other sinners. The expiation of the sin of all these sinners is made by the uttering of the name of Viṣṇu . . . . Whether uttered in calling some one who bears that name, or uttered in jest, or uttered in filling a stop in a tune while singing, or uttered in disrespect, the name of Hari has been spoken of as destructive of sins.[1]

According to the logic of this passage the efficacy of calling on the name of God is independent of all social, ethical, or moral circumstances. *Karma* and *dharma* are made inoperative when man calls upon God. By this simple act a man can revolutionize his situation in the world. When he utters the name of God he transcends ethical standards and becomes a new person existing outside the law, as it were. "Like a covetous thief, the *Prema-bhakta* loses all powers of distinguishing between good and evil."[2] In less drastic terms, devotion to God is the only true measure of a man's worth. No matter what caste a man belongs to, if he loves God he is precious, and if he denies God he is worthless.

> For the *truly low is he who does not serve the Lord*. He alone is truly mean and contemptible. There is no distinction of caste nor of creed in the matter of serving my Lord Krishna . . .
>
> And so it is written "A Brahmin may be endowed with all the twelve gifts. And yet if he be averse to the holy lotus-feet of the Lord, he is nothing. He is worse than a *Chandala* who has his life and riches, his work and speech, mind and all dedicated to the Lord. *For that Chandala makes his own life pure.* And he makes his very caste pure too, while the proud Brahmin cannot make even his own self pure, not to speak of purging his own caste of sins."[3]

The centrality of the *gopis* as paradigmatic for devotion further

---

[1]Vishnu Puri, *Bhakti-Ratnavali*, trans. A Professor of Sanskrit, p. 102; from *Bhāgavata-purāṇa* VI. 2. 7-12.

[2]Rūpa Gosvāmin, *Bhakti-rasāmṛta-sindhu*, translator's Introduction (I, xxviii).

[3]Kṛṣṇadāsa Kavirāja *Caitanya-caritāmṛta*, Antya-lilā 4. 62-64 (pp. 82-83).

underlines the radical nature of the new *bhakti* movements. While such legendary devotees as Nārada and Prahlāda are important as models, the *gopis* are far more popular and important figures. The *gopis* are low-caste, ignorant peasant women. They are not known for their religious austerity or for their ethical and social virtue. They are devotees *par excellence* precisely because they turn their backs on society and their responsibilities to it and answer the call of Kṛṣṇa's flute. They are paradigmatic because of their intense passion for Kṛṣṇa, because they ignore all barriers to be with him alone. In contrast to the *gopis* the *Bhāgavata-purāṇa* portrays the *brāhmans* as stubborn and wilful, refusing to recognize in Kṛṣṇa the Lord of the universe.[1] As was said earlier, the *gopis* particularly in Bengal Vaiṣṇavism, are carefully imitated and are felt to embody the attitude of *mādhurya-bhāva*, the most intense form of *bhakti* for Kṛṣṇa. The centrality of the *gopis* underlines again the fact that *bhakti* is understood as superior to any other religious path and may be accomplished outside, or even with a certain disdain for, society. "He who aspires to this feeling of the Gopis, renounces everything of the Vedic religion. For he works only for loving faith in the Lord Krishna."[2] When one's greed for Kṛṣṇa reaches a certain point, the injunctions of the *śāstras* and *vedas* become irrelevant.[3] The devotee, following the path of *rāgānugā*, devotes his whole mind and being to becoming a *gopi* and like the *gopis* pays little or no attention to religious law or tradition. For the passionate affair between man and Kṛṣṇa is subject to no law. It is a spontaneous affair, an "illicit" affair that transcends tradition and morality.

In the *bhakti* cults the devotional fact was clear: *bhakti* is the pre-eminent path to salvation, the path most pleasing to God as well as the most satisfying and natural to man. In *bhakti* theology this truth was substantiated by the conviction that *bhakti* is man's

---

[1]*Bhāgavata-purāṇa* X. 23 (IV, 99 ff.). The *brāhmans'* wives, however, do respond affirmatively to Kṛṣṇa. The *purāṇa* generally regards orthodox religion as useless and the *brāhmans* as stubborn. For a discussion of the social attitudes of the *Bhāgavata-purāṇa*, see Hopkins, "The Social Teachings of the *Bhāgavata Purāṇa*."

[2]Kṛṣṇadāsa Kavirāja *Caitanya-caritāmṛta*, Madhya-līlā 8. 177 (p. 171).

[3]*Ibid.* 22. 31 (p. 549).

svadharma, his essential duty.[1] Through *bhakti* alone does man realize his true *dharma*.

> It is assumed that, when the spirit is freed from all such extraneous impurities, the natural condition of the spirit is its natural *dharma*. This *dharma* is therefore not a thing that is to be attained or achieved as an external acquirement, but it is man's own nature, which manifests itself as soon as the impurities are removed . . . . as soon as the extraneous elements are wiped out, the spirit shows itself in its own true nature, and then its relation to absolute truth and absolute good is self-evident.[2]

In Bengal Vaiṣṇava philosophy, *jivas* (souls, spiritual essences) are understood to be manifestations of God's *hlādini-śakti*, his most essential self, which is nothing but pure bliss and is epitomized by Rādhā.[3] *Jivas*, however, are inhibited from expressing their true nature due to the influence of *māyā*, which often makes *jivas* averse to God. Salvation is simply the process whereby man recognizes his true nature and gives it vent in devotion to Kṛṣṇa.[4] *Bhakti* is thus not a means to an end but an end in itself. The four aims of life—*kāma*, *artha*, *dharma*, and *mokṣa*—are simply forgotten when man realizes his true nature. When man expresses himself in devotion to Kṛṣṇa, when he sports with Kṛṣṇa in ecstatic bliss, all desires are fulfilled. Man becomes rapt in the intoxicating beauty of Kṛṣṇa.[5]

Not only is *bhakti* the *svadharma* of man, it is an essential part of divine *lilā*. As was noted above,[6] the *hlādini-śakti* is the means whereby Bhagavān (Kṛṣṇa) plays with himself. By means of

---

[1]The term *svadharma* is sometimes used to refer to one's inherited, social *dharma*; see, for example, Rūpa Gosvāmin, *Bhakti-rasāmṛta-sindhu*, Eastern Division: Second Wave, *śloka* 66 (I, 118). I am using the term here, however, to distinguish between man's inherited duty (*dharma*) and his inherent duty (*svadharma*).

[2]Dasgupta, *A History of Indian Philosophy*, IV, 10-11, speaking of the *Bhāgavata-purāṇa* and the medieval *bhakti* cults.

[3]See above, Chap. II, Sec. G.

[4]De, *Vaisnava Faith and Movement*, p. 355.

[5]Rūpa Gosvāmin, *Bhakti-rasāmṛta-sindhu*, Eastern Division: Second Wave, *śloka* 24, Viśvanātha Cakravartin's commentary (I, 83).

[6]See above, Chap. II, Sec. G.

his *hlādinī-śakti*, personified as Rādhā, Kṛṣṇa enjoys his own beauty and revels in his own bliss. Man becomes a part of this love play, this divine self-dalliance when he realizes his own nature as part of the *hlādinī-śakti*. Through *bhakti*, and *bhakti* alone, man causes great delight in Kṛṣṇa, and by means of *bhakti* makes Kṛṣṇa subservient to him.[1] In *bhakti* man becomes the equal of God insofar as he becomes Kṛṣṇa's lover or playmate. Essentially, each *jīva* is a *gopī* whose innate nature is to revel with Kṛṣṇa in Vṛndāvana. "In truth every finite being is essentially an emanation or phase of Radha, to wit, a *mañjarī* or a milkmaid of Eternal Vrindabana in the prime of perennial youth."[2] The entire Vṛndāvana-*līlā*, then, is not simply a once-upon-a-time event, or simply a drama played out in heavenly Vṛndāvana, but a description of God's continuing relationship to man, a description of the mutual intoxication that is realized in man's devotion to God.

The nonutilitarian nature of *bhakti* from the *Gītā* to the Bengal Vaiṣṇavas is maintained consistently. In the *Gītā* man is told to sacrifice all his actions to Viṣṇu without regard to consequences. The devotee of Viṣṇu, while remaining in the world, lives for Viṣṇu alone, remaining indifferent to all else. In effect, the *Gītā* demands of the devotee that he surrender his pragmatic nature, that he deny his bondage to cause and effect. The *bhakta* as pictured in the *Gītā* is a man who remains in society but who has transcended society. Vis-à-vis society the devotee is desireless and selfless, something of an automaton who functions purposelessly. In a sense, the devotee plays a game—he remains in the world of desire and cause and effect but is unaffected by that world. He is simply playing a part. His essential self exists on another plane, where his whole being has been, and is being, sacrificed to Viṣṇu in devotion.

The later *bhakti* movements also emphasized the nonutilitarian aspect of *bhakti*, but from a different point of view. In the medieval *bhakti* cults devotion to God was seen as an expression of man's highest and essential nature. Thus, even *mokṣa* is

---

[1]De, *Vaisnava Faith and Movement*, p. 393, discussing Jīva Gosvāmin's *Prīti-saṁdarbha*.

[2]Krishnadas, *Krishna of Vrindabana*, p. 446.

considered an unworthy goal for the devotee.[1] *Bhakti* presupposes that man surrender his utilitarian nature, that he come to God simply to serve and enjoy him with no ulterior motive. For the *Gītā* this could be done within society, but increasingly the later *bhakti* movements found this to be difficult if not impossible. For the radical movements the idea of playing the social game was not acceptable. Tradition and society increasingly came to be seen as deceptions to be avoided. The emphasis changed from maintaining an attitude of disinterest to acquiring an attitude of rebellion. The attitude toward society, one might say, changed from one of secret humor to rebellious anger. In both cases, though, the denial of pragmatic existence is clear.

If *bhakti* denies man's pragmatic nature, it affirms his inner yearning for spontaneity and bliss. From the devotee's point of view other traditional paths fall short of fulfilling this yearning. The paths of works, knowledge, and *yoga* are too restrictive. Indeed, they are dull in comparison to the way of devotion. "The principle called knowledge is static, uniform, unchangeable and undiversified like the gaze without winking. On the contrary Love and its progressively developed states are diversified like the sidelong look of love."[2] In *bhakti*, when man has surrendered his attachment to desire and appetite, he does not remain in a state of inactive tranquility but participates in active delight. For according to *bhakti* it is not man's essential nature to immobilize himself. His *svadharma* is to revel in bliss, to dance uncontrollably under the intoxicating influence of God. In *bhakti* man's senses no longer serve pragmatic purposes but become platforms for Kṛṣṇa's dance.[3] Penetrated by God, the devotee goes into mad frenzy, weeping, laughing, and dancing. Like a love affair, to which it is repeatedly compared, the devotee's relationship to God is constantly changing, full of surprises, hidden delights, and ecstasies. It is unpredictable and spontaneous. It is an end in itself. *Bhakti* is an ovation of bliss in which the devotee and Kṛṣṇa delight and entertain one another,

---

[1]Rūpa Gosvāmin, *Bhakti-rasāmṛta-sindhu,* Eastern Division: First Wave, *śloka* 33 (I, 43).

[2]Krishnadas, *Krishna of Vrindabana*, p. 461.

[3]Rūpa Gosvāmin, *Bhakti-rasāmṛta-sindhu,* Eastern Division: Second Wave, *śloka* 234, Jīva Gosvāmin's commentary (I, 232).

charmed by each other's beauty and drawn irresistibly by each other's love. In *bhakti* man enters the ultimate felicitous state, which is participation in Kṛṣṇa's sport.

Regarding the relationship of play to religious activity, I have tried to show that *bhakti* emphasizes two characteristics of the play sphere in man's relationship to God. *Bhakti*, like play, is nonutilitarian, transcending the barriers of pragmatic existence. Like play it takes place outside the normal world, either mentally (as in the *Gītā*) or physically (as in the case of the Kannada saints and the *gopīs*). It is superfluous activity that is undertaken as an end in itself. Second, *bhakti* is spontaneous activity that is intrinsically satisfying, as it is the highest and most essential nature of man. Like play, it is also joyous, jubilant, and often merry, particularly when it is directed toward Kṛṣṇa.

Bhakti, then, seems to illustrate the fact that in his relationship to God man's nature as a player comes to the fore. Implicit in the repeated affirmations concerning the nonutilitarian nature of *bhakti* and its expression in frenzy and dance is the recognition that the appropriate meeting ground for man and God is outside the boundaries of the ordinary world, that the appropriate meeting place is the playground rather than the workshop. Or at least the implication is that the appropriate meeting ground is one of freedom and joy, where man is not bound by habit and necessity but is free to behave spontaneously.

It would be an exaggeration, nevertheless, to suggest that *bhakti* is essentially playful or that it can be reduced to or, in some way has originated in, play. For the essential characteristic of play is more often than not clearly missing in *bhakti*. Play is done for fun—it is fun, and when it ceases to be fun it ceases to be play. It is certainly possible to say that *bhakti*, particularly vis-à-vis the rollicking Kṛṣṇa of Vṛndāvana, is sometimes good fun. Dancing, laughing, and singing are certainly common expressions of devotion in the *bhakti* cults. However, awe and wonder (in the *Gītā*) and tears, longing, and loss (in the later *bhakti* cults) are also a part of the devotee's relationship to God. An unmistakable element in *bhakti* is greed for the divine, and when the divine cannot be had, devotion does not cease but continues, often painfully in tears.

Before making a final evaluation of the importance of play to cult based on the phenomena I have discussed, I should like to consider the lives of a few Hindu saints. The saints, as special practitioners of the religious, as peculiarly gifted devotees, can be regarded as embodying those qualities that are striven after by all devotees in the cult. The lives of the saints, precisely because they have been designated saints, illustrate those qualities that are cherished by man and God. The saints are those devotees who have in some way excelled in the religious quest and who are, therefore, paradigmatic for other devotees. Both their techniques and their behavior can be taken as models to imitate and achieve. It is fair to say that in the lives of the saints the essence of man's relationship to God is distilled. In the lives of the saints philosophical and theological discourse, devotional practice, and the inheritance of religious tradition are summed up and played out dramatically in such a way that we are able to separate the essential from the inconsequential. It will be pertinent, therefore, to explore the extent to which play, play techniques, and phenomena that share common characteristics with play are central to the lives of the saints.

CHAPTER IV
THE PLAY OF THE SAINTS

A. The Love-Mad Caitanya

Kṛṣṇa Caitanya (born Viśvambhara) revitalized Vaiṣṇavism in Bengal during his lifetime (1486-1533) with a minimum of organizational effort and theological comment. Although the sect produced famous missionaries (Nityānanda, Śyāmānanda, and Narottama, for example) and industrious theologians (Rūpa and Jīva Gosvāmin, Gopāla Bhaṭṭa, and others), Caitanya himself appears to have written nothing and to have spent a minimum of time trying to organize his following. Although he was reputed to have been a brilliant scholar at Navadvīp (his birthplace), his interest in scholarship seems to have disappeared entirely after he became a *sannyāsin* (in 1510). Indeed, the impact Caitanya had upon his followers appears to have stemmed from the force of his personality alone. The several biographies of his life, although they sometimes portray him as a clever rhetorician and able philosopher, frequently emphasize the dizzying effect he had on those who merely caught a glimpse of him. He is constantly portrayed as being irresistibly beautiful (his most famous epithet is Gaura, or Gaurāṅga, the fair or bright one), seized by emotion, and at times incapable of looking after himself due to his repeated swoonings.

If Caitanya contributed little or nothing to the cult as an organizer or thinker, his life became paradigmatic for devotion. Caitanya exemplified all those aspects of devotion discussed above that illustrate a positive relationship between play and cult. He repeatedly identified himself with transcendent models, manifested frenzy while performing *kīrtan*, and lived out an amazingly "useless" life because of his constant attention to wholehearted devotion to Kṛṣṇa. Indeed, it was to a great extent because of his life that these aspects of devotion became cherished by the cult. I would like, therefore, to discuss briefly various aspects of Caitanya's devotional life in a further attempt to illustrate the importance of play in man's religious activity and expression.

A distinctive feature of Caitanya's life as portrayed in his biographies and poems concerning him is the frequency with which he identified, or was identified, with Kṛṣṇa or Rādhā. Speaking of the poems written about Caitanya (*gauracandrikās*), which are sung as invocations before every performance of *kirtan*, Edward Dimock says:

> Caitanya, in the *Gaurapadas*, acts in either one of these two *bhāvas*—now he is like Kṛṣṇa, the charming light-hearted boy, mischievous, arch, playful, or like Kṛṣṇa the youth, the object of the love of the women of Navadvīp as Kṛṣṇa was the object of the love of the Gopīs at Vṛndāvana; and now he is like Rādhā, falling faint at the sight of a blue cloud, or staring mournfully at the dark waters of a river, as Rādhā at the Yamunā.
>
> . . . .
>
> . . . in the minds of these poets, everything physical that surrounded Caitanya had its reality only as a reflection of that eternal Vṛndāvana where the eternal Kṛṣṇa takes his pleasure.[1]

In the *Caitanya-caritāmṛta*, for example, the most famous of Caitanya's biographies, the author repeatedly compares the saint to Kṛṣṇa. His mother is described as being "struck with the beauty of the Baby looking exactly like Sri Krishna of Gokula, the colour only being different."[2] As a child Caitanya disobeyed his mother and ate dirt, just as Kṛṣṇa did as a child.[3] He stole food from his mother and neighbors and created a nuisance, a distinctive feature of Kṛṣṇa's youth.[4] He is said to have "performed several wild frolics in company of his friends and sported in the waters of the Ganga."[5] In his later life as a *sannyāsin* he is portrayed as leading Kṛṣṇa's famous *rāsa* dance (the circular dance that Kṛṣṇa danced with the *gopis* in which he multiplied himself).[6] During a discussion with Rāmānandarāy, an Oriyan

---

[1]Dimock, "Gauracandrikā," pp. 156, 158.
[2]Kṛṣṇadāsa Kavirāja *Caitanya-caritāmṛta*, Ādi-lilā 13. 114 (p. 165).
[3]*Ibid.* 14. 22 (p. 169).
[4]*Ibid.* 14. 36-37 (p. 170).
[5]*Ibid.* 16. 5 (p. 178).
[6]*Ibid.*, Madhya-līlā 13. 65 (pp. 291-92).

royal minister who became an ardent devotee, Caitanya appeared to him in the form of a cowherd boy with a blue complexion and holding a flute.[1] In the *Caitanya-bhāgavata* Caitanya is described as ascending Kṛṣṇa's throne in a temple and accepting adoration from his devotees.[2] And in the following poem of Jagannātha-dāsa, Caitanya is described as preparing to take the cows out to pasture:

> The youthful Gaura was engrossed in the sports of his earlier incarnation. He then desired the sport of pasturing the cattle. He called (aloud), naming Dāma, Śrīdāma and Subala [cowherd companions of Kṛṣṇa], and tears trickled down his eyes. He said, "Get ready with your staffs, horns and pipes: we shall go to the Banian tree." Then Gaurīdāsa got himself ready and came to Gaura. Brother Abhirāma gave shouts of joy and attached anklets to the feet (of Gaura). Nityananda-candra, the master, walked in front and called the cows out. All the people of Nadiyā [Navadvīp] hastened to see the sportfulness of Gaura. Taking binding ropes and milking pans Jagannāth-dāsa would accompany them.[3]

Caitanya, however, identified, or was identified, with Rādhā even more commonly than with Kṛṣṇa. It is in Rādhā's mood of *mādhurya-bhāva*, the mood of love, that Caitanya is most frequently portrayed. This is a typical description:

> The grief that the Gopis felt when the Lord Krishna went to the holy Mathura, did our Lord feel for his separation from the Lord Krishna. The delirium of the Lord's beloved Radha was repeated by the Lord. For the Lord's feeling too, like hers, gradually passed into delirium. He raved as his beloved Radha had raved when she saw the devotee Uddhava.
>
> And the Lord was always in the frenzy of holy love as Radha

---

[1] *Ibid.* 8. 223 (p. 178).

[2] Vṛndāvana-dāsa *Caitanya-bhāgavata,* Madhya Khaṇḍa 9. 12-54, pp. 571-73.

[3] In S. Sen, *Brajabuli Literature,* p. 83.

> was. And out of this deep frenzy he always considered himself as Radha.[1]

Caitanya's golden complexion is often compared to Rādhā's, and in general his beauty is praised as unsurpassable. At times he is said to have actually appeared as Rādhā before his companions:

> The Lord danced on till it was afternoon. And all the four batches [of devotees] sang till they were tired.
>
> And in this way the Lord's frenzy of love grew. It grew to such a height that all on a sudden the Lord was seen there as Radha.[2]

This remarkable phenomenon is portrayed in a Bengali lithograph that I have before me entitled "Rādhābhāve Gaurāṅga," Gaurāṅga in the Rādhā mood. Caitanya is pictured as feminine: lithe, narrow waisted, long eyed, with delicate limbs. He is wearing anklets, necklace, *śari*, garland, and earrings. His hair falls well below his waist. His lips are dark red, and he smiles softly.

The constant tendency of Caitanya to identify himself with Rādhā or Kṛṣṇa illustrates again the importance of playacting as a means of expressing devotion.[3] In the biographical works of the sect Caitanya's identification came about as a result of remembering Kṛṣṇa's sport. The mention of Kṛṣṇa's sport in song or discourse, or the thought of Kṛṣṇa, frequently triggered furious emotional responses, during which he behaved like Rādhā, or is said actually to have become Rādhā. While Caitanya's turbulent moods are sometimes described without explicit references to Rādhā, the centrality of Rādhā's love for Kṛṣṇa in his devotional life is so pervasive that there was rarely any doubt that Rādhā's love itself was being felt again in the person of Caitanya. The following poem, for example, does not mention

---

[1]Kṛṣṇadāsa Kavirāja *Caitanya-caritāmṛta*, Antya-līlā 14. 11-14 (p. 246).

[2]*Ibid.*, Madhya-līlā 14. 220 (p. 333).

[3]He is also portrayed as identifying with a cowherd boy (Kṛṣṇadāsa Kavirāja *Caitanya-caritāmṛta*, Madhya-līlā 1. 136 [p. 14], 15. 18 [p. 339]) and often played various parts in religious dramas, for example, as Lakṣmī (Vṛndāvanadāsa *Caitanya-bhāgavata*, Madhya Khaṇḍa 18. 5 ff., p. 707).

Rādhā specifically, but it is quite clear that the poet is describing a forlorn, lovesick girl, the sorrowful Rādhā who has been described in hundreds of similar poems :

> Gaura is sitting in a lonely place,
> his head bowed,
> tracing in the dust with his toe-nail.
> He cannot see, through the tears in his eyes;
> in his *māna* [a stage of love typified by pique and longing for union at the same time] his face is pale,
> and when they see (its paleness), the hearts of his companions grow heavy.
> Why doesn't he speak?
> Prem-dāsa (can only sit) with his head in his hands.[1]

What seems evident in this aspect of Caitanya's devotion was his spontaneous inclination to express his devotion according to a transcendent pattern. As the intensity of his devotional emotions increased he became less and less identifiable as the ascetic *sannyāsin* and took on more and more the characteristics of the moody, frantic, love-mad beauty of Vṛndāvana. It seems as if his personality as a *sannyāsin*, and as a male, was incapable of channeling his deepest feelings. Only as Rādhā could they be fully expressed.[2]

The frequency and ease with which Caitanya identified with Rādhā and other transcendent models is illustrated dramatically by a peculiar and distinctive feature of his life. Caitanya seems to have been only barely attached to this world. His behavior indicates he hovered somewhere between the ordinary world

---

[1]In Dimock, "Gauracandrikā," p. 160.

[2]Caitanya's identification with Kṛṣṇa might lead to some confusion at this point. It should be remembered, however, that the supreme model for devotion is the love affair between Rādhā and Kṛṣṇa, obviously a matter of mutual feelings, and that according to Bengal Vaiṣṇava doctrine Kṛṣṇa and Rādhā are both incarnate in the one body of Caitanya. Thus, Caitanya, as the physical presence of this relationship, will sometimes express the equally frenzied feelings of Kṛṣṇa for Rādhā. The mood of Kṛṣṇa, however, is rarely if ever displayed outside the life of Caitanya himself and is never encouraged in the literature and practice of the cult. The underlying assumption, apparently, is that *bhakti* is always directed toward or vis-à-vis Kṛṣṇa, and thereby a clear duality is maintained : that is, between worshiper and worshiped, man and God. To assume the identity of Kṛṣṇa is to imply the philosophical assumption of monism, which is anathema to the Bengal Vaiṣṇavas. Caitanya, it goes without saying, is considered a unique case.

and the transcendent world of Kṛṣṇa. He saw Kṛṣṇa everywhere and was reminded of Kṛṣṇa by a variety of commonplace sights. When he saw the blue neck of a peacock, for example, he was "at once put . . . in mind of his blue Lord Krishna. And he fell unconscious on the ground out of the holy ecstasy of love."[1] When he heard the flute of a cowherd boy he "forgot himself entirely in the holy frenzy of love. He fell down unconscious on the ground, his breath stopped, and foam came out of his mouth."[2] In Purī he mistook Mount Chataka for Mount Govardhana of Vṛndāvana, ran toward it, and was overcome with ecstasy.[3] Also in Purī he saw a flower garden, and it reminded him of the bowers of Vṛndāvana. He was seized by the mood of the *gopis* after Kṛṣṇa deserted them after the *rāsa* dance. "And in the same sentiment the Lord was seized with the ecstasy of search. And he looked at every tree and every creeper wheresoever he found them. And he talked unto them all reciting slokas from the speech of the Gopis."[4] Walking along the seashore in Purī Caitanya looked at the waves and "at once took the sea for the holy Yamuna. And he ran towards it. And unseen by anyone the Lord jumped into the water."[5] Unconscious in the sea he became "absorbed in the joy of that holy game that the Lord Krishna played with the Gopis in the water of the holy Yamuna."[6] In one passage Kṛṣṇadāsa sums up Caitanya's constant tendency to leave one plane for another at the slightest provocation by saying:

> He mistook every forest for the holy Vrindavana and every hill he mistook for the hill Govardhana. Every river on his way [to Vṛndāvana] he took for the holy Yamuna and on the bank of each one of them he sang and danced and wept in deep of ecstasy love.[7]

To use a familiar phrase, Caitanya behaved as though he were in but not of the world. He lived two lives: one as a *sannyāsin* who roamed the countryside with his companions and the other

---

[1] Kṛṣṇadāsa Kavirāja *Caitanya-caritāmṛta*, Madhya-līlā 17. 204 (p. 419).
[2] *Ibid.* 18. 151-52 (p. 439).
[3] *Ibid.*, Antya-līlā 14. 79-80 (p. 255).
[4] *Ibid.* 15. 28-29 (pp. 262-63).
[5] *Ibid.* 18. 25-26 (p. 308).
[6] *Ibid.* 18. 30 (p. 309).
[7] *Ibid.*, Madhya-līlā 17. 52-53 (p. 400).

as a *gopi* or Rādhā on a transcendent plane where he constantly participated in Kṛṣṇa's sports. The slightest stimulus could result in his leaving the former and entering the latter plane. The slightest stimulus could trigger within him a flood of emotions and release him from the confines of his immediate surroundings, or transform his immediate surroundings into transcendent realities. On the transcendent plane his devotional sentiments were consummated. When he entered that "other" realm his devotion found complete fulfilment. His intense devotion that came to be paradigmatic for the cult is directly associated with his ability to enter this transcendent plane almost at will. It was as Rādhā or another member of Kṛṣṇa's retinue that Caitanya's devotion was played out, suggesting again that a prerequisite to ultimately pure devotion is the ability to identify with a participant in the ongoing Kṛṣṇa drama.

Regarding the role of acting as a religious technique and the Bengal Vaiṣṇava doctrine of *rāgānugā*, Caitanya's behavior differs from the pattern discussed earlier in an important respect. There is no indication that he consciously and laboriously imitated the *gopis* generally or Rādhā particularly. His frequent possessions by Rādhā's moods and the sudden transformations in his appearance are not linked to any militant regime of remembrance, imagination, or imitation. This is significant, as it suggests that role-playing is more than a means to an end in the context of his devotion. For Caitanya the assumption of Rādhā's mood was coincidental with his most intense and complete expression of devotion. It was in no way an aspect of devotional discipline and technique but the ultimate goal of all devotional discipline and technique, pure and complete love for Kṛṣṇa.

In the technique of the actor the end in mind is loss of self and the consequent state of *anyamānas*; in the theory of *rāgānugā* the end is complete identification with a transcendent model. In both cases this state is achieved only as a result of a strenuous and disciplined regime. In the case of the actor all his bodily movements and facial expressions must be disciplined to conform to a classical model. In *rāgānugā* the mind is trained to constantly dwell on one or another of Kṛṣṇa's companions with the aim in mind to become that companion. The goal is to overcome, subdue, or completely inhibit one's own identity, to achieve loss of self. In the case of Caitanya's identification with Rādhā, however, the emphasis is not so much upon the inhibition of self as upon the extension of self. There is no doubt that Caitanya was a highly emotional person given to sudden attacks of weeping, trembling, and frenzy. This aspect of his personality is not at all inhibited by his identification with Rādhā but extended and epitomized by it. Caitanya's easy and spontaneous participation in Rādhā's moods suggests that she was not another personality that he acquired but was simply a facet of his own personality, that facet which enabled him to express his devotion most completely.

The importance of frenzy in the worship of Kṛṣṇa among the Bengal Vaiṣṇavas can partly be traced to the fact that it was the hallmark of Caitanya's devotion. Perhaps even more characteristic than his continual identification with Rādhā, with which it is intimately bound up,[1] was Caitanya's emotional fervor. He is often portrayed as experiencing several different moods in rapid succession, or at the same time.

> And the Lord passed his days in dancing as the various feelings moved him. For now it was remorse, now sorrow, now humility and now impatience, now pleasure and now patience and now again anger, that moved the Lord thus. And in all these he passed his days.[2]

> The Lord Chaitanya, that holy moon of Gauḍa at once stood up and wept.
>
> And the heart of the Lord went mad in holy love. And he began to run sometimes this way and sometimes that.
>
> And sometimes he laughed and danced and sang. And at the very next moment again he thundered.
>
> And the Lord said over and over again, "Ah poor me, Ah poor me." And as he said this his voice was choked and tears flowed from his eyes. Now, he shook and now he perspired, now he looked stiff and now his colour changed. And now again his whole body was permeated with joy.
>
> And thus all these feelings, repentance and grief, weakness

---

[1]See, for example, *ibid.*, Madhya-līlā 3. 119-25 (p. 52) and Antya-līlā 19. 30-32 (p. 324).

[2]*Ibid.*, Madhya-līlā 2. 65 (p. 37).

> and pride, joy and humility all seemed equally to overwhelm the Lord.[1]

Caitanya is rarely depicted as expressing his devotion in quiet solitude. He did not seek to calm his turbulent feelings in withdrawn meditation but gave them vent constantly and with gusto. He was repeatedly overwhelmed by emotions and gave himself up to frenzied singing and dancing and behaved like a drunkard or a madman.

> As soon as he heard such divine things from holy Mukunda [a *kīrtan*-singer who was leading a group of devotees in song], the jewel of all *brāhmans* became possessed. The Lord began to sing the name of Hari with a thundering voice. He reeled and fell down repeatedly, and none could control him. Trembling, laughing, awe, sweating, ecstasy, and thundering, all these *bhāvas* appeared at once.[2]

> Overcome by ecstasy and madness, the Lord's heart would not be still. Everything he said and did was symptomatic of madness.[3]

Caitanya appeared not to have had the ability to control himself, to contain his feelings within. His behavior did not appear premeditated, logical, orderly, or routine. He was tossed by deep emotion that racked his body. He was rent by conflicting emotions and repeatedly fell to the ground in swoons or fits of stupor. He gave expression to every nuance of feeling spontaneously and unabashedly. His behavior seemed marked by a minimum of "the conscious working of the will." His body was unwilling or unable to contain the torrent of emotions within, and it was racked by great awe and trembling, it burned like a raging fire one moment, and the next his teeth chattered like a boy's as he was overcome with great cold.[4] His emotional capacity was limitless, and his emotional expression was extraordinary. He was completely awash in a sea of sentiment, feeling, and emotion. Although he was an ascetic *sannyāsin*

---

[1] *Ibid.* 4. 196-99 (p. 80).
[2] Vṛndāvana-dāsa *Caitanya-bhāgavata*, Madhya Khaṇḍa 2. 217-19, p. 473.
[3] Kṛṣṇadāsa Kavirāja *Caitanya-caritāmṛta*, Antya-līlā 19. 62; my translation.
[4] Vṛndāvana-dāsa *Caitanya-bhāgavata*, Madhya Khaṇḍa 8. 153-59, p. 559.

he behaved like a fickle child or a love-sick girl, restless, moody, and excitable.

While Caitanya's behavior stands in direct opposition to that of the self-contained, immovable, immutable *yogin*, his frenetic activity leads in one respect to a similar end. The *yogin* through his withdrawal achieves the state of being in but not of the world. He is unaffected by his surroundings or pragmatic desires and appetites. In his self-imposed "exile" from the world and society, he is an inert, "useless" figure. As was said above, Caitanya's repeated identification with Rādhā and his apparent second sight, by which he saw Kṛṣṇa and Vṛndāvana in everything, also resulted in his being in but not of the world. During those periods of identification, ecstasy, stupor, or possession, Caitanya remained out of touch with the phenomenal world. These periods often lasted days, as, for example, when he visited Vṛndāvana. In that holy place he was almost continually in a state of ecstasy or possession, and danced from place to place.

> And at Vrindavana our holy Lord Chaitanya went from one place to another and he pleased the trees and jungles with his holy presence. And he himself was also pleased to travel hither and thither in his holy ecstasy for the Lord Krishna.
>
> . . . .
>
> And he travelled in these places dancing all along. And at last he reached Aritgrama [a place of pilgrimage near Vṛndāvana where Rādhā's tank is located] and here he recovered his senses. For so long he, though a moving figure, was unconscious, yea, quite unconscious as to what he himse f was doing.[1]

Unconscious of the world around him, possessed by the "other mind," Caitanya consistently enjoyed visions of Rādhā and Kṛṣṇa and Vṛndāvana in which he would either take part directly or enjoy the action vicariously as a spectator.[2] Eventually, toward the end of his life, Caitanya seems to have been so immersed in that transcendent world of Kṛṣṇa's sport that he could not take care of himself. Because he was likely to dart off

---

[1] Kṛṣṇadāsa Kavirāja *Caitanya-caritāmṛta*, Madhya-līlā 18. 1-2 (p. 422).

[2] *Ibid.*, Antya-līlā 14. 15-18 (p. 247), 17. 22-25 (pp. 293-95), 18. 77-79 (pp. 308-9).

in pursuit of Kṛṣṇa, provoked by the blue neck of a peacock or the color of the sky, or jump into lakes, rivers, or even the ocean (mistaken for the River Jumna), or suddenly collapse in stupors of longing for Kṛṣṇa, he had to be watched and protected constantly by his companions lest he inadvertently injure or kill himself. Near the end of his life he remained unconscious for long periods of time, or behaved as if only semiconscious, raving and weeping uncontrollably. He seems to have increasingly lost his interest in his surroundings and performed his daily chores without the slightest involvement or interest in them.

> [Caitanya]sang and danced continuously as if he were mad, but he still prayed, bathed, and ate out of habit or instinct.[1]

> In this way the Lord passed his days. And he was absorbed day and night in his love for the Lord Krishna. And he was unconscious of his ownself. And the Lord had now three conditions. At times he was altogether absorbed; on other occasions he was half conscious. And at times again he was in full consciousness. And the Lord bathed and ate and performed his duties as it were by a habit. For he was not his master. And he seemed like a machine turning always by itself like the wheel of the potter.[2]

Caitanya's life, particularly in its later stages, was a "useless" affair. As helpless as a child, as distracted as a girl in love, he was incapable of, and disinterested in, managing his day-to-day life. He was apathetic toward his duties in this world and overwhelmed with longing to be with Kṛṣṇa in that "other" realm. His actions in this world were completely without desire for fruits, as he had lost all interest in such fruits. He had transcended the barriers of pragmatic existence and behaved like an automaton. Vis-à-vis the cause-and-effect world, his life was aimless and irrelevant. His life, in fact, epitomized the qualities of genuine *bhakti* discussed earlier. He acted with complete disregard for fruits, cared nothing for social *dharma*, and acted spontaneously and unashamedly, reveling in the ecstasy of bliss. His immense impact upon his followers did not

---

[1] *Ibid.* 14. 37; my translation.
[2] *Ibid.* 15. 4-5 (p. 259).

stem from any accomplishment that could be considered pragmatically successful but, on the contrary, from the very spontaneity and uselessness of his behavior, as indicated in the following passages:

> And the Lord now stopped the dance of his devotees. And he himself began to dance as he had done every year. And Ballava saw the beauty of the Lord. He also saw the Lord's ecstasy. And as he saw these, he was convinced that the Lord himself was *the holy Lord Krishna.*[1]

A study of matters will indeed increase the knowledge of the same. But the abstruse secrets of matters will always escape you if you are bereft of the mercy of God.

> All the signs of Godhood exist fully in our Lord Caitanya; and you yourself have seen his divine ecstasy. And yet you do not believe that our Lord is the God Incarnate.[2]

> In company with his followers Gaura the handsome and superb was going to the bank of the Ganges. Looking at that beauty all my bashfulness and decorum fled away, and I became restless. O friend! manifold are the charms of Gorā's loveliness: I am a lady of a noble family, and yet I am so much perturbed, and in a moment, have become mad, as it were. My heart is pierced through and through with the darts of the Bodyless One (*i.e.*, the god of love): slander by men is at a distance . . . . In the sea of Gaura's loveliness. I shall throw down my life and my youthfulness: this is the desire of my heart. All sense of decorum and reverence for my superiors I will forsake: I will care nothing for the dignity of my family. The heart of Gokulānanda has drowned itself into the sea of that loveliness, and it does not know how to swim (back).[3]

Caitanya's beauty, dancing, and ecstasy marked him as special and implied his divinity. He was more than human as he

---

[1]*Ibid.*, 7. 62-63 (p. 156).

[2]*Ibid.*, Madhya-līlā 6. 87-89 (p. 105). Gopinātha is trying to convince Sārvabhauma of Caitanya's divinity.

[3]From Gokulānanda (seventeenth century); in S. Sen, *Brajabuli Literature*, p. 186.

reveled in those things that are irrelevant and extra vis-à-vis man's quest for achieving useful ends. His transcendence of the human sphere was not marked by cleverness, brilliance, or industry—all useful attributes in the phenomenal world—but by his superfluous characteristics: his beauty, his lack of control, his dancing and singing. As a socially productive being Caitanya was a complete failure. Vis-à-vis the pragmatic human context in which actions proceed "according to the conscious working of the will," his life was nothing more than an attractive bauble.

It would be an exaggeration to say that Caitanya's emotional and frenzied devotion is essentially playful, and therefore demonstrates his dependence upon play as a mode of expressing his relationship to Kṛṣṇa. There are, nevertheless, aspects of his peculiar style of devotion to Kṛṣṇa that bear important similarities to play. As suggested earlier, his devotion transcended the bondage of cause and effect. He cared nothing for fruits. His devotion was an end in itself, an intrinsically satisfying activity that proceeded spontaneously. The aimlessness, frenzy, and flamboyance of his life were adornments in the ordinary world. Like Kṛṣṇa's, his life was ornamental rather than functional or purposive. And it is no doubt partly because of these "extra" characteristics described above—his beauty, ecstasy, frenzy, dancing, and singing, the very uselessness of his life—that Caitanya's entire biography is referred to as play (*līlā*) in Bengal Vaiṣṇavism (see below).

It is true too, furthermore, that Caitanya often played both by himself and with his devotees, that he laughed, joked, and sported with his friends, and that this was usually done in a devotional context. In these instances there is an indication that for Caitanya devotion, or religious activity generally, was fun, that he enjoyed it immensely, that it amused him. Caitanya was particularly prone to play when he was overcome by the *bhāva* or emotion of a boy or child, as in this passage:

> For a moment he fell under the spell of boyishness and became restless. Imitating boyish pranks, he made sounds in imitation of musical instruments. He moved his feet in

various ways and laughed loudly. Under this spell, he crawled on all fours like a child.[1]

In a poem by Govindadāsa, Caitanya's playfulness is described as a concomitant to his grace and beauty:

In my mind, I am numbed—
I have just seen Gaurāṅga
going to the bathing-*ghat* with his companions;
I have just seen the beloved son of Śacī; on the road,
laughing and joking with his friends—
laughing, flirting with glance and gesture, in what game
I cannot say.
If of all lightnings one were made, and that one caught,
even that would not compare to one line of my Gaurāṅga's
body.
At the dancing of his eyes and the arching of his brows,
the heart within me leaped.
In the features of his face, the moon was glowing,
and at the sight of him, a wreath of flowers in his curly hair,
a stream of tears welled from my eyes.
He drives young women to madness, and to disgrace their
families.
But he wears clothing on that beautiful body—
it is for this that Govinda-dāsa weeps.[2]

A clear sense of fun is seen in this passage from the *Caitanya-bhāgavata*, which describes a session of *kirtan*:

The Lord said, "Now I feel joyous in my heart," and laughing, Śrības began to do *kirtan*. And then with great bliss the sound of *kirtan* was raised, and the assemblage of Vaiṣṇavas laughed with joy, rollicking in laughter. The handsome fair one danced on with great pleasure.[3]

And in this passage Caitanya's play with his devotees is reminiscent of Kṛṣṇa's sport with the *gopis* in the Jumna:

---

[1]Vṛndāvana-dāsa *Caitanya-bhāgavata*, Madhya Khaṇḍa 8. 174-75, p. 560.
[2]In Dimock, "Gauracandrikā," p. 159.
[3]Vṛndāvana-dāsa *Caitanya-bhāgavata*, Madhya Khaṇḍa 16. 19-21, p. 685.

And the band of singers from Gauda now danced. And as all met the Lord, they began to weep in the ecstasy of love. And the holy water-game proceeded.

And as the Lord Govinda played in water, the devotees all sang and danced, beat drums and other instruments of music. On the bank there was a great uproar, while in water there was the holy game. And the uproar of the singers of Gauda who sang the holy song mixed with the cry of lamentations of love: and both together made one huge uproar that filled the creation.

And the Lord now went down into waters with all his followers. And he played with them all in great joy.[1]

The importance of play in the life of Caitanya, finally, is seen by the fact that in the works and jargon of the cult his activity is consistently referred to as *līlā*. As has no doubt been noticed by now, the *Caitanya-caritāmṛta*, the famous biography of Caitanya by Kṛṣṇadāsa, is divided into three parts: the Ādi-, Madhya-, and Antya-līlās—the early, middle, and late playings. The implication is that all of Caitanya's actions were free, transcending the limitations of the pragmatic world, that none of his actions were performed because of necessity, that all his actions were done for the fun of it.[2] It is no exaggeration to say that Caitanya's mission itself was to play, to display himself aimlessly for the salvation of men. For it was his appearance, his irresistible beauty, and his useless, extra, characteristics that attracted men. In fact, Kṛṣṇadāsa's statement about the purpose of Caitanya's life on earth says just this:

> It was to liberate all, that Lord Chaitanya appeared on earth as the incarnation of grace. And it is for delivering all that He played the fun and tried boundless tricks.[3]

Caitanya appeared. And that was enough. For all his actions were full of grace, and he himself was lovely. He lived

---

[1]Kṛṣṇadāsa Kavirāja *Caitanya-caritāmṛta*, Antya-līlā 10. 44-47 (p. 195).

[2]The tendency to call all Caitanya's actions play is seen in this passage from the *Caitanya-caritāmṛta*: "I shall now enumerate the boyhood *līlās* of the Lord, / The chief among them being his study." *Ibid.*, Ādi-līlā 15. 2; my translation.

[3]*Ibid.* 7. 36 (p. 100).

spontaneously, superfluously, and beautifully. He did not appear to transform the creation but to adorn it, to set it dancing by his example and by his intoxicating influence.

> A wonderful *avatār*—Gaurāṅga—a wonderful *avatār* is made . . .
> Jagāi, Mādhāi [two ruffians of Navadvīp who later became devotees of Caitanya]—a tribute to the Master—dancing,
> The moon is dancing, the sun is dancing, and the stars are dancing, dancing,
> The denizens of hell are dancing, singing "Gaura, Gaura."
> Crowds of *bhaktas*, joyful dancing,
> the poor and broken, love-drunk, dancing,
> the dumb and blind and sick (are dancing), the out-cast in deliverance (dancing)—
> and only Vāsu Ghoṣ can say: I have been deprived.[1]

B. *Rāmakṛṣṇa the Child*

Three and a half centuries after the time of Caitanya another great saint appeared in Bengal. He was Rāmakṛṣṇa, and like Caitanya his life illustrates the importance of play in the lives of Hindu saints. Indeed, he was frequently compared to Caitanya by his devotees, who saw in his appearance and methods and expressions of devotion a reincarnation of Caitanya.[2] While Rāmakṛṣṇa was probably more attracted to Kālī than to Kṛṣṇa, and while he is invariably linked to her today (he is commonly shown with Kālī in contemporary lithographs and images), he did, in fact, worship many deities, among whom Kṛṣṇa was one of the most popular. And while Rāmakṛṣṇa has also come to be associated with the thought and methods of strict monism, he was a great practitioner of *bhakti* and employed many of those devotional techniques and expressions discussed above.

First of all, Rāmakṛṣṇa, like Caitanya, was a great actor and frequently recommended the technique of *rāgānugā* to his disciples.

---

[1]In Dimock, "Gauracandrikā," p. 160.

[2]For example, M., *Gospel of Ramakrishna*, pp. 189-90, and Swami Saradananda, *Sri Ramakrishna, the Great Master*, trans. Swami Jagadananda p. 169.

> A man can change his nature by imitating another's character. He can get rid of a passion like lust by assuming the feminine mood. He gradually comes to act exactly like a woman. I have noticed that men who take female parts in the theatre speak like women or brush their teeth like women while bathing.[1]

He himself frequently assumed various moods and roles befitting the nature of the deity he was worshiping at a particular time. When he worshiped the child Rām (Rāmlala), for example, he immersed himself in the mood of a mother. He was so successful that women soon came to disregard the fact that he was a male.

> While worshiping Ramlala as the Divine Child, Sri Ramakrishna's heart became filled with motherly tenderness, and he began to regard himself as a woman. His speech and gestures changed. He began to move freely with the ladies of Mathur's family, who now looked upon him as one of their own sex.[2]

He worshiped the child Kṛṣṇa by identifying one of his youthful disciples, Rakhal, with his object of adoration, and himself assuming the attitude of Yaśodā, Kṛṣṇa's foster mother.

> During these days Sri Ramakrishna's heart overflowed with motherly love like the love Yashoda felt for Krishna. So he kept Rakhal with him. Rakhal felt toward the Master as a child feels toward its mother. He would sit leaning on the Master's lap as a young child leans on its mother while suckling her breast.
>
> . . . .
>
> At the sight of Rakhal his eyes expressed the tender feelings of a mother, a love like that which had filled the heart of Mother Yashoda at the sight of the baby Krishna.
>
> . . . .
>
> During these days the Master looked on Rakhal as Gopala [the child Kṛṣṇa] and on himself as Mother Yashoda.[3]

[1]M., *Gospel of Ramakrishna*, p. 176.
[2]*Ibid.*, pp. 24-25.
[3]*Ibid.*, pp. 185, 195, 429.

Rāmakṛṣṇa, unlike the orthodox Vaiṣṇavas, used to dress as a woman in order to facilitate his identification with a particular feminine mood.

> He . . . now applied his mind to the discipline of the two principal devotional modes of Vatsalya and Madhura [parental and erotic] practised by the Vaishnava teachers. During that period he looked upon himself as a woman friend of the divine Mother, and engaged himself in fanning Her with a Chamara. Dressed in a woman's apparel and surrounded by ladies, he paid obeisance to the Devi during Her autumn worship . . . and on account of the absorption in feminine feelings, often forgot that he had a male body.[1]

> Engaged in the practices of the Madhura Bhava, the Master became anxious to use clothes and ornaments proper to a woman. Knowing that desire of his, the greatly devout Mathur had the pleasure of adorning him now with a precious sari, now with a skirt, a gauze scarf and a bodice. Desirous of making his female mode of dress perfect in all respects, Mathur decked him with a head of artificial hair and set of gold ornaments. . . .Adorned in such dress and ornaments, the Master gradually merged so much in the mood of the Woman of Vraja desirous to have the love of Krishna, that the consciousness that he was a male person disappeared altogether and every thought, word, or movement of his became womanly. The Master, we were told by himself, was thus in a woman's dress for six months under the faith that he was a spiritual consort of God.[2]

Rāmakṛṣṇa often used to imitate, or become possessed by, the moods of Rādhā specifically[3] and sometimes enjoyed visions of her. In one case, he is reported to have seen the figure of Rādhā approach him and enter his body, thereby marking his complete identification with her.[4]

Rāmakṛṣṇa also imitated several models and moods in the

[1]Saradananda, *The Great Master,* p. 206.
[2]*Ibid.,* pp. 233-34.
[3]*Ibid.,* p. 235; M., *Gospel of Ramakrishna,* pp. 179, 224, 445.
[4]Saradananda, *The Great Master,* pp. 236-37.

masculine mode. In his attempt to fully identify with the mood of the servant (*dāsya-bhāva*), he imitated Hanumān, the great and loyal monkey companion of Rāma.

> About this time he began to worship God by assuming the attitude of a servant toward his master. He imitated the mood of Hanuman, the monkey chieftain of the *Ramayana*, the ideal servant of Rama and traditional model for this self-effacing form of devotion. When he meditated on Hanuman his movements and his way of life began to resemble those of a monkey. His eyes became restless. He lived on fruits and roots. With his cloth tied around his waist, a portion of it hanging in the form of a tail, he jumped from place to place instead of walking. And after a short while he was blessed with a vision of Sita, the divine consort of Rama, who entered his body and disappeared there with the words, "I bequeath to you my smile."[1]

He sought success in the mood of friendship (*sākhya-bhāva*) by imitating the boy companions of Kṛṣṇa.

> During the first four years of the Master's spiritual practices when he did not accept any external help, he undertook the disciplines of the modes of Santa and Dasya and sometimes that of Sakhya like that of Sridama, Sudama and other friends of Sri Krishna at Vraja and attained success in all of them.[2]

The importance of role-playing in the devotion of Rāmakṛṣṇa in these examples could not be clearer. He seeks to attain perfection in his devotion to God by imitating transcendent models that epitomize one attitude or another. He channels his feelings for God through the roles, or by means of the roles, of those transcendent figures who are felt to best exemplify these feelings. Indeed by imitating these models these feelings are intensified and perfected until, at a certain point, he becomes possessed by the model and fully realizes the feeling in all its intensity and perfection. Rāmakṛṣṇa's devotional predilection for imitating

[1]M., *Gospel of Ramakrishna*, p. 16.
[2]Saradananda, *The Great Master*, p. 206.

models exemplifies the importance of role-playing both as a technique, wherein the model acts as a guide to devotion, and as an extension of the devotee's devotional expression, wherein the devotee so identifies with the model that he becomes that model, thereby extending his personality and enabling him to express sentiments and emotions that would be difficult or impossible to express otherwise due to certain limitations of usual personality.

Rāmakṛṣṇa, like Caitanya, did not spend his time in composing theological, or even devotional, works. He spent no time organizing a following. His religious activity, too, was characteristically emotional, and he was often described as being either intoxicated or mad.

> Like a drunkard, he would reel to the throne of the Mother, touch her chin by way of showing his affection for Her, and sing, talk, joke, laugh, and dance.[1]

> Presently Sri Ramakrishna returned from the pine grove. The devotees noticed that he was in an ecstatic mood and was reeling like a drunkard.[2]

Hṛday, the personal attendant of Rāmakṛṣṇa during his early days as priest at the Dakṣiṇeśvar temple, describes his master as having an intimate relationship with Kālī and behaving as if intoxicated while under her influence:

> I saw his bosom and eyes always reddish like those of a drunkard. Reeling in that condition, he left the worshipper's seat, and ascending the altar caressed the divine Mother by affectionately touching Her chin and began singing, laughing, joking, and conversing with Her; or, sometimes, he caught hold of Her hands and danced.[3]

Rāmakṛṣṇa himself seemed to sense the appropriateness of comparing divine ecstasy to intoxication or drunkenness. For on one occasion the sight of several drunken men in a tavern produced in him an esctatic trance. He was driving through Calcutta in a carriage when this strange incident took place:

---

[1] M., *Gospel of Ramakrishna*, p. 14.
[2] *Ibid.*, p. 523.
[3] Saradananda, *The Great Master*, p. 145.

> The noise attracted the Master's attention to the shop, and he happened to see the drunkards expressing their joy noisily. As soon as he saw their merry-making due to the drinking of wine, the memory of the blissful nature of the universal Cause arose in his mind through association. It was not the memory alone, but its direct experience also followed and he was completely filled with inebriation and his words became indistinct. That was not all. He brought out suddenly a part of his person and his right leg out of the carriage, placed his foot on the footboard and stood there. Like one drunk, he expressed joy at this, moving his hands; and making gesticulations of his body cried out loudly, "Very nice, fine enjoyment, bravo, bravo !"[1]

For Rāmakṛṣṇa the loss of inhibition brought about during intoxication, the dropping away of the mean and harsh aspects of reality, the feeling of having escaped and transcended the ordinary world that sometimes accompanies drunkenness, the joyous attitude of living for the moment were no doubt reminiscent of his own periods of ecstasy. The drunkard and the ecstatic saint both reel through the world smiling, laughing, and happy. For a time, in the case of the former, and perhaps eternally, in the case of the latter, they have given the lie to the bleak demands of the pragmatic, rationalistic, moralistic world.

Rāmakrsna's behavior also bordered on madness, and in some respects he acted as madly as his mistress, Kālī. His moods and behavior were unpredictable, and he was prone to fall into fits of ecstasy suddenly and frequently. He is described in this passage shortly after his marriage and his return to Dakṣiṇeśvar to the Kālī temple there :

> His madness reappeared tenfold. The same meditation and prayer, the same ecstatic moods, the same burning sensation, the same weeping, the same sleeplessness, the same indifference to the body and the outside world, the same divine delirium.[2]

[1]*Ibid.*, p. 538.

[2]M., *Gospel of Ramakrishna*, p. 18.

At first, in fact, Rāmakṛṣṇa was greatly concerned about his condition, for he thought that perhaps he really was going insane. He consulted several theologians and devotees, however, and was reassured that his behavior was that of a saint and not of a madman.[1] Later in his life he even told his devotees that the marks of madness were characteristic of great devotion and should not be ridiculed. "Sometimes the perfect jñani behaves like a ghoul. He does not discriminate about food and drink, holiness and unholiness. A perfect knower of God and a perfect idiot have the same outer signs."[2] Rāmakṛṣṇa suggested that such attributes of madness as a lack of interest in the world and an element of naïveté that permits foolish behavior are the result of meritorious actions in past lives: "There is such a thing as inborn tendencies. When a man has performed many good actions in his previous births, in the final birth he becomes guileless. In the final birth he acts somewhat like a madcap."[3]

Insofar as sanity is measured according to the standards of achievement in the pragmatic world, the behavior of a "drunken," ecstatic, and laughing saint who cares nothing for 'achievement" can justifiably be called mad. Madness implies that a certain distance exists between the real world and the mind of the madman, that he has in some way lost touch with the normal environment, that he has become uninvolved to the point where he can no longer function effectively. Such was the case with Rāmakṛṣṇa, and such was the case with Caitanya. Both had to be cared for lest they physically injure themselves in their "mad" fits of ecstasy in which the world simply ceased to exist for them. And, as Rāmakṛṣṇa suggests, madness sometimes implies lack of guile. The town fool is traditionally a great target for practical jokes and teasing, as he never learns suspicion and calculation. He is completely open to suggestion, completely gullible. Because he himself does not act deviously, he never suspects the plot until it is too late, and is always delightfully surprised. The saint, too, is without guile or calculation, as naïve as the town

---

[1]For example, a *brāhman* woman from East Bengal assured him that his physical symptoms, "shedding of tears, a tremor of the body, horripilation, perspiration, and a burning sensation," were all typical of great devotion and were to be seen in such cases as Rādhā and Caitanya. M., *Gospel of Rāmakrishna*, pp. 18-19.

[2]*Ibid.*, p. 792.

[3]*Ibid.*, p. 783.

buffoon in many ways, or, as we shall see later, as naïve as a child.

The devotional frenzy that was so characteristic of Caitanya was also manifest in Rāmakṛṣṇa. As has already been indicated, Rāmakṛṣṇa did not behave normally but as one drunk or mad. In the process of devotion he would frequently sing, dance, laugh, and cry, giving vent openly to his emotions in much the same way as Caitanya did. The following passage might well have been taken from a Vaiṣṇava scripture describing Caitanya, and indeed the author suggests that there is a remarkable affinity between the two:

> He joined the kirtan party of Navadvip Gosvami, Mani Sen's guru, and danced, totally forgetting the world. Every now and then he stood still in samadhi, carefully supported by Navadvip Gosvami for fear he might fall to the ground . . . The crowd seemed to become infected by the Master's divine fervour and swayed to and fro, chanting the name of God until the very air seemed to reverberate with it. Drums, cymbals, and other instruments produced melodious sounds. The atmosphere became intense with spiritual fervour. The devotees felt that Gauranga himself [Caitanya] was being manifested in the person of Sri Ramakrishna. Flowers were showered from all sides on his feet and head. The shouting of the name of Hari was heard even at a distance, like the rumbling of the ocean.[1]

Kirtan was a favorite means of devotion for Rāmakṛṣṇa, but during such devotional song fêtes Rāmakṛṣṇa did not limit his devotion to Kṛṣṇa, with whom this type of devotion is usually associated. He also worshiped Kālī by means of congregational singing that praised her with the songs of Rāmprasād or with songs composed by Rāmakṛṣṇa himself. And he betrayed in his worship of Kālī the same frenzy that Caitanya did for Kṛṣṇa. As Trailokya, one of his disciples, sang:

> Sri Ramakrishna danced, intoxicated with divine love. Many times he went into samadhi. He stood still, his eyes fixed, his face beaming, with one hand on the shoulder of a beloved

---

[1]*Ibid.*, p. 253. See also p. 599, and Saradananda, *The Great Master*, p. 482.

disciple. Coming down a little from the state of ecstasy, he danced again like a mad elephant. Regaining consciousness of the outer world, he improvised lines to the music:

"O Mother, dance about Thy devotees!
Dance Thyself and make them dance as well.
O Mother, dance in the lotus of my heart;
Dance, O Thou the ever blessed Brahman!
Dance in all Thy world-bewtching beauty!"

An indescribable scene. The exquisite and celestial dance of a child completely filled with ecstatic love of God and identified heart and soul with the Divine Mother! The Brahmo devotees danced around the Master again and again. . . . Many of them wept like children, crying "Mother! Mother!"[1]

Rāmakrṣna was also characterized by Caitanya's "second sight," by means of which he was in but not of the world, by means of which the slightest provocation would remind him of God and send him into ecstasy. The following incident took place at a fair in Calcutta:

I saw an English boy leaning against a tree. As he stood there his body was bent in three places [a famous posture of Kṛṣṇa, called his *tribhaṅga* pose]. The vision of Krishna came before me in a flash. I went into samadhi. Once, at Sihore, I fed the cowherd boys. I put sweetmeats into their hands. I saw that these boys were actually the cowherd boys of Vrindavana, and I partook of the sweetmeats from their hands.[2]

This second sight, as in the case of Caitanya, was particularly evident when he visited Vṛndāvana.

In the dusk I would walk on the bank of the Jumna when the cattle returned along the sandy banks from their pastures. At the very sight of those cows the thought of Krishna would

[1]M., *Gospel of Ramakrishna*, p. 632.
[2]*Ibid.*, pp. 231-32.

flash in my mind. I would run along like a madman, crying: "Oh, where is Krishna? Where is my Krishna?"[1]

The drunken, mad, ecstatic nature of Rāmakṛṣṇa's devotion resulted in his leading a "useless" life, a life given to spontaneous expressions of emotion, singing, dancing, and stupor. His tendency to fall suddenly into stupor or ecstasy made him incapable of looking after himself responsibly. For years his nephew, Hṛday, looked after him, and when Hṛday left him it was clear that he could not take care of himself. "On account of his frequent spiritual moods he could hardly take care of himself. The lack of an attendant caused him great inconvenience."[2] He would spend long periods during which he was completely oblivious to the world around him and had to be watched carefully lest he injure himself. His condition is aptly compared to Caitanya's:

> The enchanting form of the Master reminded the devotees of Chaitanya, another Incarnation of God. The Master passed alternately through three moods of divine consciousness: the inmost, when he completely lost all knowledge of the outer world; the semi-conscious, when he danced with the devotees in an ecstasy of love; and the conscious, when he joined them in loud singing.[3]

The point, again, is that Rāmakṛṣṇa's states left him in only tenuous touch with the phenomenal world. His life unfolded on an "other" plane. He lived primarily in a transcendent sphere where pragmatic and utilitarian activity are irrelevant. From the point of view of the ordinary working world, his life was useless, a mere ornament. In his mad frenzy he was incapable of, and in his spirit disinclined to, comfort himself according to the laws of pragmatic existence. He did not live to work but to revel in ecstasy, and so his life appeared purposeless. "The doings of Sri Ramakrishna, who was always of the nature of a boy, appeared purposeless in the eyes of ordinary people."[4] He moved as if in a dream. "The vain clamour of the world did

[1] *Ibid.*, p. 129.
[2] *Ibid.*, p. 93.
[3] *Ibid.*, pp. 189-90. See also p. 330.
[4] Saradananda, *The Great Master*, p. 127.

not reach his ears at all. Although in the world, he was not of it. The external world was now transformed for him into a dream world."[1]

The spontaneous, superfluous nature of Rāmakṛṣṇa's style of life is expressed in his relationship with his devotees, with whom he frequently joked, laughed, and played. He thoroughly enjoyed this aspect of the relative world (which he called the *līlā* aspect of reality, as opposed to the *nitya* aspect, the indivisible Whole of the Absolute) and sometimes pleaded with Kālī to let him remain in the world of men, where he could enjoy the creation and play with her.

> O Mother, let me remain in contact with men! Don't make me a dried-up ascetic. I want to enjoy Your sport in the world.[2]

> Mother, don't make me unconscious with the Knowledge of Brahman. Mother, I don't want Brahmanjñana. I want to be merry. I want to play.[3]

> Why should I say nothing but, "I am He?" I want to play various melodies on my instrument with seven holes [the human body]. Why should I say only, "Brahman, Brahman!"? I want to call on God through all the moods—through santa, dasya, vatsalya and madhur. I want to make merry with God. I want to sport with God.[4]

And Rāmakṛṣṇa never did become a "dried-up ascetic" but continued to take delight in his devotion and conveyed to his disciples the joy, and even the humor, of his relationship with the Divine. He delighted in joking and playing with his disciples as if they were his boyhood playmates.[5] "In the meantime the Master was having great fun with the boys, treating them as if

---

[1] *Ibid.*, p. 143.

[2] M., *Gospel of Ramakrishna*, p. 66.

[3] *Ibid.*, p. 373.

[4] *Ibid.*, p. 1010.

[5] Saradananda in fact calls his disciples "eternal playmates" (*The Great Master*, p. 711) and the rather stern, meditative Vivekānanda his "chief playmate in his divine sport" (p. 715).

they were his most intimate friends. Peals of sidesplitting laughter filled the room, as if it were a mart of joy."[1] Vivekānanda remembers his relationship with Rāmakṛṣṇa as being, not didactic or formal, but merry and playful:

> Why speak of spiritual exercises alone? We spent much time there in play and merriment also. At those times the Master too joined us as far as possible and added to our happiness There we ran about, climbed trees, and sitting in the swing formed by the Madhavi creeper as strong as cable, swung freely and merrily; and sometimes we picnicked, cooking our meals ourselves.[2]

Rāmakṛṣṇa even treated the Divine, in one form or another, as his playmate; he laughed, joked, and danced with Kālī and scampered about with an image of the child Rāma. Hṛday describes his master's playful attitude to Kālī.

> Uncle rose from his bed very early in the morning and collected flowers in order to make garlands for Mother Kali. At that time too it seemed to me that there was someone there whom he caressed, and with whom he spoke, laughed, joked and made merry and played the importunate child.[3]

When a wandering Vaiṣṇava monk named Jatadhari arrived at Dakṣiṇeśvar with a small metal image of the child Rāma (Rāmlala), Rāmakṛṣṇa soon became intimate with it. The monk treated the image as though it were alive and would spend hours playing with it, feeding it, reprimanding it, and cajoling it. Rāmakṛṣṇa, too, soon looked on the image as alive and began to play with it.[4] In fact, the image became so fond of Rāmakṛṣṇa that when Jatadhari prepared to leave Dakṣiṇeśvar Rāmlala refused to go, preferring to stay with his new friend.[5] The intimacy of Rāmakṛṣṇa's relationship with the Divine is striking in this remarkable incident related by Rāmakṛṣṇa himself:

> As days passed on, Ramlala's love for me went on increasing. As long as I remained with the "father" [Jatadhari], Ram-

---

1M., *Gospel of Ramakrishna*, p. 90.
2Saradananda, *The Great Master*, p. .801.
3*Ibid*·, p. 145.
4M., *Gospel of Ramakrishna*, p. 24.
5Saradananda, *The Great Master*, p. 531.

lala felt happy—he played and sported; but as soon as I came away from that place to my room, he also followed me immediately there. He did not remain with the Sadhu although I forbade him to come. I at first thought it was perhaps a fancy of my brain. How could it otherwise be possible that the boy (in the image) loved me more than him—the boy worshipped by the Sadhu for a long time, whom he loved so dearly, and served so tenderly with devotion? But of what avail were these thoughts? I actually saw—just as I see you before me—that Ramlala accompanied me dancing, now preceding, now following me. Sometimes he importuned to be carried in my lap. Again, when I took him on my lap, he would by no means remain there. He would go down to run hither and thither, collect flowers in thorny jungles or to the Ganga to swim and splash water there. I said over and over again, "My child, don't do that, you will get blisters on your soles if you run in the sun; do not remain in water so long, you will catch cold and get fever." But he did not give ear to my words, however much I might forbid him. He went on with his pranks unconcerned, as if I was speaking to someone else. He would sometimes grin and look at me with his two eyes, beautiful like the petals of a lotus, or carry on his pranks with a vengeance. He would pout both his lips and grimace and make mouth at me. . . . Findng it impossible to restrain his naughtiness I would sometimes give him a slap or two. Thus beaten, he would pout his beautiful lips and sob and look at me with tears in his eyes, when I would feel pain. I then took him affectionately on my lap and cajoled him.[1]

Man giving God "a slap or two" to subdue his contrary nature, indeed! The idea would be incredibly shocking were it not for Rāmakṛṣṇa's beautiful naïveté, his guileless nature, his perfect innocence before the gods. Or if it were not for the Bengal Vaiṣṇava insistence upon man approaching God as a lover, a fickle lover at that, who may be chided and scolded for his indifference or unfaithfulness, as is done in countless poems written in the mood of Rādhā. The relationship portrayed here

---

[1] *Ibid.*, pp. 526-27.

between man and god is free from any distance implied by majesty or power. It is spontaneous and without reserve. This is also clear in another episode in the saint's life, related in his own words, in which he plays with God:

> God talked to me. It was not merely His vision. Yes, he talked to me. Under the banyan-tree I saw him coming from the Ganges. Then we laughed so much! By way of playing with me He cracked my fingers. Then he talked. Yes, he talked to me.[1]

In somewhat less personal terms, Rāmakṛṣṇa spoke of his state during *samādhi* as a condition in which he was completely free, as a playful state:

> Sometimes the Spiritual Current rises through the spine [a reference to the *kuṇḍalini*, usually pictured as a coiled serpent at the base of the spine that crawls upward during Tantric sādhana], crawling like an ant. Sometimes, in samadhi, the soul swims joyfully in the ocean of divine ecstasy, like a fish. Sometimes, when I lie down on my side, I feel the Spiritual Current pushing me like a monkey and playing with me joyfully. I remain still.[2]

The original title of Swami Saradananda's book *Sri Ramakrishna, the Great Master*, was *Śrī Rāmakṛṣṇa-līlā-prasanga*, "About the Play of Rāmakṛṣṇa." Like Caitanya, Rāmakṛṣṇa's life was considered essentially sport, a life given over to purposeless, superfluous activity, a life that was ornamental rather than "successful." Besides the playful aspects of his life that have already been discussed, there is one more aspect of Rāmakṛṣṇa's devotion that justifies this characterization of his life, an aspect that is seen in other saints, too, but is epitomized in Rāmakṛṣṇa. Rāmakṛṣṇa saw in childhood and youth characteristics of the divine and often advised his disciples on the spiritual merits of observing children's behavior and imitating it.

> After realizing God, a man becomes like a child five years old. The ego of such a man may be called the "ego of a

[1] M., *Gospel of Ramakrishna*, p. 830.
[2] *Ibid.*, p. 829.

> child," the "ripe ego." The child is not under the control of any of the gunas. He is beyond the three gunas. . . . Just watch a child and you will find that he is not under the influence of tamas. One moment he quarrels with his chum or even fights with him, and the next moment he hugs him, shows him much affection, and plays with him again. . . Now he builds his play house and makes all kinds of plans to make it beautiful, and the next moment he leaves everything behind and runs to his mother. . . . He doesn't hesitate to come out naked before others. . . . An old man has many shackles: caste, pride, shame, hatred, and fear. Furthermore, he is bound by the ideas of worldly cleverness, calculating intelligence, and deceit.[1]

> But you must remember one thing. One cannot see God sporting as man unless one has had a vision of Him. Do you know the sign of one who has God-vision? Such a man acquires the nature of a child. Why a child? Because God is like a child. So he who sees God becomes like a child.[2]

And this mark of a man who has seen God and who enjoys God was clearly seen in Rāmakṛṣṇa himself. He was utterly simple and without guile.

> As the Master walked to the house he said to M., like a child, pointing to his shirt-button: "My shirt is unbuttoned. Will that offend Vidyasagar?"
>
> "Oh, no!" said M. "Don't be anxious about it. Nothing about you will be offensive. You don't have to button your shirt." He accepted the assurance simply, like a child.[3]

> "What do people think of me? Do they think anything in particular about me when they see me in that condition?"
>
> M: "We feel in you a wonderful synthesis of knowledge, love, and renunciation, and on the surface a natural spon-

---

[1] *Ibid.*, pp. 860-61.

[2] *Ibid.*, p. 688. See also pp. 171, 176, 208, 245, 265, 491, and 783, and Saradananda, *The Great Master*, p. 562.

[3] M., *Gospel of Ramakrishna*, p. 100.

> taneity. Many divine experiences have passed, like huge steamboats, through the deep of your inner consciousness; still you maintain outwardly this utter simplicity. Many cannot understand it, but a few are attracted by this state alone."
>
> Master: "There is a sect of Vaishnavas known as the Ghoshpara, who describe God as the 'Sahaja,' the 'Simple One.' They say further that a man cannot recognize this 'Simple One' unless he too is simple."[1]

As was noted above, Rāmakṛṣṇa often pleaded with Kālī to keep him from becoming a dried-up ascetic. He enjoyed playing with his devotees, laughing and joking with them, and being frivolous like a young boy.

> "At first I went stark mad. Why am I less so now? But I get into that state now and then."
>
> M: "You don't have just one mood. As you said, you experience various moods. Sometimes you are like a child, sometimes like a madman, sometimes like an inert thing, and sometimes like a ghoul. And now and then you are a natural person."
>
> Master: "Yes, like a child. But I also experience the moods of a boy and a young man. When I give instruction I feel like a young man. Then there is my boyishness: like a boy twelve or thirteen years old, I want to be frivolous. That is why I joke and make merry with the youngsters."[2]

> The Master was again talking and laughing, like a child, though ailing [he had recently broken his arm], sometimes forgets his illness and laughs and plays about.[3]

Rāmakṛṣṇa was without that ponderous seriousness of an adult, particularly the all-knowing *pandit* who holds formal audience. He was easily approachable, disregarding many of the traditional customs of the teacher-pupil relationship. He was entirely without pomp. He would praise or criticize without premeditation, simply, like a child.

---

[1] *Ibid.*, p. 505.
[2] *Ibid.*, p. 594.
[3] *Ibid.*, p. 384.

> There were in that state [Ramakṛṣna's spiritual state] childlike sincerity, faith, dependence, and sweetness only, with the divine Mother for their stay and support. The seriousness of an adult, the personal efforts for the observance of injunctions and prohibitions according to time, place and person, the conducting of oneself with forethought for conforming to both worldliness and godliness—none of these were to be seen in that attitude of his.[1]

His lack of pride and his distaste for formalities, his preference for teaching informally and simply, led him to repeatedly refuse requests to give lectures. "Still in an ecstatic mood, he said to me with a divine smile: 'I shall eat, drink, and be merry. I shall play and sleep. But I can't give lectures.' "[2] Sometimes he would go about completely naked, expressing a complete disregard for propriety and the unselfconsciousness of a child. "The master showed his devotees the manners and movements of a paramhamsa [a great saint, literally, 'supreme swan']: the gait of a child, face beaming with laughter, eyes swimming in joy, and body completely naked."[3]

The mark of an adult is his recognition of, and willingness to accept, responsibility, to act soberly and with forethought. To survive in the utilitarian world he must resist the impulse to act frivolously—he must observe customs and perform his duties earnestly. It is also the mark of an adult to acquire a certain skepticism, the ability to act and think critically. All these attributes were missing in Rāmakṛṣṇa and are said to be missing in all great saints. Rāmakṛṣṇa was as secure as a loved child. Safe in the care of his mother Kālī, he could act simply and openly. His naïveté and simplicity, his uncomplicated view of things, enabled him to prance off spontaneously, to take delight in simple things and experience wonder and amazement in his childlike relationship to Kālī.

The lesson of Rāmakṛṣṇa is that man must approach the divine without guile—openly, in wonder, with the simple faith of a child—and that he who has seen God and enjoys him becomes

---

[1]Saradananda, *The Great Master*, p. 143.

[2]From a letter from Aswini Kumar Dutta to M. after Dutta had asked Rāmakṛṣṇa why he didn't give lectures; M., *Gospel of Ramakrishna*, p. 1022.

[3]*Ibid.*, p. 297.

like a child, accepting grace unquestioningly. In man's love affair with the divine he is free to behave without premeditation, spontaneously and unceremoniously, to scamper about carelessly like a child. In such a relationship all things are given and received; man need no longer strive after anything. He has become, indeed, free to play, having discovered the futility of artifice, premeditation, deceit, and pragmatic effort. Rāmakṛṣṇa enjoyed the love of Kālī, and returned that love, with the wholehearted sincerity of a child. He reveled in it and celebrated it, not by building temples for her or explaining its wonder in lectures, but by laughing, singing, dancing, and playing, by acting as silly and as frivolous as a child. And indeed, as a child of the Mother, he did not act like a child, he was a child.

And, finally, the lesson of Rāmakṛṣna is that God is like a child, of simple and uncomplicated nature, who would rather have as a devotee a playmate, someone to laugh and joke with, than an empire-builder of sober and pompous character. The great saint discovered this, and so approached the divine naïvely, openly—ready to play with God, to amuse and be amused by Him in superfluous sport and aimless dalliance.

C. *Play in the Lives of Other Hindu Saints*

The characteristics that indicate the efficacious nature of play in the lives of Caitanya and Rāmakṛṣṇa also appear in many other saints. Therefore they seem typical of saintly activity as a whole. Indeed, there are passages in various Hindu scriptures suggesting that these characteristics are the marks of all genuine devotion. In his discourse on *bhakti* addressed to Uddhava in the eleventh chapter of the *Bhāgavata-purāṇa*, Kṛṣṇa says:

> Whoever, desirous of liberation, is fond of the acquisition of knowledge and is regardless of liberation, should become my devotee by renouncing all *Asramas* having characteristic signs and should wander about independent of regulations. Although senseless he should sport like a boy, although skilled he should behave like a stupid person, although learned he should talk like a maniac, and although regarding the Vedas he should act like a cow regardless of all rules.[1]

[1] *Bhāgavata-purāṇa* XI. 18. 29 (V, 204).

In a similar vein, the *Caitanya-caritāmṛta* says of the man who has deep love for Kṛṣṇa:

> Such a man sings out of deep love the sweet name of his beloved Krishna. He has no control upon himself. Now he smiles and now he weeps. Now he sings and then again he dances. He forgets himself completely and appears like [a] lunatic.[1]

And in Mahīpati's *Santavijaya* the peculiar antics of Caitanya and Rāmakṛṣṇa are seen as marks of supermen. "There are three characteristic behaviours of Supermen. They are actions like those of a child, like those of one possessed, and like those of one intoxicated."[2]

And indeed these and other characteristics that are common to Caitanya and Rāmakṛṣṇa are seen consistently in the lives of the Hindu saints. Mīrābāī (1498-1546), a Rajputana princess and devotee of Kṛṣṇa, describes herself as ecstatic and admits that she is considered mad by others:

> Mira danced with ankle-bells on her feet.
> People said Mira was mad; my mother-in-law said I ruined
> the family reputation.
> Rana sent me a cup of poison and Mira drank it laughing.
> I dedicated my body and soul at the feet of Hari.
> I am thirsty for the nectar of the sight of him.
> Mira's lord is Giridhar Nagar; I will come for refuge to him.[3]

She describes herself as intoxicated :

> Friend, I am completely dyed this (i.e., Krishna's) color.
> I drank the cup of immortal bliss, and became drunk.
> My inebriation never goes away, however many millions. . .
> of ways I try (to get rid of it).[4]

In another poem Mīrābāī says:

---

[1]Kṛṣṇadāsa Kavirāja *Caitanya-caritāmṛta*, Madhya-līlā 23. 21-22 (p. 572).

[2]Mahipati *Santavijaya* V. 7; Mahipati, *Ramdas* (*Santavijaya*), trans. Justin E. Abbott, p. 64. Cf. *Bṛhad-āraṇyaka Upaniṣad* III. 5. 1 (*Upaniṣads*, p. 221): "Therefore let a Brāhmaṇa, after he has done with learning, desire to live as a child" ("tasmād brāhmaṇaḥ, pāṇḍityaṁ nirvidya bālyena tiṣṭhāset").

[3]Mīrābāī, "Poems from Mīrābāī," *pada* 36, p. 18.

[4]*Ibid.*, *pada* 40, p. 32.

> I go to Giridhar's house.
> Giridhar is my real lover; I see his beauty and am allured.
> When night falls I go, and when day breaks I come back.
> Night and day I play with him; I please him in every way.[1]

And finally, in a striking image, Mīrābāī describes herself as a butterfly attracted to flowers that are all Kṛṣṇa and as dancing uncontrollably into the light that is Kṛṣṇa:

> As in summer blooms a garden so my spirit buds and blooms; and of every flower the name is always Krishna. As a butterfly in sunshine filled with light in blue air hovers, thus I dance. In the golden halls of Brindaban I dance before my Krishna on whose brow gleams the Tilakam. Holy Krishna. From my lips I tear concealment and my willing breasts reveal; love inflamed I dance into the Light of Blessed Krishna.[2]

Rāmdās (1601-81) of Maharashtra is described as acting like a child:

> He had first behaved like one possessed by a demon, but now he adopted childish actions. When the boys of the town gathered, he called out loudly to them: "Friends, I want to play with you for a moment." And when they heard this, a great crowd assembled. Just as one smiles on children, so Ramdas did. He played Hututu with the boys, but none could catch him. And as he played, he would repeat some blessing-bearing abhangas [devotional songs] . . . . Thus Ramdas the crazy man, like Krishna in his *avatara* form, played with the boys, but was untouched by any fault.[3]

> Then Samartha [Rāmdās] went into the forest. . . . Just as children arrange their playthings, and play with them as they feel inclined, and then throw them down, and run away, just such an one was Ramdas.[4]

---

[1] *Ibid., pada* 20, p. 14.
[2] Althaus, *Mystic Lyrics*, p. 34.
[3] Mahipati *Santavijaya* V. 43-45, 49 (pp. 67-68).
[4] *Ibid.,* XIV. 56-57 (p. 210).

He also behaved in strange and wild ways, appearing to be a madman. He came to the bank of the Kṛṣṇa River and

> there began his strange antics. He climbed the trees by the banks of the Krishna and there acted as one crazy. The boys of the town gathered in numbers to see him, and all laughed heartily at his antics. He would look at the boys and wink at them. He would break off branches and leaves, and throw them to the ground. Boys threw stones at him up in the tree, and he bore it with pleasure. He would glare at them, and make faces at them. He would let go a branch, and appear as if he were about to fall to the ground, and then would fly backwards, and sit on a topmost branch. Seeing such antics, a great crowd assembled. They all remarked that he did not seem to have the least fear for his life. While the people were talking thus, he was wildly leaping from branch to branch.[1]

> Ramdas, the god-loving *bhakta* and saint, possessed with Devotion, Knowledge, and Indifference to worldly things, was constantly wandering about in the forests, but came into the towns to beg his food. In his outer appearance he looked like a mad man.[2]

In his wildness he was said to be living frivolously:

> Suddenly. . . .Samartha appeared in the town, and a crowd assembled to look at him. They remarked: "It seems to us, his life is being spent uselessly. In appearance he is supremely beautiful. His age must be less than twenty five. One does not know with what demon or ghost he is possessed." While they were talking thus, Ramdas increased his curious antics. He made faces at the people. This made the people exclaim: "A mighty figure, indeed !". . . . As Ramdas heard these remarks, he was made exceedingly happy. He rolled his eyes and made faces at the people.[3]

The theme of madness as the mark of a great devotee or the

---

[1] *Ibid.* V. 9-15 (p. 65).
[2] *Ibid.* V. 127-28 (p. 74).
[3] *Ibid.* V. 24-28 (p. 66).

liberated man, which is clear in Rāmdās, is particularly important in the Tantric and Bengal Bāul traditions. In his quest for liberation the Tantric devotee is said to pass through six stages (*vedācāra*, *vaiṣṇavācāra*, *śaivācāra*, *dakṣiṇācāra vāmācāra*, and *siddhācāra*), during which he attains greater and greater purity. Finally, he reaches the ultimate stage, called *kaulācāra*, which is characterized by absolute freedom and total disregard for rules.[1]

> Sometimes the *kaulācāri* roams about the world as a very civil and social man and sometimes as a person who does not care anything for social customs, behaving like an outsider or outcaste. Sometimes he behaves like a goblin, moving about like an apparition, dressed in whatever clothes strike his fancy. For the *kaulācāri* there are no fixed customs, rites, or rituals. He learns to totally disregard customary distinctions such as sacred and profane places, auspicious and inauspicious times, and moral and immoral actions. With a complete sense of the final identity of things, he is a man who is totally detached and places everything on the same level: mud and sandalpaste, friend and enemy, home and the burial ground, gold, silver, and money and a piece of grass.[2]

A good example of the Tantric *kaulācāri* is to be found in the life of the nineteenth-century Bengali saint Bāmākhepa (Bāmā the mad one). This amazing man was particularly fond of Kālī and used to live in the burning grounds along the Dvarka River.

> This was the place where Bāmā used to carry on his *sādhana*.

[1]Swami Nigamānanda Sarasvatī, *Tantrik Guru* (Bengali), p. 37. See also R. C. Majumdar (ed.), *The History and Culture of the Indian People*, Vol. IV: *The Age of Imperial Kanauj*, pp. 320-21, and *Kulārṇava-tantra* II. 7, 8 for a delineation of these stages.

[2]Sarasvatī, *Tantrik Guru*, p. 37. For a discussion of the importance of madness and anti-social behavior among the Tantrics, see Daniel H. H. Ingalls, "Cynics and Pāśupatas: The Seeking of Dishonor," *Harvard Theological Review*, LV, No. 4 (October, 1962), 281-98. See also Rao, *Elements of Hindu Iconography*, II, Part I, 24-30, for a description of the practices of the Pāśupatas, Kālāmukhas, and Kāpālikas—Śaivite sects whose members often betray signs of divine madness. Rao suggests that the members of these sects in large measure base their aberrant, mad behavior on Śiva, the paradigm of divine madness. *Ibid.*, p. 30.

> He himself was like the great *yogin* Śiva: tall, dark, and completely naked. Due to the excessive use of wine and *gāñja* [a type of marijuana] his large eyes were the color of blood-red flowers. But to observant eyes he appeared what he truly was, a divine child, self-forgetful, with eyes sparkling with inner joy. To these eyes was revealed that divine child peeping out of his dark body. His companions were a pack of dogs, habitual dwellers in the cremation ground, who played all around him, completely unafraid of him. He, too, played with them, sometimes petting them and sometimes chasing them away. When devotees came to have *darśan* [sight] of him, they were puzzled by his actions, which were like those of a child or a ghoul. He would sometimes ask those who came to see him, "Are you boys carrying any intoxicants with you? If so, bring them out, and let's have some fun."[1]

His behavior is consistently described as being naïve, simplistic, capricious,[2] and absent minded.[3] His disregard for the world and its conventions was not so much rebellious as it was naïve. He was so absorbed in devotion to Kālī that he cared for nothing else. Consequently, he could barely manage to cope with normal life and appeared idiotic.

As for the Bāuls, the very name means madness.[4] They are minstrels who have given up life in the normal world to wander the countryside singing in praise of God. Their clothes are made from cast-off Muslim and Hindu rags patched together. They sing and dance wildly and are generally rather bizarre in appearance.[5] And many great Bāuls bear the honorific title of *khepā* (the mad one).[6] As was suggested earlier in connection with

---

[1]*Bhārater-sādhak* (Bengali), ed. Śaṅkarnāth Roy, I, 239-40.

[2]*Ibid.*, p. 240.

[3]*Ibid.*, p. 248.

[4]Dimock, *The Place of the Hidden Moon*, p. 250.

[5]Each year the Bāuls do manage to get together, wandering to the same place at the same time. At Jayadeva's birthplace in West Bengal, Kenduli, the Bāuls gather on Jayadeva's birthday each year (in January) and celebrate the event with much singing and dancing. This is the easiest way to see the Bāuls in their native, rural setting.

[6]At the Kenduli *mela* (festival) it was interesting to hear Caitanya referred to as the greatest of Bāuls, the greatest of the madmen. The gist of a song

the frenzy and ecstasy of the Bengal Vaiṣṇavas, the madness of the Bāuls can best be understood in relationship to the deity they worship. Their madness is not an end in itself but the effect of the mad god they adore. Edward Dimock says:

> The Bāul cannot help his madness; he is maddened by the sound of Krsna's flute, and, like a Gopī, caring nothing for home or for the respect of the world, he follows it: "I hear its sound, and maddened I leave everything and run to hear . . . . I leave my house and run away, abandoning my house and home."[1]

The *Bhaktamāl* of Nābhā Dās, the most famous and comprehensive account of Indian saints, is full of examples of those characteristics that suggest the efficacious nature of play in the lives of saints. Bhābuk Brāhman used to worship Kṛṣṇa in the form of a child by assuming the mood of a parent. He would collect toys for the child and play with him.

> In this *bhāva* he reared the Lord as a son and used to put him on his lap to feed him. He used to dress the Lord with many ornaments, clothes, garlands, and other things and used to put *tilak* marks on his nose. He used to kiss and embrace the Lord, making him dance and play, and he used to dance with the Lord.[2]
>
> Whenever some attractive thing caught his eye, wherever he was, he would collect it and keep it carefully for Gopāl. He brought Gopāl tops, rattles, bats and balls, colored shells, dolls, earthen pots and pans, and all kinds of toys and gave them to him with gladdened heart so Gopāl could play with them.[3]

Kṛṣṇadās Sādhu, who lived in a cave, is described as being

---

sung by Gopāldās Bāul on the second night of the *mela* was: Caitanya was the Bāul of Bāuls (*bāuler bāul āmār caitanya gosāi*), the best of Bāuls. Caitanya was born in Navadvīp to taste the love feelings of Rādhā. He was the greatest of the *khepās*, and Advaita, Nityānanda and others joined in his madness, and he spread this intoxication for God among all.

[1]Dimock, *The Place of the Hidden Moon*, p. 252, containing a song of the Bāul Padmalocana.

[2]Nabha Das, *Bhaktamāl*, p. 143.

[3]*Ibid.*, p. 143.

"perpetually madlike and constantly enthralled by the joy of love for Kṛṣṇa."[1] Kharoga Sen, on the occasion of the Rās Līlā, a festival held in the autumn to celebrate Kṛṣṇa's circular dance with the *gopīs*, was once seized by love and began dancing like a madman. He danced so enthusiastically that he fell down dead "and immediately entered the eternal *līlā* of the *rāsa*, dancing, laughing, and joking with Kṛṣṇa" in heavenly Vṛndāvana.[2] Haridās Banik realized that he was soon to die and undertook a pilgrimage to holy Vṛndāvana so that he might die there and join Kṛṣṇa in heaven. Halfway to his goal he became weakened to the point of death, whereupon Vṛndāvana itself moved to him. "Upon his death he entered the *rāsa* dance as a *gopī*, having cast off his old body, and became fully engaged in dalliance with Kṛṣṇa."[3] Karametibāī, the daughter of a *brāhman*, is described as being repeatedly seized by love for Kṛṣṇa, during which she would break out in tears and laughter and behave like a mad woman. After living in Vṛndāvana for some time she is said to have achieved the status of a *gopī*.[4]

Bilvamangal, whose biography is a favorite theme of Bengali folk theatre (*jātrā*), is often described as being intoxicated or drunk day and night due to his love for Kṛṣṇa.[5] Bilva had blinded himself when the sight of a woman distracted him from concentration on Kṛṣṇa. When he was permitted as a reward to have a spiritual vision of Kṛṣṇa, Bilva was overcome with seizure. "Then there appeared on him all the eight physical signs of seizure, of being possessed by *bhāva*: ecstasy, tears, and so on. He repeatedly rolled on the ground, stood up, and fell again, or sang and danced."[6] Kṛṣṇa is also described as teasing and playing with the blind saint:

> He [Bilva] laughed and tried to catch him, but Kṛṣṇa moved away again. The Lord was playing with his devotee. Then,

[1] *Ibid.*, p. 296.
[2] *Ibid.*, p. 292.
[3] *Ibid.*, p. 290.
[4] *Ibid.*, pp. 291-92.
[5] *Ibid.*, p. 140.
[6] *Ibid.*, p. 141.

in fun and full of the *rasa* of humor, the Lord played with his devotee with zest.[1]

Vittaldās, who lived at Mathurā near Vṛndāvana, was fond of *kirtan* and, overcome with bliss whenever he heard or sang it, would swoon and fall unconscious. He became so enthusiastic on one occasion that he fell off the roof on which he was dancing.

> Unconscious with the bliss of love, he could not control himself. After a while he regained consciousness, yet he went on dancing like one completely forgetful of the external world. He danced under the spell of the *bhāva* of love. He wasn't aware of how his feet moved or where he was or that there were others present. On a sea of bliss that flooded his mind no trace of memory of his normal life floated. Whooping and whirling, dancing up and down, he suddenly fell off the roof . . . . and survived without injury of any kind.[2]

The queen of Madhav Singh of Jaipur in Rajasthan was so impressed with the devotion of her maid-servant that she herself began worshiping an image of Kṛṣṇa. She assumed the attitude of Kṛṣṇa's lover and would spend hours feeding, bathing, and even rebuking him. She arranged sports for the images of Rādhā and Kṛṣṇa, and while she played with the images she would become overcome with love and break into dance, laughter, or tears. She was finally blessed with the sight of the two images playing.[3]

Tukārām (1607-49) is described as celebrating Kṛṣṇa's birthday by dressing up as the holy child and dancing and singing with other devotees:

> For seven days this festival of *kīrtan* continued. Remembering . . . Kṛṣṇa's birthday . . . the *sādhus* began playing with curd and mud. Among the *sādhus* some dressed up as Nanda, some as Yaśodā, some as the baby Kṛṣṇa. Tukā took the part of baby Kṛṣṇa, and whoever played whatever part, Tukā immediately composed verses on it and thereby made

[1] *Ibid.*
[2] *Ibid.*, p. 223.
[3] *Ibid.*, p. 287.

the whole show more impressive. Visitors and *sādhus* alike were beside themselves with joy. And after many days, seeing Vṛndāvana vivified before them in their mind's eyes, all became fulfilled. Tears of joy flooded many eyes and overflowed many breasts. Famous grey-haired *sādhus*, like boys, with utter simplicity, sang and danced and enjoyed the festival of the Lord.[1]

Alibhagavan is described as having been continually drunk under the influence of love for Kṛṣṇa: "He stands and then falls down repeatedly, as if perpetually drunk, and he had a great desire to see Vṛndāvana."[2] Upon reaching that holy place he was intoxicated by everything he saw and swooned and trembled.

> He saw the *rāsa* ground on the bank of the Jumna, a place of unparalleled beauty, rare in the universe. As soon as he went there he had a metamorphosis and became a female. Being possessed by the *bhāva* of the *gopis*, completely identifying himself with them, he forgot his male body. With the *gopīs* "he" saw Rādhā and Kṛṣna and became absolutely charmed. With eyes full of wonder "he" looked all around. The *gopīs* dragged "him" by the hand and drew "him" near, and full of love they laughed and joked with "him."[3]

A few more examples from the life of one more saint should suffice to illustrate that play and phenomena which share important characteristics with play are common in the lives of Hindu saints. Nityagopāl (1834-1911), a contemporary and acquaintance of Rāmakṛṣṇa, displayed the kind of frenzy typical of Caitanya.

> Any song on God would throw Him into the blessed state of superconsciousness. . . . At such times he would also be dissolved into ecstasies and dance like *Mahaprabhu Sri Sri Gouranga Deva* [Caitanya] overwhelmed with divine emotions; and a torrent of tears would flow incessantly down His eyes.[4]

---

[1] Jogindra Nāth Bose, *Tukārām-carit* (Bengali), p. 132.
[2] Nābhā Dās, *Bhaktamāl*, p. 229.
[3] *Ibid.*
[4] Srimat Swami Nityapadananda Abadhuta, *Sri Sri Nityagopal*, p. [5].

At Vṛndāvana he was continually and violently agitated with emotions and repeatedly passed out in ecstasy. Drawn by his fervent devotion, Rādhā herself appeared to Nityagopāl and led him to the Nikunja Bana (where she and Kṛṣṇa had dallied). "But Thakur [Nityagopāl] was quite reticent about what had followed His entrance into the bower. This has made it impossible for us to touch upon the details connected with it."[1] If we cannot be certain that Nityagopāl sported with Rādhā in that bower, it is clear that he played with Kālī.

> Now commenced the *pujah* of *Yoga-Maya* [Kālī] before an image at the sight of which Thakur said giggling, "Oh! Mad One, I shall cut off Thy tongue [images of Kālī are almost always shown with lolling tongue] and hold in My grasp the garland of heads Thou sustainest." Again, the image became enlivened and animated with life, assumed a sitting posture on the lap of the Yogacharya and indulged in a loud laughter, bent on sports and plays.[2]

Like Rāmakṛṣṇa, Nityagopāl saw in the behavior of children a paradigm to be imitated by all who sought liberation.

> "Great *Siddha purushas* . . . can live in the world quite unaffected like infants and little children.
>
> Little children sometimes wear clothes and sometimes remain naked. They are free in both conditions. The conduct and behaviour of *Siddha purushas* can be likened to theirs. In all conditions they remain free from the fetters of *Maya*."[3]

And also like Rāmakṛṣṇa he acted like a child, either capriciously and wildly or simply and without guile. He once assumed the state of a divine child, reminiscent of Kṛṣṇa, and demanded a particular kind of sweet. "He was sulkily insistent on the satisfaction of the childish desire. Nothing could intercept His caprice."[4] And when bathing he

> would indulge in a regular sporting in water in a state of

[1] *Ibid.*, p. 73.
[2] *Ibid.*, p. 221.
[3] *Ibid.*, "Some Pronouncements of the Yogacharya," p. [xii].
[4] *Ibid.*, p. 276.

ecstasy. He would sometimes sprinkle and throw water like a child and sometimes indulge in such amusements as would prevail upon the observing devotees to think that Thakur would recall the parts He played in His past careers [an allusion either to Kṛṣṇa, Caitanya, or both].[1]

Hindu saints are portrayed as having either partially or entirely transcended the human sphere. They do not behave normally or naturally; indeed, they are sometimes supermen. They seem to hover above the turmoil and tumult of the human sphere unaffected by their environment. Given the slightest provocation they are prone to fall into trance, stupor, ecstasy, tears, or laughter. They have about them the aura of an "other" world that is typified by their behavior as madmen and children. Much like the gods, and unlike men, they seem to act spontaneously and not as the result of "the conscious working of the will." They are prone to prance off in silly and superfluous capers. They are often entirely without guile. They are often incapable of managing their own affairs or even of looking after their own physical welfare. Indeed, to designate a devotee's life "useless" or "frivolous" is to accord him honor in the logic of Hindu hagiology. Among men, in fact, the saints are great players, capable of acting without thought for the future, without premeditation, spontaneously and joyfully. Under the intoxicating influence of God there is nothing to be achieved. For the saints, striving is finished and life is joy. And the saints express this in play, by treating the world about them as their playground and considering themselves playmates of the gods.

D. *The Place of Play in Medieval Hindu Cult*: *Summary*

The preceding two chapters illustrate clearly that play is associated with medieval Hindu cult in a positive way. I should like now to summarize this association and draw some conclusions about the place of play in cult generally.

From the materials discussed it appears that play may be related to cult in three general ways: (1) as a technique of cult, as a vehicle or mode of expression for cultic and devotional activity; (2) as a context in which the divine may be approached

[1] *Ibid.*, pp. 296-97.

and enjoyed, as an appropriate atmosphere in which the divine-human relationship can flourish; and (3) as a phenomenon that embodies many of those characteristics that are central to cultic activities—a phenomenon, therefore, that is regarded as peculiarly religious and clearly divine.

1. The role of play as a technique of cult is seen most clearly in *rāgānugā* and other forms of devotion that employ role-playing on the part of the devotee. The emphasis in *rāgānugā* is to lose oneself in the identity of another, to become, as far as possible, a member of Kṛṣṇa's Vṛndāvana retinue. The follower of this path, like the actor in classical Indian dance-drama, seeks to tame certain aspects of his individuality. The ideal is to imitate a transcendent model and by so doing to give up one's unique identity. Playacting, then, functions as a technique whereby one may transcend his individuality, his limited position in space and time.

The technique of playacting may be understood to achieve more than just the denial of selfhood. As the cases of Caitanya and Rāmakṛṣṇa make clear, role-playing may also be a means of extending the devotee's devotional potential. As has been suggested, the role-playing may function as a means of magnifying certain devotional sentiments of the devotee, of distilling or epitomizing them. In this case the result of role-playing is not the denial of self, the curbing of individuality, but the extension of it. By imitating Rādhā, for example, Caitanya does not necessarily experience loss of self but rather experiences intensification of his innermost self. By taking on her mood his basically unstable and intense emotionalism is heightened. His devotional capacity is expanded, but not as the result of prior loss of self. It seems clear to me, particularly in the case of the saints, that playacting is a means of having several personalities at once, by means of which devotion may be expressed in a great variety of ways. Each role or model acts as a vehicle by means of which various aspects of the devotee's devotional feelings can be epitomized. There is not, as a result of this however, a permanent, or in many cases even a temporary, loss of self. Role-playing, then, may be a means both of taming certain aspects of individuality and of intensifying others. It may function to abolish self or to expand self.

2. The role of play as an appropriate context in which the divine-human relationship may flourish is seen both in cultic activities per se and in the mythological models of the cult. Caitanya and Rāmakṛṣṇa frequently played with their devotees, and at times played with the gods. In the Holī festival playful revel with other devotees and with Kṛṣṇa is characteristic. One does not perform or even celebrate Holī, one plays it. In these examples of pure play in cult it is clear that man and god may meet appropriately on the playground as well as in the temple. The joy of the relationship, its blissful and often wild nature, impels (as it were) man to express himself in play. Pure play, too, is paradigmatic for the Kṛṣṇa cult. For Kṛṣṇa himself is a great player, frolicking endlessly in eternal Vṛndāvana, while his heaven is a sporting ground *par excellence.* In the case of several saints it is clearly stated that upon death they entered heavenly Vṛndāvana, where they joined in Kṛṣṇa's sport. Salvation or release in the Kṛṣṇa cult is defined as achieving a state in which one plays eternally.

The importance of understanding the mythology of the sect from the point of view of classical aesthetic theory also suggests the importance of play as an appropriate context for the divine-human relationship. Rūpa and Jīva Gosvāmin saw in Kṛṣṇa and Rādhā the ideal hero and heroine and emphasized the fact that the mythology of the sect was not simply a once-upon-a-time thing, but that it happens eternally, that Kṛṣṇa's Vṛndāvana sport is an eternal, ongoing drama. The devotee, in the view of Rūpa and other *pandits* of the sect, is put in the position of enjoying a dramatic or theatrical performance of which Rādhā and Kṛṣṇa are the central figures. Like the aesthetic connoisseur, the devotee, by means of certain inherent sensibilities, may relish or taste the bliss of the theatrical creation whenever it is conjured up in song, recitation, or within his own imagination. By relishing the performance the devotee, like the aesthetic connoisseur, finds release. He experiences *bhakti-rasa* as a result of enjoying the ongoing drama of Rādhā and Kṛṣṇa. In Rūpa's scheme all devotees comprise an audience at a theatrical performance. The overall context of Kṛṣṇa's relationship to his devotees, therefore, is basically a theatrical one. The relationship takes place in the play sphere, in a sphere that is outside the ordinary, in a sphere where amusement, enjoyment, and fun are sought after.

3. The third type of relationship does not involve activities that can be called pure play but activities that are often associated with play, or phenomena that share important characteristics with play. Song and dance, for example, are basic to the Bengal Vaiṣṇava cult, and while these may not justifiably be called pure play, they are superfluous and joyous activities.[1] Their centrality in the life of the cult emphasizes the importance of activities that imply no necessary future, that are done as ends in themselves. Frenzy and ecstasy are canonical marks of Kṛṣṇa devotion. In his relationship to Kṛṣṇa the devotee often acts like a wild man who has lost all inhibition. Madness and childlike behavior illustrate man's detachment from the ordinary world, his proclivity for aimless, pure activity that is beyond the realm of necessity and prediction in his relationship to Kṛṣṇa. Both the madman and the child are held up as models in the cult, and the saints are frequently pictured as behaving in both of these modes. *Bhakti* itself is consistently said to be nonutilitarian, spontaneous, joyous activity. There is a rebellious flavor in much of *bhakti* literature that emphasizes the meeting of man and God outside the realm of the ordinary religious and moral order.

From these examples alone it is possible to say that play is considered a peculiarly appropriate means of expressing man's relationship to the divine, or that it is the kind of activity that is compatible with the religious sphere. All those characteristics

---

[1]Huizinga, in fact, considers dance and especially music essentially play. While music and dance are often intrinsically satisfying, nonutilitarian, and may even be done for fun pure and simple, they can be considered essentially play only if we are willing to reduce art to play. In fact, art and play are similar in a great many and essential ways. The primary difference, however, is seen in their respective intentions. The intention of play is fun, while the *raison d'être* of art is the creation of beauty. Play, of course, is often beautiful; it is frequently full of grace, harmony, rhythm, and sheer beauty. And art may often be carried out as a form of amusement, a pastime that is done for fun. So the two phenomena may at times appear identical. This is not the same thing, however, as saying that one may be reduced to the other or that one arises from or necessarily produces the other. This is the same criticism that I made of Huizinga's postulate concerning the origin and development of cult in play. Unless one keeps clearly in mind the *raison d'être* of a particular phenomenon, characteristics are likely to be confused with essentials. See Huizinga, *Homo Ludens*, chap. x.

that typify the above phenomena are embodied in play. It is spontaneous, superfluous, joyous, outside the realm of the ordinary, and intrinsically satisfying. In fact, of course, it is clear that play is regarded in medieval Hindu cult as divine activity. The gods are great players, and the traditional means of signifying that a saint's life participates in the divine is to call all his activities *līlā*.

The materials discussed from the *bhakti* cults, however, do not appear to justify the conclusion that religious activity generally or devotion specifically necessarily arise from and in play. To a very great extent the playful elements in the Kṛṣṇa *bhakti* cults can be understood as reactions to the frolicking, merry god who is worshiped. Kṛṣṇa is a great player who presides over a heavenly playground. The members of his retinue are not his subjects but his playmates. While it is certainly true, as Huizinga asserts, that play in and of itself may lead to freedom and joy, perhaps even a holy freedom and a sacred joy, the primary fact in medieval Hindu cult is not the play itself but the Divine Player. It is he who incites and excites his devotees to frenzy and who ultimately accepts his devotees as eternal playmates in his heavenly playground. Play may indeed be efficacious in and of itself, without any vertical referent being implied, but in the *bhakti* cults *līlā* is holy because the God who is worshiped reveals himself as the Divine Player *par excellence*. The "other" in the Kṛṣṇa *bhakti* cults is expressed, revealed, and enjoyed in sport, play, and dalliance. And the unavoidable conclusion is, therefore, that he who cannot or will not play must forever be denied entrance to Kṛṣṇa's paradise.

CHAPTER V

PLAY IN NON-HINDU TRADITIONS

A. *Cosmic Time and the Insignificance of History in Hinduism*

Before bringing this study to an end, I should like to comment briefly on the Hindu concepts of time and history and their relevance to the appropriateness of play as a positive phenomenon in the Hindu tradition. My purpose is to demonstrate that while (1) the Hindu view of time and history is compatible with play as divine or religious activity, (2) examples from other traditions show that non-Hindu traditions which do not share this view of time and history illustrate that we cannot assume that the importance of play in Hinduism is simply the result of certain cosmological presuppositions.

The Hindu concept of time is at once infinite and cyclical. Time has no beginning and no end, and history repeats itself eternally. Man's span of years is so insignificant given the Hindu view of time that such terms as "achievement," "accomplishment," and "success" are almost laughable. Against the Hindu view of cosmic time, anything that one might accomplish, even the establishment of a kingdom, is hopelessly dwarfed.

The impact of the Hindu concept of time and history upon the significance of individual achievement is illustrated in the story of Indra's humiliation (for even the might of the gods is insignificant against the background of cosmic time). Befitting his position as leader of the gods, Indra commanded Viśvakarmā, the architect of the gods, to build him a magnificent castle appropriate to his regal position. No matter how hard Viśvakarmā worked, no matter how splendid his creations, however, Indra was not satisfied and continued to press his master-builder to erect even more magnificent structures. In despair, Viśvakarmā went secretly to Brahmā, whose realm lies even above Indra's, and requested that Brahmā relieve him of his impossible task. Brahmā consoled Viśvakarmā and promised that something would be done. Brahmā, in turn, went to Viṣṇu, who resides in the highest heaven, and put the case before him. Viṣṇu indicated that he would take care of the problem. A few days later a beautiful young boy appeared at Indra's palace and requested an audience with the divine king. When Indra boasted about his palace and his extravagant plans for future construction, the boy remarked casually that he had yet to see an Indra complete such a task. Somewhat taken aback, Indra asked the boy what he knew of other Indras, whereupon the boy (Viṣṇu in disguise) instructed Indra on the infinite number of Indras that had preceded him and on the infinite number of worlds in the infinite universes that are ruled by innumerable Indras. During the discourse a long procession of ants marched through the hall of audience, and the boy, seeing them, broke into laughter. Perplexed, Indra asked why the boy was laughing. The boy told the great god that he was amused, as it had been revealed to him that each ant in the procession at one time had also been an Indra. Each ant at one time, through endless lives of merit, had achieved Indra's position and had subsequently, through lack of merit, fallen to its present lowly state. And so Indra was humbled and was only persuaded not to give up his throne and become an ascetic by the pleading of his wife and the counsel of his priest, Brihaspati.[1]

According to the Hindu view of time, each world cycle is divided into four *yugas*: *kṛta* (1,728,000 years), *tretā* (1,296,000), *dvāpara* (864,000), and *kali* (432,000). Each *yuga* diminishes in length of time, because each represents a decline in virtue. The mythical cow representing *dharma* stands on four legs during the *kṛta yuga*, three during the *tretā yuga*, two during the *dvāpara yuga*, and on only one leg during the *kali yuga*, the age in which we are now entangled and in which morality and virtue are at an ebb. Each cycle of four *yugas* is known as a *mahāyuga* and comprises 4,320,000 years. One thousand *mahāyugas*, or 4,320,000,000 years, is equal to one day of Brahmā, or one *kalpa*. Each day of Brahmā sees the creation of the world and each night (equal in length to one day of Brahmā), its dissolution. Each day sees the reiteration of all those primordial myths of Viṣṇu's world-saving *avatāras*. Each day sees the gradual decline of the world and its eventual destruction. But even this incredible

[1] *Brahma-vaivarta-purāṇa*, Kṛṣna Janma Khaṇḍa 47 (Part II, pp. 310-12). The story is retold with certain elaborations by Zimmer, *Myths and Symbols*, pp. 3-11.

span of time is made insignificant when we learn that there is even a greater cycle that revolves around the lifetime of Brahmā. Brahmā lives for one hundred Brahmā years of Brahmā days and nights ($4{,}320{,}000{,}000 \times 2 \times 365 \times 100$), or for the incredible time of 311,040,000,000,000 human years. At the end of his lifetime all things become totally dissolved, including Brahmā himself. And for a Brahmā century nothing exists but primeval substance. At the end of this time, the great cycle begins again and, we may assume, continues endlessly.[1]

Humble and insignificant indeed is man against this background. Individuality is meaningless given the view that each man is continually reborn, enjoying (or enduring) lives as Indras and ants. Uniqueness is this view is nonexistent, as all things and beings, some time in the course of infinitely recurring time, have occurred many times before. For the Hindu, time is not to be used preciously but is to be transcended. An individual biography in the Hindu view is not a once-for-all thing but merely a link in an endless chain. The emphasis, then, in Hindu soteriology is upon release from the wheel of *karma* and *saṁsāra* (actions and rebirth), release from that which binds man to this endless, and therefore wearisome, cycle of ages. One way of gaining release is to act without regard for fruits, to disengage oneself from the world of cause and effect, a theme that pervades *bhakti* theology and literature. Any action that results from desire, that serves pragmatic ends or bears fruit, only keeps the individual tied to the great wheel.

Given these presuppositions, play may be seen as the type of activity that leads to release. For play accomplishes nothing. In play there is no striving or premeditation, no expectation of pragmatic reward. Play is activity that is free from necessity, free from cause and effect, and so *karma* does not accrue as a result of it. In order to play, man must surmount or ignore the utilitarian demands of his circumstances and act spontaneously, uselessly, and frivolously. Given the above view of time and

---

[1]Zimmer, *Myths and Symbols*, pp. 13-19. The very names of the four *yugas* (*kṛta*, *tretā*, *dvāpara*, and *kali*) indicate a playful attitude toward time and history, for the names of the *yugas* are the names for various throws at dice, which suggests that time and history are one big, cosmic dice game—the amusement of the gods. See M. Eliade, *Images and Symbols*: *Studies in Religious Symbolism*, trans. Philip Mairet, p. 63.

history, abstention from work and abstention from hankering after achievement and success in the phenomenal world may be seen as activities that lead to release. Play presupposes such abstention and therefore may be regarded as an appropriate activity of saints and gods, who, though also bound to the wheel, are further than ordinary men on their way to ultimate release from the "moon dream of history."

B. Play outside the Hindu Tradition

There are indications in other religious traditions that play is regarded both as divine activity and as soteriologically efficacious activity for man. I would like to give a few examples in order to argue the point that play in Hinduism is not regarded as a positive religious activity *simply* because of any particular circumstances that are unique to India or the Hindu tradition. For even in traditions where the Hindu concepts of time and history are foreign, in which work and accomplishment are extolled (notably the Judaic-Christian) there are indications that play bears a positive relationship to religion. First of all, then, let me give a few examples from non-Hindu traditions exclusive of the Judaic-Christian tradition, which I shall treat separately.

In Greek mythology Zeus is sometimes portrayed as playing with toys. In a cave on Mount Ida in Crete, where he was born, Zeus is given a wonderful ball to play with by his nurse, Adrastea.[1] Apollo, too, is sometimes described as a playful child: "And they, even gold-tressed Leto and wise Zeus rejoiced in their great hearts as they watch their dear son [Apollo] playing among undying gods."[2] In a fragment of Heraclitus the world is said to be governed by a child at play. "The Aeon is a child at play, playing draughts. The kingly rule is as a child's."[3] Philo of Alexandria describes divine activity as aimless: "The divine Logos goes circling in his round, he whom many men

---

[1]Apollonius of Rhodes, *The Voyage of Argo* (*The Argonautica*), trans. E. V. Rieu, iii. 131 ff. (pp. 112-13).

[2]Homeric Hymn III (Apollo), ll. 204-6; *Hesiod, the Homeric Hymns and Homerica*, trans. Hugh G. Evelyn-White, p. 339.

[3]Quoted in Hugo Rahner, S.J., *Man at Play*, trans. Brian Battershaw and Edward Quinn, p. 14. Cf. above, Chap. V, Sec. A, n. 2.

call Chance."[1] Plotinus' description of divine creation is similar to the Hindu in its conception of creation as resulting from the overflow of God's bliss and of the phenomenal world as His playground. "All things are created by the life of the all in its fullness, and by living it creates gay multiplicity; it never ceases, but continues without pause to call into being lovely, well-formed, living playthings."[2]

Dionysus, however, is the clearest example of the divine player in Greek mythology. He is said to play with "tops of different kinds and dolls with moving limbs, apples too, the beautiful golden ones of the clear-voiced daughters of Hesperus."[3] His very nature is wild and uncontrollable, and his impact upon man is shattering. He is "a wild and boistrous spirit"[4] who creates pandemonium and a "stupifying din."[5] Like Kālī, he is at once terrifying and sublime—completely unpredictable. Indeed, he is a mad god who bounds through the forest, reluctant to enter the civilized world.[6] He is associated with the teeming, "wet" element of nature, with wine, ecstasy, song, and dance. Like Kṛṣṇa, he is an intoxicated and intoxicating god who maddens and incites women with the sound of his flute.[7]

The great and mighty Allah is also associated with frivolity and wildness in the *Gulshan I Raz* of the fourteenth-century Sūfī Sa'd ud Din Mahmud Shabistari. He is said to bring forth the world in the twinkling of an eye.[8] As his creation, the world is said to be a "dizzy whirl,"[9] having only "a simulated existence, / Its state is but an insubstantial pageant and a farce."[10] As to the inscrutable actions of Allah, "causation is inapplicable to the acts of God."[11] Like Dionysus and Kṛṣṇa, he appears intoxicated and intoxicates man as well.

---

[1] *Quod Deus sit immutabilis* 172-76; quoted *ibid.*, p. 15.
[2] *Enneads* III, 2. 15; quoted *ibid.*, pp. 15-16.
[3] Orphic fragment; quoted *ibid.*, p. 17.
[4] Walter F. Otto, *Dionysus*: *Myth and Cult*, trans. Robert B. Palmer, p. 134.
[5] *Ibid.*, p. 92.
[6] *Ibid.*, p. 133.
[7] *Ibid.*, p. 94.
[8] Sa'd ud Din Mahmud Shabistari, *Gulshan I Raz*: *The Mystic Rose Garden*, trans. E. H. Whinfield, p. 1.
[9] *Ibid.*, p. 17.
[10] *Ibid.*, p. 50 .
[11] *Ibid.*, p. 55. The man who has known god in Islam, in this case the Sūfī

Heavenly beauty descends from the unseen world,
Descends like some licentious reveller,
Sets up its flag in the strong city of earthly beauty,
Throws into confusion all the world's array.[1]
With a frown He lays waste the creature world,
With a kiss He restores it again every moment.
Because of His eye our blood is ever boiling,
Because of His lip our souls are ever beside themselves.
By a frown of His eye He plunders the heart,
By a smile on His lips He cheers the soul . . .
By a frown He finishes the affair of the world,
By a kiss He ever and anon revives the soul.[2]

In a fantastic passage, the author describes the whole world as the winehouse of Allah and the entire creation as being intoxicated by his influence:

The whole universe is as His winehouse,
The heart of every atom as His winecup.
Reason is drunken, angels drunken, soul drunken,
Air drunken, earth drunken, heaven drunken.
The heavens giddy with this wine are reeling to and fro,
Desiring in their heart to smell its perfume.
The angels drinking it pure from pure vessels,
Pour the dregs of their draught upon this world.
The elements becoming light-headed from that draught
Fall now into the fire, now into the water.
From the scent of its dregs which fell on the earth,
Man ascends up till he reaches heaven.
From its reflection the withered body becomes a living soul,
From its heat the frozen soul is warmed to life and motion.
The creature world is ever dizzy therewith.[3]

Jalāluddin Rumi, shares this feeling of transcending causation. Jalāluddin sings: "I have put duality away, I have seen that the two worlds are one; / One I seek, One I know, One I see, One I call. / I am intoxicated with Love's cup, the two worlds have passed out of my ken; / I have no business save carouse and revelry." Quoted in Reynold A. Nicholson, *The Mystics of Islam*, p. 96.

[1]Sa'd ud Din Mahmud Shabistari, *Gulshan I Raz*, p. 62.

[2]*Ibid.*, p. 73.

[3]*Ibid.*, p. 80.

Again, there is the image of God creating the world out of bliss that intoxicates, of God creating the world and then reveling madly in it.

From a certain point of view it is also possible to detect a playful theme in those great "gods" of Mahāyāna Buddhism, the *bodhisattvas*. The *bodhisattva* has gained enlightenment and so is free from the wheel of life, the wheel of cause and effect. But he has postponed his entrance into *nirvāṇa* until all sentient beings are also freed. The *bodhisattva* is still in the world but completely unattached to it. He "returns to society and adopts its conventions without 'attachment' "; he "*plays* the social game instead of taking it seriously."[1]

> Buddhism sees the fully liberated man as a Bodhisattva, as one completely free to take part in the cosmic and social game. When it is said that he is in the world but not of it, that he returns to join in all its activities without attachment, this means that he no longer confuses his identity with his social role—that he plays his role instead of taking it seriously. He is a Joker or "wild" man who can play any card in the pack.[2]

For the *bodhisattva* the phenomenal world is a comedy in which he has elected to play a role. Indeed, the concept of the *bodhisattva*, his situation of being in but not of the world, has been called a "meta-comedy."[3] The *bodhisattva's* actions are purposeless, completely free from desire or appetite. He moves in the world as an actor on a stage, never involving his essential self in the action.

There is a playful spirit, too, in the Taoist concept of the Way. In the *Tao Tê Ching* of Lao-tzu it is written of the Tao:

> The model [or, law] of man is the earth;
> The model of the earth is heaven;
> The model of heaven is the Tao;
> The model of the Tao is spontaneity.[4]

---

[1]Alan W. Watts, *Psychotherapy East and West*, p. 55.

[2]*Ibid.*, p. 70.

[3]Gerald Heard coined the term, cited *ibid.*, p. 71. See also Zimmer, *Philosophies of India*, p. 554.

[4]Trans. Ch'u Ta-kao (London: Buddhist Society, 1937), vs. 25; quoted

In these same traditions there are indications that play may be an efficacious activity for man. Plato suggests that man is "a plaything in the hand of God, and truly this is the best thing about him."[1] The maenads, the women devotees of Dionysus, are as wild and mad as the god they worship. They are torn from their homes at the sound of his flute, dash to the forest, and join Dionysus in ecstatic dancing. They are pictured as raving women with disheveled hair.[2] They care nothing for law or custom and dance and sing as if intoxicated. In their madness they are said to tear apart wild animals.[3] In their frenzy to revel with their god in the forest, they are reminiscent of the *gopis*. There is nothing normal about them; their actions take place in a world apart. They have transcended law, morality, and custom in their ecstasy for Dionysus.

In Taoism the school of Pure Conversation (*ch'ing t'an*) emphasized the importance of behaving openly and spontaneously, without regard for custom or ceremony. The sages of this school turned their backs on worldly advantages such as money and power. Their behavior is described in the term *feng liu* (wandering from convention, literally, "wind-floating"). *Feng liu* is best exemplified in the Seven Sages of the Bamboo Grove, who lived during the third century A.D. Juan Chi (210-63) drank heavily through his mother's mourning and refused to observe convention. He and his brother Juan Hsien used to drink wine from a huge bowl on the ground, as they believed cups to be an "unnatural sophistication," and did not mind when pigs trotted over for a taste.[4] The most celebrated drinker among the Seven Sages was Liu Ling (221-300). His servant used to follow him around with a flask in one hand and a shovel in the other—the flask for when he wanted a drink and the shovel in case he fell and died. Liu Ling also liked to go about

in Watts, *Psychotherapy East and West*, p. 186. The Chinese is *tzu-jan*. Arthur Waley translates the term as "the Self-so," the "unconditioned," or the "what-is-so-of-itself." *The Way and Its Power*: *A Study of the Tao Te Ching and Its Place in Chinese Thought*, p. 174.

[1]*Laws*: 803BC; quoted in Rahner, *Man at Play*, p. 13.

[2]Otto, *Dionysus*, p. 134 and Pl. VI.

[3]*Ibid.*, pp. 108-9.

[4]Holmes Welch, *Taoism*: *The Parting of the Way*, p. 124.

naked in his home, refusing to dress even in the presence of company. He considered the whole world his clothing.[1] The Seven Sages believed in following every impulse, as their model was the Tao, and "the model of the Tao is spontaneity." Their actions were completely unpremeditated and free from the necessities imposed by custom and propriety. In the *Chuang-tzu* we read that the ancient Taoist sages acted in the same way:

> The pure men of old acted without calculation, not seeking to secure results. They laid no plans. Therefore, failing, they had no cause for regret; succeeding, no cause for congratulation. And thus they could scale heights without fear . . . They did not know what it was to love life and hate death. They did not rejoice in birth, nor strive to put off dissolution. Quickly come, and quickly go;—no more . . . This is what is called not to lead the heart astray from Tao, nor to let the human seek to supplement the divine.[2]

The Taoist sages behaved without guile, and in fact the *Chuang-tzu* holds up the example of the child as paradigmatic for those who seek to follow the Tao :

> Can you be like a newborn child? The baby cries all day and yet his voice never becomes hoarse; that is because he has not lost nature's harmony. . . . The baby looks at things all day without winking; that is because his eyes are not focused on any particular object. He goes without knowing where he is going, and stops without knowing what he is doing. He merges himself with his surroundings and moves along with it. These are the principles of mental hygiene.[3]

Completely unattached to the pragmatic and ceremonial world, the Taoist sage glides through his environment encountering no opposition. In his freedom he does not know desire or necessity. He is a "wind-floating" spirit whose actions are performed without regard for fruits.

There is a similar spirit in Zen Buddhism, which is in many

---

[1] *Ibid.*, pp. 124-25.

[2] *Chuang-tzu,* trans. H. A. Giles (Shanghai, 1926), 6; quoted in Watts, *Psychotherapy East and West*, pp. 77-78.

[3] *Chuang-tzu*, 23; quoted *ibid.*, p. 189.

ways a kindred tradition to Taoism. Speaking of Zen and other Asian religious traditions, Alan Watts says: "The ways of liberation make it very clear that life is not going anywhere, because it is already *there*. In other words, it is playing, and those who do not play with it have simply missed the point."[1] A favorite illustration of the unenlightened man in Chinese Ch'an Buddhism is the man in search of an ass—and riding upon an ass. Enlightenment is not to be found by striving after it, through goal-directed activity. It is not to be found through conscious effort but by remaining open and realizing that enlightenment is in all things, that it can be found while carrying water or cleaning one's teeth just as well as during meditation in the monastery. Zen *sādhana* is the ability to remain self-satisfied under any and all circumstances, to act without calculation or care for the future. In Zen, *sādhana* is purposeless, nonsensical, a game played between teacher and student in which the teacher seeks to demonstrate to the student that it is in fact a game. "The presence of purpose in the mind is a hindrance."[2] The teacher seeks to guide the student not so much by words or logical argumentation as by startling him. "As the shrine of satori is approached, words fall away to silence, or sudden laughter, or a biff on the jaw."[3] Both laughter and humor are used in Zen as "oil in the machine" of *sādhana*, as it were. For "humour is sanity, a release of interior tension with a sudden vision of the fun of things."[4] By shocking or startling the pupil the Zen master seeks to undo at a stroke those inward knots that strangle the student and have come about as the result of intense striving after enlightenment. In Zen, spontaneity is the way of enlightenment. To gain enlightenment means to be entirely open, somewhat in the manner of the Taoist sages.

> Keep the emotions where they belong, for they have no part in "right" actions, and none at all in thought. But do not repress them. If yours is an emotional temperament, use them, develop them. . . . Take them for a run at times. Sing, shout, get excited, whether with great beauty, a local football

---

[1] *Ibid.*
[2] Christmas Humphreys, *Zen Buddhism*, p. 84.
[3] *Ibid.*, p. 110.
[4] *Ibid.*

match or, best of all, great fun. . . .It is the excitement itself, letting off steam, which matters.[1]

Finally, Zen assumes a certain childlike simplicity and enthusiasm. It is not, after all, a highly esoteric, complicated tedious business.

Look children,
Hail-stones !
Let's rush out ![2]

says one of Bashō's poems. Let's revel in the here and now and give the lie to the future.

Perhaps you now smile condescendingly, assuming that Zen is for the child at play. So it is, for the child at play, though it has less knowledge, has far more wisdom than its parents, but the power of a child is greater than the oldest adult can control . . . Zen is child-like in the sense that of such are the Kingdom of Heaven, but it is a reveille and not a lullaby, a challenge to the whole of man to become what he is.[3]

C. Play in the Judaic-Christian—"Post-Christian" Tradition

There is a strain in Western thought that extols work and orderly progression toward ends that is highly suspicious of anything that hints at idleness or frivolity. In Western thought it is common to consider pointless activities like play a mere waste of time. This is particularly clear in the Christian polemic against play and idleness. Addressing his fellow Christians Ambrose writes :

Joking should be avoided even in small talk, so that some more serious topic is not made light of. "Woe upon you who laugh now; you shall mourn and weep" (Luke 6. 25), saith the Lord: are we then looking for something to laugh at, so that we may laugh now but weep hereafter? I maintain that not only loose jokes, but jokes of any kind

[1]*Ibid.*, p. 158 .
[2]Quoted *ibid.*, p. 81.
[3]*Ibid.*

> must be avoided—except perhaps when our words are full of sweetness and grace, not indelicate.[1]

Such popular sayings as "The Devil makes work for idle hands" and "Life is real, life is earnest, but the grave is not its goal" may be associated with the Protestant ethic of industry and work, but early Christian writers had clearly grasped the point too. John Chrysostom, in a sermon given in Antioch in 390, exhorts his congregation:

> This world is not a theatre, in which we can laugh; and we are not assembled together in order to burst into peals of laughter, but to weep for our sins. But some of you still want to say : "I would prefer God to give me the chance to go on laughing and joking." Is there anything more childish than thinking in this way? It is not God who gives us the chance to play, but the devil.[2]

The sobriety in these passages is certainly not atypical of Western piety and the estimate of the place of play in man's religious quest. Perhaps the more typical position, however, is seen in Aquinas. Following Aristotle's model of the *eutrapelos*, the man who strikes a balance between humor and seriousness, Aquinas says:

> There is some good in playing, *in as much as it is useful for human life*. As man needs from time to time to rest and leave off bodily labours, so also his mind from time to time must relax from its intense concentration on serious pursuits: this comes about through play. Hence Aristotle says that man obtains in this life a kind of rest from his anxieties and preoccupations in playful conversation.[3]

The much heralded (and misnamed) "post-Christian" era of our time is almost equally suspicious of idleness and frivolity, although such inhibitive traditions as the Puritan are roundly condemned as crippling to the development of the "whole" man. In our time leisure, and what to do with it, has become a serious

---

[1] *De officiis* I. 23. 103; quoted in Rahner, *Man at Play*, p. 97.
[2] *Commentary on Matthew*, Homily 6. 6; quoted *ibid.*, p. 98.
[3] *In decem libros Ethicorum Aristotelis ad Nicomachum*, lib. iv, lect. 16; quoted *ibid.*, p. 99.

problem. It is assumed that leisure is really not for idleness at all but must be "utilized creatively."

> We read or go to concerts to improve our minds; we relax in order to improve our work; we worship God to improve our morals; we even get drunk *in order to* forget our worries. Everything that is done playfully, without ulterior motive and second thought, makes us feel guilty, and it is even widely believed that such unmotivated action is impossible. You *must* have a reason for what you do.[1]

Perhaps modern man's suspicion of the superfluous and frivolous is the result of his middle age. For after all, as we have been told in the rather pretentious proclamation, in our time, finally and at long last, "Man has come of age." Childhood is now behind us, and we are free to behave as adults. We are free to see things as they really are, without comfort and succor, without resort to superstition and myth. In our adulthood we are free to look at ourselves, free from the misconceptions and traditional presuppositions of our youth. And while this realization is accepted with great clamor and applause, there seems nevertheless a certain joylessness in its ultimate acceptance and practice. For man is now free to behave "authentically," and he who has not grasped the very serious nature and responsibility of living in the glory of his new freedom as an adult is felt to still cling to his frivolous youth in an attempt to avoid his new responsibilities. Now is the time when man as a species can finally take himself seriously, and if the species develops a racial ulcer because of too heavy a dose of *Angst*, that is also a part of coming of age.

The world around us, too, has ceased to behave frivolously. It has now been established that nothing around us or about us happens without good cause. The heavens are no longer to be wondered at but charted. Man is no longer to be marveled at but dissected. Nature is no longer to be reveled in but utilized, or cultivated for future utilization. It is this age that has witnessed Einstein's dogmatic and persistent quest for a "Unified Field Theory" despite the discovery of the Quantum Theory. It is this age that speaks when Einstein says: "I cannot believe

[1] Watts, *Psychotherapy East and West*, p. 107.

that God throws dice with men."[1] If man has outgrown his frivolous childhood, then God has outgrown his too.

Despite the Christian polemic against frivolity, the celebration of work as a means to salvation, and modern man's staid, middle-aged outlook on things, there is another strain in the Judaic-Christian tradition that runs counter to the mainstream and that has also survived the species' coming of age. While it may be considered subversive in some quarters, and probably represents a minority opinion, there is a tradition that hints at the efficacious nature of play, and even suggests that God himself may play from time to time.

In Zechariah's vision of a new age, of the New Jerusalem, it is said: "And the streets of the city shall be full of boys and girls playing."[2] The two Carthaginian martyrs, Perpetua and Felicitas, are told upon arriving before the throne of God: "*Ite et ludite*—go and play!"[3] In the *Lives of the Fathers*, which deals with the biographies of early Church leaders, it is written of one of the patriarchs: "It was revealed to Paphnutius that a certain joker would be his companion in heaven."[4] If man is not entirely free to play in this vale of tears, when that new age dawns, or when man is finally through with his life of toil, he will realize a new mode of being in which he will be free from strife and work and in which he will be free to play.

There are also indications that the Judaic-Christian God, often stereotyped as a stern, somber, authoritarian figure, is believed to play. In Proverbs, the Wisdom of God speaks:

When he established the heavens I was there,
  when he drew a circle on the face of the deep,
when he made firm the skies above,
  when he established the fountains of the deep,
when he assigned to the sea its limit,
  so that the waters might not transgress his command,
  when he marked out the foundations of the earth,

---

[1]Quoted in Edgar Ansel Mowrer, "The Open Universe," *American Review* (USIS, New Delhi), III, No. 2 (January, 1959), 88 (first published in the *Saturday Review*, April 19, 1958).

[2]8:5 (R.S.V.).

[3]Rahner, *Man at Play*, p. 61.

[4]Quoted *ibid.*, p. 104.

then I was beside him, like a master workman [another
reading is "little child"[1]];
and I was daily his delight,
rejoicing[2] before him always,
rejoicing in his inhabited world,
and delighting in the sons of men.[3]

The idea of the Wisdom of God, or the Logos, playing is more clearly expressed in some early Christian writings. Gregory Nazianzen says: "For the Logos on high plays, stirring the whole cosmos back and forth, as he wills, into shapes of every kind."[4] Cornelius a Lapide is equally explicit in his commentary on Prov. 8:31: "The Son is called a child because of his proceeding everlastingly from the Father, because in the dewy freshness and spring-time beauty of his eternal youth he eternally enacts a game before his Father."[5] The seventeenth-century German mystic Angelus Silesius says of creation:

The all is just a sport
That Godhood chose to make:
It brought the Creature forth
For its own Godly sake.[6]

Meister Eckhart also speaks of the play of God, of self-dalliance within the Godhead:

> There has always been this play going on in the Father-nature . . . from the Father's embrace of his own nature there comes this eternal playing of the Son. This play was played eternally before all creatures . . . .The playing of the twain

[1]The Hebrew word is *amōn*, "master workman." The meaning "little child" seems to have arisen in Rabbinic tradition, where the word was taken as *amun*, 'nursling." See *Midrash Rabbah* (to Genesis [Bereshith] 8:2), trans. H. Freedman and Maurice Simon, I. 56.

[2]The Hebrew word is *SāHaQ*, which may also mean dancing, laughing (or laughing at), playing a musical instrument, making sport. See, for example, II Sam. 6:5 and 6:21.

[3]Prov. 8:27-31 (R.S.V.).

[4]Carmina I. 2, 2, vss. 589-90; quoted in Rahner, *Man at Play*, p. 23.

[5]*Commentaria in Proverbia* 8. 31, Nota tertio, Mystice; quoted *ibid.*, p. 23.

[6]Quoted in Mowrer, "The Open Universe," p. 95.

is the Holy Ghost in whom they both disport themselves and he disports himself in both. Sport and players are the same.[1]

Henry Suso, another German mystic, who lived in the thirteenth and fourteenth centuries, extends the idea of divine dalliance to Mary and God. From his *Little Book of Eternal Wisdom* is this passage, spoken by the Servant to Mary: "Ah, thou art God's, and He is thine, and ye two form an eternal, infinite play of love, which no duality can ever separate."[2] Suso suggests other themes that were discussed vis-à-vis the Hindu gods. He describes, for example, the incredible, irresistible, and intoxicating beauty of God. Eternal Wisdom speaks:

> I am the throne of heavenly bliss, The crown of joy and happiness. My eyes are so clear, My mouth so gentle, My cheeks are so bright and rosy, and all My person so fair and lovely and altogether perfect, that if, until the Last Day, a man were to remain in a fiery furnace, for the sake of a mere glimpse of Me, he would still not have deserved it.
>
> See, I am so charmingly adorned in bright raiment, so beautifully surrounded with the variegated hues of living flowers, of red roses, white lilies, fair violets, and of all bright meadows, the gentle flowerlets of all fair pastures are like a rough thistle, as compared with My adornment.
>
> In the Godhead I play a game of joy; it gives the angel host of happiness the most. A thousand years do seem to them a fleeting dream. All the heavenly hosts fix their eyes on Me with a new wonder, and gaze upon Me. Their eyes are fastened on Mine; their hearts are inclined toward Me; and their soul is bowed to Me without intermission. Blessed be he who dances the dance of joy and heavenly bliss by My side, who in complete security will pace, holding My fair hand, for all eternity! One little word, that sounds so clear from My sweet mouth, surpasses all the songs of angels, the melody of all harps, and of all sweet instruments. Ah, look, I am so dear to love, so lovely to embrace and so tender

[1]Quoted in Coomaraswamy, "Lilā," p. 98.

[2]Henry Suso, *Little Book of Eternal Wisdom and Little Book of Truth*, trans. James M. Clark, p. 113.

> for the loving soul to kiss, that all hearts should be fit to break with longing for Me.[1]

Speaking of his own relationship with God, Suso says that at times he experienced laughter. "He sang during this time so completely into God, the Eternal Wisdom, that he could not speak of it. At times he had a loving converse with God, then a lamentable sighing, at times silent laughter."[2] Suso describes the effect of God upon his devotees as intoxicating. In his *Little Book of Truth*, Truth says:

> It happens, no doubt, that, when the good and faithful servant enters into the joy of his Lord, he becomes intoxicated with the immeasurable abundance of the Divine house. For in an ineffable manner, it happens to him as to a drunk man, who forgets himself.[3]

Suso also says that "the actions of a truly abandoned man are his inaction, and his work is to be inactive, for in his actions he remains at rest, and in his work he remains at leisure."[4] This sounds like a description of the ideal *bhakta* who acts without regard for fruits. And, finally, Suso describes the *coelum empyreum*, the heaven of fire, which is far above the ninth heaven, as a playground:

> Now, look thyself at the fair heavenly meadow, ah, the whole joy of summer is there, the fields of bright May, the valley of true happiness! Here one sees the happy glances exchanged by lovers; here are harps and fiddles; here they sing, and leap and dance, and play all joyful games. Here there is abundant joy, gladness without sadness, for ever and a day.[5]

Another image in the Christian tradition that runs counter to the stereotype of the stern, authoritarian God and the theme of working out one's salvation in somber, calculated earnest is

---

[1] *Ibid.*, pp. 72-73.
[2] From his autobiography; quoted *ibid.*, p. 33.
[3] *Ibid.*, p. 185.
[4] *Ibid.*, p. 207.
[5] *Ibid.*, p. 90.

the figure of the dancing Christ. Perhaps reflecting on Prov. 8:31 Saint Bernard wrote:

> Jesus the dancer's master is,
> A great skill at the dance is his,
> He turns to right, he turns to left;
> All must follow his teaching deft.[1]

Saint Bernard's vision is that of a dancing god, a god whose redemptive biography is an invitation to the dance, an invitation to transcend the bondage of sin and death, not in somber, earnest, plodding denial of the festive but in joyous dance. The following hymns rejoice in the same image—Christ the Redeemer, the Great Dancer who came to earth to teach man how to celebrate, who danced out rather than worked out his biography:

> To-morrow shall be my dancing day:
> I would my true love did so chance
> To see the legend of my play,
> To call my true love to my dance:
> (Refrain): Sing O my love, O my love, my love;
> This have I done for my true love.
>
> Then was I born of a virgin pure,
> Of her I took fleshly substance;
> Thus was I knit to man's nature,
> To call my true love to my dance: (Refrain)
>
> In a manger laid and wrapped I was,
> So very poor, this was my chance,
> Betwixt an ox and a silly poor ass,
> To call my true love to my dance: (Refrain)
>
> Then afterwards baptized I was;
> The Holy Ghost on me did glance,
> My Father's voice heard from above,
> To call my true love to my dance: (Refrain)

---

[1]Quoted in Geradus van der Leeuw, *Sacred and Profane Beauty: The Holy in Art*, trans. David E. Green, p. 30.

Into the desert I was led,
Where I fasted without substance;
The devil bade me make stones my bread,
To have me break my true love's dance: (Refrain)

The Jews on me they made great suit,
And with me made great variance,
Because they loved darkness rather than light,
To call my true love to my dance: (Refrain)

For thirty pence Judas me sold,
His covetousness for to advance;
"Mark whom I kiss, the same do hold,"
The same is he shall lead the dance: (Refrain)

Before Pilote the Jews me brought,
Where Barabbas had deliverance;
They scourged me and set me at nought,
Judged me to die to lead the dance: (Refrain)

Then on the cross hanged I was,
Where a spear to my heart did glance;
There issued forth both water and blood,
To call my true love to my dance: (Refrain)

Then down to hell I took my way
For my true love's deliverance,
And rose again on the third day,
Up to my true love and the dance: (Refrain)

Then up to heaven I did ascend,
Where now I dwell in sure substance,
On the right hand of God, that man
May come unto the general dance: (Refrain)[1]

I danced in the morning
  when the world was begun,

[1]Percy Dearmer, R. Vaughan Williams, and Martin Shaw (eds.), *The Oxford Book of Carols*, no. 71, "My Dancing Day," pp. 154-55. "The text seems to go back earlier than the seventeenth century." *Ibid*., p. 155, editor's note.

And I danced in the moon,
 and the stars and the sun,
And I came down from heaven
 and I danced on the earth,
At Bethlehem I had my birth.
(Chorus): Dance, then, wherever you may be,
"I am the Lord of the Dance," said he,
"And I'll lead you all wherever you may be,
And I'll lead you all in the Dance," said he.

I danced for the Scribe,
 and the Pharisee,
But they would not dance,
 and they wouldn't follow me,
I danced for the fishermen,
 for James and John,
They came with me and the dance was on. (Chorus)

I danced on the Sabbath
 and I cured the lame,
The holy people said
 it was a shame,
They whipped and they stripped
 and they hung me high,
And they left me there on a cross to die. (Chorus)

I danced on a Friday,
 when the sky turned black,
It's hard to dance
 with the devil on your back,
They buried my body
 and they thought I'd gone,
But I am the dance and I still go on. (Chorus)

They cut me down,
 and I leap up high,
I am the life
 that'll never, never die.
I'll live in you if
 you'll live in me,

I am the Lord of the Dance, said he. (Chorus)[1]

It is not within the scope of this study to examine the importance of dance vis-à-vis the Christian tradition.[2] What is clear from these few examples, however, is that the dance—that most superfluous, extra, beautiful, joyous activity—has been associated with God's redemptive act and, further, that man himself is invited to dance his way to salvation, to swing, sway, and leap under the Great Dancer's direction.

The themes of play, celebration, dance, and festivity have recently been taken up by contemporary theologians and writers, to the extent that a "theology of play" is now somewhat in vogue.[3] Harvey Cox, for example, sees as fundamentally necessary to man's religious expression festivity and celebration, without which man would remain trapped and bound by the bleak realities of his historical existence.

> The religious man is one who grasps his own life within a larger historical and cosmic setting. He sees himself as part of a greater whole, a longer story in which he plays a part. Song, ritual, and vision link man to this story. They help him place himself somewhere between Eden and the Kingdom of God; they give him a past and a future. But without real festive occasions and without the nurture of fantasy man's spirit as well as his psyche shrinks. He becomes

---

[1]Sydney Carter (words and music), "The Lord of the Dance," from the recording *Robert Edwin Sings "Keep the Rumor Going."*

[2]See E. Louis Backman *Religious Dances in the Christian Church and in Popular Medicine*; Margaret Fisk Taylor, *A Time to Dance*: *Symbolic Movement in Worship*; and "Religion and the Dance."

[3]Gabriel Fackre, *Humiliation and Celebration*; Romano Guardini, *The Spirit of the Liturgy*, trans. Ada Lane; Walter Harrelson, *From Fertility Cult to Worship*; Sam Keen, *Apology for Wonder*; Sister Corita Kent, *Footnotes and Headlines*: *A Play and Pray Book*; William F. Lynch, S.J., *Christ and Apollo*: *The Dimensions of the Literary Imagination* and *Images of Hope*: *Imagination as Healer of the Hopeless*; David L. Miller, *Gods and Games*: *Toward a Theology of Play* and "Salvation and the Image of Comedy: Pirandello and Aristophanes," *Religion and Life* (Summer, 1964); Robert Neale, *In Praise of Play*; Josef Pieper, *In Tune with the World*: *A Theory of Festivity*, trans. Richard and Clara Winston; Rahner, *Man at Play*; and Watts, *Beyond Theology*.

> something less than a man, a gnat with neither origin nor destiny.[1]

For Cox, Nietzsche's identification of the devil with the "spirit of gravity" is particularly true today.[2] Festivity, celebration, dance, and joy have become disassociated from the liturgy specifically and from the Church generally, and because of this the spirit of the devil, not the spirit of God, now lives in the churches. Our churches, Cox says, have become musty and cold, barren of joy—indeed, he implies, they have become coffins for the Dead God.

What is needed, he suggests, is both a recognition of festivity and celebration as fundamental to the Church's life in the world and an appreciation of Christ the Harlequin. The hymns of the dancing Christ quoted above tend to paint Christ as a buffoon—a clown who danced his way to the cross and mocked those who mocked him.

> The clown refuses to live inside the present reality. He senses another one. He defies the law of gravity, taunts the policeman, ridicules the other performers. Through him we catch a glimpse of another world impinging on this one, upsetting its rules and practices.[3]

For Cox, Christ is to be seen as the Harlequin, "the joke in the middle of the prayer. . . . He is the spirit of play in a world of calculated utilitarian seriousness."[4] He transcends this world and opens us to an "other" world by "dancing his way to the cross," as the hymns suggest, by mocking pomposity and gravity, by playing the clown.

There is a growing "secular" literature, too, that supports the position that man's physical, psychical, and spiritual well-

---

[1]Harvery Cox, *The Feast of Fools: A Theological Essay on Festivity and Fantasy*, p. 14.

[2]"Do not cease dancing, you lovely girls ! No killjoy has come to you with evil eyes, no enemy of girls. God's advocate am I before the devil: but the devil is the spirit of gravity. How could I, you lightfooted ones, be any enemy of Godlike dances? Or of girls' feet with pretty ankels ?" Nietzsche, *Thus Spoke Zarathustra*; quoted *ibid.*, p. 48.

[3]*Ibid.*, p. 150.

[4]*Ibid.*, p. 145.

being is dependent upon fantasy, celebration, and play, that without these extras man must shrivel and die.[1] And the sociologist Peter Berger suggests that it is precisely in these "extra" phenomena that one finds hints (rumors) of that "other" world of the divine. Berger argues that, despite the reported death of the supernatural in our time, there are phenomena that may be empirically measured that demonstrate the likelihood of God's continued good health. Berger points to five human phenomena that he says are by no means rare but prototypical, and he suggests that they are "signals of transcendence." Two of these phenomena are relevant to this study: the author's arguments from play and the comic. In both of these typically human phenomena there is implied, according to Berger, a vertical referent. In play, he says, man steps out of the ordinary world and out of ordinary time and denies his finite place in the world.[2] In a similar vein, Berger argues that man's sense of humor reflects "discrepancy, incongruity, incommensurability"; it reflects "the imprisonment of the human spirit in the world," while at the same time mocking that imprisonment.[3]

And even if it is true that man has finally grown up, there are those who stubbornly insist that if growing up means adapting and accepting a closed universe in which the miraculous and wondrous are *a priori* ruled out, they will have no part of it. There are those who yearn for those days when the universe was open, when the unexpected and unimagined were possible, when the world was full of surprises and nothing could be predicted confidently.

An article published in the *Saturday Review* suggests that men are basically prone to be either mental agoraphobes (fearing open spaces), or mental claustrophobes (fearing confinement). The former, following Einstein, seek confidently the final key to the absolute predictability of the universe, while the latter rejoice every time the former encounter a setback. For the

[1]See, for example, Norman O Brown, *Life against Death*; Roger Caillois, *Man and the Sacred*, trans. Meyer Barash; Roy L. Hart, *Unfinished Man and the Imagination*; Andre Maurois, *Illusions*; and Jean Paul Sartre, *The Psychology of Imagination*.

[2]Peter Berger, *A Rumor of Angels*: *Modern Society and the Rediscovery of the Supernatural*, pp. 72-75.

[3]*Ibid.*, pp. 86, 87.

claustrophobes, the author says, are believers in an open universe and see "spontaneity as the salt of life" and rebel at the very possibility of a closed universe.[1] The author himself is a self-confessed claustrophobe, and his concluding comment reflects the undying spirit of rebellion in man that affirms his conviction that inwardly he is free and that the world around him will never cease to be filled with wonderful surprises. He says that while scientists may some day demonstrate that such phenomena as dream, trance, second sight, prophetic vision, and insight (we might add play, humor, and dance, among other things) are perfectly understandable and predictable, there is no guarantee that some great, new surprise will not come along and thoroughly upset their applecart. "Even determinists may, by some twist of fate, turn out to be *right for a time, a given place and a certain class of events*. Right, that is, until immortal Shiva, wearying of man's pedantry, once more varies the steps of his immortal dance."[2]

There is also the example of the hippies, who proclaim that if contemporary society is representative of man's coming of age, they will have nothing to do with becoming adults. Their creed of drop out, tune in, implies that in modern society man is denied the possibilities of freedom, wonder, and joy. Their brilliant clothes, their quest for ecstasy (erotic or drug induced), their joy in flowers and superfluous adornment indicate their conviction that life is not a trust but a gift that is to be reveled in. The hippie vision of the ideal world is summed up in a description of "The Happy Village," a place beyond this world where men are free to play. The description is offered by the hippie brother of the hero of a short story that appeared in *Playboy*. The brother has a faraway look in his eyes and is under the influence of drugs.

> "Where are you at?" I asked again.
> "I'm in the happy village."
> "Where?"
> "The Happy Village!"
> I said I didn't know where that was.
>
> Allen bolted upright, his eyes flashing, and brushed the hair from his face. "It's where things are done for you to make

[1]Mowrer, "The Open Universe," p. 96.
[2]*Ibid.*, p. 98.

you feel good. I love you," he said. "Both of you. Now dig it. There's this village: beautiful, verdant, recreational facilities, free love, civil liberties, everything, man. What you do there is ball, explore caves, discover little animals, yoga, puppet shows, *dancing*, always dancing—I mean, like, all you do is *play*. And the food has nothing to do with hunger, just with taste. And you're all kids. Freaking freely. Big ones, skinny ones, old, young. But all kids. This is called the Happy Village. That's where I am. Now, the world is two scenes. Outside the village is practically everyone alive pulling on this rope—in rags, BO, some of them getting trampled, like a giant gang of Volga boatmen, get it? It's like a huge tug of war, except the other side is hooked onto the sun or something—the center of the universe! And these guys are holding the planet up in orbit. They're being whirled around this center and having a bitch of a time, but they know that if they let go, then the world goes hurtling off into space and there's no more gravity. So that's the big gig in the world, pulling on this rope. I mean, like, it's the *only* gig. So all the time, these guys are always beckoning to the kids on the border pastures of the village, dig? Come on, this cat says, what do you think you're doing *gamboling* on the green when if we don't get some help here pretty fast the whole world is gonna fly off into space? So a lot of the kids, when they go in for the evening hootenanny or whatever, start thinking to themselves, what *am* I doing just *playing* all the time instead of becoming a Volga boatman or something? They start thinking a man has to be a *man*. So most of them sooner or later say goodbye to the village and pack up their trinkets in an old kit bag and they cross the border and get on the rope line. Pulling. In fact, that's how everybody got tugging on there in the first place. Once everybody lived in the village. Almost everybody. But a few guys, here's the gritty, a few kids, I mean, *stay in the village*. To play. Then after a while, they die. The guys on the line die, too. Everybody dies, but the village cats, they go happy into that good night."[1]

[1]Jacob Brackman, "Dance with a Stranger," *Playboy*, XIV, No. 12 (December, 1967), 305 (author's emphasis).

CONCLUSION

The Hindu gods are frequently depicted as playing in a variety of ways. They are often shown as being intoxicated, mad, or as acting aimlessly and frivolously. One of the most popular gods of Hinduism is pictured as an adolescent cowherd boy who sports endlessly with his friends and lovers. For many he is the supreme manifestation of the divine. Play is clearly an activity that is considered appropriate to the gods. It conveys their otherness, their transcendence of the finite sphere, by appearing motiveless and entirely free. Through play the gods reveal their nature as completely unconditioned. Through play, too, the nature of the gods is revealed as blissful and beautiful. The term *līlā* is almost synonymous with divine activity generally, and with Kṛṣṇa's activity specifically. It is also a term that is commonly used to describe the activity of the saints.[1] Indeed, the useless, playful nature of the saints marks them as being suspended somewhere between the divine and human spheres. They have transcended the ordinary world and are free to play as the gods do.

The examples of pure play in cult are not as common as they are in the divine sphere, but play, nevertheless, is clearly seen as an appropriate technique of cult and as an appropriate context for the divine-human relationship. While the examples of man in cult participating in pure play, in the kind of freewheeling sport that typifies the divine, are few, a variety of other cultic activities and phenomena make it clear that play embodies all those characteristics that are treasured by man in his relationship to the divine. The relative lack of play in cult compared to the divine sphere does not necessarily suggest that it is not esteemed as appropriate; it suggests that man does not burst forth in play with the same facility as the gods. This is understandable, as man is a finite, bound creature who must strive to soar freely as the gods do. Because of his limitations and inhibitions man is

[1]In addition to those works already cited, note the title of Mahipati's *Bhaktalīlāmṛta* ("The Eternal Līlā of Devotees"), a Marāthi account of the saints similar to the *Bhaktamāl*. Mahipati Marathi, *Bhaktalilamrita*, trans. Justin E. Abbott and J. F. Edwards.

not as likely to prance off in reckless play as the gods are. He is in the position of striving after that essential spontaneity and freedom that presuppose the playful nature of the divine.

I should like, finally, to make a few remarks concerning the underlying religiousness, or "otherness" of play, to comment on those essential qualities of play that make it so appropriate to man's experience and understanding of the "other" sphere in which the gods revel and in which he longs to be immersed. In seeking to explain the apparent universal urge of man to play, Huizinga has suggested that play answers man's "imperishable need . . . to live in beauty," his "need of rhythm, harmony, change, alteration, contrast and climax."[1] Because play is intrinsically satisfying, serving no other purpose than its own, which is to have fun, to act freely and superfluously, because play is irresponsible and permits man to behave both heroically and foolishly, it is certainly a beautiful thing compared to enforced routine and habit. The aimless display, prancing, dancing, and frolicking of primal play, the excitement of competition in sports, furthermore, suggest and fulfil man's thirst to be constantly moving and restless, his need for excitement and revelry. It seems there is in man an eternal child who refuses to be still, who persistently urges him to dart off, skipping and jumping in useless, restless activity. Man's love of color, music, beauty, excitement, the ornamental and decorative, contests and games implies an undying, inward spirit of youth, an essential immaturity.[2] In a variety of activities, but particularly in play, this rambunctious spirit finds fulfilment.

I would suggest that man's religious activity answers a similar need, or perhaps answers the same need in a different way. Bound by limitations of desire, appetite, and circumstance, aware of his limited position, man seems to possess a kind of psychological or spiritual claustrophobia. He is not content to remain a prisoner, bound by his own limitations. He seeks to participate in something "other," something outside or beyond himself, something that can explode the limited condition of his species,

---

[1]Huizinga, *Homo Ludens*, pp. 63, 75.

[2]Note the comment of a priest whom Andre Malraux met in the French Resistance: "The fundamental fact is that there's no such thing as a grown-up person." *Anti-Memoirs*.

biography, and society. An almost universal characteristic of man's religious activity, therefore, is a vertical referent, an indication of a dimension that transcends the ordinary and hints at the extraordinary.

I have indicated earlier that Huizinga's postulate, that man's awareness of the sacred originated and developed in play, cannot be shown to be necessarily the case. I have argued that the basic intentions of play and cult are different and that both represent irreducible, primal phenomena. It is clear, nevertheless, that in play man may taste the divine, that he may find the kind of joyous activity he associates with the "other" realm of the gods. For play is an extra activity that is irrelevant to man's nature as a finite creature bound to the earth. It is an ornamental thing whose only justification for being is aimless display. When man plays he behaves as foolishly, arrogantly, and superfluously as a strutting peacock. He laughs at his predicament of being a mortal creature bound to the inevitable wheel of birth, suffering, and death. Indeed, he transcends that wheel, escapes its bondage by reveling in the moment. For play yields the attitude that life is not a business to be worked out but an affair to be danced out. In play man gives vent to his unquenchable spirit of youth that affirms that he is inwardly free. In play man denies the joylessness of inactivity and ordered life and prances about carelessly and freely. In play man affirms that life is sufficient unto itself, a gift to be enjoyed, not a trust to be guarded with sober and somber countenance. He affirms that life is to be celebrated, not simply tolerated. In play man affirms and experiences the fact that life is enough, that it is not necessary to improve upon it or work at it. In play man becomes complete and self-satisfied, as the gods are.

When man plays he becomes a god by denying his mortal circumstances and predicament; he becomes completely free to act as frivolously and spontaneously as the mad, intoxicated gods of the Hindus.

> To play is to yield oneself to a kind of magic, to enact to oneself the absolutely other, to pre-empt the future, to give the lie to the inconvenient world of fact. In play earthly realities become, of a sudden, things of the transient moment, presently left behind, then disposed of and buried in the past;

> the mind is prepared to accept the unimagined and incredible, to enter a world where different laws apply, to be relieved of all the weights that bear down, to be free, kingly, unfettered and divine. Man at play is reaching out . . . for that superlative ease, in which even the body, freed from its earthly burden, moves to the effortless measures of a heavenly dance.[1]

This estimate of play, finally, written by a child of the West, a priest of the Roman Catholic Church, may perhaps be taken as a commentary on these words of Jesus: "Truly, I say to you, unless you turn and become like children, you will never enter the kingdom of heaven."[2]

---

[1]Rahner, *Man at Play*, pp. 65-66.
[2]Mt. 18:3 (R.S.V.).

SELECTED BIBLIOGRAPHY

Agni Purāṇam: A Prose English Translation. Translated by Manmatha Nāth Dutt Shastrī. Chowkhamba Sanskrit Studies, Vol. LIV. 2 vols. Varanasi: Chowkhamba Sanskrit Series Office, 1967.

Agrawala, Vasudeva S. *Matsya Purāṇa—a study (An Exposition of the Ancient Purāṇa-Vidyā).* Varanasi: All-India Kashiraj Trust, 1963.

———. *Vāmana Purāṇa—a Study (An Exposition of the Ancient Purāṇa-Vidyā).* Varanasi: Prithivi Prakashan, 1964.

Althaus, Paul. *Mystic Lyrics from the Indian Middle Ages.* Translated by P. Althaus. London: George Allen & Unwin, 1928.

Apollonius of Rhodes. *The Voyage of Argo (The Argonautica).* Translated by E. V. Rieu. Baltimore: Penguin Books, 1959.

Archer, William G. *The Loves of Krishna in Indian Painting and Poetry.* New York: Macmillan Co., 1957.

Backman, E. Louis. *Religious Dances in the Christian Church and in Popular Medicine.* London: George Allen & Unwin, 1952.

[Bādarāyaṇa.] *The Brahma Sūtra: The Philosophy of Spiritual Life.* Translated and edited by S. Radhakrishnan. London: George Allen & Unwin, 1960.

Basavaṇṇa. *Vacanas of Basavaṇṇa.* Edited by H. Deveerappa. Translated by L. M. A. Menezes and S. M. Angadi. Sirigere, Mysore: Annana Balaga, 1967.

Basham, A. L. *The Wonder That Was India: A Survey of the Culture of the Indian Sub-continent before the Coming of the Muslims.* New York: Grove Press, Inc., 1954.

Berger, Peter. *A Rumor of Angels: Modern Society and the Rediscovery of the Supernatural.* Garden City, N.Y.: Doubleday & Co., 1969.

The Bhagavad Gitā. Translated by Franklin Edgerton. Harper Torchbook; Cloister Library. New York: Harper & Row, 1964.

[*Bhāgavata-purāṇa.*] *The Srimad-Bhagavatam of Krishna-Dwaipayana Vyasa.* Translated by J. M. Sanyal. 5 vols. 2d ed.

(Vols. I, IV, V); 3d ed. (Vols. II, III). Calcutta: Oriental Publishing Co., 2d ed., n.d.; 3d ed., 1965.

The Bhakti Sutras of Narada. Translated by Nandlal Sinha. Sacred Books of the Hindus, Vol. VII. Allahabad: Sudhindra Nath Vasu, 1911.

Bhandarkar, R. G. *Vaiṣṇavism, Śaivism and Minor Religious Systems*. Varanasi: Indological Book House, Antiquarian Book-sellers & Publishers [1966].

Bhārater-sādhak. (Bengali.) Vol. I. Edited by Śaṅkarnāth Roy. Calcutta: Writer's Syndicate, 1956.

Bharati, Agehananda. *The Tantric Tradition*. London: Rider & Co., 1965.

Bhaṭṭācārya, Siddheśvara. *The Philosophy of the Srīmad-Bhāgavata*. Vol. I: *Metaphysics*; Vol. II: *Religion*. Vishva-Bharati Research Publication. 2 vols. Santiniketan: Visva-Bharati, Vol. I, 1960; Vol. II, 1962.

Bhavnani, Enakshi. *The Dance in India: The Origin and History, Foundations, the Art and Science of the Dance in India—Classical, Folk and Tribal*. Bombay: D. B. Taraporevala Sons & Co., 1965.

Bose, Jogindra Nāth. *Tukārām-carit*. (Bengali.) Calcutta: City Book Society, 1901.

Bose, Manindra Mohan. *The Post-Caitanya Sahajiā Cult of Bengal*. Calcutta: University of Calcutta, 1930.

Bose, Nirmal Kumar. *Cultural Anthropology*. Calcutta: India Associated Publishing Co., 1953.

Brackman, Jacob. "Dance with a Stranger." *Playboy*, Vol. XIV, No. 12 (December, 1967).

Brahma-Vaivarta Puranam. Part I: *Brahma and Prakriti Khandas*; Part II: *Ganesa and Krishna Janma Khandas*. Translated by Rajendra Nath Sen. Sacred Books of the Hindus, Vol. XXIV. Allahabad: Sudhindra Nath Vasu, Part I, 1920; Part II, 1922.

Brahma-vaivarta-purāṇam. (Sanskrit.) Śrīmaddvaipāyanamuni (praṇītam). Ānandāśramasanskrita-granthāvaliḥ, Granthāṇkaḥ 102. 2 vols. N. p.: Ānandāśramamudranalaya, 1935.

Brown, Norman O. *Life against Death*. Vintage Paperback. New York: Random House, 1960.

Caillois, Roger. *Man, Play, and Games*. Translated from the

French by Meyer Barash. New York: Free Press of Glencoe, 1961.

———. *Man and the Sacred.* Translated by Meyer Barash. Glencoe, Ill.: Free Press, 1959.

Cakravartin, Narahari. *Bhakti-ratnākara.* (Bengali.) Edited by Rāmanārāyaṇa Vidyāratna. Murshidabad ed. Berhampur: Rādhā-ramaṇ Press, 1888.

Campbell, Joseph. *The Masks of God: Primitive Mythology.* New York: Viking Press, 1959.

Carpenter, Joseph. *Theism in Medieval India.* London: Constable & Co., 1926.

Carter, Sydney (words and music). "Lord of the Dance." In *Robert Edwin Sings "Keep the Rumor Going" (Accompanied by Instrumental Trio).* AV-106. New York: Avant Garde Records, n.d.

Chakravarti, Chintaharan. *Tantras: Studies on Their Religion and Literature.* Calcutta: Punthi Pustak, 1963.

Chandidās. *Love Songs of Chandidās, the Rebel Poet-Priest of Bengal.* Translated from the Bengali by Deben Bhattacharya. London: George Allen & Unwin, 1967.

Chaudhuri, Nirad C. *The Continent of Circe.* Paperback. Bombay: Jaico Publishing House, 1965.

Coomaraswamy, Ananda K. *The Dance of Shiva: Fourteen Indian Essays.* Rev. ed. New York: Noonday Press, 1957.

———. "Līlā." *Journal of the American Oriental Society,* LXI (1941), 98-101.

Cox, Harvey. *The Feast of Fools: A Theological Essay on Festivity and Fantasy.* Cambridge, Mass.: Harvard University Press, 1969.

Das, Sambidananda. *Sri Chaitanya Mahaprabhu.* (English.) Madras: Sree Gaudiya Math, 1958.

Das, Sudhendukumar. *Sakti or Divine Power.* Calcutta: University of Calcutta, 1934.

Dasgupta, Shashibhusan. *Obscure Religious Cults.* Rev. 2d ed. Calcutta: Firma K. L. Mukhopadhyay, 1962.

Dasgupta, Surendranath. *A History of Indian Philosophy.* Vol. IV: *Indian Pluralism.* London: Cambridge University Press, 1966.

"Daśamahāvidyā." In Basu, Nāgendranāth (ed.). *Viśvakoṣa.*

(A Bengali encyclopedia.) Calcutta: Nāgendranāth Basu [1908?]. VIII, 405-18.

De, Sushil Kumar. *Ancient Indian Erotics and Erotic Literature.* Calcutta: Firma K. L. Mukhopadhyay, 1959.

———. *Bengal's Contribution to Sanskrit Literature and Studies in Bengal Vaisnavism.* Calcutta: Firma K. L. Mukhopadhyay, 1960.

———. *Early History of the Vaisnava Faith and Movement in Bengal from Sanskrit and Bengali Sources.* Calcutta: Firma K. L. Mukhopadhyay 1961.

———. *History of Sanskrit Poetics.* 2 vols. Calcutta: Firma K.L. Mukhopadhyay, 1960.

———. *Sanskrit Poetics as a Study of Aesthetic.* Berkeley: University of California Press, 1963.

Dearmer, Percy; Williams, R. Vaughan; and Shaw, Martin (eds.). *The Oxford Book of Carols.* 24th impression. New York: Oxford University Press, 1961.

Deming, Wilbur S. *Ramdas and the Ramdasis.* London: Oxford University Press, 1928.

Devanandan, Paul David. *The Concept of Māyā: An Essay in Historical Survey of the Hindu Theory of the World, with Special Reference to the Vedānta.* London: Lutterworth Press, 1950.

[*Devī Bhāgavata.*] *The Srimad Devi Bhagavatam.* Translated by Swami Vijnanananda. Sacred Books of the Hindus, Vol. XXVI. Allahabad: Sudhindra Nath Vasu, 1922.

[*Devī Bhāgavata.*] *Śrīmad Devībhāgavatam Mahāpurāṇam.* (Sanskrit.) Varanasi: Pāṇḍeya Rāmateja Śāstrī, Paṇḍit Pustakālay, 1965.

De Zoete, Beryl. *The Other Mind: A Study of Dance in South India.* New York: Theatre Arts Books, 1960.

Dimock, Edward C., Jr. "The Place of Gauracandrikā in Bengali Vaiṣṇava Lyrics." *Journal of the American Oriental Society,* LXXVIII (July-September, 1958), 153-69.

———. *The Place of the Hidden Moon: Erotic Mysticism in the Vaiṣṇava-sahajiyā Cult of Bengal.* Chicago: University of Chicago Press, 1966.

———. "A Study of the Vaiṣṇava-sahajiyā Movement of Bengal." Ph.D. dissertation, Harvard University, Cambridge, Mass., 1959.

Dimock, Edward C., and Jahan, Roushan. "Bengali Vaisnava

Lyrics: A Reader for Advanced Students." Mimeographed. South Asian Languages Research Program, University of Chicago, June, 1963.

Dimock, Edward C., and Levertov, Denise (trans.). *In Praise of Krishna: Songs from the Bengali.* Garden City, N.Y.: Doubleday & Co., 1967.

Dutt, Kanai Lal, and Purkayastha, Kshetra M. *The Bengal Vaishnavism and Modern Life.* Calcutta: Sribhumi Publishing Co., 1963.

Dutta, Aksoy Kumar. *Bhāratbarser-upāsak-sampradāya.* (Bengali.) Calcutta : Sanskrit Press Depository, 1888.

Eliade, Mircea. *Images and Symbols: Studies in Religious Symbolism.* Translated by Philip Mairet. New York: Sheed & Ward, 1961.

———. *Mephistopheles and the Androgyne: Studies in Religious Myth and Symbol.* Translated by J. M. Cohen. New York: Sheed & Ward, 1965.

Eliot, Charles. *Hinduism and Buddhism: An Historical Sketch.* 3 vols. London: Routledge & Kegan Paul, 1921.

Fackre, Gabriel. *Humiliation and Celebration.* New York: Sheed & Ward, 1969.

Farquhar, J. N. *Modern Religious Movements in India.* Delhi: Munshiram Manoharlal, Oriental Publishers Booksellers, 1967.

———. *An Outline of the Religious Literature of India.* Delhi : Motilal Banarsidass, 1967.

Fink, Eugen. *Spiel als Weltsymbol.* Stuttgart: W. Kohlhammer Verlag, 1960.

Forster, E. M. *A Passage to India.* New York: Harcourt, Brace & Co., 1924.

Garuḍa-purāṇam. Translated into English prose by Manmatha Nath Dutt Shastrī. 2d ed. Varanasi: Chowkhamba Sanskrit Series Office, 1968.

Ghose, Shishir Kumar. *Lord Gauranga.* Bhavan's Book University. Bombay: Bharatiya Vidya Bhavan, 1961.

Ghosh, J. C. *Bengali Literature.* London: Oxford University Press, 1948.

Glasenapp, Helmuth von. *Madhva's Philosophie des Vishnu Glaubens.* Vol. III. Bonn: Kurt Schroeder, Verlag, 1923.

Gonda, J. *Aspects of Early Viṣṇuism.* 2d ed. Delhi: Motilal Banarsidass, 1969.

———. *Change and Continuity in Indian Religion.* The Hague: Mouton & Co., 1965.

———. *Four Studies in the Language of the Veda.* 's-Gravenhage: Mouton & Co., 1959.

Grierson, George A. "Rādhāvallabhīs." In Hastings, James (ed.). *Encyclopaedia of Religion and Ethics.* Edinburgh : T. & T. Clark, 1908-21. X, 559-60.

Growse, F. S. *Mathura: A District Memoir.* N.p.: North-Western Provinces and Oudh Government Press, 1883.

Guardini, Romano. *The Spirit of the Liturgy.* Translated by Ada Lane. London: Sheed & Ward, 1930.

Harivamsha. Translated by Manmatha Nath Dutt. Calcutta: Elysium Press, 1897.

Harrelson, Walter. *From Fertility Cult to Worship.* New York: Doubleday & Co., 1969.

Hart, Roy L. *Unfinished Man and the Imagination.* New York : Herder & Herder, 1968.

Hein, Norvin. "The Rām Līlā." In Singer, Milton (ed.). *Traditional India: Structure and Change.* Bibliographical Series, Vol. X. Philadelphia: American Folklore Society, 1959. Pp. 73-98.

Hesiod, the Homeric Hymns and Homerica. Translated by Hugh G. Evelyn-White. New York: G. P. Putnam's Sons, 1920.

Hiriyanna, M. *Outlines of Indian Philosophy.* London: George Allen & Unwin, 1932.

Hooper, J. S. M. *Hymns of the Alvars.* London: Oxford University Press, 1929.

Hopkins, Thomas J. "The Social Teachings of the *Bhāgavata Purāṇa.*" In Singer, Milton (ed.). *Krishna: Myths, Rites, and Attitudes.* Honolulu: East-West Center Press, 1966. Pp. 3-22.

———. "Vaiṣṇava Bhakti Movement in the *Bhāgavata Purāṇa.*" Ph.D. dissertation, Yale University, New Haven, Conn., 1960.

Huizinga, J. *Homo Ludens: A Study of the Play-Element in Culture.* Beacon Paperback. Boston: Beacon Press, 1955.

Humphreys, Christmas. *Zen Buddhism.* Paperback. New York : Macmillan Co., n.d.

Hymns to the Goddess. Translated from the Sanskrit by Arthur and Ellen Avalon [John Woodroffe and Lady Woodroffe]. 3d ed. Madras: Ganesh & Co., 1964.

Ingalls, Daniel H. H. "Cynics and Pāśupatas: The Seeking of Dishonor." *Harvard Theological Review*, LV, No. 4 (October, 1962), 281-98.

Isherwood, Christopher. *Ramakrishna and His Disciples.* London: Methuen & Co., 1965.

Iyer, K. Bharatha. *Kathakali: The Sacred Dance-Drama of Malabar.* London: Luzac & Co., 1955.

Jayadeva. *Gita-Govinda. The Loves of Kṛṣṇa & Rādhā.* Translated from the Sanskrit by George Keyt. Bombay : Kutub-Popular, 1940.

———. *The Song of Divine Love* (*Gita-Govinda*). Translated by Duncan Greenlees. Madras: Kalakshetra Publications, 1957.

Jensen, Adolf E. *Myth and Cult among Primitive Peoples.* Translated by Marianna Tax Choldin and Wolfgang Weissleder. Chicago: University of Chicago Press, 1963.

Jīva Gosvāmin. *Bhakti-saṁdarbha.* (Bengali.) Edited by Bhakti Vilās Tīrtha Mahārāj. Calcutta: Caitanya Research Institute, 1963.

———. *Śrikṛṣṇa-saṁdarbha.* Translated into Bengali by Śrī Pran Gopan Gosvāmin. Navadvīp: Rajani Kanta Nāth, 1332 B.S. [1925].

———. *Śrī Śrī Gopāla-campū.* Translated into Bengali by Rasabihāri Sāṁkhyatīrtha. Murshidabad: Published under the patronage of the Rāja of Kasimbazar, Murshidabad, 1317 B.S. [1910].

Jung, C. G. "On the Psychology of Eastern Meditation." Translated by Carol Baumann. In Iyer, K. Bharatha (ed.). *Art and Thought: Issued in Honor of Dr. Ananda K. Coomaraswamy on the Occasion of His 70th Birthday.* London: Luzac & Co., 1947. Pp. 169-79.

Kabir. *One Hundred Poems of Kabir.* Translated by Rabindranath Tagore and Evelyn Underhill. London: Macmillan & Co., 1967.

Kane, Mahāmahopādhyāya Pandurang Vaman. *History of*

Dharmaśāstra (*Ancient and Mediaeval Religious and Civil Law in India*). Vol. V, in 2 parts. Poona: Bhandarkar Oriental Research Institute, Part I, 1958; Part II, 1962.

Karmarkar, A. P., and Kalamdani, N. B. *Mystic Teachings of the Haridasas of Karnataka.* Dharwar, Mysore: Karnataka Vidyavardhaka Sangha, 1939.

Kavi-karṇapūra. *Gauragaṇoddeśa-dipikā.* Translated into Bengali by Rāmanārāyaṇa Vidyāratna. Edited by Ramdev Misra. Murshidabad: Rādhā-ramaṇ Press, 1922.

Keen, Sam. *Apology for Wonder.* New York: Harper & Row, 1969.

Kennedy, J. "The Child Krishna, Christianity and the Gujars." *Journal of the Royal Asiatic Society of Great Britain and Ireland* (1907).

Kennedy, Melville. *The Chaitanya Movement: A Study of Vaishnavism of Bengal.* Calcutta: Association Press (Y.M.C.A.); London: Oxford University Press, 1925.

Kent, Sister Corita. *Footnotes and Headlines: A Play and Pray Book.* New York: Herder & Herder, 1967.

Kerenyi, C. *The Religion of the Greeks and Romans.* Translated by Christopher Holme. London: Thames & Hudson, 1962.

Kingsbury, F., and Phillips, G. E. *Hymns of the Tamil Śaivite Saints.* Heritage of India Series. Calcutta: Association Press; London: Oxford University Press, 1921.

Krishnadas. [Charuchandra Guha.] *Krishna of Vrindabana.* Calcutta: Bengal Library Book Depot, 1927.

Kṛṣṇadāsa Kavirāja. *Govinda-līlāmṛta.* Translated from the Sanskrit into Bengali by Saccidāndana Gosvāmin Bhaktiratna of Navadvīp. Vṛndāvana: Printed under the patronage of Banamali Roy and published by Nityasvarup Brahmacārī at Śrī Daivokinanda Press, 1908.

———. *Śrī Śrī Caitanya-caritāmṛta.* (Bengali.) 5 vols. Calcutta: Published by Manoranjan Caudhuri at Sādhana Prakāśanī, 1963.

———. *Sri Sri Chaitanya Charitamrita.* Translated into English by Nagendra Kumar Ray. 6 vols. 2d ed. Calcutta: Nagendra Kumar Ray, 1959.

Lal, Kanwar. *The Cult of Desire: An Interpretation of Erotic Sculpture of India.* Delhi : Asia Press, 1966.

———. *Immortal Khajuraho.* Delhi: Asia Press, 1965.

Leeson, Francis. *Kama Shilpa*. Delhi: Asia Press, 1965.

Leeuw, Geradus van der. *Sacred and Profane Beauty*: *The Holy in Art*. Translated by David E. Green. New York: Holt, Rinehart & Winston, 1963.

Lynch, William F., S.J. *Christ and Apollo*: *The Dimensions of the Literary Imagination*. New York: Sheed & Ward, 1960.

———. *Images of Hope*: *Imagination as Healer of the Hopeless*. Baltimore: Helicon Press, 1965.

M. [Mahendranath Gupta.] *The Gospel of Sri Ramakrishna*. Translated from the Bengali by Swami Nikhilananda. New York: Ramakrishna-Vivekananda Center, 1942.

Mackichan, D. "Vallabha, Vallabhāchārya." In Hastings, James (ed.). *Encyclopaedia of Religion and Ethics*. Edinburgh: T. & T. Clark, 1908-21. XII, 580-83.

Macnicol, Nicol. *Indian Theism from the Vedic to the Muhammadan Period*. London: Oxford University Press, 1915.

Mahābhārata. (Sanskrit.) Edited by Vishnu S. Sukthankar *et al*. Poona: Bhandarkar Oriental Research Institute, 1933.

The Mahabharata of Krishna-Dwaipayana. Translated by K. M. Ganguly. Published by Pratap Chandra Roy. 12 vols. Calcutta: Oriental Publishing Co., n.d.

[*Mahānirvāṇa-tantra*.] *The Great Liberation* (*Mahānirvāna Tantra*). Translated by Arthur Avalon [John Woodroffe]. 4th ed. Madras: Ganesh & Co., 1963.

Maharaj, Srimat Bhakti Vilas Tirtha Goswami. *Sri Chaitanya's Concept of Theistic Vedanta*. Madras: Sree Gaudiya Math, 1964.

Mahipati Marathi. *Bhaktalilamrita*. Translated into English by Justin E. Abbott and J. F. Edwards. Poona: Aryabhushan Press, 1935.

———. *Bhaktavijaya*. Translated into English by Justin E. Abbott and Narhar R. Godbole. 2 vols. Poona: Aryabhushan Press, 1933.

———. *Ramdas* (*Santavijaya*). Translated into English by Justin E. Abbott. Poona : Aryabhushan Press, 1932.

Majumdar, A. K. *Caitanya*: *His Life and Doctrine*: *A Study in Vaiṣṇavism*. Bombay: Bharatiya Vidya Bhavan, 1969.

———. "Early History of the Vaisnava Faith." *Indo-Asian Culture*, XI, No. 3 (1963), 249-54.

Majumdar, R. C. (ed.). *The History and Culture of the Indian*

People. Vol. IV: *The Age of Imperial Kanauj*. Bombay: Bharatiya Vidya Bhavan, 1955.

Mallik, Girindra Narayan. *The Philosophy of Vaiṣṇava Religion*. Punjab Oriental Sanskrit Series, No. XIV. Lahore: Punjab Sanskrit Book Depot, 1927.

Māṇikka-Vācagar. *The Tiruvācagam: or, "Sacred Utterances" of the Tamil Poet, Saint, and Sage Māṇikka-Vācagar*. Translated by G. U. Pope. Oxford: Clarendon Press, 1900.

[*Manu-smṛti*.] *The Laws of Manu*. Translated by G. Bühler. Sacred Books of the East, Vol. XXV. Delhi: Motilal Banarsidass, 1967.

The Mārkaṇḍeya Purāṇa. Translated by F. Eden Pargiter. Bibliotheca Indica: A Collection of Oriental Works. Calcutta: Baptist Mission Press for the Asiatic Society of Bengal, 1904.

Marriott, McKim. "The Feast of Love." In Singer, Milton (ed.). *Krishna: Myths, Rites, and Attitudes*. Honolulu: East-West Center Press, 1966. Pp. 200-212.

[*Matsya-purāṇa*.] *Śrīmanmatsya Mahāpurāṇam*. (Sanskrit.) Bombay: Published by Śivadulare Vājapeyī at Śrī Venkateśvar Steam Press, 1938.

Matsya Purāṇam. Translated by A Taluqdar of Oudh. Sacred Books of the Hindus, Vol. XVII, in 2 parts. Allahabad: Sudhindra Nath Vasu, 1916.

Maurois, André. *Illusions*. New York: Columbia University Press, 1968.

Midrash Rabbah. Vol. I. Translated by H Freedman and Maurice Simon. London: Soncino Press, 1939.

Miller, David L. *Gods and Games: Toward a Theology of Play*. New York: World Publishing Co., 1970.

———. "Salvation and the Image of Comedy: Pirandello and Aristophanes." *Religion and Life* (Summer, 1964).

Mīrābāī. "Poems from Mīrābāī." Translated by S. M. Pandey and Norman H. Zide. Mimeographed. University of Chicago, 1964.

Misra, Janardan. *The Religious Poetry of Surdas*. Königsberg: University of Königsberg, 1934.

Mitra, Khagendranāth. *Kirtan*. (Bengali.) Śāntiniketan: Viśvabhārati, 1945.

Mookerjee, Ajit. *Tantra Art: Its Philosophy and Physics.* New Delhi: Ravi Kumar, Kumar Gallery, 1966.

Mowrer, Edgar Ansel. "The Open Universe." *American Review* (USIS, New Delhi). Vol. III, No. 2 (January, 1959).

Müller, F. Max. *Ramakrishna: His Life and Sayings.* London: Longmans, Green, & Co., 1898.

Mukerjee, Radhakamal. *The Lord of the Autumn Moons.* Bombay: Asia Publishing House, 1957.

Mukherji, S. C. *A Study of Vaiṣṇavism in Ancient and Medieval Bengal—upto the Advent of Chaitanya (Based on Archaeological & Literary Data).* Calcutta: Punthi Pustak, 1966.

Mukhopadhyay, Prabhat. *The History of Medieval Vaishnavism in Orissa.* Calcutta : R. Chatterjee, 1940.

[Mulji, Karsandas.] *History of the Sect of Mahārājas, or Vallabhāchāryas, in Western India.* London: Trübner & Co., 1865.

Nābhā Dās. *Bhaktamāl.* Translated from the Hindi into Bengali by Kṛṣṇadās Babaji. Edited by Upendranāth Mukherji. N.p.: Basumati Sāhitya Mandir, 1924.

Nandikeshvara. *The Mirror of Gesture. Being the Abhinaya Darpana of Nandikeshvara.* Translated by A. K. Coomaraswamy and Gopala K. Duggirala. Cambridge, Mass.: Harvard University Press, 1917.

Narahari-dāsa. *Narottama-vilāsa.* (Bengali.) Edited by Rāmanārāyaṇa Vidyāratna. Murshidabaded. Berhampur: Rādhā-ramaṇ Press, 1328 B.S. [1918].

Narottama-dāsa. *Prema-bhakti-candrikā.* (Bengali.) Edited by Rādhika Nāth Śarma. N.p.: Rādhika Nāth Śarma, 1899.

———. *Vairāgya-nirnaya.* (Bengali.) Title page missing.

Nāth Rādhāgovinda. *Śrī Śrī Caitanya-caritāmṛta Bhumika.* (Bengali.) Calcutta: Published by Jatīndra Bimal Caudhurī at Śrī Guru Library, 1958.

———. "A Survey of the Caitanya Movement." In Bhattacharyya, Haridas (ed.). *The Cultural Heritage of India.* Vol IV: *The Religions.* Calcutta: Ramakrishna Mission Institute of Culture, 1956. Pp. 186-200.

Neale, Robert. *In Praise of Play.* New York: Harper & Row, 1969.

Nicholson, Reynold A. *The Mystics of Islam.* London: Routledge & Kegan Paul, 1966.

Nityapadananda Abadhuta, Srimat Swami. *Sri Sri Nityagopal*

(*Known Also as the Yogacharya Sri Srimat Abadhuta Jnanananda Deva*). Nabadwip, Nadia, West Bengal: Mahanirvan Math, 1948.

O'Flaherty, Wendy Doniger. "Asceticism and Sexuality in the Mythology of Śiva." *History of Religions*, VIII, No. 4 (May, 1969), 300-337; IX, No. 1 (August, 1969), 1-41.

Ortega y Gasset, José. *Toward a Philosophy of History*. New York : W. W. Norton & Co., 1941.

Otto, Walter F. *Dionysus: Myth and Cult*. Translated by Robert B. Palmer. Bloomington: Indiana University Press, 1965.

Payne, Ernest A. *The Shaktas: An Introductory and Comparative Study*. Religious Life of India. Calcutta: YMCA Publishing House; London : Oxford University Press, 1933.

Pieper, Josef. *In Tune with the World: A Theory of Festivity*. Translated by Richard and Clara Winston. New York: Harcourt, Brace & World, 1965.

Prabodhānanda Sarasavatī. *Ānanda-vṛndāvana-campū*. (Bengali.) Title page missing. Probably published late nineteenth century.

———. *Vṛndāvana-mahimāmṛta*. Translated into Bengali by Haridās Babaji. Vṛndāvana: Bhagavāndās Babaji, 1936.

Puṇyānanda-nātha. *Kāma-kālā-vilāsa*. Translated by Arthur Avalon [John Woodroffe]. Madras: Ganesh & Co., 1961.

Pusalker, A. D. *Studies in the Epics and Purāṇas*. Bombay: Bharatiya Vidya Bhavan, 1963.

Rahner, Hugo, S.J. *Man at Play*. Translated from the German by Brian Battershaw and Edward Quinn. New York : Herder & Herder, 1967.

Ramanuja, Jatīndra. "Kīrtan." *Bhāratakoṣa*. (A Bengali encyclopedia.) [Calcutta]: Bangīya Sāhitya Pariṣad, n.d. Vol. II.

Ramanujan, A. K. "Medieval 'Protestant' Movements." Lecture, Introduction to Indian Civilization, University of Chicago, February 7, 1966.

———. (trans.). *Speaking of Śiva*. Baltimore: Penguin Books, 1973.

———. (trans.). Unpublished translations of Liṅgāyata devotional poetry. University of Chicago, n.d.

Rama Prasada's Devotional Songs: The Cult of Shakti. Translated by Jadunath Sinha. Calcutta: Sinha Publishing House, 1966.

Randhawa, M. S. *Kangra Paintings of the Gita Govinda.* New Delhi : National Museum, 1963.

———. *Kangra Paintings on Love.* New Delhi: National Museum, 1962.

Rao, T. A. Gopinatha. *Elements of Hindu Iconography.* 2 vols., each in 2 parts. 2d ed. New York: Paragon Book Reprint Corp., 1968.

Raychaudhuri, Hemchandra. *Materials for the Study of the Early History of the Vaishnava Sect.* Calcutta: University of Calcutta, 1936.

"Religion and the Dance." Report of a consultation on the dance sponsored by the Department of Worship and the Arts, National Council of Churches of Christ, November 16, 1960.

Reyna, Ruth. *The Concept of Māyā : From the Vedas to the 20th Century.* Bombay: Asia Publishing House, 1962.

[*Ṛg-veda.*] *Hymns of the Ṛgveda.* Translated by Ralph T. H. Griffith. Chowkhamba Sanskrit Studies, Vol. XXXV. 2 vols. 4th ed. Varanasi: Chowkhamba Sanskrit Series Office, 1963.

Rolland, Romain. *The Life of Ramakrishna.* Calcutta: Advaita Ashrama, 1954.

Rūpa Gosvāmī. *Bhakti-rasāmṛta-sindhuh.* Vol. I. Translated into English by Tridaṇḍi Swāmī Bhakti Hṛdaya Bon Mahārāj. Vrindaban: Institute of Oriental Philosophy, 1965.

———. *Dāna-keli-kaumudī.* Translated into Bengali by Rāmanārāyaṇa Vidyāratna. Murshidabad: Published by Brājanāth Misra at Rādhā-ramaṇ Press, 1339 B.S. [1932].

———. *Laghu-bhāgavatāmṛta.* Translated into Bengali by Śrī Pran Gopan Gosvāmin. Edited by Śrī Balai Cand Gosvāmin Calcutta : Śrī Śrī Mahāprabhu Mandir, 1304 B.S. [1897].

———. *Lalita-mādhava.* Translated into Bengali by Satyendranāth Basu. N.p.: Published by Satiścandra Mukherji at Basumati Sāhitya Mandir, n.d.

———. *Stava-mālā.* Collected by Jīva Gosvāmin. Edited by Baladeva Vidyābhūṣaṇa. Translated into Bengali by Rāmanārāyaṇa Vidyāratna. Murshidabad: Ramdev Misra, 1913.

———. *Ujjvala-nīlamaṇi.* Edited by Rasabihāri Sāṁkhyatīrtha. Translated into Bengali by Rāmanārāyaṇa Vidyāratna. Murshidabad: Ramdev Misra, 1919.

Sa'd ud Din Mahmud Shabistari. *Gulshan I Raz: The Mystic Rose Garden.* Translated by E. H. Whinfield. London: Trübner & Co., 1880.

Sanyal, Nisikanta. *Sree Krishna Chaitanya.* Vol. I. Madras: Sree Gaudiya Math, 1933.

Saradananda, Swami. *Sri Ramakrishna, the Great Master.* Translated from the Bengali by Swami Jagadananda. Madras: Sri Ramakrishna Math, 1952.

Sarasvatī, Swami Nigamānanda. *Tantrik Guru.* (Bengali.) Jorhat, Assam: Sarasvatī Mati, 1959.

Sartre, Jean Paul. *The Psychology of Imagination.* New York: Philosophical Library, 1948.

The Saundaryalahari: or, Flood of Beauty. Edited and translated by W. Norman Brown. Harvard Oriental Series, Vol. XLIII. Cambridge, Mass.: Harvard University Press, 1958.

Sen, Dinesh Chandra. *Chaitanya and His Age.* Calcutta: University of Calcutta, 1924.

———. *Chaitanya and His Companions.* Calcutta: University of Calcutta [1917].

———. *History of Bengali Language and Literature.* Calcutta: University of Calcutta, 1954.

———. *The Vaisnava Literature of Medieval Bengal.* Calcutta: University of Calcutta, 1917.

Sen, Sukumar. *History of Bengali Literature.* New Delhi: Sahitya Akademi, 1960.

———. *A History of Brajabuli Literature: Being a Study of the Vaisnava Lyric Poetry and Poets of Bengal.* Calcutta: University of Calcutta, 1935.

Shāradātilakatantram. In Avalon, Arthur (ed.). [John Woodroffe.] *Tantrik Texts.* Vol. XVI, Part I. London: Luzac & Co., 1933.

Shastri, Prabhu Dutt. *The Doctrine of Maya.* London: Luzac and Co., 1911.

Singer, Milton (ed.). *Krishna: Myths, Rites, and Attitudes.* Honolulu: East-West Center Press, 1966.

———. "The Rādhā-Krishna *Bhajanas* of Madras City." In Singer, Milton (ed.). *Krishna: Myths, Rites, and Attitudes.* Honolulu: East-West Center Press, 1966. Pp. 90-138.

———. (ed.). *Traditional India: Structure and Change.* Bibliographical Series, Vol. X. Philadelphia: American Folklore Society, 1959.

Sūrdās. "The Poems of Sūrdās for Advanced Students of Hindi." Translated by S. M. Pandey and N. H. Zide. Mimeographed. University of Chicago, 1963.

Suso, Henry. *Little Book of Eternal Wisdom and Little Book of Truth.* Translated by James M. Clark. London: Faber & Faber, 1953.

Tagore, Rabindranath. *Gitanjali (Song Offerings).* Translated from the Bengali into English prose by Rabindranath Tagore. London: Macmillan & Co., 1967.

———. *Sādhanā: The Realisation of Life.* New York: Macmillan & Co., 1913.

Taylor, Margaret Fisk. *A Time to Dance: Symbolic Movement in Worship.* Philadelphia: United Church Press, 1967.

Thompson, Edward J., and Spencer, Arthur Marshman. *Bengail Religious Lyrics, Śākta.* Calcutta: Association Press (Y.M. C.A.); London: Oxford University Press, 1923.

Tirtha, Tridandibhikshu Bhakti Pradip. *Sri Chaitanya Mahaprabhu.* (English.) Rev. 2d ed. Calcutta: Gaudiya Mission, 1947.

Tulsī Dās. *Kavitāvali.* Translated into English by F. R. Allchin. London: George Allen & Unwin, 1964.

———. *The Petition to Rām: Hindi Devotional Hymns of the Seventeenth Century (Vinaya-patrikā).* Translated by F. R. Allchin. London : George Allen & Unwin, 1966.

[*Upaniṣads.*] *The Principal Upaniṣads.* Edited and translated by S. Radhakrishnan. London: George Allen & Unwin, 1953.

Vaudeville, Charlotte. "Evolution of Love Symbolism in Bhagavatism." *Journal of the American Oriental Society,* LXXXII (March, 1962), 31-40.

Vidyāpati. *Love Songs of Vidyāpati.* Edited by W. G. Archer. Translated by Deben Bhattacharya. London: Geroge Allen & Unwin, 1963.

———. *The Songs of Vidyapati.* Translated by Subhadra Jha. Banaras: Motilal Banarsidass, Oriental Publishers & Booksellers, 1954.

The Vishṇu Purāṇa. Translated by H. H. Wilson. 3d ed. Calcutta: Punthi Pustak, 1961.

Vishnu Puri. *Bhakti-Ratnavali.* Translated by A Professor of Sanskrit. Sacred Books of the Hindus, Vol. VII. Allahabad: Sudhindra Nath Vasu, 1912.

Vṛndāvana-dāsa. *Caitanya-bhāgavata.* (Bengali.) Edited by Bhaktisidhānta Gosvāmin Thakur. Calcutta: Gauḍīya Maṭh, 1936.

Waley, Arthur. *The Way and Its Power: A Study of the Tao Tê Ching and Its Place in Chinese Thought.* 5th impression. London: George Allen & Unwin, 1965.

Watts, Alan. *Beyond Theology: The Art of Godmanship.* New York: Pantheon Books (A Divison of Random House), 1964.

———. *Psychotherapy East and West.* New York: Pantheon Books, 1961.

Welch, Holmes. *Taoism: The Parting of the Way.* Beacon Paperback. Rev. ed. Boston: Beacon Press, 1966.

White, Charles. "Bhakti as a Religious Structure in the Context of Medieval Hinduism in the Hindi Speaking Area of North India." Ph.D. dissertation, University of Chicago, 1964.

Woodroffe, John. *Śakti and Śākta: Essays and Addresses.* 6th ed. Madras: Ganesh & Co., 1965.

Zannas, Eliky. *Khajurāho.* 's-Gravenhage: Mouton & Co., 1960.

Zimmer, Heinrich. *The King and the Corpse: Tales of the Soul's Conquest of Evil.* Edited by Joseph Campbell. Bollingen Series, Vol. XI. Washington, D.C.: Pantheon Books, 1948.

———. *Myths and Symbols of Indian Art and Civilization.* Edited by Joseph Campbell. Harper Torchbook; Bollingen Library. New York: Harper & Row, 1962.

———. *Philosophies of India.* Edited by Joseph Campbell. Meridian Books. Cleveland: World Publishing Co., 1956.

INDEX